SEX WITHOUT CONSENT

EDITED BY MERRIL D. SMITH

SEX WITHOUT CONSENT

Rape and Sexual Coercion in America

New York University Press • *New York and London*

NEW YORK UNIVERSITY PRESS
New York and London

© 2001 by New York University

Library of Congress Cataloging-in-Publication Data
Sex without consent : rape and sexual coercion in America / edited by Merril D. Smith.
p. cm.
Includes bibliographical references and index.
Contents: "None of the women were abused" : indigenous contexts for the treatment of women captives in the Northeast / Alice Nash — "Playing the rogue" : rape and issues of consent in seventeenth-century Massachusetts / Else Hambleton — Sexual consent and sexual coercion in seventeenth-century Virginia / Terri L. Snyder — Coerced sex and gendered violence in New Netherland / James Horner Williams — Rape, law, courts, and custom in Pennsylvania, 1682–1800 / Jack Marietta and G. S. Rowe — "The law should be her protector" : the criminal prosecution of rape in Upper Canada, 1791–1850 / Patrick J. Connor — "I was very much wounded" : rape law, children, and the Antebellum South / Diane Miller Sommerville — "A most detestable crim" : character, consent, and corroboration in Vermont's rape law, 1850–1920 / Hal Goldman — "In the marriage bed woman's sex has been enslaved and abused" : defining and exposing marital rape in late-nineteenth-century America / Jesse F. Battan —Race, honor, citizenship : the Massie rape/murder case / Bonni Cermak — "Another negro-did-it crime" : black-on-white rape and protest in Virginia, 1945–1960 / Lisa Lindquist Dorr — Sexual coercion and limited choices : their link to teen pregnancy and welfare / Robert Cherry — Rape on campus : numbers tell less than half the story / Julie Campbell-Ruggaard and Jami Van Ryswyk.
ISBN 0-8147-9788-1 (cloth : alk. paper) — ISBN 0-8147-9789-X (pbk. : alk. paper)
1. Rape—United States—History. 2. Sex crimes—United States—History. 3. Sex discrimination in criminal justice administration—United States.   I. Smith, Merril D., 1956–
HV6561 .S47 2001
364.15'32'0973—dc21   2001003460

New York University Press books are printed on acid-free paper, and their binding materials are chosen for strength and durability.

Manufactured in the United States of America

10 9 8 7 6 5 4 3 2

For my sisters,

   Lynne, Lori, Linda, Michele, and Hannah

Contents

Acknowledgments

Grateful thanks to the many people who offered ideas, suggestions, and friendship while I was working on this book. In particular, I would like to thank Else L. Hambleton and Ann Wolff for permitting me to vent my frustrations in numerous e-mails. Jennifer Hammer, my editor at New York University Press, promptly answered my many questions and did not grumble at my delays. Thanks to Despina Papazoglou Gimbel, also at NYU Press, for once again guiding my manuscript through copyediting. A special thank you to the staff of the West Deptford Public Library who cheerfully obtained obscure books for me when I was working and provided me with leisure reading when I wasn't. The men and women of the National Park Post Office went beyond the call of duty in making sure I got my mail.

This book is a collaborative effort, and I could not have done it without the contributions of the authors of the essays included here. Thank you for coming through with great essays.

As always, thanks to Doug, Megan, and Sheryl just for being in my life.

And to J.W., thanks for the chocolate.

Introduction

Studying Rape in American History

Merril D. Smith

SINCE THE PUBLICATION of Susan Brownmiller's pathbreaking book, *Against Our Will*, rape has become a significant topic of research. Although Brownmiller's work has been criticized for weaknesses in its historical analysis,[1] it opened the subject up to serious examination "by uncovering the existence of rape as an important element in world history."[2] The aim of this book is to examine rape in what is now the United States from the time of early contact between Europeans and Native Americans to the present. Two questions need to be addressed here. First, why examine rape in American history? Second, can we put rape in historical perspective?

By exploring the experience, the prosecution, and the meaning of rape in American history, we add a larger dimension to the study of crime and punishment, as well as to gender relations, gender roles, and sexual politics. Limiting this book to what is now the United States, with the addition of one essay on Upper Canada, is partly a matter of practicality—a detailed history of rape in the world would take several volumes.[3] The essays included here, however, explore changes in rape law over three centuries, cover a wide area geographically, and analyze topics and situations that are unique or relevant to the history of the United States, such as interracial encounters due to colonization and slavery, and rape on contemporary college campuses.

The study of rape can and should be put into a historical context. As the essays in this book make clear, what individuals thought about rape and how it was prosecuted depended very much upon their society and backgrounds. For example, in her essay in this volume, Else L. Hambleton notes that though there are certain constants in the experience of rape, the belief system of Puritan Massachusetts affected who made complaints about rape, who was prosecuted for the crime, and how they were punished. For one thing, judges and juries believed that a woman could not conceive from a rape. Thus, no matter how good the character of the woman nor how credible her story, if she became pregnant, Puritans assumed the woman must have consented to sexual intercourse. In such cases, the victim of the crime might be punished herself—for fornication.[4]

The perception of women's and men's natures and ideas about their proper roles differs and changes throughout the centuries and places studied here. Women were variously considered "lustful daughters of Eve," pure or asexual creatures, and demure but willing temptresses. Sometimes these notions coexisted at a particular time or depended upon the race, ethnicity, or class of the women involved. Similarly, men might be considered the "protectors" of women, hapless victims caught in their snares, or lust-filled beasts. These ideas about women and men, in turn, colored the perception of rape throughout American history and the formulation of rape laws and prosecutorial procedures.

In exploring rape over the centuries of American history, we see some similarities in the experiences of *all* female victims, who might be of any age, class, race, or ethnicity, and who might be raped by strangers or acquaintances. Some examples from this book include a group of men who raped an intoxicated fifteen-year-old girl to "make a woman of her," a young woman raped by soldiers, an immigrant woman who was raped after accepting a ride from a stranger, and a young mother who was accosted after a neighbor escorted her home from a tavern. In another case, a college frat party was the scene of the crime. Although these incidents appear similar to accounts one can read in the newspapers almost any day in the United States, only the last one occurred in this century. Each, however, involved a woman or girl compelled to have sex against her will.[5]

The short title of this volume is *Sex without Consent*, and this is the theme that binds the essays together—women, children, or men forced into sexual encounters. Whether the rapes discussed here were accomplished by threats or violence is irrelevant—all were coerced in some fashion. Although the topics overlap, some of the essays focus more on

rape law and its prosecution, while others are more concerned with so-
cietal issues. All, however, focus on what rape meant at a particular
time and place in American history, or what it means today.

In this book, I am defining the word "rape" broadly to include
sodomy, child molestation, and instances of sexual coercion that were
not actually prosecuted as rape. The meanings of rape and consent
changed and evolved throughout the time periods studied here, and
so do the classifications of its victims and the willingness of societies
to take legal action in their defense. Today, for example, most people
consider rape to be a crime against women. Indeed, few men notify
authorities after they are raped, and they seldom seek help at college
or community rape crisis centers. Partly this is because they perceive
these centers to be only for women—and sometimes they are correct.
However, some men may be reluctant to report attacks because they
fear being labeled as homosexuals. Julie Campbell Ruggaard and
Jami Van Ryswyk inform us that most same-sex male rapists identify
themselves as heterosexual, and sometimes the rapes they commit are
done "as a gay-bashing tool when the perpetrator knows or suspects
the victim to be homosexual." Clearly, at the start of the twenty-first
century more needs to be done for both the female and male victims
of sexual attacks.[6]

In the seventeenth century, men who were assaulted may have been
just as reluctant to come forward for fear of being prosecuted as willing
participants in sodomy, a capital crime, although the sodomy cases
were seldom brought to trial, and even fewer men were executed for the
crime.[7] James Homer Williams's essay examines three cases of men who
were charged with molesting boys. He concludes that in New Netherland the courts stepped in to regulate breaches in morals and to preserve public order. However, authorities were less concerned with protecting women, children, servants, Africans, and Indians from physical
harm. Officials intervened only when the cases seemed extraordinary,
such as in sodomy cases, or when they threatened the property rights of
white men, as in the molestation of their servants.

In contrast, Terri L. Synder argues that in seventeenth-century Virginia, some white women took matters into their own hands. Though
few rape cases came before the courts, women took "command of the
public forum of the courtroom" in order to clear their reputations when
they had been accused of fornication. In this public setting, before their
neighbors, they were able to "control definitions of sexual consent and

sexual coercion," and in the process they were able to "obtain retribution" and "restore their honor."

The definition of rape and rape victims is even more elusive in Native American cultures. Using a combination of Wabanaki oral tradition and European travelers' accounts, Alice Nash argues that when indigenous women were taken captive by other indigenous people, they were considered sexually available, but captured European women were not. Nash contends that "new cultural possibilities emerged" when Englishwomen taken captive were adopted as sisters in Wabanaki households and thus were made "unavailable" as sexual partners to the men in those households.

Defining the crime of rape is one problem. Bringing charges and prosecuting is another. Throughout the three centuries studied here, courts and cultures have had to decide whether they would trust a woman's report of rape. And women have had to decide whether they think family, neighbors, judges, and juries would believe their stories. Since rapes are generally not witnessed by others and physical evidence of the crime may be lacking, prosecution often depended on the woman's word against the man's. Thus, the credibility of a rape victim was of prime importance, and her credibility depended on her character. As Hal Goldman's essay makes clear, what was admissible evidence concerning a woman's character, such as her past sexual behavior, varied enormously from state to state in the nineteenth and early twentieth centuries, as did determinations of consent. Goldman finds that in Vermont, the courts were much more willing to consider a woman-centered perception of sexual assault. In contrast, he notes neighboring New York "was relentlessly hostile to female accusers."

Consent was a crucial aspect of any rape prosecution. Questions about and rulings on consent tell us a great deal about how a society views women. Rape laws of the past required a woman to "prove" she had resisted by yelling and calling out, and they frequently required two witnesses to testify if a rape was to be prosecuted. At the other extreme, marital rape laws did not exist in the United States until very recently. Indeed, both laws and legal authorities agreed that in marriage a woman lost her right to refuse sexual intercourse with her husband. In taking her wedding vows, she was consenting to marital sexual relations. This implied consent meant that a husband could not be accused of raping his wife. In the late nineteenth century, these legal opinions matched the beliefs of the general public, and many women internal-

ized these views. As Jesse F. Battan notes, "law and ideology thus mitigated against resistance, and shame and reticence discouraged disclosure." However, in his essay on the Free Lovers, he demonstrates that
they "brought marital sexual abuse to popular awareness and subsequently to the historical record." Although their campaign against marital rape did not change laws, their periodicals gave women a forum in
which to express their feelings and describe experiences that were normally kept hidden in late-nineteenth-century society.

The rape of a married woman by someone *other* than her husband
was considered a serious crime in colonial America, particularly in New
England, because it injured the *husband* and threatened the sanctity of
the marital bonds. Even if she had not consented, a married woman
might be suspected of committing adultery.[8] In the case of an unmarried
woman, her adultery would not be an issue (although it might be for
her assailant, if he was married), but the courts still had to determine
whether she had given consent. In general, female children under ten
years old were considered too young to consent. Several of the essays in
this book examine sexual attacks on female children. For example, Jack
Marietta and G. S. Rowe note that seven of thirty-three rapes in Chester
County, Pennsylvania, between 1682 and 1801 involved children. Marietta and Rowe further observe that some of the prescriptive literature of
the mid-eighteenth century described girls as young as fourteen as sexual temptresses.

Whether a young girl was considered a victim or an instigator of a
sexual episode depended not only on her age, but also on her race and
class, and where and when the crime occurred. Diane Miller Sommerville's study reveals that the age of consent varied widely in the antebellum South. However, she states that some states enacted laws establishing two different ages of consent based on race. In Tennessee, for
example an eleven-year-old white girl "would have been deemed
legally incapable of understanding consent in the context of sexual relations with a slave, but perfectly capable and hence responsible for
having sexual relations with a white man."

The issue of race is a factor in a number of these essays. While Sommerville observes differences in the treatment of white and black victims and offenders in the antebellum South, Lisa Lindquist Dorr explores the legal system of post–World War II Virginia. Examining
changes in the ways Americans viewed women and women's sexuality,
she observes that "white women, who previously had near-absolute

power to accuse and convict black men of rape, saw that power limited as white men became distrustful, not of their willingness to accuse black men falsely, but rather of their willingness to accuse *any* man of rape at all." Black women faced even greater scrutiny of their characters, but "beliefs about women's sexuality hindered all women in achieving vindication through the legal system."

Bonni Cermak calls for a further analysis of interracial sexual assaults, including studies of those involving Asians, Native Americans, and Hispanics. Her essay uses the Massie rape/murder case to explore rape, race, and citizenship in 1930s Hawaii. The mixed-raced population of Hawaii, which included Japanese, Chinese, and Filipino residents, as well as native Hawaiians and the white elite, combined with its status as a U. S. territory, complicated the two trials in this case. Cermak uses the Massie Incident to examine "the nature of citizenship and its connections to ideologies of race and sexuality in Hawaii during the interwar period."

Race and sexuality come together differently in economist Robert Cherry's essay. Cherry applies a "benefit-cost" model to look at "individual decisions that put women at risk." Because poor black women often live in neighborhoods where they must accept more risks in their daily lives, they make choices that wealthy women of all races do not have to make. For example, they may have to take public transportation instead of cabs and live in buildings without doormen. They may also live in situations in which there is a culture of sexual coercion.

Besides examining who commits rapes and who is raped, these essays look at where rapes occur. Although people often associate rape with urban crime, many of the rape cases described in this book occurred in rural settings. And many of the rapes, if not most, were committed by assailants known to the victim. Since for most of its history the United States was predominantly rural or made up of small towns, perhaps this should not be surprising. Certainly women were raped in Philadelphia, New York City, and other cities.[9] Yet Patrick J. Connor's study of Upper Canada uncovered only six rapes in urban areas between 1791 and 1850. Connor suggests that the anonymity of urban life and more stringent expectations concerning women's behavior may have made it more difficult for these women to attempt a prosecution on rape charges. At the same time, the isolation of agrarian communities made women vulnerable to potential attacks. Sommerville finds a similar pattern in the antebellum South, especially for children. Such activities as berry picking or gathering eggs made young girls the easy targets of prospective rapists.

College campuses, whether urban or not, are also the site of many rapes. As Campbell-Ruggaard and Van Ryswyk have documented, the number of campus rapes is greatly underreported. For one thing, methods of collecting statistics and reporting crimes vary from school to school. In addition, some students may feel that the assault was not really a "crime," and so they do not report it to authorities. As Campbell-Ruggaard and Van Ryswyk note, many college rapists do not even consider themselves to be rapists. They do not believe that they really *forced* their partners into having sex.

This perception by a rapist that the woman he rapes actually wanted intercourse is noted in many of the essays in this book. However, it is difficult to know whether the purpose of such testimonies is merely to defend rapists' actions to the courts, or whether they truly believe the women they raped wanted sex and just needed "persuasion." If it is difficult to understand the motivations of rapists now, this is even more so in the past when records may have been lost or cultural biases obscured testimonies. I have arranged the essays here in roughly chronological order because, though there are constants in the *experiences* of rape and even in the attitudes of some rapists, the laws regarding rape have changed over the centuries. In many other ways, of course, the twenty-first century is far different from the seventeenth, and these differences affect the study of rape.

Still, rape has not been eliminated, any more than murder has. Brownmiller declared that rape was "a conscious process of intimidation by which all men keep all women in a state of fear." In contrast, evolutionary biologists Randy Thornhill and Craig T. Palmer claim that "human rape arises from men's evolved machinery for obtaining a high number of mates in an environment where females choose mates."[10] It seems to me that rape is a complex crime encompassing both sex and violence. Some rapes are perhaps more sexually motivated; others are very definitely hostile acts and displays of power against women (or men or children). I believe, for example, that an unplanned "date rape" differs—at least in motivation—from an organized policy of ethnic cleansing by Bosnian Serbs who forcibly impregnated Muslim women, and that these differences should be discussed and analyzed.[11] The historical context of rape needs to be examined, and I hope this book will spark some discussion of the topic.

NOTES

1. Susan Brownmiller, *Against Our Will: Men, Women, and Rape* (New York: Fawcett Columbine, 1975). Criticisms include Edward Shorter, "On Writing the History of Rape," *Signs: Journal of Women in Culture and Society* 3 (Winter 1977): 471–482. For a critique of Shorter, see Heidi Hartman and Ellen Ross, "Comment on 'Writing the History of Rape,'" *Signs: Journal of Women in Culture and Society* 3 (Summer 1978): 931–935. Roy Porter, "Rape—Does It Have Historical Meaning?" in *Rape*, ed. Sylvana Tomaselli and Roy Porter (Oxford: Basil Blackwell, 1986), 216–236. Evolutionary biologists Randy Thornhill and Craig T. Palmer devote a number of pages in their recent book to criticizing Brownmiller. See *A Natural History of Rape: Biological Bases of Sexual Coercion* (Cambridge: MIT Press, 2000), esp. chapter 6.

2. Hartmann and Ross, "Comment," 932.

3. Since Canada was a British colony, just as the United States was, many of its laws and practices were similar to those of colonial America. Patrick J. Connor's essay on Upper Canada permits us to compare and contrast Canadian and U.S. laws and practices. In addition, Upper Canada's rural setting was similar to that of much of the United States during this time period.

4. See the essay by Else L. Hambleton in thụis book. Also see her essay, "The Regulation of Sex in Seventeenth-Century Massachusetts: The Quarterly Court of Essex County vs. Priscilla Willson and Mr. Samuel Appleton," in *Sex and Sexuality in Early America*, ed. Merril D. Smith (New York: New York University Press, 1998), 89–115. The belief that pregnancy cannot result from a rape persists in our own time.

5. The examples are from essays by Jack Marietta and G. S. Row (eighteenth-century Pennsylvania), Patrick J. Connor (eighteenth-century Upper Canada), Hal Goldman (nineteenth-century Vermont), Terri L. Snyder (seventeenth-century Virginia), and Julie Campbell-Ruggaard and Jami Van Ryswyk (1990s college campus).

6. All quotations unless otherwise cited are from the essays referred to in this book.

7. For a thorough discussion of sodomy in early America, see Thomas Foster, "Locating Sodomy in Massachusetts, 1690–1765," unpublished paper presented to the Sexuality in Early America conference, Philadelphia, June 1–3, 2001. Also see Richard Godbeer, "'The Cry of Sodom'; Discourse, Intercourse, and Desire in New England," *William and Mary Quarterly* 52 (April 1995): 259–286.

8. For a discussion of rape and sodomy laws in colonial America, see Mary Beth Norton, *Founding Mothers and Fathers: Gendered Power and the Forming of American Society* (New York: Vintage Books, 1997), 347–357.

9. See, for example, Christine Stansell, *City of Women: Sex and Class in New*

York (New York: Alfred A. Knopf, 1986); Marybeth Hamilton Arnold, "'The Life of a Citizen in the Hands of Woman': Sexual Assault in New York City, 1790–1820," in Kathy Peiss and Christina Simmons, eds., *Passion and Power: Sexuality in History* (Philadelphia: Temple University Press, 1989); Claire Anna Lyons, "Sex Among the 'Rabble': Gender Transitions in the Age of Revolution, 1750–1830" (Ph.D. dissertation: Yale University, 1996).

10. Brownmiller, *Against Our Will*, 15. Thornhill and Palmer, *A Natural History of Rape*, 190. For another view, see Frans B. M. de Waal's review of *A Natural History of Rape*, in the *New York Times*, April 2, 2000.

11. Anne Barker analyzes rape during war in her article, "Justice Delayed," *Michigan State University Journal of International Law* 8 (Summer 1999): 453–485.

I

"None of the Women Were Abused"

Indigenous Contexts for the Treatment of Women Captives in the Northeast

Alice Nash

LONG BEFORE THE first New England captives were carried to Canada in the seventeenth century, Wabanaki men took captives in intertribal warfare. A close examination of Wabanaki oral tradition, in conjunction with European travel accounts from the Northeast in the early contact period, suggests that when indigenous women were taken captive by other indigenous people they became wives, concubines, or slaves to their captors, sexually available within culturally defined limits. In contrast, when Englishwomen were taken captive during the intercolonial wars of the seventeenth and eighteenth centuries, all reports indicate that they were never subjected to rape, or sex without consent.[1] Even Cotton Mather omitted rape from his litany of the horrors that English captives could expect. In *Good Fetch'd Out of Evil* (1706) he wrote, "Tis a wonderful Restraint from God upon the Bruitish Salvages, that no *English Woman* was ever known to have any Violence offered unto her *Chastity*, by any of them."[2]

To reconcile these two scenarios, bear in mind that categories of analysis that seem important to us—including gender and sexuality—embody historically and culturally specific ideas that may actually impede our understanding. The operative category here has less to do with male sexuality or desire than with insider/outsider status, and specifically how outsiders might be incorporated into the group. The complicating factor is colonization. Wabanaki peoples responded to the contingencies of colonization in creative ways that allowed new cultural possibilities to emerge—such as the practice of adopting some Englishwomen taken captive as sisters, a relationship that made them explicitly unavailable to men in their adopted households—without letting go of older ways.

This essay is an exploration of the indigenous context of captivity among the eastern Algonquian-speaking peoples of the Northeast, with a narrow focus on Wabanaki peoples in the area known to colonial New Englanders as "the eastern frontier"—a region that encompasses present-day Maine, Nova Scotia, New Brunswick, and southeastern Quebec. The term "Wabanaki," meaning "People of the Dawnland," is used today to designate five linguistically and culturally related tribal groups (Abenaki, Penobscot, Passamaquoddy, Maliseet, and Mi'kmaq). There are important differences, past and present, between them, but to keep things simple in this essay I use "Wabanaki" when making generalizations and other terms as appropriate.

Wabanaki oral tradition, used as a complement to European explorer accounts, offers a way to examine the meaning of captivity as it figures in Wabanaki stories about themselves.[3] The majority of the sources used for the following discussion of women captives in the early contact period relate to the Mi'kmaq, the easternmost of the Wabanaki peoples, and their near neighbors. Mi'kmaq oral histories collected and published during the late nineteenth century by Protestant missionary Silas Rand describe a series of conflicts that took place over several generations prior to 1600 between the Mi'kmaq and the Kwetej, an Iroquoian group who once lived along the St. Lawrence River and on the Gaspé Peninsula.[4] Published accounts by French and English explorers report on intertribal conflicts in the two decades before 1620. These sources make it clear that there was extensive contact between the Mi'kmaq and their Wabanaki neighbors. Because they share broad cultural characteristics, related languages, and histories that include intermarriage as well as captive taking, I bring in evidence related to Maliseet, Passamaquoddy, Penobscot, or Abenaki peoples when it seems useful, knowing that there is a risk of conflating very different practices.

It is important to be specific about time, place, and which groups of people are involved because not all Indians are alike, and cultures change over time.[5] Due to the influence of two early and much reprinted articles, "The White Indians of Colonial North America," by James Axtell, and "War and Culture: The Iroquois Experience," by

Daniel K. Richter, much of the academic literature on captives and captive taking draws heavily on accounts of Iroquoian practices.[6] While this is fine when talking about Iroquoian peoples—that is, people whose languages are part of the Iroquoian language family, including members of the Iroquois Confederacy (Mohawks, Oneidas, Onondagas, Cayugas, Senecas and Tuscaroras) as well as the Huron or Wendat on the north side of the St. Lawrence River—it is problematic when generalized to the eastern Algonquian speakers living east of the Hudson River and south of the St. Lawrence. This distinction is supported by the recent work of Evan Haefeli and Kevin Sweeney in their analysis of the 1704 attack on Deerfield, Massachusetts, where French, Mohawk, Huron, Pennacook, Cowassuck, Pigwacket, and St. Francis Abenaki forces fought with very different motives and treated their captives in culturally and politically contextualized ways.[7] Other seeming inconsistencies in the historical record may be resolved by paying more attention to chronology. A diachronic analysis of Iroquoian and eastern Algonquian practices around captive taking and the treatment of captives suggests that there was some convergence by the mid-eighteenth century, in part due to their shared history of relations with the French and English colonies.[8]

The most important distinction here is that Wabanaki warfare was not characterized by the particular Iroquoian ritual known as the mourning war, in which Iroquois men, often at the urging of female relatives, conducted raids on enemy tribes for the express purpose of taking captives. Some of these captives were tortured and even killed as a way of purging grief for a deceased family member. Others were adopted through a ritual of resuscitation or requickening, in which the deceased was brought back to life in the person of the adoptee. As Daniel Richter and others have pointed out, the Iroquoian mourning war complex spun out of control as mortality rates from epidemic disease, warfare, and war-related famine escalated through the seventeenth century, creating a harsh cycle of raid, retaliation, and more grief to assuage.[9]

Wabanaki peoples sometimes adopted captives, but taking captives expressly for adoption was never the major goal of warfare. In the early contact period—from about 1500 to 1620, before the arrival of epidemics and Pilgrims brought irreversible changes to the land and its people—Wabanaki warriors went on raids for vengeance and honor. Captive taking was more a by-product than a primary goal when making war. Captives might be tortured or killed to avenge the dead, a means of purging violent emotions and restoring balance within the community. Captives could also be used as envoys, hostages, gifts, or slaves, practices that predated the arrival of European colonists and continued through the eighteenth century.[10]

The range of possible uses for captives expanded over time. Older practices persisted in intertribal warfare, but new practices emerged when the captives were not Indian. While some English captives, especially young children, were adopted into Wabanaki families, Wabanaki people more often used them to take care of their own, living relatives. For example, they sought to trade English captives for Indians being held prisoner in New England, or to ransom them for cash or goods that could benefit either individuals or the group.[11] In general—and this aspect of captive taking remains consistent over time—captives were taken during raids and distributed as needed, a fluid practice with a range of possible outcomes that depended heavily on circumstance.

In Wabanaki stories about the time before Europeans came, captives are portrayed as dangerous people. Women, in particular, are dangerous to their captors because their husbands and families are expected to follow in search of revenge, whether or not that meant actually freeing the women. A man might take a captive woman for his wife, only to have her betray him at the earliest possible opportunity. Yet captive taking also enhanced a warrior's prestige, partly because it challenged the enemy's ability to protect and care for his family, partly because the work performed by captive women—cooking food, tanning skins, and making clothing and other utilitarian or ceremonial items—helped men to demonstrate their status to others.

The Mi'kmaq oral histories collected by Silas Rand do more than simply narrate events. Like other forms of prescriptive literature, they offer a model of how women should behave if captured by enemies. In one instance, a Kwetej war party attacked a Mi'kmaq village and captured the chief's wife while the men were away. The Mi'kmaq chief and one other warrior set out to bring her back. When they came to the enemy camp, they found the warriors asleep and the captive woman sitting up by the fire, mending moccasins. Her husband slid his belt under the side of the wigwam. Recognizing it (perhaps she had made it herself), the woman got up quietly and went outside to meet him. With her help, the two men killed all their enemies and brought the woman home.[12] Another story, told with many variants, features a captive

Wabanaki woman traveling on a river with her captors. In one version collected by Rand, a Mohawk war party took two Maliseet women just above the Grand Falls on the St. John River. The Mohawks, not noted (at least in Wabanaki stories) for their skill as canoeists, lashed several canoes together to form a raft and let it float downstream. Toward evening they slept, assured by their captives that the river would stay calm. The women slipped away just before the raft went over the falls and all their captors were killed. According to Rand, "They stripped the slain of their clothing and ornaments, and gathered much spoil; then they danced all night for joy, and were highly honored by their nation."[13]

It is notable that in both these stories the women seem to accept their fate calmly; there is no special emphasis on women captives as sexually vulnerable, emotionally distraught, or helpless. There is a shared expectation between captors and captives about how a woman should behave. Instead of tying her up or taking steps to prevent her escape, the captors take it for granted that she will do women's work such as mending moccasins or keeping watch while the men sleep. Clearly, "captive" should not be confused with "prisoner," that is, someone held against her will through physical restraint or incarceration in the Euro-American sense of the word. Later accounts by English captives report that some women were given the freedom to visit their children in other villages, and men might be given guns to go hunting. The persistent practice of giving captives considerable autonomy suggests that for the most part it worked, and that not every captive woman brought death and destruction to her captors. Nevertheless, the potential for disaster was there.

Women captives might adapt to their new circumstances, but stories insisted that they should never forget their grief and rage. In another episode of warfare between the Mi'kmaq and the Kwetej, a Mi'kmaq woman was captured, and her husband killed, by a Kwetej raiding party. The Kwetej chief, a powerful shaman, took the captive woman as his wife. She went along, of course, at least on the surface. Soon after a group of hunters from her village, returning home from the winter hunt, met the Kwetej party on the river. They recognized the woman and immediately understood what must have happened. Without acknowledging her presence, the Mi'kmaq chief invited the Kwetej party to camp and feast with him. Through clever tactics—cleverness being perhaps more important than brute strength for successful warriors—the Mi'kmaq men eventually killed all their enemies except for the chief and the captive woman. The Kwetej chief, a man of considerable spirit power, tried to escape by turning himself into a loon, only to be defeated in the end by the greater spirit power of the Mi'kmaq chief. The Mi'kmaq chief then told the woman to claim her husband's scalp, which had been taken by the enemy, and give it a proper burial. The woman took a knife, ripped open her captor's chest, and thrust the scalp inside. This, she declared, would be her husband's grave.[14] The passion depicted in the ending to this story belies the seemingly calm acceptance of captivity displayed by women who became the "wives" of their captors.

Conforming on the surface, hiding their emotions, captured women might wait years for the opportunity to escape or get revenge. If their kin failed to rescue them, captive women could always raise their sons in a subversive manner. One story tells how a Mi'kmaq woman, pregnant at the time of her capture, got revenge on her Kwetej captors, even though they took her far away into Canada. The Kwetej chief made her his wife and became so fond of her that he adopted her son, the child of her Mi'kmaq husband. The woman learned the Kwetej language and seemed to have forgotten her past. The son grew up excelling in all things, and it soon became clear that he had unusual spirit power (which Rand described as "magic"). When the son turned seventeen, his mother told him the truth about his father. She told him about her homeland, taught him the language, and spoke about the relatives left behind, including her two brothers and his true father's older sister. The young shaman decided to avenge his father and return to his own people. The woman made him a map of the Mi'kmaq country and a tiny pair of snowshoes in the Mi'kmaq style so that he would know their tracks. When the time came, the young shaman used his power to put the village into a deep sleep. He killed his stepfather and seven subchiefs, taking their scalps with him. Angry Kwetej warriors killed the woman in revenge, but the son escaped. He found his people by their tracks and, after another series of adventures, lived out his life among them in great honor.[15]

In sum, captive women posed a potential danger to the households and communities in which they lived. As these stories prescribe what Mi'kmaq women should do if captured, they also *describe* the risks inherent in bringing other women into Mi'kmaq households as captives. Captives, in general, might betray their captors or try to escape, even if they were incorporated by marriage or adoption. Captive women might also compete with local women for attention from men, arousing resentment and anger. Men with captive women in their households risked disaster for themselves and their people, especially when the women came from prominent families who could rally support to avenge, if not rescue, them.

The disruptive potential of captive women depicted in Mi'kmaq oral tradition may also be seen in European explorer accounts from the early contact period. Frenchman Marc Lescarbot described several incidents involving Armouchiquois captives living in a Mi'kmaq village near Port Royal on the Bay of Fundy around 1607. The Armouchiquois, sometimes identified as eastern Abenakis, but more likely a group affiliated with the Massachusett-speaking people further south, lived at the mouth of the Saco River on the Gulf of Maine.[16] Both Lescarbot and Samuel de Champlain describe a series of incidents between the Mi'kmaq and the Armouchiquois that culminated in a raid in which the Mi'kmaq living at Port Royal, led by the centenarian shaman-chief Membertou, traveled south with some four hundred allied warriors in search of revenge after Membertou's son-in-law, Panounias, was killed by some Armouchiquois men. Perhaps coincidentally, perhaps not, we know that two years before his death Panounias had an Armouchiquois "wife" in addition to his high-status wife, the daughter of Membertou.[17] Given the ongoing pattern of raid and counterraid between the Mi'kmaq and the Armouchiquois that is evident in these accounts, and the number of captives available for ransom on either side, it seems likely that the Armouchiquois woman was in fact a concubine or captive wife.

Lescarbot's account makes it clear that both sides took captives in war, and the captives display the kind of behavior described in the oral traditions above. In one instance, two Armouchiquois captives living in Membertou's village escaped by making a birchbark canoe and crossing the Bay of Fundy to the mainland, then making their way home on foot. In another case, a captive Armouchiquois woman living with the Mi'kmaq helped one of her countrymen to escape and gave him a tinderbox that she had stolen from Membertou's cabin. Lescarbot does not tell us why the woman stayed behind, but she would have been better off had she gone. When the escape was discovered, the hapless woman was taken to a camp four or five leagues distant from Port Royal. There she was executed by the "wives and daughters" of her Mi'kmaq captors. According to Lescarbot, the Mi'kmaq deemed it appropriate for a woman to be executed by other women. He wrote:

Kinibech-coech, a young maid of eighteen years of age, plump and fair, gave her the first stroke in the throat, which was with a knife. Another maid of the same age, handsome enough, called Metembroech, followed on, and the daughter of Membertou, whom we called Membertouech-coech, made an end of her. . . . This is their form of justice.[18]

The statement that one of Membertou's daughters struck the killing blow and the fact that the captive woman stole a tinderbox from Membertou's cabin suggest that she lived as a slave in Membertou's household.

This killing or execution highlights something deemphasized in the stories above: the vulnerability of a captive woman in an enemy camp. Men with captive women in their households could mistreat them with relative impunity, although other members of the household might intervene.[19] Women who found favor with a male captor ran the risk of alienating other women in the community. Separated from her own kin, a woman could not rely on their protection or support.

The question of whether or not indigenous women taken captive in intertribal warfare were raped is tricky because, at this time at least, there is not enough information to determine how Wabanaki people in the early contact period defined rape or even consensual sex. In oral tradition, captive women seem to make the transition to the role of "wife" with little resistance, although they might harbor thoughts of violent revenge. Linguistic evidence suggests that captive women were defined as sexually available. In his early eighteenth-century Abenaki dictionary, missionary Joseph Aubery defined "slave" as *A8akkañn* (ah-wahkan, the *8* being pronounced as *w* or *ou*), and listed related words that meant "a lewd, lascivious person" and "I am in the midst of the act . . . this sounds bad, as meaning in the middle of a passionate sin."[20] However, this does not tell us how sex might have been negotiated or coerced, or what would happen to a woman who said no.

In general, sex and violence were not equated as a measure of manhood or prestige for Wabanaki men. Unrestrained violence in warfare or against one's enemies brought approval for men, but a lack of restraint in sexual matters produced only scorn. A man who mistreated a woman beyond a socially sanctioned degree would be viewed with contempt. Still, captive women had very little protection if a man wanted to abuse them.[21]

The absence of specific references to what we would call rape does not, of course, prove anything. Evidence from oral tradition indicates that Wabanaki peoples used euphemisms when speaking of almost anything that could disrupt the balance of harmonious social relations within their small, face-to-face communities, as well as between groups, including both warfare and marriage. In some cases the silence around sexual matters may reflect the fact that those who collected and wrote down stories, such as missionary Silas Rand, edited the texts to conform to their own sensibilities. In other cases, storytellers may have censored themselves. Wabanaki peoples, like other indigenous peoples across North America, enjoy a rich repertoire of cautionary tales and humorous stories about sexual foolishness and bodily functions that get expurgated for outsiders, who might be offended or judge them by the standards of Christian morality. For example, in one story as published by Rand, a young woman found a neckbone and "treated it with contempt."[22] Some fifty years later, anthropologist Elsie Clews Parsons heard the same story from an old Mi'kmaq woman who said that the young woman in the story "sat" on the bone. The storyteller's daughter protested that the correct verb should be "pissed." The old woman conceded this to be true but added, "Nicer to say sit."[23]

Framing the question in terms of whether or not captive women were raped is less useful, in this instance, than exploring the range of possibilities for how captive women might be treated. A statement made by L'kimu, a Mi'kmaq shaman-chief who spoke to the Abbé Pierre Antoine Simon Maillard in 1740 about what life was like before the Europeans came, suggests a clear distinction between captive women who were slaves or concubines, and captive women who became wives. L'kimu described how the task of preserving the fire, especially in winter, was entrusted to the war-chief's women. A fire that lasted the full span of three moons became sacred and magical to them, and the woman who had been its guardian during the last days of the third moon was "showered with a thousand praises." If she was not already the war-chief's principal wife, she became so. If she was a concubine, she had the right to choose a husband from all those who gathered to honor her.[24] Lest there be any doubt about the meaning of the word "concubine" in this context, L'kimu claimed that the men who prayed to the sacred fire asked (at least in the English translation of the French transcriber's text) to "become strong and vigorous and always able to know [their] slave-women and the wives of [their] bed."[25] Thus, captive women could change their status by demonstrating personal or spirit power and contributing to the welfare of the group.

The sources suggest that adult captives were most often treated as slaves, that is, as people who had no basis for claiming reciprocal obligations in the community. In a sense, captives experienced social death; they could have been killed instead of taken, and unless something happened to change their status, their fate lay in the hands of their captors. Marc Lescarbot reported that the Mi'kmaq killed enemy warriors but showed "humanity and mercy towards their enemies' wives and little children, whose lives they spare[d], but who remain[ed] their prisoners to serve them, according to the ancient right of servitude."[26]

It should be noted that the institution of indigenous slavery among Wabanaki peoples in the early contact period differs from the model put forth by sociologist Orlando Patterson in his cross-cultural study of slavery in 186 societies across time and space.[27] Patterson's emphasis on indigenous slavery as an extreme relationship of dominance and subordination, or power and powerlessness, reflects a non-Wabanaki view of how power works. Among Wabanaki peoples in the early contact period, power was never fixed. It derived more from the spirit than from physical strength and hence was not intrinsically gendered, although given the gender-based division of labor in Wabanaki society, people generally demonstrated power in gendered ways. The ideal was balance rather than equality or hierarchy. People with less power had to rely on others for food, for social stability, and for protection from supernatural forces. Individuals who earned a reputation for being able to demonstrate power consistently, and whose power encompassed the well-being of others so that they in turn could achieve stability and parity in their own lives, became leaders. One reason why the experiences of captives taken by Wabanaki peoples were so diverse is that the institution was fluid, and captives who demonstrated power could alter their status.

The context of captive taking changed dramatically during the seventeenth century because English captives could be used by Wabanaki peoples to mediate relations with French and English colonists, even as captive taking continued to be a source of prestige for warriors. The families of English captives were willing to pay ransoms to get their relatives back, creating an economic incentive. During King Philip's War (1675–76), Massachusetts raised 340 pounds in public funds to ransom captives taken from Hatfield and Deerfield, but in later wars, Massachusetts instead offered to pay soldiers a bounty of eight pounds for every English captive brought back to New England, in addition to "what benefit they [could] make" from taking plunder and captives. Economics and diplomacy came together when the French started to pay money for English captives. In an extension of aboriginal practices, warriors could turn captives over to their French allies instead of to someone in the village. So, for example, in 1675 Benoni Stebbins reported that the Norwottocks from the middle Connecticut River told him that they were living in Canada and expected to receive eight pounds apiece for the captives.[28]

The most famous of the seventeenth-century English captives, Mary Rowlandson, was taken from Lancaster, Massachusetts, in 1675, during King Philip's War. The narrative of her captivity among the Nipmuc, Narragansett, and Wampanoag people of southern and central New England, published in 1682, became an instant bestseller. Perhaps hoping to squash rumors that she had become the wife of a Nipmuc man known to the English as One-Eyed John, Rowlandson wrote:

> I have been in the midst of those roaring Lyons, and Salvage Bears, that feared neither God, nor Man, nor the Devil, by night and day, alone and in company: sleeping all sorts together, and yet not one of them ever offered me the least abuse of unchastity to me, in word or action. Though some are ready to say, I speak it for my own credit; But I speak it in the presence of God, and to His glory.[29]

The Reverend William Hubbard may have been thinking of Rowlandson in his own account of the attack on Lancaster when he commented that, "to prevent Mistakes, let it here be observed, that none of the Women were abused."[30]

One way to reconcile the evidence that indigenous women taken captive were defined as sexually available to their Wabanaki captors while Englishwomen were not is by looking at how the related practice of adoption also changed over time. Adopting outsiders as a way of incorporating them into the kin group other than through marriage was not limited to captives, and the practice highlights the way in which kinship structured social relations. A relatively early example from 1652 tells us that the priest Gabriel Druillettes was adopted by the Abenaki community at Narantsouak (Norridgewock, Maine) as a father. This gave the young man—in his early thirties at the time—a position of respect in the community that he otherwise would not have had, although Druillettes and other European "fathers" soon learned that this kin term did not convey the same authority that it has in patriarchal societies.[31] Children, of course, were easily incorporated as sons and daughters, and the literature contains many examples of Iroquoian and Wabanaki people who refused to give them up. In some cases older youth and men were also adopted as sons, a position within the household that did not challenge the older men and women who benefited from the age hierarchy within Wabanaki society. Adult men might also be adopted as "brothers" by their captors, a more egalitarian relationship than "son."

The adoption of adult women taken captive could be an indigenous practice that predates the early contact period, but the evidence suggests that it was uncommon at best. Captive women were readily incorporated into households as slaves or concubines, and the fact that they were not kin gave their captors a certain freedom that might include harsh treatment, physical abuse, and forced sexual intimacy (here I include women who may have complied but would not have chosen to be in that situation). But captive women could also be incorporated into the kin group through marriage, sometimes as a second or third wife, and apparently this was a common practice.

When the pool of captives expanded to include Englishwomen, however, other variables were introduced that favored the practice of adopting women as sisters, a relationship that enmeshed them in reciprocal obligations but also defined them as sexually unavailable within their new households. Thus when Susannah Johnson, a married woman, was taken captive to the Abenaki mission of St. Francis in 1754, she was adopted as a sister by her master, Joseph-Louis Gill (himself the child of two English captives, born and raised among the Abenakis), which allowed them to live together without impropriety.[32] These adoptions also gave other women in the kin group a say in regulating potential marriages.

Not all Englishwomen taken captive were formally adopted. As slaves they could still live within Wabanaki households and do work, although the cultural definition of work was not frozen in time any more than the ritual practice of captive taking was. English captives might perform the same tasks as Wabanaki women—cooking, scraping hides, gathering firewood, and the like—but their captors were quick to make use of new skills. Francis Card, taken near the Kennebec River in Maine in 1676, reported on the welfare of other English captives after his own return, saying, "Such of the Women as were gifted at knitting and sewing, were improved to make Stockings and Garments for their Pateroons."[33] The wife of Phinehas Hull, taken near York, Maine, in August 1690, was valued for her skill in writing. During a negotiated captive exchange at Sagadahoc in 1691, her captors, who included "John Hawkins, an Indian Enemy Captain," were reluctant to part with her since "they had employed her in the place of a secretary."[34] This is not to say that all Englishwomen made good additions to a household. Susannah Johnson reported that she "was a novice at making canoes, bunks, and tumplines, which was the only occupation of the squaws [women]."[35] She succeeded better at milking cows and making shirts for her adopted brother. However, suffering from physical weakness after giving birth during the forced march to Canada, she earned the epithet "no good squaw" from her adopted sister when, instead of working, she "strolled gloomily about, looking sometimes into an unsociable wigwam, at others sauntering into the bushes, and walking on the banks of brooks."[36]

Overall, Wabanaki peoples were somewhat picky about who they adopted; certainly the warriors who traveled for days and weeks with newly captured men, women, and children had an opportunity to observe the captives, perhaps judging how well they would fit in if adopted. Once adopted, captives might still be ransomed or released when diplomatic or economic pressure forced their new families to give them up. Whether or not adult captives stayed permanently in Wabanaki communities had little to do with anyone making a "choice" about transculturation. Of over six hundred English captives taken by Wabanaki warriors prior to 1763, less than 3 percent—all children when captured, all but one taken before 1726—are definitely known to have become "white Indians."[37] Yet many captives formed affective bonds with their Indian families, and returning to New England did not mean that all contact between them ceased.

Englishwomen who were captured were treated differently from indigenous women captives because the practical consequences of treating the former as concubines, or harming them in other ways, introduced new considerations. The French, who allied with Wabanaki peoples against the English, providing guns and supplies and establishing mission villages where Wabanaki women and children could be relatively safe from English raids, shared a common cultural imperative with the English: to keep white women away from Indian men. However, the ways in which they articulated their concern suggests that the greater danger lay in temptation, especially for teenage girls, rather than force. Most of the Englishwomen brought to Wabanaki villages were ransomed as soon as possible by French priests, government officials, or local merchants, or by family members who offered cash incentives and used political pressure to secure their release.[38] Further, after 1689 English captives were generally taken to Catholic mission villages, where Christian ideals required Wabanaki people to live monogamously and made it a sin for a man to keep more than one wife or a concubine.[39]

In conclusion, folklore and oral tradition suggest that in the early contact period captive women were treated as slaves, people without kin ties to their captors who could be tortured, killed, or exploited for labor and services, including sex. This is supported by the sexual implications of the Abenaki word for slave as well as the 1740 statement by L'kimu, the Mi'kmaq shaman-chief, who differentiated between sexually available slave women, or concubines, and wives. Women who were accepted as "wives" had more control over their own lives than slaves because they could invoke reciprocal ties of kinship with others in the community.

This runs counter to the notion that all captives were adopted, a generalization which reflects the fact that much of the academic literature on captives and captive taking in the Northeast conflates Iroquoian and eastern Algonquian practices. Instead, the new practice of adopting adult women captives is a marker of how Wabanaki peoples adapted to a changing world. It seems likely that the practice of adopting captives became increasingly important in the late seventeenth century due to the influence of Christian beliefs, as well as the diplomatic implications of how captives were treated. Through adoption, Englishwomen could be incorporated into households in relationships that defined them as sexually unavailable to their male captors. The seeming ease with which the sexual implications of captivity disappeared once the pool of captives included Englishwomen, suggests that it was never central to the practice.

NOTES

I would like to thank Neal Salisbury and Susan Sleeper-Smith for their comments, and Merril Smith and Alden Vaughan for their particular encouragements, without which this essay would never have been finished.

1. See James Axtell, *The Invasion Within: The Contest of Cultures in Colonial North America* (New York: Oxford University Press, 1985), 310–11; Alden T. Vaughan and Daniel K. Richter, "Crossing the Cultural Divide: Indians and New Englanders, 1605–1763," chapter 10 in Alden T. Vaughan, ed., *Roots of American Racism: Essays on the Colonial Experience* (New York: Oxford University Press, 1995), 339 n129; Neal Salisbury, ed., *The Sovereignty and Goodness of God: Together with the faithfulness of his promises displayed: being a narrative of the captivity and restoration of Mrs. Mary Rowlandson and related documents* (Boston: Bedford Books, 1997), 107 n82. Note that the most common explanations in the literature, such as a cultural prohibition against warriors having sex while on the warpath, contain an implicit assumption that rape is a natural corollary of war and that its absence, rather than its presence, must be explained.

2. Quoted in Vaughan and Richter, "Crossing the Cultural Divide," 243.

3. See Gordon M. Day, "Oral Tradition as Complement," *Ethnohistory* 19 (1972): 99–108.

4. Silas T. Rand, *Legends of the Micmacs*, Wellesley Philological Publications (New York: Longmans, Green, and Co., 1894).

5. Cf. Ira Berlin, "Time, Space, and the Evolution of Afro-American Society on British Mainland North America," *American Historical Review* 85 (1980): 44–78.

6. James Axtell, "The White Indians of Colonial North America," *William and Mary Quarterly*, 3rd. ser., 32 (1975): 55–88; Daniel K. Richter, "War and Culture: The Iroquois Experience," *William and Mary Quarterly*, 3rd ser., 40 (1983): 528–59.

7. Evan Haefeli and Kevin Sweeney, "Revisiting *The Redeemed Captive*: New Perspectives on the 1704 Attack on Deerfield," in Colin G Calloway, ed., *After King Philip's War: Presence and Persistence in Indian New England* (Hanover, N.H.: University Press of New England, 1997), 32–34, 52–53.

8. Pauline Turner Strong, *Captive Selves, Captivating Others: The Politics and Poetics of Colonial American Captivity Narratives* (Boulder, Colo.: Westview Press, 1999), 82.

9. Richter expands on his earlier work in Daniel K. Richter, *The Ordeal of the Longhouse: The Peoples of the Iroquois League in the Era of European Colonization* (Chapel Hill: University of North Carolina Press, 1992), 30–74.

10. Alice Nash, "The Abiding Frontier: Family, Gender and Religion in Wabanaki History, 1600–1763," Ph.D. dissertation, (Columbia University, 1997), 95–106, 253–60.

11. See, for example, Emma Lewis Coleman, *New England Captives Carried to Canada between 1677 and 1760 during the French and Indian Wars*, 2 vols. (Portland, Maine: Southworth Press, 1925), 1: 69, 142, 425, 2: 11–12, 21–22, 55–56, 136–38, 140–44, 152–53, 184, 225–27.

12. Rand, *Legends of the Micmacs*, 137–38; see also 139–40, 219–22. Story told to Rand in Micmac by Michael Snake, n.d.

13. Rand, *Legends of the Micmacs*, 344; see also 139. In an Abenaki variant from Odanak, Quebec, dated December 28, 1922, Louis Napoleon Obomsawin told A. Irving Hallowell a story told to him by Sabbatis Hannis, who "heard it from someone else." An Abenaki woman, captured by Mohawks, tricked them into going over the falls on the Vermillion River, a branch of the St. Maurice River in Quebec. A. Irving Hallowell Collection, Mss. 26, Series II, Box 1, folder 6, American Philosophical Society, Philadelphia.

14. Rand, *Legends of the Micmacs*, 126–36. The story was told to Rand in Mi'kmaq by Jacob Mitchell, Charlottetown, Prince Edward Island, 1848.

15. Rand, *Legends of the Micmacs*, 169–78. The story was told to Rand by a daughter of Peter Toney of Pictou; she heard it from her father's eldest brother, Francis John Toney.

16. Emerson Woods Baker, "Trouble to the Eastward: The Failure of Anglo-Indian Relations in Early Maine," Ph.D. dissertation (College of William and Mary, 1986), 22.

17. Marc Lescarbot, *The History of New France*, ed. H. P. Biggar, 3 vols. (Toronto: Champlain Society, 1907–1914), 368–69; "The Defeat of the Armouchiquois Savages by Chief Membertou and His Savage Allies, in New France, in the Month of July, 1607," trans. Thomas H. Goetz, in William Cowan, ed., *Papers of the Sixth Algonquian Conference, 1974* (Ottawa: National Museum of Man, Mercury Series, Canadian Ethnology Service Paper No. 23, 1975), 141–79.

18. Lescarbot, *History of New France*, 3:216–17.

19. Lescarbot, *History of New France*, 3:215. Some of the violent behavior chronicled by seventeenth-century writers should clearly be ascribed to the derangement of particular individuals, perhaps due to grief, rather than cultural norms. When Mehitable Goodwin's Abenaki master lost control and was about to kill her, his horrified friends intervened and persuaded him to let them ransom her. Cotton Mather, "The Condition of the Captives," in Alden T. Vaughan and Edward W. Clark, eds., *Puritans among the Indians: Accounts of Captivity and Redemption, 1675–1724* (Cambridge: Belknap Press, 1981 [1684]), 141.

20. *Matsa8ékkañs8inno* [mat-sa-WEHK-kan-sa-winno] and *nedampta8ékkañsi* [neh-dam-pi-ta-WEHK-kan-si], respectively. Joseph Aubery, *Father Aubery's French Abenaki Dictionary*, trans. Stephen Laurent (Portland, Maine: Chisholm Bros. Publishers, 1995), 10.

21. Nash, "The Abiding Frontier," 170–73.

22. Rand, *Legends of the Micmacs*, 165.

23. Elsie Clews Parsons, "Micmac Folklore," *Journal of American Folklore* 38 (1925): 65; see also commentary by Ruth Holmes Whitehead, *Stories from the Six Worlds: Micmac Legends* (Halifax, N.S.: Nimbus Publishing Limited, 1988), 219–20, 234–36.

24. Pierre Antoine Simon Maillard, letter orig. pub. as "Lettre à Madame de Drucourt," in *Les Soirées Canadiennes* (Québec: Brousseau Frères, 1863), trans.

Margaret Anne Hamelin and excerpted in Ruth Homes Whitehead, *The Old Man Told Us: Excerpts from Micmac History* (Halifax, N.S.: Nimbus Publishing Limited, 1991), 9–14.

25. Maillard, "Lettre à Madame de Drucourt," in Whitehead, *The Old Man Told Us*, 12.

26. Lescarbot, *History of New France*, 3:215.

27. Orlando Patterson, *Slavery and Social Death: A Comparative Study* (Cambridge: Harvard University Press, 1982), 1–3, 9–10. For a compelling application of Patterson's work, see William A. Starna and Ralph Watkins, "Northern Iroquoian Slavery," *Ethnohistory* 38 (1991): 34–57, especially pp. 36–37.

28. Increase Mather, "Quentin Stockwell's Relation of His Captivity and Redemption," in Vaughan and Clark, *Puritans among the Indians*, 89; General Court of Massachusetts, June 7, 1690, in Ernest Myrand, *Sir William Phips devant Québec: histoire dun siege* (Montreal: Librairie Beauchemin, 1925), 179; Peter R. Christoph and Florence A. Christoph, eds., *The Andros Papers, 1674–1676: Files of the Provincial Secretary of New York during the Administration of Governor Sir Edmund Andros, 1674–1680*, 3 vols. (Syracuse, N.Y.: Syracuse University Press, 1989), 1:254–55.

29. Salisbury, *Sovereignty and Goodness of God*, 107.

30. William Hubbard, *The History of the Indian Wars in New England*, 2 vols., rev. and supp. by Samuel Drake (Bowie, Md.: Heritage Books, 1990, facs. repr. 1864 [1677]), 2:48.

31. Reuben Gold Thwaites, ed., *The Jesuit Relations and Allied Documents: Travels and Explorations of the Jesuit Missionaries in New France, 1610–1791*, 73 vols. (Cleveland: Burrows Brothers Co., 1896–1901), 38:27–31, 33, 35.

32. Susannah Willard Johnson, *A Narrative of the Captivity of Mrs. Johnson, containing an Account of Her Sufferings during Four Years, with the Indians and French* (Walpole, N.H.: David Carlisle, 1796), 65.

33. Hubbard, *History of the Indian Wars*, 2:201.

34. Coleman, *New England Captives*, 1:171.

35. Johnson, *A Narrative*, 66.

36. Johnson, *A Narrative*, 69.

37. Nash, "The Abiding Frontier," 276 (Table 5.1).

38. Nash, "The Abiding Frontier," 270–71, 288–93. Note that none of the adult Englishwomen captured by Wabanaki men stayed permanently with their captors.

39. Nash, "The Abiding Frontier," 225–29.

2

"Playing the Rogue"

Rape and Issues of Consent in Seventeenth-Century Massachusetts

Else L. Hambleton

THERE ARE CONSTANTS in the female experience of rape. The typical rape victim in the seventeenth century, as today, was unmarried, employed, knew her attacker, and was unlikely to report the assault. Her assailant, in the unlikely event of prosecution, offered a defense as effective in the early modern world as today: the sexual activity had been consensual; there had been no struggle; and, he would assert, her sexual reputation was such that no reasonable man could have expected to meet with a refusal.

These constants, however, mask significant differences. The physical and psychological effects of rape were exacerbated by the Puritan conflation of chastity and femininity. Public knowledge of the loss of virginity reduced a rape victim's marriageability. Shame, too, was a powerful incentive to silence. In addition, the Puritan belief in predestination meant that as women who successfully resisted rapists credited God for their salvation, those who failed felt the full weight of God's abandonment. These women had little to gain and much to lose by reporting a sexual assault.

Rape victims faced additional difficulties. First, the seventeenth-century belief in female inferiority and the concomitant application of a sexual double standard led to conflicting notions of the seriousness of the crime of rape.[1] Grand jurymen had the power to ignore a complaint, or they could lay a charge along a continuum of criminality from fornication, which penalized the victim too, through assault, or lewd and lascivious behavior, to attempted rape or rape. Grand jurymen were influenced by the class, the age, the marital status, and the reputation of the female victim and the man she accused. Second, the ideological construction of women as the "lustful daughters of Eve" imbued everyday female behavior with sexual meaning.[2] A smile while mutually engaged in fieldwork could be construed as an invitation. Third, the language of sexuality, the discourse of intercourse, privileged male aggressiveness over female submission. In consensual sexual intercourse, women "submitted" or "suffered" men to "use" or "occupy" their bodies for the purpose of "begetting children upon" them.[3] Fourth, rape was difficult to prove. Two witnesses and an outcry were required. Even in cases where the rules of evidence appear to have been satisfied, a guilty verdict was not certain. Fifth, the narrow legal definition of rape conveyed the belief that if a woman conceived as the result of coerced sexual intercourse she had been a willing participant. The Massachusetts Bay Court of Assistants used an English jurisprudence manual, Michael Dalton's *The Countrey Justice,* when they constructed their law code. Dalton defined rape as violent nonconsensual sexual intercourse. The issue of consent was paramount to Dalton. If a woman had consented after the fact, or if she had consented to intercourse out of fear for her life, her attacker was to be charged with rape. Dalton believed, though, and Puritan judges and juries agreed with him, that:

> [if] a woman at the time of the supposed rape do conceive with child by the Ravisher, this is no Rape, for a woman cannot conceive with child, except she doth consent.[4]

This presumption of consent upon conception made a world of legal difference to young women in seventeenth-century Massachusetts. All these factors meant that a decision to lay a rape charge was never cut-and-dried, and a verdict of guilty was never a foregone conclusion.

Rape was a capital offense, but men were reluctant to hang other men for engaging in heterosexual sexual activity including rape. Only fourteen men were tried for rape and three men for attempted rape by the Massachusetts Court of Assistants between 1630 and 1692. One might conclude, then, that sexual violence against women was limited. However, these low numbers are evidence *not* that sexual violence was rare in seventeenth-century Massachusetts but that women were reluctant to report incidents, and that those responsible for administering criminal justice, from the grand jurymen of the local quarterly courts to the justices of the Massachusetts Court of Assistants, were predisposed to see the use of force as an extreme, but not necessarily illegal, expression of normal male sexual activity. Only those cases in which the victim was married, where the issue of consent could be bypassed, or cases in which the victim was ten years of age or less and incapable of consent, resulted in guilty verdicts from Puritan juries.[5]

An understanding of the sex ways of Massachusetts is integral to any examination of the dynamics of rape prosecutions in seventeenth-century Massachusetts. It was illegal for unmarried women and men to engage in consensual sexual intercourse in seventeenth-century Massachusetts. For much of the eighteenth century as well the potential for criminal prosecution remained for women who bore bastards. Single women who were raped were seen as involuntarily participating in an illegal act for which Puritan women were more likely to be prosecuted than their male partners, and if convicted, to be sentenced more severely than their male partners, even if they were of equivalent social status.[6]

Puritans had moral and economic reasons for criminalizing extramarital sexual intercourse. First, sex between single women and single or married men was explicitly prohibited in the Bible which was foundational to Puritan jurisprudence. As well, Covenant theology promised Puritans that in return for obeying His commandments and eschewing sin, God would see to it that Massachusetts prospered. While frequent and satisfying sexual intercourse was the right and duty of husband and wife to each other, marriage was the only appropriate venue for fully consummated coitus.

The economic imperative for prohibiting extramarital sexual intercourse was considerable, as evidenced by a 1668 amendment to Massachusetts fornication law that privileged the collection of child support payments from putative fathers over prosecuting men for fornication. Bastards represented a potential drain on town resources. Moreover, there was the economic cost borne by employers in the form of lost or more limited production from pregnant female servants. For these reasons, Puritans successfully controlled extramarital sexual activity through a combination of criminal prosecutions of single women who bore illegitimate children, some of their partners, and couples whose first child arrived within thirty-two weeks of marriage, and through cultural impediments that mediated against premarital sex.

That Puritans successfully limited coitus outside marriage is evident from the number of persons prosecuted for fornication. In the forty-five-year period prior to 1686 in Essex County, Massachusetts, there were an average of 2.3 illegitimate fornication prosecutions and 3.3 pre-marital fornication prosecutions annually.[7]

The central issue for the Court in rape and attempted rape prosecutions seems not to have been that sexual intercourse was accomplished through violent means, but that it had occurred at all. The generally light sentences given to single male rapists and attempted rapists when the victim was unmarried, both in the Court of Assistants and in the Essex County Quarterly Court, suggest that a certain level of coercion was an acceptable part of sexual activity when both participants were single.

Depositions filed in the fornication prosecution of Elizabeth Emerson of Haverhill in 1685–6, open a door into the past that allows us to listen to a disparate group of seventeenth-century women discussing rape and their understanding of the conditions necessary to conception. The discussion was heated: it was during the course of an argument that the diverse viewpoints were presented. The participants were twenty-one-year-old Elizabeth Emerson, who was in labor, her mother, Hannah Emerson, her sister, Hannah Dustin, the midwife, Johanah Corliss, and at least three neighbors—Liddia Ladd, Mary Neff, and Johanah Haseltine.

The quarrel began when Corliss assumed her legal role and asked Emerson to name the baby's father. The required paternity statement had taken on increased significance because when Emerson and her father had gone to the magistrate during her pregnancy to lay formal charges against Timothy Swan, she had claimed that Swan had raped her in her parents' new bedchamber, which Swan had asked to see. The neighbors greeted this claim with skepticism. Goodwife Corliss asked why she hadn't scratched him or kicked him. Goodwife Haseltine asserted that she would have made "ye towne ringe of it before ye morning."[8]

The four Puritan matrons—Corliss, Haseltine, Neff, and Ladd—espoused an assertive response. A reading of this deposition alone suggests they were giving Emerson good advice and that there was a community expectation that rape victims should struggle vigorously and call out. However, a cumulative reading of depositions describing similar incidents indicates that most young women lacked the necessary confidence in the system to test the strength of the neighborhood belief in their chastity by making a charge. Emerson had already violated the Puritan ideal of femininity as a teenager when some unspecified misdeed or act of rebelliousness had provoked her father to beat her so severely that he was prosecuted by the quarterly court of Essex County.[9]

Depositions in this case provide evidence of the Puritan expectation that conception would occur only if the intercourse was consensual, and that it would not happen if the young woman had been a virgin before intercourse. Goodwife Hazeltine stated that "it was impossible or very unlikely for a maide to be with childe at ye first, being forced."[10] These women were not informed solely by simple folk beliefs about the origin of babies. Early modern English medical texts advised that a female orgasm promoted conception. It is hardly surprising that they, like Puritan juries composed of men, believed that conception would not occur as the outcome of rape.

The depositions in the Emerson case also confirm that claims of rape might be met with disbelief if the claimant had a damaged reputation and a weak story.[11] She had failed to cry out and she had not made a timely accusation of rape. Swan was not charged with rape or fornication, although he was required to pay child support for Emerson's daughter, whom she named Dorothie after Swan's sister. Six years later, in 1691, Emerson committed infanticide after giving birth secretly to illegitimate twin daughters rather than face a second fornication prosecution. She was hanged in June 1693.

Puritans looked not to traditional English common law, in which heterosexual rape was a capital crime, but to the Bible when they drew up their first law code for the Massachusetts Bay Colony. Mosaic law was the more complex of the two systems; the penalties for rape depended on the marital status of the victim. The Bible prescribed death by stoning for rape in cases where the victim of rape or attempted rape was either married or engaged. The rape of a married or engaged woman was a capital offense because sexual intercourse with her was an injury to her husband and/or fiancé. Puritan adultery statutes further justified the death penalty for the rape of a married or engaged woman.

Mosaic law enjoined marriage between the victim and her rapist in cases where the woman had no prior attachment. The Puritans, to their credit, given their devotion to the idea of establishing a Commonwealth governed by biblical precepts, did not think that marrying a rape victim to her rapist was an appropriate or fair remedy. Nor did they think that capital punishment was appropriate in the case of the rape of a single woman because of the issue of consent. They were caught between Mosaic law, which was inadequate in this instance, and English common law, which was too secular for their religious Commonwealth. Furthermore, there was no Mosaic precedent for the rape of a child.[12]

The first recorded rape case tried in New England reflects this judicial uncertainty. In 1636, an indentured servant, Edward Woodley, broke into a neighboring house and assaulted a female servant. He was charged with attempted rape, swearing, and housebreaking, sentenced to be whipped thirty stripes, to spend a year in prison at hard labor, and to wear an iron collar.[13] Four months later, the Court ordered him released to his master if the woman he had assaulted would declare herself to be free of fear from him. As an indentured servant, he was not free to marry his victim, thus marriage was not a possible alternative to punishment.

The Court was forced to include a law specifically addressing the issue of child rape in 1641 following the discovery that two young girls, Sarah and Dorcas Humfrey, both under the age of ten, had been sexually abused for a period of three years by their father's servants. The Court learned that nothing in the colony's current law code prohibited either consensual or nonconsensual sexual activity between adults and children and moved swiftly to close this loophole. They revised the rape statute to make sexual intercourse with a child aged ten or less a capital crime. The rape of an engaged or married woman was also a capital crime, but the punishment for raping a single woman was left to the discretion of the judges. It could be capital punishment, but a lesser punishment could be levied, depending on the circumstances.

The Court rationalized its decision to levy the death penalty in cases where the victim was aged ten or less in two ways. Mosaic law mandated the death penalty for sodomy and bestiality. As with sexual intercourse between men, or with animals, intercourse with children could not possibly be fruitful and was therefore unnatural. John Winthrop articulated their reasoning, saying "it should be death for a man to have carnal copulation with a girl so young, as there can be no possibility of generation, for it is against nature as well as sodomy and buggery."[14] This logic cut two ways. Dorcas also accused two of her brothers, but since neither of them had reached puberty, they were not charged. The second rationale was that children aged ten or less were incapable of consent. However, the Court was not comfortable with this second line of reasoning and when a new law code, *The Laws and Liberties of Massachusetts*, was issued in 1648, the only rape law that remained in force involved married and single women over the age of ten, as girls that age or less were deemed incapable of understanding enough either to consent or actively not to consent.[15]

This law sufficed until 1669, when Patrick Jeannison raped eight-year-old Grace Roberts. Judges wanted to hang Jeannison, but they found that there was no legal provision for capital punishment since his victim was under ten years of age. They referred the case to the General Court, which decided that since the rape of a child was a more heinous crime than the rape of a single woman, they could infer that capital punishment was legal in this case and in other cases involving children.[16]

In only seventeen instances between 1636 and 1692 did local grand juries refer suspected rapists to the Massachusetts Bay Court of Assistants for prosecution. Fourteen of them were prosecuted for rape; three more were prosecuted for attempted rape. The prosecutions occurred in two clusters. The first cluster occurred between 1636 and 1642 when three men were tried for rape and two men for attempted rape. The second cluster occurred after a twenty-five-year interval which saw no recorded prosecutions for rape or attempted rape in the Court of Assistants. Twelve of the seventeen cases tried by the Court of Assistants between 1636 and 1692, or 70 percent, occurred in a fifteen-year period between 1667 and 1683.[17] During the twenty-five-year hiatus between the two clusters of Court of Assistants rape and attempted rape prosecutions, eight men were tried for attempted rape in the Essex County Quarterly Court. Presumably men were also prosecuted for attempted rape in other Massachusetts County quarterly courts. But these courts had jurisdiction over minor offenses, and punishment they imposed was limited to whipping or to a maximum fine of 10 pounds, which evinces the reluctance of Puritan grand juries to treat the rape of a single woman as anything other than aggressive consensual sexual intercourse.

In the first cluster of rape prosecutions, between 1636 and 1642, all the assailants and four of their victims were unmarried young persons. Four of the men were indentured servants; the age of the fifth (seventeen) suggests he was too. Four of the women they assaulted were teenaged servants. The fifth, Mary Greenfield, was a seven-year-old who lived with her family. The punishments levied by the

Court during this period were consistent. Two attempted rapes in 1636 and 1639 were punished by whipping and a short prison term. In the 1639 case the attempted rapist was ordered to compensate his female victim with 5 pounds. In 1641, Jonathan Thing, Mary Greenfield's rapist, was whipped, and ordered to pay the victim's father 20 pounds within three years.

In 1642, the Court of Assistants tried two indentured servants, Robert Wyar and John Garland, for rape. The verdict clearly illustrates the reluctance of Puritan judges and juries to punish young men who engaged in coitus with single women with the death penalty and their propensity to treat coerced sexual intercourse as consensual coitus. There had been enough evidence to initiate a prosecution; the will to convict was lacking.

> Robert Wyar & John Garland beeing indited for ravishing two yong girles, the fact confessed by the girles and the girles both upon search found to have bin defloured, and filthy dalliance confessed by the boyes; the Jury found them, not guilty, with reference to the Capitall Law. The Court judged the boyes to bee openly whipped at Boston, the next market day, and againe to be whipped at Cambridge on the Lecture day and each of them to pay 5lb a peece to their master in service. It was also judged that the two girls Sarah Wythes and Ursula Odle, being both guilty of that wickednes, shall bee severely whipped at Cambridge in the presence of the Secretary.[18]

This verdict indicates that Puritan juries were reluctant to convict men of rape if they believed there was a possibility that their partners had consented to coitus.

Although there are only five cases in this initial cluster of rapes and attempted rapes, they provide us the first opportunity to assess the attitudes of the elected representatives to the Court of Assistants to sexual violence. All five men were whipped; but so were two of the single women who reported being raped. Compensatory payments were made on four of the five occasions, but in only one case was the payment made to the victim. None of the rapists or attempted rapists suffered a penalty more severe than that paid by a man who fathered an illegitimate child during consensual coitus. The explicit identification of chastity and femininity, and the implicit construction of women as innately more sexual than men made it difficult for an unmarried woman who had been raped to secure a conviction.

There had always been a dissonance between Puritan religious ideology that ascribed chastity as the defining female characteristic and popular cultural beliefs about women. The early modern ideology of women as the instigators of sexual activity was the more powerful. Under both belief systems, however, women were responsible for protecting themselves from aggressive male sexual behavior. As Massachusetts was increasingly drawn into the Atlantic community, early modern English economic and social values competed with the Puritan ideal. The adoption of the Halfway Covenant in 1662 to make church membership more inclusive was symptomatic of a general decline in religious fervor. Fornication prosecutions increased in number, due not to any intensification of already strenuous efforts by the Puritans to control sexuality in the face of a changing moral climate, but to the fact that greater numbers of couples were engaging in extramarital sexual activity despite the social controls long in place in the Puritan community.[19] Prosecutions for rape at the superior court level also resumed. The second cluster of rape and attempted rape cases occurred after a twenty-five-year interval with no recorded prosecutions at the superior court level. Seventy percent of rape and attempted rape prosecutions occurred between 1667 and 1683. The five men who were hanged for rape were executed during this fifteen-year period. In 25 percent of the cases, the female victim was also declared culpable, and these cases were referred back to county quarterly courts and prosecuted as fornication. In the final rape case prosecuted by the Court of Assistants in 1683, the case was referred to the Suffolk County Quarterly Court, although the defendant, Christopher Portingall confessed, and a vaginal examination of the victim indicated penetration had occurred. The Court of Assistants had effectively abrogated their responsibility to try rape cases as capital crimes when the victims were single women.[20]

Four of the defendants in this second cluster were nonwhite. Three of them, Tom Indian, Twenty Rod, and Samuel Indian were tried in the four-year period prior to King Philip's War (1675–76). All of them were convicted. While drunk, Twenty Rod brutally raped a nine-year-old native American child. He was ordered deported to the Caribbean and sold. Tom Indian raped a married native American woman and was hanged. Samuel Indian was found guilty of the attempted rape of a fifty-two-year-old Puritan woman, Mary Bacon. His fate is unrecorded. The fourth was an African American, Basto Negro, who raped his master's three-year-old daughter in 1676. His master, Robert Cox, petitioned the Court to have Basto, who had been sentenced to hang, released to him. In each of these cases, the victim was either a child or a married woman. So the cases clearly came under the jurisdiction of the Court of Assistants where they were tried.

No young man, whether white, African American, or native American, was executed for raping an unmarried woman. Whippings, fines, and, in one case, the wearing of a symbolic noose, were imposed as punishments. The law allowed judges discretion in sentencing unless the victim was married or, for restricted periods of time, aged ten or less, and judges exercised their option. Judges were predisposed to assume that the victim had consented, had provoked her rape through seductive behavior, or that coitus had resulted from consensual petting that got out of control. In the exception that proves the rule, William Cheney, a middle-aged, married, and prosperous Dorchester farmer, was executed for the rape of his unmarried maidservant in 1681. In his case the presumption of aggressive male sexual activity occurring within a courting context could not be supported.

Although the number of prosecuted rape cases is too low to draw definitive conclusions about the prevalence of sexual violence in seventeenth-century Massachusetts, some inferences can be drawn. First, the very fact that the number of rape prosecutions is so limited indicates that the likelihood a woman who was raped would report it to the authorities was low. The consequences of a public admission of loss of virginity were severe. Only three of the ten women who were unmarried at the time of their rape can be definitively shown to have married later.[21] One of them, Ursula Odle, was fourteen when she was raped in 1642. Grace Roberts had been eight at the time of her assault. In both these instances, considerable time elapsed between their rape and their marriage. A third woman, Elizabeth Holbrook, who was nineteen when she was raped, did not marry until she was thirty-two. A loss of chastity, however involuntary, represented a significant bar to future marriage.

Second, there was a risk to accusing a man of rape. Five of the nine single women who laid a charge of rape or attempted rape that was prosecuted in the Court of Assistants were subsequently charged with fornication. For example, when Alice Burwood, a Boston servant, went to the authorities in 1638 and told them that John Bicker-staff, also a servant, had raped her, she was censured to "bee whipped for yielding to Bickerstaffe without crying out and conceal-ing it 9 or 10 dayes."[22] It cannot have been much comfort to her that Bickerstaff was whipped fifteen lashes to her ten. Her employer was so affronted by her sexual activity and the subsequent stain on her character that a court order was required to force him to receive her back into his house after the whipping. In 1676, Benjamin Simonds was prosecuted for raping Elizabeth Pierce, but convicted of at-tempted rape. The verdict was overturned three months later and both Pierce and Simonds were convicted of fornication.[23]

Efforts were also made to intimidate witnesses. A twenty-seven-year-old married woman, Mary Ash, was harassed by her rapist and his brother. In an attempt to frighten her and confuse her about which brother had been the actual rapist, Samuel Guild and his brother John appeared repeatedly before her at her house wearing identical clothes. This behavior did not help Samuel. He was hanged because the woman he had raped was married. There were no issues of consent to muddy the waters: Guild was guilty of adultery, also a capital offense.

Third, the justices followed the letter of the rape law in all but two instances. A married tinker, Thomas Waters, was charged with raping thirty-nine-year-old Bethiah Johnson. Although Waters was acquitted, he was ordered to leave Massachusetts within 10 days.[24] He had previ-ously been prosecuted for lying, swearing, and theft, and the authori-ties may have welcomed an excuse to expel him. William Cheney, as mentioned above, was hanged, but he had compounded the rape with an escape attempt, and his age and status precluded returning him to the community unpunished. All the defendants who were executed, with the exception of Cheney, had raped either a child or a married woman. Cheney and Waters were also the only rape defendants who were married. The 1673 rape trial of Peter Croy, a twenty-year-old French servant, demonstrates the difficulty of securing a conviction, given the rules of evidence and the reluctance of the Court of Assistants to punish youthful male defendants to the full extent of the law despite a preponderance of evidence and the youth of the victim.[25] His victim was a thirteen-year-old servant, Sarah Lambert, who, with her fifteen-year-old sister, Mary, had gone at nightfall to collect cattle owned by Mistress Pod, their employer, from Ipswich's day pasture. Croy was searching for his master's cows in the same darkening field.

Lambert provided a graphic description of sexual violence in her testimony:

> Peter Croy came to her and tooke her by the middle and threw her downe on the ground and tooke up her coates and lay upon her belly shee cryed out to her sister that was not farr off and hee stopped her breath with his hand on her throat. He lay upon her a long time and she felt his member in her body which did hurt her and afterward she felt wet upon her shift and that her privy parte did burne.[26]

Her sister, Mary, added that she had seen "his naked privityes, the agitation and thrashing of his body upon my sister."[27] An additional witness, John Divan, Croy's thirteen-year-old companion, reported that he had heard Sarah cry out, "you french curr, lett me alone," that he had accused Croy of "playing the rogue with Pods girle," and that Croy had enjoined his silence.[28] The testimony of Mary Lambert and John Divan met an important Puritan evidentiary requirement. Both could attest that Sarah Lambert had cried out. Only Mary Lambert, however, could provide direct eyewitness testimony because Divan had arrived as Croy straightened his clothes. The testimony of two eyewitnesses or a confession was required to convict in capital cases.

The sequence of events over the next few days can be learned from Peter Croy's testimony. Sarah and Mary Lambert did not tell their employer, Mistress Pod, about the rape until the following morning. This was not the timely disclosure hoped for by the court. Mistress Pod waited a further four days before informing a magistrate. Whether she was inhibited by the harm that public awareness might cause Lambert's sexual reputation, or by fear that the news might place her household in a negative light is unknowable. Croy claimed that Mistress Pod had gone to the magistrate out of fear that Lambert might be pregnant.

Two panels were assembled eleven days after the alleged rape. Lambert's body was examined by a committee of women who determined that she had been penetrated by "this or some other man." Croy and the other witnesses were questioned by a grand jury. Croy provided a statement which allows a unique insight into his actions. He admitted that his intent was to have sexual intercourse with Sarah Lambert:

> I confesse I would have beene naught with ye wench whether she would or no but was hindered from carnall knowledge of her body by

reasons John Dyd come and called to me which made me rise up before I could comitt ye act nor can it be comprehended that I could in that time easily committ ye act

1. because my clothes were all up and I was not naked with her nor did I ever fully enter hir body
2. her sister or herselfe might easily have hindered
3. there were no signes of her being deflowered that were seene or observed.
4. If I had committed the act I humbly conceive I could not leagally be charged with it by Sarah or Dame Pod
   1. because Sarah never spake of it either to John Divan when he came to us or any Else
   2. Nor did shee speake of it to her Dame till next morning and hir Dame did not complaine to any officer till foure days after and that was only for feare she should prove with his child and then shee should be undone for ever of the deed.[29]

This statement was sufficient to bind Peter Croy over to the Massachusetts Court of Assistants on a charge of rape. Croy, however, recanted this statement at his trial. The requirements for conviction in a capital crime were strict and they had not been met. Lambert was no longer a virgin, but there was only one direct eyewitness, reporting had been delayed, and Croy refused to confess. No official verdict survives but since Croy was charged with not wearing his noose around his neck at the Essex County Quarterly Court in Ipswich in May 1674, it appears he was convicted of rape, but given only symbolic capital punishment. Wearing a noose served the dual function of shaming Croy and warning the community that there was a convicted rapist in their midst.

Rape and attempted rape cases prosecuted by the Massachusetts Bay Court of Assistants and the county quarterly courts provide concrete evidence of the incidence of sexual violence in seventeenth-century Massachusetts. There is, however, a third category of sex prosecutions that indicates the impossibility of a rape or attempted rape charge if the victim conceived as a result of coerced sex. Depositions filed by women who bore illegitimate children and who were subsequently prosecuted for fornication in the Essex County Quarterly Court indicate that, as Dalton had stated and popular opinion confirmed, conception "proved" to the Puritans that a victim had consented to sexual intercourse and had received pleasure from the act.

Forty-five percent of women who bore illegitimate children between 1640 and 1685 in Essex County were between the ages of 15 and
twenty and worked away from home when they conceived.[30] The potential for sexual abuse was considerable in an economic system where
production occurred in a patriarchal household containing a husband
and wife, sons, daughters, apprentices and servants, both male and female, and every person worked, ate, worshiped, and slept (often in the
same room) as part of a family unit. When an unmarried woman conceived, no matter how vile the physical assault had been, how virtuous
she had been perceived to be in the past, or how many witnesses there
were to attest to the fact that she had been forced, there was no possibility of a rape prosecution. The fornication trial of Anne Chase of Salisbury in 1670 is typical. Although her father was a prosperous carpenter, Chase worked as a servant in the busy household of her maternal
uncle, Henry Wheeler and his wife, Abigail. In December 1669, Chase
gave birth to an illegitimate child. Chase told her midwife, Elignor Bayley, that Abigail Wheeler's twenty-one-year-old brother, John Allen,
was the father of her child.

> [He] met her by ye way as shee was going to her lodging, and suddenly
> laide hands on her; and shee told him hee would wrong her: his answer
> was, hee would right her againe: shee saide that shee would Cry out,
> he tould her that hee would stop her mouth, and hee forced her against
> ye Railes, and shee being in a sore fright was not able to cry out.[31]

Chase was not a stranger to Bayley. She had worked for Bayley for two
years, and Bayley attested that "shee never saw any light or unseemly
carriage in all that time."[32] Still, Bayley did not believe Chase's version
of the circumstances under which she had conceived. Bayley further
testified that:

> This shee [Chase] Constantly affirmed, beeing in labor and extremity
> about six dayes and in Appearance at ye pointe of death I often told
> her that it was likely her paines continued the longer, because Shee
> had not spoken ye truth; her constant answer was, that if shee dyed for
> it shee had spoken ye truth and nothing els.[33]

The Essex County Quarterly Court concurred with Bayley. Anne Chase
was convicted and sentenced to be whipped or to pay a fine. Allen was

not charged with fornication, nor was he required to pay child support for Chase's son, whom she named John Allen.[34] The inherent dissonance between the conditions under which women like Chase conceived and their expectations of what was necessary for conception must have been considerable. The legal assumption that conception implied consent deprived Chase and other young women of the traditional support of the women's community during labor. The midwife arrived as inquisitor, not comforter.

The number of rape and attempted rape prosecutions in the Massachusetts Bay Colony Court of Assistants does not reflect the true incidence of sexual violence in seventeenth-century Massachusetts. There was no incentive for single women to report incidents of sexual violence. The cultural expectation of female chastity enjoined silence. Moreover, the practical considerations were considerable. The loss of sexual reputation and concomitant marriageability and the knowledge that an accusation of rape might result in a mutual fornication prosecution precluded making a rape public. Sarah Lambert belatedly reported her rape to the authorities. Would she have done so without the prodding of Mistress Pod? It is not surprising that seven of the seventeen prosecuted cases involved children ten years of age or less or married women.

While rapes and attempted rapes were not prosecuted with vigor, there is no indication that sexual violence against women was pervasive in seventeenth-century Massachusetts. This was a society that monitored young people closely and socialized them to view sexual intercourse as the province of married persons. The low number of persons convicted of fornication indicates that extramarital sexual activity was not widespread, and it can be inferred that levels of coerced sexual intercourse were correspondingly low. Nor do the circumstances surrounding the reported rapes fit common theoretical assumptions about rape. These rapes were not the enforcement arm of patriarchy under threat. The patriarchal order was firmly entrenched and unquestioned. Neither were they an expression of generalized hatred of women, as the depositions do not record extensive physical injuries beyond the genital area. Certainly Puritan men indicated through their deliberations and verdicts from the bench and the jury box that they believed rape to be a sexual offense.

Grand juries were reluctant to characterize acts of coerced sexual intercourse as capital crimes. They proved this every time they prosecuted rapes or attempted rapes at the county quarterly court level where corporal punishment or a fine was the only punitive remedy. The juries of the Court of Assistants were equally reluctant to draw fine distinctions between coerced and consensual intercourse when both the defendant and the victim were unmarried and the maximum penalty was capital punishment. Four of fourteen rape cases were reduced to fornication and the women were prosecuted as well. Four more cases involved children, which would be considered aberrant sexual activity in any century, and two more involved married women. Of the four remaining cases, three defendants were whipped, fined, or both. The one remaining defendant, William Cheney, gained the unenviable fate of being the only man in seventeenth-century Massachusetts to be hanged for the rape of an unmarried woman. He had compounded his initial crime by stabbing the constable who came to arrest him and attempting to escape on the constable's horse.

The degree to which Puritan justices regarded rape and attempted rape as the end point on a continuum of sexual offenses can be illustrated by a pair of sentences issued by the judges of an Essex County Quarterly Court session meeting in Ipswich in September 1681. Twenty-one-year-old William Nelson was tried for the attempted rape of a child, Mehitabel Avis. There was a witness, the testimony of Mehitabel Avis, and an admission of guilt from Nelson. Nelson was sentenced to be severely whipped. The defendants who preceded Nelson to the dock, John Ring and Martha Lamson, were also sentenced to be severely whipped. Their crime had been consensual sexual intercourse unsanctioned by marriage.[35]

NOTES

1. In sex cases involving consensual sexual intercourse women bore greater responsibility than men for engaging in extramarital sexual activity. In Essex County, Massachusetts, 104 women and 35 men were prosecuted for fornication following the births of illegitimate children between 1640 and 1685. Women were prosecuted more often than their male partners, and were punished more severely even when both participants were of equivalent rank. Else L. Hambleton, "A World Filled with a Generation of Bastards: Pregnant Brides and Unwed Mothers in Seventeenth-Century Massachusetts" (Ph.D. dissertation, University of Massachusetts at Amherst, 2000), 82.

2. It was commonly believed that women possessed greater sexual ap-

petites than men. Anne Laurence, *Women in England, 1500–1760: A Social History* (New York: St. Martin's Press, 1994), 66.

3. Garthine Walker, "Rereading Rape and Sexual Violence in Early Modern England," *Gender and History* 10 (April 1998): 6.

4. Michael Dalton, *The Countrey Justice* (London: Company of Stationers, 1618), 350–351. Dalton's definition of rape was predicated on contemporary scientific understanding of the mechanics of conception: a mutual orgasm was required.

5. Men who raped married women were guilty of adultery, also a capital crime.

6. Hambleton, "A World Filled with," 82.

7. Ibid., 46. I conducted a group study of women prosecuted for fornication or bastardy, and men prosecuted for fornication or named in paternity cases in Essex County, Massachusetts, between 1640 and 1692. I analyzed prosecution and conviction rates, sentencing patterns, and socioeconomic and attitudinal data. While a few persons may have escaped prosecution, I crosschecked the published Vital Records and local genealogies and I conclude that the error rate is no greater than 10 percent.

8. From the WPA transcription of the records of the Essex County Quarterly Court, property of the Supreme Judicial Court, Division of Archives and Records Preservation, on deposit at the Peabody Essex Museum, Salem, Massachusetts, 46–131–1. I have changed j to i, f to s, v to u, and brought superscripts down, but otherwise have retained the original spelling in these quotations.

9. Michael Emerson was fined and bound to good behavior for "cruel and excessive beating of his daughter with a flail swingle and for kicking her." George Francis Dow, *Records and Files of the Quarterly Courts of Essex County*, vol. VI, Massachusetts (Salem, Essex Institute, 1917), 141.

10. Ibid.

11. Emerson's older sister, Mary, had been charged with fornication in 1683, along with her husband, Hugh Mathews, following the birth of their first child within thirty-two weeks of marriage. A previous familial prosecution for fornication increased the likelihood that other siblings would face charges of sexual misconduct. Hambleton, "A World Filled with," 138.

12. Under English common law, coerced or consensual intercourse between adult males and children under the age of ten was rape. Edgar J. McManus, *Law and Liberty in Early New England: Criminal Justice and Due Process, 1620–1692* (Amherst: University of Massachusetts Press, 1993), 31.

13. John Noble, *Records of the Court of Assistants of the Colony of Massachusetts Bay*, vol. II (Boston: Suffolk County, 1904), 64–65.

14. Lyle Koehler, *A Search for Power: The "Weaker Sex" in Seventeenth-Century New England* (Urbana: University of Illinois Press, 1980), 95.

15. Holly Brewer argues that since justice-of-the-peace manuals defined rape as sexual intercourse with a woman without consent, rapists received lesser sentences when their victims were aged ten or less because children were ineligible to consent. Holly Brewer, "Constructing Consent: How Children's Status in Political Theory Shaped Public Policy on Virginia, Pennsylvania, and Massachusetts before and after the American Revolution," (Ph.D. dissertation, UCLA, 1994), 261–162.

16. *Records of the Court of Assistants of the Massachusetts Bay,* vol. III, 200.

17. Between 1641 and 1665, twenty-three women and fifteen men were convicted of fornication in the Essex County quarterly courts following the birth of an illegitimate child. Between 1666 and 1685, the period that coincides with the second phase of rape prosecutions in the Massachusetts Bay Court of Assistants, eighty-one women and twenty men were convicted of fornication. A 1668 amendment to Massachusetts Bay fornication law released men from fornication convictions in order to legalize the collection of child support payments without a formal admission of paternity. These figures indicate both an increased level of sexual activity and the degree to which Puritans considered women to be responsible for the initiation of sexual intercourse. Hambleton, "A World Filled with," 66.

18. *Records of the Court of Assistants,* vol. II, 121. Wythes was seventeen, Odle fourteen. Odle is the only woman in this initial cluster whose marriage can be traced.

19. The number of prosecutions for consensual sexual intercourse also increased dramatically during this period. Between 1640 and 1665, 23 Essex County women were convicted of fornication following the births of illegitimate children. Between 1666 and 1685 the number more than tripled to 81. Similarly, the number of couples convicted of fornication following the birth of their first child within thirty-two weeks of marriage quadrupled from 28 to 123 during the same period. Hambleton, "A World Filled with," 46.

20. *Records of the Court of Assistants,* vol. I, 230.

21. Clarence Almon Torrey, *New England Marriages Prior to 1700* (Baltimore: Genealogical Publishing Company, 1985). The 30 percent marriage rate is comparable to that of women who were convicted of illegitimate fornication. Ninety-eight percent of Essex County women married.

22. *Records of the Court of Assistants,* vol. II, 79.

23. The most likely reason for the reversal of the attempted rape verdict is that Pierce was discovered to be pregnant.

24. *Records of the Court of Assistants,* vol. I, 158.

25. Croy had a poor reputation prior to his trial for rape. The previous year he had been convicted of stealing wine and other foodstuffs from his master and partying with a group of similarly placed young male servants.

26. Suffolk County Court files, #1254.

27. Ibid.
28. Ibid.
29. Ibid.
30. Hambleton, "A World Filled with," 48.
31. WPA transcription, 16–128–1.
32. Ibid.
33. Ibid.
34. Allen and his wife were convicted of fornication four years later when their first child was born within thirty-two weeks of their marriage. *Records and Files*, vol. V, 408.
35. *Records and Files*, vol. VIII, 15. They were, however, given the option of paying a fine. The fine was to be reduced if they married and Martha Lamson's sexuality contained. They did not marry.

3

Sexual Consent and Sexual Coercion in Seventeenth-Century Virginia

Terri L. Snyder

IN SEVENTEENTH-CENTURY VIRGINIA, matters of sexual consent and coercion rarely came to the attention of the courts. Those few white women who sought to prosecute white men for sexual assault or rape faced formidable barriers to success. For African American slave women, the situation was, of course, worse. They could not seek legal redress for sexual violations; raping a slave was not a criminal act. Moreover, rumors of sexual misconduct often swirled around the victims of sexual coercion, casting doubts on their character. A white woman in Virginia walked a legal and social tightrope: successfully prosecuting a white man for sexual coercion was highly unlikely, but taking no legal action could damage her reputation.[1]

If she could not confidently prosecute for sexual coercion, how might a woman convince her neighborhood that she had not freely consented to sexual relations? In her study of sexual coercion in British North America, Sharon Block argues that sexual coercion was more than an act of power. Establishing and proving that sexual coercion had occurred depended on who controlled the definition of the act.[2] When a woman stood before the assembled magistrates, juries, and spectators in county courtrooms in colonial Virginia, she could seize that power, simultaneously defending herself, wrestling the meaning of consent away from others, and defining it in her own terms. In doing so, she framed a narrative that would vindicate her. This essay explores the strategies employed by women in two cases in which sexual consent was fundamentally, although not directly, at issue. When they took command of the public forum of the courtroom, an admittedly rare event, white women could use that forum to their advantage, even against white men, and control definitions of sexual consent and sexual coercion. Rightly deployed, women's narrative strategies could successfully obtain retribution, clear their names, and restore their honor.

In 1662 Ann Collins, an indentured servant, stood before the court in York County, Virginia, on the routine charges of fornication and out-of-wedlock pregnancy. Instead of mutely receiving her sentence, as did most women in her situation, Ann Collins spoke out in her own defense. She was at a clear disadvantage in offering her relatively extended confession: she was a servant, pregnant, and unmarried in defiance of the law, standing in a courtroom full of legal authorities who would judge her and neighbors whose tongues would wag over her sentence. Still, she wanted the assembled individuals to understand *how* her consent was extracted and *why* she had engaged in the illegal act of sexual intercourse outside marriage.

Collins presented a narrative of a bad bargain, and in recounting the circumstances under which her sexual consent was obtained, she controlled the terms of the contract, and therefore the definition of consent. From her point of view—a viewpoint that she wanted those assembled at court to share—sexual consent was strictly quid pro quo. Ann Collins viewed the exchange between her and Robert Pierce, her sexual partner, as a more or less contractual one: she consented to sex, and he consented to free her. More importantly, her story was framed to show that her consent was obtained by fraudulent means. In other words, Pierce bargained in bad faith. She wanted the court to understand, as she herself did, that this constituted a form of coercion. She framed the story to shift blame from herself to her partner.

Ann Collins's confession was explicit. She began by explaining that she would never have "yielded" to Pierce's entreaties for sex, but eventually was persuaded to do so. Why? To put the matter simply, Pierce made significant promises to Collins. "Hee told mee that hee would free mee from my master whatsoever it would cost him and that hee had stocke cattle servants and a plantacon and that I should ride his Mare and then your Mistress will thinke much [of you]." Collins constructed herself as open, perhaps even susceptible, to an offer, and recounted the terms of the contract made between herself and Pierce. She agreed to sex, and with a romantic flourish Pierce agreed to free her "whatsoever it would cost him" and make her rich. While Pierce did not make a clear marriage offer, Collins may well have inferred such a promise or at least felt it expedient that the court think that she had done so. Her narrative strategy, then, was deployed to illustrate how the two of them had struck an agreement. Motivated by a longing for freedom, mobility, and status, Collins thought—and wanted the court to think—that she had traded sex for a better chance.³

After noting the terms of the bargain, Collins provided further details that no doubt cemented the perception that she was a victim of sexual coercion. Pierce, it seems, was the only party who had benefited from their contract. She stood before the court unmarried, unfree, and pregnant, while Pierce had only profited from their arrangement. Collins conveyed the one-sided nature of their bargain by offering up the particulars of their sexual relationship. After obtaining her consent, she explained, Pierce took "a bout" with her at "the fireside and sometimes in the tobaccoe house milke house and orchard at spring sometimes 8 or 9 times a day." Her argument was never explicitly stated, and yet clearly she used the frequency of intercourse between them as an index of coercion. Under the most egregious circumstances, she held up her end of the bargain, allowing him to "take a bout" with her whenever and wherever he liked.⁴

As a servant, unprotected by her own family and surrounded by a master's family with whom she apparently experienced conflict, sex was about the only commodity that Ann Collins possessed. She could, however, notify the community that she had traded it under false pretenses. True, she had consented to sexual intercourse under the terms Pierce offered. Had she known that Pierce would fail to keep his promises, she declared, she would never have "yielded" to his sexual entreaties.

Unfortunately, Collins's narrative strategies had no effect on her treatment at the hands of the legal authorities. Both Collins and Pierce paid penalties, but hers, as was consistent with Virginia statutes, was the steeper of the two. Her term of service was extended by two and a half years, and Pierce was ordered into custody for failing to provide a bond of security. By law, he owed five hundred pounds of tobacco or six months' service for his crime.⁵

Finally, Ann Collins's narrative also allows us to see how Pierce established mastery over her. He was not her master, but his references to his multiple sources of power—*his* land, *his* stock, and, most importantly, *his* ability to free her—were the means by which he created opportunities for coercing her. Sharon Block argues that masters

used their power over unfree laborers to redefine coercive into consensual sexual relations, and Robert Pierce was surely engaged in a
similar act.[6] Just as surely, however, Ann Collins's narrative of consent attempted both to deflect rumors that she was sexually dissolute
and project considerable negative weight on the neighborhood's assessment of Pierce. Putting the terms of the consent at the very center
of her story may have vindicated Collins in the eyes of her neighbors.
She wanted them to know that it was Robert Pierce, rather than she,
who bargained in bad faith.

Telling her story did not alter the terms of her sentence, nor could
it have been expected to do so, but it did allow her to clarify for her
audience the terms under which her consent was given. Despite her
legal sentence, Ann Collins's story went some distance toward restoring her honor. She no doubt feared local censure for her out-of-wedlock pregnancy, but if she did not come forward on her own behalf,
no one else would do so.[7] Besides, in telling her story she had nothing
to lose and everything to gain. Ann Collins may have been saddled
with her legal sentence, but her narrative illustrated the coercive elements used to obtain her consent, casting greater aspersions upon her
partner than on herself.

What were a woman's choices when she was a victim of direct sexual
assault or rape? Rape was a capital offense in colonial Virginia, and
rapes were tried in a bifurcated system. The rights of white defendants
were rigorously protected. Their cases were tried at the General Court
that had jurisdiction over criminal offenses affecting life and member.
The cases of white defendants were heard first by a grand jury, which
decided whether or not sufficient evidence existed to proceed. If the
grand jury recommended further prosecution, their cases were then
heard by petit juries. Juries were required to reach unanimous verdicts.[8]
After 1692, Virginia's lower courts of Oyer and Terminer, where procedures and standards of evidence were much less rigorous, tried slave
defendants.[9] It was therefore the rare woman who was able to obtain a
conviction for rape against a white man in Virginia's General Court.

Who was likely to obtain convictions for sexual assault in the seventeenth century? In Virginia and Maryland, English law was adopted
without revision, and although laws governing rape were revised in
some New England colonies, rape remained a capital crime during the
colonial period.[10] In the seventeenth century, Puritan jurists also relied

on the veracity of women's words, a trend that was clearly not echoed by Chesapeake magistrates. Among Puritans, men were assumed to have a "proclivity for lying," and women, despite their personal histories, were largely believed.[11] In the Chesapeake, rather than give credence to a woman's word, magistrates doubted it, unless her assailant was black.[12]

Since most of the records of Virginia's superior court, the General Court, are lost for the colonial period we cannot know the precise number of rape convictions that were attempted or obtained.[13] Extant records, however, reveal that there were no successful prosecutions for rape or attempted rape in Virginia's General Court prior to 1670. Kathleen Brown finds that at least one woman obtained a successful conviction for the lesser charge at the county level.[14] All told, then, convictions of white men for rape or the lesser charge of attempted rape were comparatively rare in colonial Virginia. However, because the rate of violent crime, including rape, in the colony was certainly no lower than that of England, it is essential to recognize that incidents of rape or sexual coercion largely went unreported.

White women had good reason to feel hesitant about accusing a white man of rape. Making such a charge was risky, and women could lose their homes, their places in their community, or suffer punishment or reprisals.[15] Did she have any alternatives? Were there means other than direct accusation that women might employ to vindicate their reputations and restore their honor? The case of Elizabeth Hansford Burt demonstrates one woman's strategy to control the terms of sexual coercion and define the act of rape.

In the early 1690s, Elizabeth Hansford Burt was at the very center of two controversies in her York County, Virginia, neighborhood. Elizabeth was married to Richard Burt, a man of apparently middling status and good reputation who occasionally was paid by the county for capturing runaways and served as a juror for York County.[16] The couple had at least one child. In the first controversy Richard and Elizabeth were sued for trespass. The suit claimed that Elizabeth did "violently assault, bruise, and beat" Mary Peeters, perhaps causing her to miscarry. The jury concurred with the plaintiff, and the Burts were ordered to pay a hundred pounds of tobacco in damages—far less than the damages sought by Peeters, who asked for five thousand pounds.[17]

The second controversy began on August 24, 1692, when Richard and Elizabeth Burt attended the York County court, although neither had any apparent business there. After court, they retired to the French Ordinary, where they sat drinking with one of their neighbors, John Eaton. Eaton, like Richard Burt, also captured runaways for the county, and he had been appointed as a juror for York in May 1692, when Richard Burt was discharged. Moreover, he had served as a juror in the trespass suit brought by the Peeters against the Burts. The night wore on, and Elizabeth complained that it was late and that she "did not well know how to goe home with her childe." Eaton offered to carry them home on his horse, so "at the stocks" Eaton hoisted her and her child up behind him. According to Elizabeth, however, what began as a ride through the Virginia night ended up as a rape, for she claimed that John Eaton had "ravished her upon the road," despite her screams and protests, while she held fast to her child.[18]

The exchange two days later between Burt and her uncle, Captain Charles Hansford, reveals the difficulties women faced in successfully prosecuting rape, and especially their struggles persuading authorities that sex without consent had occurred. Elizabeth went to see Captain Hansford, not because he was her uncle, but because he was a York County magistrate. She directly asked him for a "warrant" for John Eaton. His skepticism was immediately apparent in his reply, "Fy Betty, as soon as you are out of one troublesum busines to goe into an other," clearly a reference to the July trespass suit. Hansford's deposition reveals that on several occasions, he attempted to deter her. But Elizabeth Burt would not be deflected.

After she asked for a warrant, Hansford requested that she clarify "the matter with you and John Eaton." At this point, she had asked for a warrant but had not specified its charge. Hansford deposed to the court that he had a cold and was "something thick of hearing," but "as near" as he could "apprehend" it, Elizabeth Burt had said that John Eaton "would have laine with her a coming from Court." Attempting to define the terms of the act, the magistrate suggested that Eaton "did not intend itt, though he profered itt." In other words, although Elizabeth Burt had claimed that Eaton had physically raped her, Hansford suggested that Eaton had simply made an offer of sex. Burt defined rape, and Hansford's redefinition effectively decriminialized the act. Yet Elizabeth Burt stood firm, replying that "indeed [Eaton] did do itt" and that she would swear an oath to it. Swearing an oath was a serious matter: it meant that she was willing to stake her reputation on this claim or risk perjury charges for being forsworn.[19]

Further exchanges between Elizabeth Burt and Charles Hansford reveal that issues of physical strength, force, and protest were key elements of the legal and cultural definitions of nonconsensual sex. Certainly Elizabeth Burt understood this. Without any prompting from the magistrate, she declared that she was "not of a man's strength and he did force me." Hansford replied that he "thought such a thing could not possibly be for shee was near as strong as John Eaton and that he could not doe itt except shee was willing." They struggled over this element, and Burt reiterated her claim that Eaton "did do itt against her will." They would return to the issue of force before their conversation ended.[20]

At this point, however, Hansford switched gears, focusing first on the element of verbal protest and second on the presence of witnesses. Both were crucial elements in defining sex without consent in early America.[21] Why did she not "hollow out"? She claimed that she did "hollow" two or three times. Was there no "company neare"? Where was her husband? She replied that he was a good way behind. How did it "come to passe" that she was with John Eaton? Here, the magistrate voiced suspicion, one that would be shared by members of the community, about a wife traveling with a man who was not her husband after a night of drinking. She answered that Eaton had offered to carry her home on his horse. If Hansford was attempting to dissuade her from filing a warrant, thus far he had failed to do so. Burt's answers consistently defined the act as rape: she was forced, she cried out, and the act occurred in an area remote from other witnesses. Again, the magistrate switched tactics. Stymied by her responses, unable to position her story outside definitions of rape, he returned to the issue of physical force.[22]

Captain Hansford asked for more specific details of the act of rape itself. Had Eaton tied her? Did he throw her down? What had she done with her child? She replied that Eaton had not tied her, but "threw her on her knees but shee recover'd again and he did itt standing." A few days later, when Burt told her story to Elizabeth Buce, the same woman who had offered a damning deposition against Burt in the Peeters trespass case, she revealed more particulars about physical force. She disclosed that Eaton clapt one hand "about the small of her back" and with the other "held up her cloaths." Eaton importuned her to lie down but Burt would not, and, instead "cryed out and called to her husband twice." "Wrenching her thighs asunder with his knees," Eaton proceeded with the rape, while Elizabeth struggled and held fast to her child.[23] All the elements of a rape are present in Burt's story, but the details of physical force would have been the most persuasive to an early American jury. It is puzzling, then, that Hansford ultimately concluded that Burt's story "did not lye under the [circum]stances of a rape" and refused to grant her warrant. He cautioned her to say nothing about the event.

On the face of it, Hansford's stance is curious. He asked for details that are key elements in early modern definitions of rape, and Elizabeth Burt supplied them. Yet he refused to grant a warrant. Why? Elizabeth Burt was suspect because of her encounter with Mary Peeters.[24] Burt was angered by Peeters's remark about Burt's father, one of Nathaniel Bacon's followers executed by Governor Berkeley after Bacon's Rebellion. She struck Peeters in the face, beat and scratched her, and finally threw her against a bedstead. Peeters claimed that the beating caused a miscarriage.[25] Since all those details had been disclosed at a trial only a month earlier, perhaps Hansford thought that Burt would lack credibility before a jury, and so he refused the warrant.

In addition, Hansford, like other county magistrates, denied or delayed executing warrants after hearing complaints.[26] One suspects that in seventeenth-century Virginia, where prosecutions for rape, as well as for petty, capital, or felonious crimes, were rare, the refusal of a magistrate to sign a warrant would have put an end to any hope for conviction and vindication. It is quite likely that in the face of a magistrate's refusal, many women would shrink from further legal action. Only the most persistent of women—and men, for that matter—succeeded in getting themselves heard in the forum of the court. Elizabeth Burt was one such woman.

Captain Hansford may have refused her warrant, but Elizabeth Burt never wavered from her assertion that she been raped. Moreover, she wanted that fact acknowledged in a public forum. When Captain Hansford told Burt that she could not have been raped unless she was willing, she fired back that "if such things be suffered shee should be counted John Eaton's whore." The damage to her reputation was unacceptable to Elizabeth Burt, and so she sought the restitution of her honor. Her strategy, initially, was to tell her neighbors about the rape. In addition to Captain Hansford, Burt certainly repeated the story to Elizabeth Buce and John Buce, Sr., and she appears also to have told it to others as well.[27]

In early colonial Virginia, as in early modern culture in general, women's gossip and their ability to circulate stories about themselves and their neighbors was a means of exercising power in a society in which they had little access to institutionalized sources of power. The restrictions of coverture were great: once married, women were civilly dead—although, as we have seen, not when they committed crimes. It goes almost without saying that women could not vote, hold public office, or have access to formalized structures of power in early American communities. But they could, and they did, gossip. "Reputations," as Mary Beth Norton has argued, "were sustained and lost in the early colonies primarily through gossip," and women were "major wielders of gossip."[28] If Elizabeth Burt was publicly counted as "John Eaton's whore," she would be a target of gossip. However, if she could channel the talk, she might redefine the act as a coercive one and thereby restore her reputation. Captain Hansford may have had some sense of this when he urged her to "be sure to say noe more of itt."[29] Not only did he wrangle with her over the definition of rape, but he wanted her account of it censored.

More was at stake here. Captain Hansford understood the power of gossip in Virginia neighborhoods. That is why the very next day, *after* he had denied Elizabeth Burt's request for a warrant and *after* he had told her to "say noe more of itt," he paid a visit to John Eaton. He rather vaguely mentioned to Eaton that he was "sorry to hear what" he had heard of him. Eaton wanted to know what the magistrate meant. Assuming his role as justice and inquisitor, Hansford directly asked, "What did [you do] to Betty Burt acoming from Court?" "Nothing," was Eaton's response. Hansford then told Eaton that Burt would swear a rape against him, and Eaton panicked. "By God," he lamented, "shee will undoe me then." He confessed to Hansford that he had put his hand up her coates "as high as her knees," but he did not know whether "she be man or woman." There is no evidence to suggest that the men conversed further.[30]

John Eaton then devised a strategy of his own: he decided to file a defamation suit against Richard and Elizabeth Burt in order to quell her gossip. Eaton had a fair amount of experience at the local court. He had successfully prosecuted cases, served on five juries, including the one that decided *Peeters v. Burt*, and recently had been appointed as a grand juror.[31] He also had some contact with a lawyer and may have consulted with him on this matter.[32] The odds of succeeding against the Burts must have seemed good to him, particularly when weighed against the unwelcome possibility of standing as a defendant in a rape trial. Because Elizabeth Burt had accused him of committing a crime, Eaton did have a suitable case for a defamation suit according to the terms of English law.[33] Still, it was a risk: she would be exonerated if she could convince the jury that the words she spoke were true. However, if he took no action, the accusation of rape, even if it remained in the realm of gossip, would seriously damage his reputation. Defending one's honor and reputation were at the very center of defamation cases.[34]

On September 26, 1692, Eaton's defamation suit against the Burts was tried by a jury in the York County court. His suit alleged that "ever since 24 August last past," Elizabeth Burt "from time to time hath most malitiously and falsely defamed" him by "publishing and declareing amongst her neighbors and others that Eaton by force and violence . . . ravisht her . . . as she was returning home." In part, the words of the suit were formulaic.[35] Yet *someone* had been talking, and most likely it was Elizabeth herself. John Buce testified that he went to see the Burts on August 26—two days after the alleged rape and the same day that Elizabeth Burt went to Captain Hansford for a warrant—because he had heard "news," including the "strange news" that John Eaton had "lay" with Elizabeth Burt "the other night comeing from Court." Elizabeth answered that it was "very true, soe he did."[36] It is impossible to know whether Burt's visit to Captain Hansford occurred before or after she spoke to the Buces, but clearly the neighborhood was buzzing at the story.

When it came time to try John Eaton's suit, a jury was impaneled and the charges against Elizabeth Burt were read. When asked for her plea, she replied "not guilty." She waited until all Eaton's evidence had been presented and sworn, and then "in open Court before the jury att the barr" offered her defense. There, standing before the entire court, she did "possatively owne and declare" that Eaton had "offered much rudenes to her with diverse perswasions to lett him ly with her, and that shee called out but yett nevertheless the plaintiff by striveing and compultion had the use of her body as she stood upright with her child in her armes." The clerk noted that she tendered her oath "severall times" to confirm the truth of her words.[37]

The jury found for Elizabeth Burt and dismissed the suit. However, they offered no damage awards to the Burts, although in other defamation suits won by defendants in the York court, juries did indeed award damages.[38] Elizabeth Hansford was vindicated, but the lack of damages as well as the fact that, as Kathleen Brown points out, Richard Burt did not press further charges of rape on behalf of his wife, suggest that the vindication was somewhat tepid.[39] Still, John Eaton's service on York juries slowed considerably; having served on five juries prior to bringing charges against the Burts, he served on only one jury in the following year.[40]

Elizabeth Burt and Ann Collins managed extraordinary feats in the legal climate of seventeenth-century Virginia. Standing as defendants, and outside the courtroom as well for Burt, they used the occasion of a legal suit to offer narratives about sexual consent and sexual coercion. Had they opted for a more direct prosecution of their grievances, they would have had little hope of redress. In order to succeed in vindicating their reputations and restoring their honor, qualities largely based on their sexuality, they had to "owne," as Elizabeth Burt put it, the terms of sexual consent and sexual coercion. By putting these matters at the very heart of their stories, both women constructed dramas of dependency, subjugation, and victimization that conformed to notions of the ideal woman. Ironically, telling their stories before the court gave them a cultural agency that they otherwise would not have possessed.[41] Although they were on risky ground, both women seem to have understood the legal system well enough to proceed with confidence. Court days doubled as social gatherings in the early Chesapeake—recall that Elizabeth Burt had attended court with no apparent legal business at hand on the day that the alleged rape occurred—and provided women with opportunities to observe the court at work.[42] Both Ann Collins and Elizabeth Burt seem to have used their observations of the local legal system, as well as their understanding of community networks, to frame their pleas. Placing their own narratives at center stage gave them the power to define sexual consent and sexual coercion in a patriarchal system. In doing so, they recouped their reputations against potential losses.

NOTES

1. Kathleen M. Brown finds one white woman in seventeenth-century Virginia who successfully prosecuted a white man for the lesser charge of attempted rape. See Kathleen M. Brown, *Good Wives, Nasty Wenches, and Anxious*

Patriarchs: Gender, Race, and Power in Colonial Virginia (Chapel Hill: University of North Carolina Press, 1996), 209 (Butt v. Gully), and 193–194, 207–211 (for an analysis of rape in colonial Virginia). Irmina Wawrzyczek examines women's unsuccessful attempts to prosecute for rape in seventeenth-century Virginia and documents the damage to the reputations of victims of sexual coercion. See Irmina Wawrzyczek, "The Women of Accomack versus Henry Smith: Gender, Legal Recourse, and the Social Order in Seventeenth-Century Virginia," *Virginia Magazine of History and Biography*, 105 (Winter 1997): 5–26. For a comparative analysis of rape in colonial America, see Sharon Block, "Coerced Sex in British North America, 1700–1820" (Ph.D. dissertation, Princeton University, 1995); and Mary Beth Norton, *Founding Mothers and Fathers: Gendered Power and the Forming of American Society* (New York: Alfred A. Knopf, 1996), 347–358. For discussion of rape in other British North American colonies, see Cornelia Hughes Dayton, *Women before the Bar: Gender, Law, and Society in Connecticut, 1639–1789* (Chapel Hill: University of North Carolina Press, 1995), 231–284; and Barbara Lindeman, "'To Ravish and Carnally Know': Rape in Eighteenth-Century Massachusetts," *Signs* 10 (Autumn 1984), 63–83.

Clearly, white women were more successful in prosecuting African American men for sexual crimes. After 1700, "black men were three and a half times more likely to be executed" for rape than were their white counterparts. See Block, "Coerced Sex in British North America," 123 (quotation), 123–178; and Philip Schwarz, *Twice Condemned: Slaves and the Criminal Laws of Virginia, 1705–1865* (Baton Rouge: Louisiana State University Press, 1988), 159–160.

2. Sharon Block, "Lines of Color, Sex, and Service: Comparative Sexual Coercion in Early America," in Martha Hodes, ed., *Sex, Love, Race: Crossing Boundaries in North American History* (New York: New York University Press, 1999), 143.

3. York County, Virginia Deeds, Orders, Wills (hereafter cited as YCDOW), no. 3, f. 149. See also Brown, *Good Wives, Nasty Wenches, and Anxious Patriarchs*, 202–203.

4. YCDOW no. 3, f. 149.

5. The punishment for female servants found guilty of fornication was two years' extra service, plus an additional six months to repay the fine of five hundred pounds of tobacco to the parish; male servants paid the same fine or served an additional six months. See William Waller Hening, *The Statues at Large; Being a Collection of All the Laws of Virginia*, vol. II (New York, R. and W. and G. Bartow, 1823; reprint, Charlottesville: University Press of Virginia, 1969), 114–115.

6. Block, "Lines of Color, Sex, and Service," 143–148.

7. Sharon Block finds that women were extremely reluctant to report rape, not on account of shame, but for fear of reprisals. See Black, "Coerced Sex in British North America," 87–122.

8. Bradley Chapin, *Criminal Justice in Colonial America, 1606–1660* (Athens: University of Georgia Press, 1983), 40–47.

9. Because of the bifurcated system, white women were more likely to obtain rape convictions in the eighteenth century, but only because black men stood accused. At least nineteen black men were charged with rape between 1670 and 1767; twelve were executed for their crime. See Brown, *Good Wives, Nasty Wenches, Anxious Patriarchs,* 209–210. In contrast, eight white men were tried for rape before Virginia's General Court in the eighteenth century: five were acquitted, one pardoned, and two hanged. See Hugh F. Rankin, *Criminal Trial Proceedings in the General Court of Colonial Virginia* (Charlottesville: University Press of Virginia, 1965), 219–222. On the justice system in colonial Virginia, see Oliver Perry Chitwood, *Justice in Colonial Virginia* (Baltimore: Johns Hopkins University Press, 1905), 44–47. On the courts of Oyer and Terminer, see Schwarz, *Twice Condemned,* 17–18, 25–26; and Block, "Coerced Sex in British North America," 127–133.

10. Norton, *Founding Mothers and Fathers,* 347–349.

11. Dayton, *Women before the Bar,* 238–240 (quotation on 239).

12. Ibid. , 246–247.

13. Virginia's General Court records survive for sixteen years, although they are supplemented with notes and excerpts from the years 1640 through the 1680s. See H. R. McIlwaine, ed., *Minutes of the Council and General Court of Colonial Virginia, 1622–1632, 1670–1676* (Richmond: Virginia State Library, 1924).

14. James Horn, *Adapting to a New World: English Society in the Seventeenth-Century Chesapeake* (Chapel Hill: University of North Carolina Press, 1994), 354–355. On the successful conviction for attempted rape at the county court level, see Brown, *Good Wives, Nasty Wenches, Anxious Patriarchs,* 209.

15. Block, "Coerced Sex in British North America," 85–122.

16. In 1690–91 Richard Burt attended a Court of Claims and proved that he had taken up a runaway, for which he was given a thousand pounds of tobacco by the Virginia General Assembly. See YCDOW 9, ff. 19, 37; he was sworn in as a grand juror on July 29, 1691. See YCDOW 9, f. 42. He was discharged on May 24, 1692. See YCDOW 9, f. 141. However, Burt did not serve on any jury during his tenure.

17. YCDOW 9, ff. 156–159.

18. Deposition of Elizabeth Buce, YCDOW 9, ff. 175.

19. Deposition of Charles Hansford, YCDOW 9, ff. 174–175.

20. Deposition of Charles Hansford, YCDOW 9, ff. 174–175.

21. Block, "Coerced Sex in British North America," 179–213.

22. Deposition of Charles Hansford, YCDOW 9, ff. 174–175.

23. Deposition of Elizabeth Buce, YCDOW 9, ff. 175.

24. Brown, *Good Wives, Nasty Wenches, and Anxious Patriarchs,* 208.

25. Depositions of Thomas Buce and Elizabeth Buce, YCDOW 9, ff. 158–159.

26. See, for example, the case of Mary Rawlins described by Terri L. Snyder, "'As If There Was Not Master or Woman in the Land': Gender, Dependency, and Household Violence in Virginia, 1646–1720," in Christine Daniels and Michael V. Kennedy, eds., *Over the Threshold: Intimate Violence in Early America* (New York: Routledge, 1999), 228–229.

27. In addition to the Buces and Captain Hansford, the story may also have been told to Dr. Richard Starke, Isaack Sedwicke, and Thomas Chamberlaine, all of whom were summoned to give evidence for John Eaton against Richard and Elizabeth Burt. See YCDOW 9, f. 174. The only surviving depositions are from Hansford and the Buces.

28. Norton, *Founding Mothers and Fathers*, 253 (quotation), 253–269 (on the social function of gossip).

29. Deposition of Charles Hansford, YCDOW 9, ff. 174–175.

30. Deposition of Charles Hansford, YCDOW 9, ff. 174–175.

31. For Eaton's jury service, see YCDOW 9, ff. 53–54, 99, 144, 155, 156; for his own suits, see ff. 40, 52, 110; for his appearance as a witness, see ff. 28, 41.

32. Isaack Sedwicke, or Sedgwicke, acted as a lawyer in York County. See YCDOW 9, f. 172 for a reference to "Isaack Sedgwicke" as an attorney, and YCDOW 9, f. 174, where "Isaack Sedwicke" is listed as providing evidence for John Eaton in his defamation suit against Richard and Elizabeth Burt.

33. According to Nina Dayton, after 1665 slander had to either make an accusation of criminal behavior, a debilitating condition, or professional incompetence, if it was to be actionable. See Dayton, *Women before the Bar*, 301–302.

34. This point is made by several historians. See Dayton, *Women before the Bar*, 285–292; Norton, *Founding Mothers and Fathers*, 253–261; Horn, *Adapting to a New World*, 364–366.

35. *Eaton v. Burt*, YCDOW 9, ff. 173–174; see, for example, the language in the defamation suits of *Dormer v. Rigon*, YCDOW 3, f. 138, *Hill v. Slate*, YCDOW 9, f. 99–102; *Hide v. Delony*, YCDOW 10, ff. 9–10.

36. Deposition of John Buce, YCDOW 9, f. 176.

37. *Eaton v. Burt*, YCDOW 9, f. 173.

38. In *Hill v. Slate*, February 24, 1691/92, the defendant was awarded a thousand pounds of tobacco in damages, a very substantial award. This was a case, however, where adultery and attempted murder were at issue. See YCDOW 9, ff. 99–102. John Eaton served on this jury.

39. Brown, *Good Wives, Nasty Wenches, and Anxious Patriarchs*, 208.

40. For Eaton's jury service prior to his defamation suit, see YCDOW 9, ff. 53–54, 99, 144, 155, 156; for his service thereafter, see YCDOW 9, f. 224.

41. Laura Gowing, *Domestic Dangers: Women, Words, and Sex in Early Modern London* (Oxford: Clarendon Press, 1996), 234.

42. On court day, see Lorena S. Walsh, "Community Networks in the Early Chesapeake," in Lois Green Carr, Philip D. Morgan, and Jean B. Russo, eds., *Colonial Chesapeake Society* (Chapel Hill: University of North Carolina Press, 1988), 233–237: Darrett B. Rutman and Anita H. Rutman, *A Place in Time: Middlesex County, Virginia, 1650–1750* (New York: Norton, 1984), 87–93, 125–127.

4

Coerced Sex and Gendered Violence in New Netherland

James Homer Williams

VIOLENCE PERVADED NEW Netherland. This Dutch colony in the Hudson and Delaware valleys was frequently at war with its Indian and European neighbors and feared constantly that another military conflict was at hand. In addition, court records reveal that more personal violence was, if not an everyday occurrence, common enough. Both women and men filed charges of assault, slander, and physical violence. These cases litter the colony's records from the late 1630s to the English takeover in 1664.

More extraordinary for their scarcity and the reactions to them recorded by the court secretaries were the cases involving child molestation, rape, and sodomy. These crimes clearly crossed the line from ordinary gendered crime to extraordinary, even abominable, offenses. They occurred with sufficient regularity to allow us to gauge the society's thoughts and feelings toward these crimes and to see how people separated in their own minds "ordinary" offenses from intolerable ones.

Since it is included in a volume on rape in America, one might expect this essay to have much to say about rape in New Netherland. My research in the scores of cases of gendered violence, however, has uncovered only a handful of rape cases, and nearly all of those deal with adults molesting children. The absence of reported rapes is not surprising, for rape has often gone unreported in modern times. Garthine Walker has pointed out the rarity of rape cases in early modern England—about 1 percent of indicted felonies—and the even greater scarcity of convictions, although a majority of guilty rapists were hanged.

Attempted rape was a misdemeanor and "formed only a tiny majority of prosecutions."[1]

Walker indicts social historians for making the history of rape "a non-history, a history of absence." It is tempting to do the same for New Netherland, for a void exists between the numerous cases of gendered violence, such as slander and beatings, and the extreme instances of sex crimes, such as the rape of children. In a colony with nearly every other sort of coerced sex (bestiality cases are absent) and gendered violence, it remains a puzzle that so few man-woman rape cases were prosecuted, or occurred at all. Using more than a hundred rape cases across England in the seventeenth century, Walker succeeds in giving voice to victims of rape.[2] The task is more difficult in New Netherland.

In seeking a solution to this puzzle, this essay recognizes that issues of sex and violence in early modern Europe and North America must be understood within the world of gendered power that determined political, economic, and social relationships in European societies. As they colonized societies across the globe, Europeans attempted to order their new worlds as they knew the old worlds at home.[3] In New Netherland, Dutchmen sought to impose a male-dominated system on Indian peoples accustomed to a matrilineal and matriarchal order. If they succeeded, it was only with those Algonquian and Iroquois people who strayed into Dutch territory. More successful, perhaps, was the imposition of European cultural norms on Africans, slave and free, in the colony, though so little is known about the inner workings of African society in New Netherland as to make any statement only speculative. Clearly, though, Africans lacked power in this society.

This essay explores a range of gendered violence and sex crimes in New Netherland. What the colony's court records make clear is that Dutch ideas about power were transplanted largely intact to North America. The peculiarities of the colony's government, as well as the presence of Indians and Africans in the Dutch domain, forced adaptations in the application of criminal codes. The argument, then, is that gendered power, as revealed in violent crime, operated in an identifiably Dutch way. But just as the Dutch varied from their European neighbors, so too did New Netherlanders differ from their nearest competitors, the English in the Chesapeake and New England.

Seventeenth-century European courts, whether in Europe or the colonies, assumed the responsibility of maintaining community order.

Therefore, courts adjudicated all manner of disorderly crimes, including those between men and women, adults and children, and Africans, Indians, and Europeans. Because New Netherland was an outpost of the Dutch West India Company (WIC), company employees promulgated and enforced its laws. Ultimate authority lay in the company's Amsterdam chamber since this division of the company had financed and planted New Netherland in 1624. As the population grew, a few communities gained their own local courts from which appeals could be made to the colony's director-general and his council, which as one body behaved as executive, legislature, and supreme court.

The WIC was a chartered corporation governed by prominent men in the Dutch Republic. It also had a decidedly Calvinist tone, since it was founded in 1621 with the explicit purpose of competing with, and it was hoped, overtaking the Spanish Catholic empire in the Americas. Beneath the rhetoric, however, the WIC was primarily interested in profit. Seldom did it let religion stand in the way. Company chambers authorized colonial directors-general to operate within the large confines of Dutch law and custom and according to the directors-generals' interpretation of the best interests of the company. Given the stamp of personality they could leave on a colony, directors-general are an important factor for the historian to consider.

In a general sense, the WIC transported Roman Dutch law to its outposts. Company officials, the evidence in New Netherland occasionally suggests, decided cases after referring to legal tracts and manuals, most notably Hugo Grotius's *Introduction to Dutch Jurisprudence* (1631). To these codifications of law, company chambers in the Netherlands and officers in the colonies added regulations and ordinances to meet the specific circumstances from place to place. In New Netherland, these laws addressed, among other mundane topics, illicit trade, taverns, and antisocial behavior. Judging by the frequency with which they were reissued, many of the laws seem regularly to have been ignored.[4]

Grotius, who towers over the history of Dutch jurisprudence, classified crime in a hierarchy of gravity. Gendered crimes are absent from the most serious type of crime—those "against God and Government," including regicide, treason, and sacrilege. Nearly as serious were "crimes against life." Murder and manslaughter were punished by beheading, hanging, burning, or banishment, while crimes short of death, such as assault and "drawing blood," were commonly punished by a fine "tailored to the extent of the injury." As we will see, this was the practice in New Netherland.[5]

Less serious was the third category, "offenses against liberty," such as riot, rape, burglary, and abduction. The punishment for such crimes ranged from death to banishment, or whipping and fines. The fourth category in Grotius's schema is crimes "against honor and reputation," reflecting the importance Europeans gave to these social attributes. Though this category includes relatively petty offenses, such as defamation and slander, it also includes the majority of sex crimes— adultery, incest, prostitution, and sodomy—which could be considered "extremely serious." Indeed, the severest penalties imposed in New Netherland were for sodomy. While the lesser sex crimes might only merit an appropriate fine or reparation to the victim, adultery could lead to banishment, and sodomy to death.[6] So, while classified in a less serious category—significantly the one dealing with "honor and reputation"—sodomy brought Grotius full circle to the most severe type of crime, that against God and government, and to the most severe punishment, death.

Our investigation of coerced sex and gendered violence in New Netherland begins with the least severe category (and leaves the consideration of sodomy to later). Several types of cases fall within the category of offenses "against honor and reputation": public deviance, marriage regulation, adultery, fornication, prostitution, and slander. Decisions in these cases frequently cited the court's concern with public scandal and its desire to maintain public order. This can be seen in such seemingly small matters as the case of Abraham Crabaat, who was fined six guilders (about one good beaver skin) for walking through the streets of Beverwijck (present-day Albany) dressed as a woman. The court further warned that he and anyone else who attempted to cross-dress would be punished "as an example to others."[7]

More commonly, the desire to enforce public order involved preserving the institution of marriage, and in some instances, forcing couples into it. Four cases of marriage regulation illustrate this. In 1642, for instance, Adriaen Pietersz tried to arrange a marriage with Elsjen Jans, age seventeen, with the help of her mother. Elsjen objected, saying, "I do not know the man." "But finally, upon the request, persuasion and desire of her mother she accepted [his] troth," Elsjen testified. She then declared that she had changed her mind and had "no desire to marry, the more so as she does not know the young man." As a symbol of her change of heart, she returned in court the man's pledge of troth, a hand-kerchief, presumably ending her obligation. A month later, however, Pietersz returned to court, but this time he was the defendant, for he had carried off Elsjen, a servant girl, during the night from her master's land "with firing guns and muskets." The "pretended bride" appeared in court and testified to her willingness to marry, yet the court ordered her return. It could not sanction the running away or theft of servants.[8]

Twelve years later at Fort Orange (present-day Albany), the court ordered Klaes Ripsz to marry an unnamed woman, referred to only as "the sister [of] the wife of Teunis Jacopsz." After admitting in court to fathering a child with her, to promising to marry her, and to having the banns proclaimed, Ripsz explained that he was waiting to hear from his father, "whom he has written about it." The minister, elder, and deacon present to prosecute the case found this excuse "absurd" and cited the risk of delay, for the mother, who was sick in bed, could die, and leave the child illegitimate, or become pregnant again. "We come to the posi-tive conclusion," the church officers declared, "that in order to avoid all scandal, to prevent further excesses, to promote good order, to maintain justice and finally to fulfill our bounden duty," the couple must be mar-ried. The court agreed, "condemn[ing] the defendant to marry the aforesaid person even this day" at her house, where she was bedridden. Ripsz had "nothing but frivolous excuses to offer and therefore was put in irons."[9] The court expressed no concern for the sick woman, who went unnamed. Instead, it focused on the public scandal that might de-velop and the charge the public might incur if the woman died with il-legitimate children. It coerced a reluctant couple into marriage.

In addition to marriage propriety, officials were devoted to the pre-vention of illegitimate births. One example will suffice here. In July 1645 Marry Willems, widow of Willem Willemsz, "brings a child into court and says that [Jan Haes] is its father." Haes denied the charge and somehow "proved that she went with other men." Persuaded of Willems's loose behavior, the court "ordered that said Marry shall de-part from New Netherland." Two aspects of the case are peculiar. First, the punishment of banishment seems unusually harsh, given that Willems's husband was dead. Although it coincides with Grotius's pre-scription for adultery, banishment was usually reserved for repeat of-fenders and as a reduced penalty for murder. On the other hand, the court ordered Haes to make Willems "a small present."[10] Perhaps this gift was meant to cover the possibility that Haes could have been the father and therefore was potentially responsible for the baby, or perhaps the court just wanted to ensure that Willems was not completely destitute in her banishment.

A fourth type of behavior against honor and reputation was "carnal intercourse," or adultery and fornication. This type of consensual sexual behavior was obviously related to the third, for extramarital sex often led to illegitimate children. But colonial officials abhorred consensual extramarital sex because of the threat they thought such sexual behavior posed to public order and the sanctity of marriage.

Of the eight cases uncovered in this category, two involve men who promised to marry women but then backed out of the engagement after having sex. Both cases have unclear endings, although such piggish behavior clearly disturbed the courts.[11] More interesting is the case of Elisabet Feax, whose attempts to alienate the property that her former husband had provided for their four children compounded her adulterous relationship with another man. Divorced some years before the case in 1648, Feax had "lived and kept company with her lover . . . and, as the witnesses declare, has also had carnal conversation with him, contrary to all good laws." This case pierced to the heart of the community's interest in regulating consensual adult relations, the court believed. "Both for the maintenance of justice and the preservation of the minor children and fatherless orphans," the court declared Feax "incompetent and powerless to dispose of any property, whether belonging to her former husband or her children," and appointed curators to look after such property. Feax was exercising the right that Dutchwomen enjoyed to control property, but the court trumped her rights with its own concern for her immoral behavior. "Although she deserves a much heavier penalty and punishment," the decision continues, "we nevertheless, out of special favor and for a private reason us thereunto moving, consent that with her children she may dwell and live at" Greenwich, one of the Dutch towns closest to English territory to the east of New Amsterdam, "provided that she remain separated both as to bed and board and common intercourse from her lover, Willem Hallet, and abstains from keeping company with him, on pain of corporal punishment." For his part in the affair, the court banished Hallet from the colony and confiscated "his pretended effects . . . for the benefit and advantage of his child procurated by her."[12]

More interesting still is the order by the director-general and council of the colony in 1654 to break up what they considered a red-light district in New Amsterdam. After allegedly receiving many complaints about three married women who lived on the same street, behaved badly, and practiced "dissolute lifestyles," the colony's ruling body ordered the fiscal, a law enforcement officer, "to notify the aforesaid woman and other consorts of theirs, passed by here unnamed for propriety's sake," (though the women and their husbands were listed), "that they either have to change their way of living" or else face banishment. "The fiscal is further ordered," the record continues, "to keep a close watch on the aforesaid women and their associates; and if during the night any other whores or whoremasters are found with the aforesaid persons at other places or uncommon places among the English," they were to be arrested and brought before the council.[13] That the sex seemed to be between Englishmen and Dutchwomen may have irritated the court's sense of morality even more.

The women's street, the Heere Wech, remained seedy, apparently, given the behavior of Samuel Cromstock and Anna Tchuys, wife of Nathaniel Tchuys, reported in a case a few months later in August 1654. Cromstock confessed to being found at night against the clapboards or fence near Jan Vinje's house lying on top of Anna, who "had her clothes pulled up and her body bared" while he "had his pants undone." Anna was not one of the three married women named in the earlier case, but she seemed to have absorbed her neighbors' bad morals. Cromstock was also married, so the couple was punished together and equally by being placed in the public pillory and fined.[14]

All the cases so far could easily have taken place in a seventeenth-century village in the Netherlands or England, or any part of western Europe, for that matter. A few other cases of "carnal intercourse," however, assure us that we are in America and make the cases different. These deal with the mingling of Europeans, Indians, and Africans, a possibility still new for most Dutchmen and women in the mid-1600s. Cases in this category penetrate to the heart of power issues in New Netherland, for here gender, class, and race intersected.

The council of New Netherland prohibited "adulterous intercourse with heathens, blacks, or other persons" in an ordinance in 1638. By "heathens" the council apparently meant Indians (none of whom had become Christians), but what it meant by "other persons" is unclear. If it was a sweeping prohibition on adultery in all forms, it was the only one ever passed in the colony. Evidence of cross-cultural intercourse does not survive from earlier years in the colony, perhaps because most of those records were destroyed. The passage of a prohibitive ordinance, however, suggests that the council perceived a problem with cross-cultural sexual relations, and a case in late 1638 bears this out. Nicolaes Coorn, a sergeant in the WIC's service, was charged with theft and adultery. Coorn, "who by reason of his office was in duty bound to set a good moral example to his soldiers," had allegedly been trading with the Indians for beaver skins axes issued to him for cutting wood. He had also "at divers times had Indian women [*wildinnen*] and Negresses [*swartinnen*] sleep entire nights with him in his bed, in the presence of all the soldiers." For these crimes, Coorn was demoted to private for the remainder of his service to the company.[15]

Coorn's carnal intercourse with Indian and African women was apparently consensual, but there is one case of violence against an Indian woman. In 1639 two men testified that they saw Claes, a cabin boy, "throw down" an Indian woman, sit on her, and draw his knife with the intention of cutting the belt around her waist. Claes's reason for doing this is not clear in the record. He was probably robbing the woman, but he may also have been attempting sexual contact. The outcome of the case does not survive.[16]

Then there is the unusual case of Elias Silva, one of the two dozen or so Jews who lived for a few years in Manhattan during the mid-1650s. What makes the case unusual, and intriguing, is the intersection of prejudice toward Jews and Africans. Jan Gerritsen, a brewer, appeared in New Amsterdam's local court in 1656 and accused Silva, always labeled a Jew in the records, of detaining Gerritsen's "negress or slave" and having "carnal conversation with her." The court gave the parties several weeks to submit written testimony. Silva was apparently jailed in the meantime. Unfortunately, the New Amsterdam records do not preserve the outcome of the case.[17] We do not know if Silva was convicted and, if so, if his punishment was more severe for being a Jew, or for having sex with another man's servant. Both are distinct possibilities.

Finally, verbal assault or slander frequently accompanied physical attacks and was considered as serious, if not more so, for the damage it could do to one's reputation. In eight cases of slander involving women, the common elements include a quarrel (between a woman and a man, or between two women) in which a woman is called a whore and whoever made that charge is accused of lying. The husband or father of the accused whore follows with a lawsuit to protect his wife's or daughter's honor. For example, in 1645 Egbert van Borsum appeared before the council at the request of Catelyn Trico. Borsum witnessed a brawl when Trico asked Paulus van der Beeck, a surgeon, "Why do you beat my daughter?" Van der Beeck accused Trico of lying, and she retorted, "You lie like a villain and a dog." When she raised her hand at him, the surgeon struck Trico and "then called her a whore and a wampum thief." When he could not prove the slanderous remarks in court, but instead said "that he has nothing to say against her that reflects on her honor or virtue," the court fined van der Beeck and warned him against slandering Trico again.[18]

In an extensive study of court cases in the city of New Amsterdam from 1653 to 1674, Linda Biemer calculates that women were involved in 16.5 percent of all court cases but in less than 1 percent of criminal cases. "Women certainly did not constitute a criminal class," Biemer concludes,[19] but, as we have seen, they did not hesitate to exercise their rights under Roman Dutch laws. Historians have made too much, perhaps, of the differences between English and Dutch law regarding women. Though significant, the differences did not lead to equality for women. Economically, married Dutchwomen could retain more property rights than Englishwomen typically enjoyed, but Dutch "women in no sense held a position equivalent to that of men," according to Rudolf Michel Dekker.[20]

Where they did nearly equal Dutchmen, Dekker says, was in their criminality, "which is unusual in comparison to the rest of Europe." Dutchwomen had a reputation that their criminal behavior confirmed; foreigners believed them to be "noisy, violent, and given to drink, but also independent and firm."[21] The impression that one gets from glimpses of women in the court records of New Netherland matches this view. Of course, since troublesome women were most likely to be a party in a suit, they are probably overrepresented. But we have no other sources from which to form our impression of women in New Netherland: no newspapers, no diaries, and only a few letters from women in the elite Rensselaer family.[22]

We move now to the second-lowest category of offenses in Dutch law, those against liberty. Here belong the rape cases. In the single case of attempted rape involving adults, Weyntjen Teunes, the wife of Harck Syboltsen, testified that Adam Roelantsz "by force tried to have intercourse with her at her house and also immodestly attacked her, of which the marks are said to be still visible on her body."

Considering the "serious consequence" of Roelantsz's action, the court condemned him to be flogged publicly and banished from the colony. The severity of the punishment suggests that the court viewed rape more seriously than Grotius. Or, like the English, the court may have thought the rape of a married woman far more serious than the rape of a single woman. The court's logic was clearer when it suspended the sentence: Roelantsz was "burdened with four small motherless children" and the winter was approaching. We do not know if the sentence was ever carried out.[23]

A similar decision occurred in one of the three cases that survive in the records of men molesting girls. In early 1648, thirty-year-old Willem Gilfoordt, from the West Country of England, faced charges of the "violation and rape" of eleven-year-old Maria Barents. The court proceedings were recorded in unusual detail and reveal the officers' disgust with Gilfoordt. A month after the initial charge, the court ordered "the midwives and some reputable women" to examine Barents. A week later, apparently convinced of Barents's injuries at the hands of Gilfoordt, the court convicted him of uncovering the girl, throwing her down into the cellar, untying his breeches, placing himself upon her, and "attempting for about a quarter of an hour to have carnal conversation with her." He failed in his "evil purpose," however, "as the girl was too young." He had confessed "without torture or irons." Viewing this "a matter of very serious consequence, which in a country where justice prevails can not be suffered or tolerated, but ought to be severely punished, in order that the children of honest people may not be dishonored and led away from the path of virtue," the director-general and council ordered Gilfoort to be "severely flogged" with rods and to be banished forever from the colony.[24]

"The delinquent deserves greater and severer punishment," the record continues, but extenuating circumstances had come to the court's attention. Soon after Gilfoort's rape of her, Maria Barents had willfully consented to "conversation" with Willem Gerritsz Wesselsz. In essence, the men of the court implied that Barents was a slutty eleven-year-old and was at least partially to blame for Gilfoort's actions. Her later actions mitigated his rape and the punishment for it. Wesselsz was punished too, for though his sex with Barents was consensual (which of course begs the question of whether eleven-year-olds can consent to sex), it was still fornication. In exchange for his promise of good behavior and work sawing lumber for the WIC for the next year (for which he would be paid), Wesselsz was "graciously pardoned."[25]

Another case of child molestation made its way from the Fort Orange court to New Amsterdam, for the crime was apparently so serious that the officers wanted Petrus Stuyvesant's "very wise opinion and order thereon." Frans Gabrielsz van Delft had confessed to molesting a girl about seven years old, well below any age of consent at the time. Stuyvesant and his council referred the case back to the local court for trial, and it sentenced Gabrielsz to be whipped at the whipping post on October 14, 1652. In this case, there was no talk of the victim's complicity, nor was Gabrielsz banished.[26]

The third case involving a man and a girl lies somewhere between molestation and rape. It also raises class issues, for the girl was a servant of the colony's director. Referred to as a "servant girl," Anna Tymens was old enough to produce a child with the defendant in the case, Gerrit Tides. Tymens had given birth on October 9. Shortly before or after that, Tides appeared at ten o'clock in the evening and "attempted to sleep with her which she refused." He then "tried to force his will upon her by threatening her with an unsheathed knife." Tides confessed to carnal conversation with Tymens but denied knowing anything about using a knife against her. Near the end of October the case reached a verdict. Here we find that Tides was the thirty-three-year-old trumpeter and household servant of Director-General Stuyvesant, and he was married. By "deflowering" and impregnating Tymens, one of Stuyvesant's maids, Tides had not only committed adultery but had "brought dishonor, scandal and shame to his master's house." Therefore, Stuyvesant and his councillors meted out a harsh sentence: Tides would be "severely beaten with rods" and forced to pay 300 guilders (more than a year's pay) to the father of "the deflowered maid."[27] That the crime had taken place under Stuyvesant's nose, and had brought him dishonor, was clearly the central issue here. Had Tymens been another gentleman's pregnant servant, the penalty would probably have been much less.

Several examples so far have demonstrated the fuzzy lines between Grotius's classes of crime. Honor and reputation were concerns that transcended all levels of crime. The protection of honor and reputation was often the court's primary concern, and it may explain the severity of punishments better than any other single factor. As Scott

Christianson suggests, "the system was highly discretionary, and discretion itself constituted an important mechanism of social control."[28]

In Grotius's hierarchy, the next highest class of crimes was those against life, including threats on life such as assault. We have seen how a slander crime in the lowest class (honor and reputation) could escalate into a physical assault. Of the ten cases of this type, a clear-cut distinction between attacks on men and attacks on women never emerges. There are few expressions of moral outrage when women are beaten. On the other hand, there were instances when men went unpunished for beating women. A double standard existed in New Netherland.[29]

Whether the man beating a woman was her husband or someone else, the court punished the man but not severely. In 1642, for instance, Michiel Picet and Nicola Boet beat the unnamed wife of a man referred to only as Touchyn. The record does not relate the circumstances, but it does say that the court ordered the two men to "pay the surgeon" an unspecified sum, presumably for his treatment of the unnamed woman, and to give 20 florins (about two and a half beaver skins) "to the woman for her pain." Twelve years later, two men broke down Merten de Brouwer's door looking for beer. One of the men, Seeger Cornelisz, hurled "many vile and abusive words" at Merten and his wife, who Cornelisz accused of being a whore and lying "in the thicket" with Frans Thomasz. They extinguished the lamp, then Jacob van Loosdreght "wanted forcibly to get on the woman's bed and that coming near the bed, he did not hesitate to grab and touch her, but did so." A witness collaborated the story, except for the assault on Merten's wife. The resolution of the case was never recorded. In a third case, a neighbor charged that Jacob Hap had "scandalously beaten and bloodied his wife and thrown firebrands at her." The neighbor went to court not to object to the beating but because the sparks had flown through a partition door into his house. Hap admitted that he "beat his wife and drew blood." Nevertheless, he was not punished. Revealing its attitude toward domestic violence, the court declared Hap's action "not punishable because it happened between man and wife."[30]

The court was less reluctant to intervene in households when men abused servants, particularly girls. Property rights were at stake in these cases. Jan van Hoesem filed suit against Jochim Wesselen Backer in 1657 when Backer allegedly kicked van Hoesem's daughter in the groin, causing an injury that made the girl unable to work. Backer answered that the girl, his servant, had smarted off to his wife after she had admonished the "young maiden" to "mend her ways." Offended, Backer's wife kicked the girl "in the behind." The case dragged on for two months, during which time van Hoesem testified that his daughter had "discharged much blood contrary to nature and for a long time was confined to her bed, suffering great pain." The court condemned Geertruy Jeronimus, Backer's wife (a Dutchwoman usually did not take her husband's surname), to pay 30 guilders for the girl's pain.[31] This fine, of course, was in addition to the work that Backer and Jeronimus lost while their servant girl was recuperating, and it fits the accepted Dutch practice of levying fines in relation to the perceived offense.

The greatest indignation expressed in a case of assault against a woman came in 1660, when the court in Fort Orange heard the case against Hendrick Anderiesen, who, "without a word of altercation, beat and mistreated Lijsbet, the wife of Gerrit Bancken." The court said that "such excesses in a place where justice prevails cannot be tolerated" and ordered the defendant to be confined. What prompted this outrage was probably that Lijsbet was pregnant and that Anderiesen had beaten her with his fists and kicked her. Unfortunately, no resolution of the case exists in the court records, which end shortly thereafter.[32]

Women in New Netherland, therefore, were not immune from the violence that pervaded their society. With a few exceptions, they could appeal to the judicial system for protection from slanderous words and physical assaults. They could also expect their behavior to be regulated closely, particularly when they engaged in extramarital sex, bore illegitimate children, or otherwise threatened male domination of society.

Finally we come to three cases of men molesting or raping boys in New Netherland. Perhaps it should not be startling that the number of men sexually abusing girls was about the same as the number of men molesting boys. What does seem odd, however, is that the two sodomy cases in the colony involved African boys, one with a European man, the other with an African man.

In the molestation case, Nicolaes Gregory Hillebrant, a native of Prague, faced charges of molesting Pieter Adriaensen, the son of Henderick Jochemsen's wife. Hillebrant admitted to being in Jochem Ketluyn's garden with the boy, and to having "his male member out of his pants, but for the need to relieve himself." He denied being on his knees in the garden, but he admitted to being in front of the boy and to having his hand on him. He answered no when asked if he had tried "to undo the boy's pants by force" and "whether, when the boy refused and screamed, he did not threaten to beat him with a stick, which he had with him?" Then he admitted that Rutger Jacobsen had come along and asked, "What are you doing there, you scoundrel?" Thus interrupted, Hillebrant left the garden and followed Jacobsen down the street, allegedly threatening Jacobsen if he said anything about what he had just seen. The court's last question was whether Hillebrant had insisted on drinking with Jacobsen so much that bystanders became suspicious. "What's wrong with you, Nicolaes? Have you got something on your conscience?" they asked. Having interrogated Hillebrant and recorded his answers, the Fort Orange court decided that, since he was a company employee, Hillebrant should be sent to the director-general and council. The case was returned to the local court for trial, and the outcome is unclear.[33]

More notorious was the sad demise of a prominent company official who died while on the run from sodomy charges. Harmen Meyndersz van den Bogaert, the former commissary of Fort Orange, fled justice after being accused of sodomizing Tobias, a Negro boy slave (*Neger jongen slave*) belonging to the WIC. Nothing else is known about Tobias, but we do know the details of van den Bogaert's death. He had fled to an Indian village, and Hans Vos, an officer of the court, found him "in an Indian house," which he set on fire "in defending himself." Van den Bogaert was dead, but the fire caused a strain in Dutch-Indian relations, for it burned all the winter provisions, wampum, and pelts in the village. The Indians demanded restitution, and the director-general and council were forced to agree to their demands.[34]

The most intriguing rape case of all occurred within the African community of New Amsterdam in 1646. "Some Negroes" had come forward and accused Jan Creoly, "Negro slave of the honorable Company," of committing "sodomy by force" with ten-year-old Manuel Congo, "also a Negro." The two were brought together and questioned. Congo, "without being threatened in any way," confessed to the accusation. Then the prisoner Creoly, "without torture and while free from irons," admitted that he had committed sodomy with the boy Congo "and that he had also committed the said heinous and abominable crime on the island of Curaçao." In levying its punishment, the court explored the biblical injunctions against sodomy and the need to punish this sin for which

God Almighty overthrew Sodom and Gamorrah [sic] of the plain and exterminated the inhabitants from the earth. (Genesis, ch. 19. See also God's covenant, Leviticus, ch. 18, v. 22; and in the same chapter, v. 29, God says: "For whosoever shall commit any of these abominations, even the souls that commit them shall be cut off from among their people.") For which reason such a man [as Creoly] is not worthy to associate with mankind and the crime on account of its heinousness may not be tolerated or suffered, in order that the wrath of God may not descend upon us as it did upon Sodom.

With this logic the court moved sodomy into the category of crimes against God and therefore condemned Creoly "to be brought to the place of justice to be strangled there to death and his body to be burned to ashes, as an example to others."[35]

This sentence is not astonishing, for the punishment for sodomy and bestiality in Calvinist societies at the time was harsh and rested on similar Old Testament beliefs.[36] More remarkable is the source of the accusation, the African community. Its willingness to inform on one of its own indicates two things: the Africans' own disgust with Creoly's actions and their inability to stop him without Dutch intervention. The astonishing part of the case was what followed, the punishment of the victim, Manual Congo. Because both Creoly and Congo had testified that the sodomy had occurred by force, "without the consent of the boy," the director-general and council decided that he could live. "Although according to law a person with whom sodomy has been committed deserves to be put to death," the court decided that "in view of the innocence and youth of the boy," he need only be brutally scarred emotionally. "We have ordered that he be brought to the place where Jan Creoly shall be executed and that he be tied to a post, with wood piled around him, and be made to view the execution and be beaten with rods." There was no relief from this cruelty, which was completed on June 25, 1646.[37]

New Netherland was a violent place in which men and women struggled for power and in which honor meant a great deal. When conflicts occurred, male jurists mediated and attempted to preserve public order and morality, even at the expense of individual rights and wellbeing. West India Company courts ordered persons under their jurisdiction to be beaten with rods. They even ordered a ten-year-old boy to watch the execution of his rapist with wood piled around his feet. He could not have known that the flames would not be lit around him next. White victims were luckier, though they were far from receiving full protection from the courts. It was these courts, after all, that told a battered wife that her husband's actions were between him and her. It was these courts that lightened the sentence of a rapist because the eleven-year-old girl he attacked had sex "voluntarily" with another man soon thereafter.

How do we explain this bizarre system of justice? How could the Dutch leaders be so callous, even cruel? First, we should remember that the Dutch behaved in ways not out of the ordinary for their day. This was a hierarchical world in which crimes and people all had a slot. The Dutch in New Netherland were not significantly different from their neighbors, but they were not identical either. As Scott Christianson puts it, "The New Netherlanders seldom seem to have approached the harsh intolerance of their Puritan neighbors in Massachusetts. Instead, their legal system of social control was more dynamic, more flexible."[38] The Dutch were somewhere between Puritan zeal and the looser mores of Chesapeake society, and if truth be told, their leaders were the zealots while the ordinary folk seem to have been much less interested in morality.

Within the hierarchies of New Netherland, white men fared best. Their world of privilege allowed them the benefit of the doubt, while women, children, Africans, and Indians were looked upon with suspicion. Male leaders apparently saw women and girls as essentially sexual creatures who lured men, Eve-like, to evil acts. Thus, the loose women of the Heere Wech were to blame, not their male customers. Thus, the eleven-year-old girl who was raped had actually invited her attack with her willingness to engage in sex with adult men. And thus the slave boy was spared execution, though not ritual psychological torture, for being the unwilling victim of sodomy.

Though rape cases in New Netherland were few, they open a window into the psychology of gender and power in this society. Courts felt it their obligation to regulate sexual behavior and to preserve the institution of marriage. In some ways, such as property rights, men and women seem to have been equal before the law, but in others, particularly those incidents involving violent attacks on women and children, or the crossing of cultural boundaries, more was at stake. Biblical injunctions applied and forced Dutch leaders to take extreme measures to preserve their colony, they thought, from a wrathful God. In the meantime, women were at risk of falling victim to male violence, and the courts stepped in only when forced to keep the peace.

NOTES

1. Garthine Walker, "Rereading Rape and Sexual Violence in Early Modern England," *Gender and History* 10, 1 (April 1998): 1–25, quotation on 1.

2. Ibid.

3. The keenest analysis of gendered power in the early English colonies is Mary Beth Norton, *Founding Mothers and Fathers: Gendered Power and the Forming of American Society* (New York: Alfred A. Knopf, 1996).

4. Charles T. Gehring, trans. and ed., *Laws and Writs of Appeal, 1647–1663* (Syracuse, N.Y.: Syracuse University Press, 1991).

5. Scott Christianson, "Criminal Punishment in New Netherland," in *A Beautiful and Fruitful Place: Selected Rensselaerswijck Seminar Papers*, ed. Nancy Anne McClure Zeller (Albany, N.Y.: New Netherland Publishing, 1991), 84.

6. Ibid.

7. Charles T. Gehring, trans. and ed., *Fort Orange Court Minutes, 1652–1660* (Syracuse, N.Y.: Syracuse University Press, 1990), 101.

8. Kenneth Scott and Kenn Stryker-Rodda, eds., Arnold J. F. van Laer, trans., *New York Historical Manuscripts: Dutch*, vol. 4, *Council Minutes, 1638–1649* (Baltimore, Md.: Geneaological Publishing Co., 1974), 160–61, 165–66, 168.

9. *Fort Orange Court Minutes*, 162–64. On January 21, 1655, the court summoned Ripsz again and fined him 50 guilders after he admitted to lying when he recanted his earlier testimony. Ibid., 171. Courts also dissolved marriages. In 1656 Frenchman Jan Picolet was relieved of his promise to marry Catryne Jans, a Swede, after she became pregnant with a soldier and because she had not disclosed the affair to Picolet. Charles T. Gehring, trans. and ed., *New York Historical Manuscripts: Dutch, Volumes XVIII–XIX: Delaware Papers (Dutch Period): A Collection of Documents Pertaining to the Regulation of Affairs on the South River of New Netherland, 1648–1664* (Baltimore, Md.: Genealogical Publishing Co., 1981), 61–63. In another case, a long-running scandal in the province of New Netherland captured from the Swedes, the courts declared null and void the marriage of the Lutheran pastor left behind after New Sweden fell to the Dutch in 1655. Lars Lock, the only clergy in the province, had married himself to a young woman and then claimed he did not realize the Dutch would consider this irregular. They did. Ibid., 196, 241, 243–54.

10. *Council Minutes, 1638–1649*, 271.

11. Case of Jannitjen Martens and Jan from Meppelen, ibid., 167; case of Lijsbet Rosekrans and Rut Adriaensz, *Fort Orange Court Minutes*, 44–45, 53.

12. *Council Minutes, 1638–1649*, 486–88.

13. Charles T. Gehring, trans. and ed., *Council Minutes, 1652–1654* (Baltimore, Md.: Genealogical Publishing Co., 1983), 137.

14. Ibid., 172, 180–81.

15. *Council Minutes, 1638–1649*, 33–34. Similar issues were raised in Dutch South Africa. See Yvette Abrahams, "Was Eva Raped? An Exercise in Speculative History," *Kronos* 23 (1996): 3–21.

16. Kenneth Scott and Kenn Stryker-Rodda, eds., Arnold J. F. van Laer, trans., *New York Historical Manuscripts: Dutch*, 3 vols., *Register of the Provincial Secretary* (Baltimore, Md.: Genealogical Publishing Co., 1974), 1:177.

17. Berthold Fernow, ed., *The Records of New Amsterdam from 1653 to 1674 Anno Domini*, 7 vols. (New York: Knickerbocker Press, 1897), 2:76, 82, 90.

18. *Register of the Provincial Secretary*, 2:286; *Council Minutes, 1638–1649*, 254–55.

19. Linda Biemer, "Criminal Law and Women in New Amsterdam and Early New York," in *A Beautiful and Fruitful Place*, 73–82, quotation on 74. Of the 43 criminal cases Biemer identified with women, there were 14 thefts, 10 violations of liquor laws, 9 assaults, 2 cases regarding runaway slaves, 3 cases involving weights and measures, 1 illegal baptism of a child, 1 case of littering, 2 cases of "whorish life and behavior," and 1 of indecent exposure.

20. Rudolf Michel Dekker, "Getting to the Source: Women in the Medieval and Early Modern Netherlands," trans. Marybeth Carlson, *Journal of Women's History* 10, 2 (Summer 1998): 165–88.

21. Ibid., 171.

22. While not copious in the Netherlands, either, information on women is more abundant and includes Herman W. Roodenburg, "The Autobiography of Isabella de Moerloose: Sex, Childrearing and Popular Belief in Seventeenth Century Holland," *Journal of Social·History* 18, 4 (Summer 1985): 517–40. For more on women in New Netherland, see Sherry Penney and Roberta Willenkin, "Dutch Women in Colonial Albany: Liberation and Retreat," *de Halve Maen* 52, 1 (Spring 1977): 9–10, 14–15, 52, 2 (Summer 1977): 7–8, 15; David E. Narrett, "Dutch Customs of Inheritance, Women, and the Law in Colonial New York City," in *Authority and Resistance in Early New York*, eds. William Pencak and Conrad Edick Wright (New York: New York Historical Society, 1988), 27–55; and Martha Dickinson Shattuck, "Women and Trade in New Netherland," *Itinerario* 18, 2 (1994): 40–49. An imaginative fictional recreation of the life of the New Amsterdam woman Gretje Reyniers, based partly on several court cases, is Michael Pye, *The Drowning Room* (New York: Granta Books, 1996).

23. *Council Minutes, 1638–1649*, 350–51; Norton, *Founding Mothers and Fathers*, 351.

24. *Council Minutes, 1638–1649*, 478, 482–84.

25. Ibid., 485–86. For a discussion of similar cases among the English colonists, see Norton, *Founding Mothers and Fathers*, 351–58. The age of consent

in English law was generally ten years. The Dutch in New Netherland never specified an age of consent, but this case suggests their thinking on the matter was close to the English.

26. *Fort Orange Court Minutes*, 25–28; *Council Minutes, 1652–1654*, 40.

27. The original is damaged at this point. Exactly to whom Tides would pay the 300 guilders is missing. It is my assumption that it would be a parent. *Council Minutes, 1652–1654*, 186, 196.

28. Christianson, "Criminal Punishment in New Netherland," 84.

29. Bernard Capp offers a flip side to the double standard debate in "The Double Standard Revisited: Plebeian Women and Male Sexual Reputation in Early Modern England," *Past and Present* 162 (1999): 70–100. Capp found that women, using the importance of male reputation against lovers and errant husbands, could succeed in seeking financial compensation or retribution in the courts.

30. *Council Minutes, 1652–1654*, 178; *Fort Orange Court Minutes*, 145. In a New Amsterdam case, the court jailed Nicolaas Boot for "shutting up" his wife "in her house without order or authority, nailing to the windows and doors, and also beating her." The court intervened when the wife, Merritje Joris, complained of Boot's drunken behavior. The court did not seem to object to the punishment as much as Boot's assuming "unto himself the authority of the Magistracy" in punishing her himself. *Records of New Amsterdam*, 2:335, 338. English colonists held similar attitudes about wives' subordination to husbands; physical punishment was acceptable as long as it was "lawfull and reasonable correction." Only Massachusetts Bay and Plymouth colonies prohibited spousal abuse, the former declaring that "no man shall strike his wife, nor any woman her husband." Norton, *Founding Mothers and Fathers*, 72–74.

31. *Fort Orange Court Minutes*, 278–79, 288, 293.

32. Ibid., 524.

33. Ibid., 404–5. The literature on sodomy in the English world is growing. See Colin L. Talley, "Gender and Male Same-Sex Erotic Behavior in British North America in the Seventeenth Century," *Journal of the History of Sexuality* 6, 3 (1996): 385–408; Cynthia Herrup, "The Patriarch at Home: The Trial of the 2nd Earl of Castlehaven for Rape and Sodomy," *History Workshop Journal* 41 (1996): 1–18; Richard Godbeer, "'The Cry of Sodom': Discourse, Intercourse, and Desire in Colonial New England," *William and Mary Quarterly*, 3d Ser., 52, 2 (1995): 259–86; Michael Warner, "New English Sodom," *American Literature* 64, 1 (1992): 19–47; and Robert F. Oaks, "'Things Fearful to Name': Sodomy and Buggery in Seventeenth-Century New England," *Journal of Social History* 12 (1978–79): 268–81.

34. *Council Minutes, 1638–1649*, 480–81.

35. Ibid., 326–27.

36. Norton, *Founding Mothers and Fathers*, 347; A. H. Huussen Jr., "Straf-

rechtelijke Vervolging van 'Sodomie' in de Republiek," *Spiegel Historiael* 17, 11 (1982): 547–52. Huussen notes that the decentralized nature of Dutch government in the Republic and the absence of sodomy cases in the records make generalizations about this crime in the Netherlands impossible. A fully cross-cultural interpretation of sodomy would include Angel Rodríguez Sánchez, "La Soga y el Fuego: La Pena de Muerte en la España de los Siglos XVI y XVII," *Cuadernos de Historia Moderna* 15 (1994): 13–39; Pierre Hurteau, "Catholic Moral Discourse on Male Sodomy and Masturbation in the Seventeenth and Eighteenth Centuries," *Journal of the History of Sexuality* 4, 1 (1993): 1–26; and Jens Rydström, "Tidelagaren och den Homosexuelle Mannen: Två Typer I den Svenska Rättshistorien," *Historisk Tidskrift* 4 (1998): 510–21.

37. *Council Minutes, 1638–1649,* 327–8.

38. Christianson, "Criminal Punishment in New Netherland," 84.

5

Rape, Law, Courts, and Custom in Pennsylvania, 1682–1800

Jack Marietta and G. S. Rowe

IN DEPICTING THE behavior of past peoples, historians of crime may employ a variety of records. One of them is the law. The legal code of a society depicts behavior that that society (or some portion of it) desires and requires. And if all men and women behaved altruistically or submissively, the laws would afford a rather comprehensive portrait of people's lives. But no society is completely altruistic or submissive and most contain at least a few members who violate the laws. They leave another record for historians, the record of crime and criminals and of the enforcement of the law. Between the legal and criminal records exists a dialectic of model conduct and intolerable behavior. But the dialectic is more complicated, and yet more records enter the picture. There is public and private prescriptive literature such as newspapers, periodicals, manuals, guides, and instructions. More oblique sources about behavior include fiction, humor and parody, and personal letters and gossip. These, too, offer clues about desirable or undesirable behavior, what is tolerated and prohibited, and what is popular and unpopular. Significantly, they can all bear upon the question of law enforcement and crime. They help disclose how laws are being enforced—effectively, zealously, impartially, or perhaps not at all. All can enter the dialectic, and historians should examine them in the attempt to synthesize a picture of the past. In the following treatment of rape in Pennsylvania before 1800, various kinds of resources are employed in a kind of dialogue in order to construct a history of rape in that province and state.

First there are the law codes of Pennsylvania and their treatment of rape. Anger over the severity of England's law and judiciary as well as

William Penn's psyche helped to shape Pennsylvania's initial penal code. Inequities in seventeenth-century England arising from the criminal code and courts' conduct encouraged legal reform.[1] Convinced that they were being unfairly targeted by the laws and magistrates, English Quakers joined the chorus for penal reform.[2] Penn not only urged legal change in England, but subsequently sought to ensure that his New World colony would embrace more enlightened precepts and practices. When he departed for Pennsylvania in September 1682 he took with him the vision of a criminal code that would redefine crime and chart for government a different course from that of the mother country.[3]

Criminal statutes in Pennsylvania were hammered out during meetings in Pennsylvania in December 1682.[4] The "Great Law," emanating from the Chester meeting that same month, and modified in subsequent assemblies,[5] was the mildest criminal justice system of any of the English colonies.[6] Its goal was leniency rather than severity, rehabilitation rather than vengeance.[7]

From their colony's founding, Pennsylvanians exhibited a disposition toward individual worth and autonomy unique among the English colonies. Their attitudes regarding human goodness and individual worth embraced females as well as males. Quaker theology celebrated the equality of the sexes in spiritual matters, and by accepting women as equals in their church, Friends also extended to them greater equality within the household and the community than did their neighbors.[8] Pennsylvania's earliest criminal code reflected the Friends' faith in personal virtue—male or female—and in individuals' capacity to be rehabilitated if temporarily seduced into improper behavior. It also reflected Quaker forbearance and appreciation of the sanctity of life. Not only was it briefer than most colonial codes, but it was also more humane.[9] Still, those responsible for its formulation were more interested in the entire body of laws than in particular crimes. Thus, in 1682, penalties for rape came about not from a specific discussion of that offense, but as a result of a general feeling that the number of capital crimes in England should be greatly reduced in Pennsylvania.

Among English capital offenses proclaimed noncapital in Pennsylvania was rape. The 1682 statutes declared that males convicted of rape were to be whipped with no specific number of lashes prescribed, and were to forfeit one-third of their estate to the victim, or if the victim were a minor, to her parents. They were also to suffer imprisonment with hard labor for one year. A second conviction carried a life sentence.[10]

Magistrates heard almost nothing of rape in Pennsylvania's first two decades. In 1685, Sussex County's Richard Gill forced his way into the house of John Giles and "endeavor[ed] to Ravish" Giles's wife, Johanna. A jury found him guilty and fined him 20 shillings. Nearly a decade later another attempted rape was registered when Chester County's Ruth Colvert complained that Owen Mack Daniel had tried to force her.[11] Admittedly, other cases occurred in those years that today would be deemed rape or attempted rape, but were not included in rape statistics for this study. For example, Philip Conway of Bucks County was convicted in 1687 of "Attempting to lye with Cloverdale's wife" after Jane Cloverdale testified that Conway twice had come to her home "and did Say he . . . would fuck her either by night or by day."[12] In 1689 Francis Smith was indicted for assault because he "did Comitt an assault upon Mary ye wife of James Bayless . . . and there did violently force [her] to ye Bed Side in her sd Husbands House with an intent to have Committed fornication with her." Four years later, Phillip Yarnell approached Elizabeth Woodyard and thrust her hand "into his Codpise and would have her to feele his members how they went limber or stifer."[13] Though today these incidents would be viewed as rape or sexual coercion, each was prosecuted under a different rubric. It was not until 1700 that the first rape (in their terms) was prosecuted in Pennsylvania.[14]

Considering the few instances of rape appearing in dockets, it is surprising that Pennsylvania's sexual assault statutes were dramatically rewritten less than twenty years after the colony's founding. In 1700, the year of the first rape prosecution, the legislature proclaimed that hereafter rape by white men was to be punishable by thirty-nine lashes and a seven-year prison term. The convicted rapist was also to forfeit his entire estate if single, one-third if married. Should he be convicted a second time, the defendant was to be castrated and branded on the forehead with the letter R.[15]

By the 1700 statutes African American men guilty of the rape of a white woman were to lose their lives. Attempts by black men to ravish white females were to bring thirty-one lashes, branding, and exile. The legislation made no mention of sanctions for black men who sexually assaulted African American women. Black rapists, like black offenders generally, were to be tried in discrete courts—in "Negro Tryals"—and without a jury.[16]

The severity of Pennsylvania's 1700 rape statutes, insofar as they related to white men, astonished British authorities. Arguing that castration was "a punishment never inflicted by any law in any of Her Majesty's dominions," the Privy Council struck down the laws, demanding that they be rewritten with less traumatic penalties.[17] Satisfactory revisions were not agreed upon until 1705. In that year, the revised criminal code declared that rape was to be punished by thirty-one lashes (eight fewer than previously), seven years' hard labor, and the forfeiture of one's entire estate if single, one-third if married. Sanctions for a second offense were to be life imprisonment and branding, rather than castration and branding. The 1705 legislation retained the death penalty for Negroes guilty of ravishing white women. A combination of whipping, branding, and exile were prescribed for attempts to rape.[18]

Though the records reveal little more than a half-dozen rape trials immediately following 1705, penalties for the act became even more severe in 1718. Legislation in 1718 proclaimed that anyone guilty of rape must forfeit his life, and for the next three-quarters of a century the death penalty held for a conviction of rape for both white and black males when white females were victims. Politics, rather than concerns over rape, shaped the 1718 statutory overhaul. Enemies of Friends, both in Pennsylvania and England, groused that Quaker criminal sanctions not only deviated from England's but failed to deter aberrant behavior. Nonetheless, it was Quaker jurors and justices refusing to take an oath to the king, ignoring practices and forms of English law, and their resistance to corporal and capital penalties that rankled more. Anglicans and other non-Quakers boycotted courts and railed against Quaker participation in the colony's judicial system. To breathe life into the crippled judiciary, Lieutenant-Governor William Keith forged a settlement where, in return for Quakers agreeing to embrace harsher criminal sanctions and mete out more severe justice, they could legally substitute affirmations for oaths in public proceedings. This understanding, which pushed Pennsylvania's criminal sanctions into greater conformity with those of England, appealed to British authorities as well as to Pennsylvania's diverse constituents. But it was a package deal; under Keith's goad virtually all of England's criminal penalties were adopted. There was no sustained discussion of individual offenses. Rape quietly became capital along with a range of other infractions.[19]

The harsher 1718 law did not reduce the already low incidence of prosecuted rape. Quite the contrary. A decade after the law declared rape a capital offense, Isaac Norris complained that, "in my memory we could Safely go to bed with our doors open but now Robberies, house-breaking, Rapes, and other crimes are become Common."[20] In the sixty-eight years between Pennsylvania's statute overhaul in 1718 and its important penal revisions in 1786, sixty sexual assault cases were tried: thirty-seven rape cases and twenty-three attempted rapes.

The September 1786 "Act for Amending the Penal Laws of This State" redrew the landscape of the penal code by substituting "continued hard labor, publicly and disgracefully imposed" for persons convicted for many crimes heretofore capital.[21] Nonetheless, legislators chose not to change the state's rape provisions. Six years earlier, in the "Act for the Gradual Abolition of Slavery," Pennsylvanians had proclaimed that "the offenses and crimes of negroes and mulattoes as well slaves and servants and [sic] as freemen," would be adjudicated in mainstream courts. "Tryals for Negroes" were abolished. Though this act provided greater legal safeguards for black males accused of rape, it did not alter the penalty for that crime.[22]

Several high profile cases occurred following 1786. Watched especially closely by the public was the case of Alice Clifton, a sixteen-year-old black girl accused of killing her illegitimate infant. Evidence at her infanticide trial established that Clifton had been repeatedly raped by John ("Fat John") Shaffer, a married white man.[23] Despite doubts of obtaining a conviction, authorities subsequently charged Shaffer with the rape of Clifton, and in raucous proceedings in February 1788, tried him. Before "a great crowd" that pushed and shoved until "one of the windows was broke," a jury exonerated Shaffer.[24] One appalled observer, William Bradford, a former prosecutor, observed that white Pennsylvanians were not yet ready to see a white man hang for the rape of a black woman, even for repeated assaults upon a black youngster.[25]

In 1794 the legislature removed the capital designation for rape. In April that year, "An Act for the Better Preventing of Crimes and for Abolishing the Punishment of Death in Certain Cases," eliminated the death penalty for all crimes except murder in the first degree. Rape hereafter was to be punished by a sentence of ten to twenty-one years in prison.[26] The 1794 enactment was the last brushstroke in the legislative portrait of rape prior to the nineteenth century in Pennsylvania.

But the legislative portrait is not the only rendering available to us.

Figure 5.1
Charges of Rape and Attempted Rape

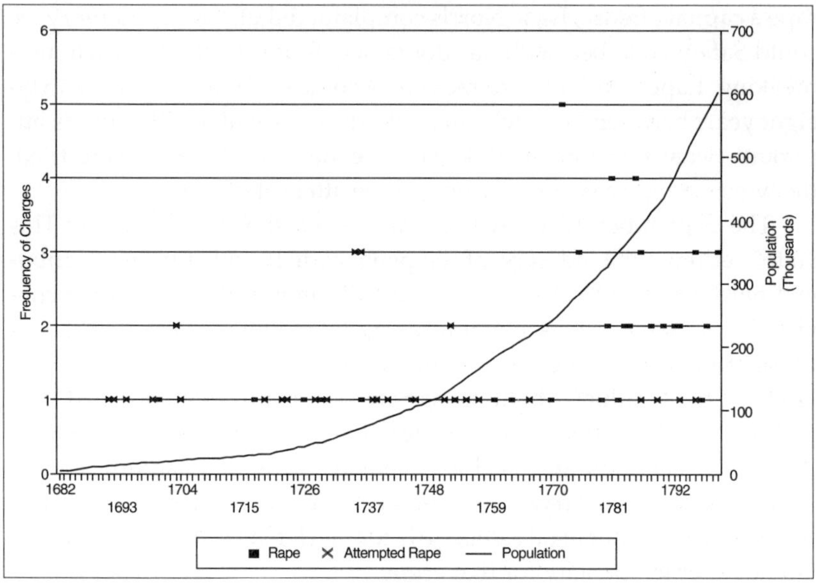

A statistical analysis of court dockets and auxiliary records reveals a second portrait of rape in early Pennsylvania. Only fifty-six prosecutions for rape appear in almost one hundred twenty-five years in court records—less than one prosecution per year. Another thirty-eight prosecutions were for attempted rape or assault with intent to ravish. In addition, twenty cases centering on abusive sexual interactions—incest, sexual cruelty to a spouse, child molestation—appear in the dockets. Prior to 1801, sexual assaults made up only 0.01 percent of the total prosecutions in Pennsylvania.[27]

Figure 5.1 and Table 5.1 illustrate that charges of rape crowded the last three decades of the eighteenth century. But as the figure also illustrates, the increase in rape charges was roughly correlated with the increase in provincial population after 1750. The figures show as well a curious shift in the balance between rape and attempted rape. Before 1770, rapes were outnumbered by attempted rapes, 10 to 29; abruptly thereafter, through 1800, rapes outnumbered attempted rapes by 47 to 9. In Chester County the court dockets are almost entirely complete and population data are the best in the province and state. There, the crime rate per 100,000 can by computed for rape, and the only decades when it rose to one per 100,000 or higher were the 1770s at two, and the next two decades at one. In 1682–1717 charges averaged 0.06 per year; in 1718–1793, 0.58 per year; in 1794–1801, 1.57 per year.

Of the fifty-six defendants formally charged with rape, almost one in four (24.6 percent) were voted *ignoramus* by grand juries—a high rate that meets or exceeds all but one of the major categories of crime in Pennsylvania. Another nine cases (16.0 percent) were dropped by the

Table 5.1

Rape Charges and Resolutions

	Charges	Ignoramus	Default[1]	Conviction	Acquittal	Unknown
1700	1		1			
1717	1	1		1		
1726	1	1				
1729	1			1		
1734	1			1		
1736	1			1		
1739	1	1				
1743	1			1		
1745	1			1		
1753	1					1
1760	1					1
1763	1		1			
1770	1			1		
1772	5			4		1
1775	2		2			
1779	1		1			
1780	2	1			1	
1781	4			1	3	
1782	1			1		
1783	2			1	1	
1784	2	1			1	
1785	4	2		1	1	
1786	3	1		2		
1788	2			1	1	
1790	2	1			1	
1792	2		1			1
1793	2		1	1		
1795	2	1	1			
1796	3	2		1		
1797	1	1				
1798	1					1
1800	3	1		1	1	
Total	57	14	8	20	10	5

[1] Default includes the state declining to prosecute, accommodating the case outside court, or failing to prosecute the case to resolution.

public prosecutor or victims or were arbitrated out of court—another high rate of default in prosecution. Twenty-eight, or half the total, went to trial; eighteen were convicted, which was 31.6 percent of all rape accusations and 64.3 percent of defendants tried. That is a high rate of conviction, but not as high as that for crimes against property. No rape defendant refused to contest the charge. The severe punishment awaiting such a choice surely precluded submitting to the court. As noted earlier, rape was removed from the list of capital crimes in 1794. The change could conceivably have led to more indictments and convictions, if we presume that the prospect of executing the accused daunted grand and petit juries before 1794. However, that was not the case. Before 1794, grand juries indicted in 80.4 percent of rape accusations; from 1794 to 1800, they indicted in 54.4 percent. Before 1794, petit juries convicted in 34.8 percent of the cases they heard, but from 1794 to 1800, they convicted in only 18.2 percent. The close of the century appears to have been a time of greater tolerance of sexual aggression, possibly a time of increased skepticism and diminished sympathy for the pleading of women complaining of rape.

In the case of attempted rape, the outcomes of the judicial process show some differences with plain rape. First, whereas no man accused of rape pleaded guilty, 23.7 percent of the accused in attempted rape did so—the punishment for being found guilty was obviously less after 1794. Without a view into the interchanges between prosecutors and the accused, some accused must have agreed to the reduced charge of attempted rape. Attempted rape or sexual assault was more easily proved than rape, adding an incentive for the prosecutor to take that alternative to the defendant. Grand juries were more apt to indict in attempted rape, by an additional margin of 14.1 percent. But then petit juries found only a small additional 5.2 percent of attempted rapists guilty.[28]

One particular statistical pattern stands out, that involving youngsters. A doleful number of rapes and attempted rapes were upon children. Chester County witnessed thirty-three rapes and attempted rapes between 1682 and 1801. The astonishing fact is that seven of the thirty-three recorded rapes, or one in five, was upon a minor. All were age twelve or younger. We have no assurance that the surviving court papers, which contain the data on victims, comprise a representative or random sample so that one in five was the case in Chester or in Pennsylvania. But the extant papers were not chosen for preservation by some astonished functionary fascinated by the record of sexual crimes;

Table 5.2
Attempted Rape Charges and Resolutions

	Charges	Ignoramus	Default[1]	Pleaded Guilty	Conviction	Acquittal
1691	1			1		
1692	1		1			
1694	1			1		
1699	1			1		
1703	2		2			
1704	1			1		
1719	1			1		
1722	1	1				
1723	1			1		
1728	1			1		
1730	1					1
1735	3				3	
1736	3		2			1
1738	1				1	1
1739	1				1	
1741	1				1	
1746	1				1	
1751	1			1		
1752	2				2	
1753	1				1	
1755	1				1	
1757	1			1		
1766	1				1	
1786	1				1	
1789	1	1				
1793	1	1				
1796	1		1			
1800	5	1	1		2	1
Total	38	4	7	9	14	4

[1] Default includes the state declining to prosecute, accommodating the case outside court, or failing to prosecute the case to resolution.

Table 5.3
Resolutions of Rape and Attempted Rape Charges

	Rape (%)	Attempted Rape (%)
Ignoramus	24.6	10.5
Default	15.8	18.5
Unknown	10.5	0
Guilty	31.6	36.8
Pleaded Guilty	0	23.7
Not Guilty	17.5	10.5
	100	100

the rape case papers appear among records of very routine thefts, liquor violations and other business. The survival of records of rape and its victims, therefore, while not random, is still accidental and amounts to a clue that children were unusually at risk. To underscore another fact about the data on rape and its victims, they are from Chester County, an area with the highest concentration of nonviolent people in early America, mostly the Quakers. The area offers the best prospect in America for low rates of rape and other violent crimes. Secondly, if Quakers and other nonviolent people in Chester County set any effective example of self-restraint in their home county, counties without this peaceful leavening doubtless were even worse.

Court papers describing assaults on Chester children detail actions as depraved as most times or places could supply. In December 1754 Mary Gordon of West Nottingham Township asked a neighbor for help in harvesting hay. The neighbor ordered his servant Jonathan McVay to help Gordon. Later, Gordon was away from her house, leaving behind her children and McVay. Upon returning, she heard her eight-year-old daughter Jane crying. When she got to the house, Jane told her that McVay had "murdered" her; he had climbed onto her back and penetrated her. A witness, Elizabeth Scott, testified that she came upon Mary acting bereft of her senses. Scott questioned her and the two entered the Gordon house, where Scott saw blood on the floor and on Jane's clothes. Jane's six-year-old brother, who had witnessed the rape, recounted the events to Scott.[29]

The youngest victim was Lydia Bird, age four. Her grandmother, Ann Babb, had put her to bed. An hour later, Patience Clayton came running to Babb to tell her that a drunken Thomas Hemphill had fallen upon the child in bed and was smothering her. When Ann ran to the child, she found Hemphill on top of Lydia with his pants down and Lydia struggling and screaming. Babb pulled him off the child and pushed him down a flight of stairs. Being discovered and kicked about seemed to bring the drunken Hemphill to his senses, for he told Babb he deserved no better treatment than the thrashing she had given him.[30]

Other than cases of victimized children, the most brutal rape was upon a Native American woman. The assault in 1722 exhibited the presumed sexual drive of the perpetrator, but surely much more. Since the victim was Native American and the rapist showed no inclination to rape her surreptitiously or to avoid apprehension, his racism and depreciation of women lay open to view. At least two witnesses had observed the principal perpetrator, James Browne, a shoemaker from Kennet, lying out of doors with an Indian woman named Great Hills. Thomas Pryor testified that later, while he was idly standing around, Browne happened by and asked him if he were interested, Browne "would show him A sight." He took Pryor to Great Hills, who was lying on the ground on her belly with her matchcoat up around her waist. Browne threw a knife to Pryor, who cut and peeled a stick with it. Then Browne rolled the woman over and used both his hands to spread her genitals while Pryor thrust the stick into her.[31]

Despite Norris's 1728 lament about the frequency of rapes and the numerous assaults upon children, on the surface the crime appears not to have been a problem since less than one case per year occurred.[32] Visitor Francois La Rochefoucauld-Liancourt observed in 1793 that women could travel unattended anywhere in Pennsylvania, even at night, without suffering sexual assault.[33] His safe-travel comment, while not a reflection on the volume of rape proceedings, does help to corroborate the infrequent prosecutions. But there is narrative evidence to the contrary and evidence from better-informed persons. William Bradford, who spent a lifetime as lawyer, prosecutor, and judge in Pennsylvania, observed that "there is scarce any crime which escapes punishment so often as that of rape."[34] Bradford was pointing to the "dark figure" of crimes, offenses that did not get reported to public authorities and did not get punished.[35]

The judicial record on rape in most English continental colonies and subsequent American states suffered from underreporting and underprosecution and Pennsylvania was probably not an exception. For a variety of reasons many sexual assaults went unrecorded. Even so, Pennsylvanians understood that sexual coercion was widespread. Judges, prosecutors, jurors, and defendants knew that rape was often either permitted to go unpunished or was prosecuted and punished under less daunting rubrics.[36] Or it was dealt with as a civil action. Victims certainly knew of unreported and untried rapes. Ministers knew, lawyers knew, relatives knew. So did humorists.[37] According to Bradford, rape cases were largely determined "by the rank, situation, and character of the victim." Where females were undistinguished in rank or station, juries frequently ignored "positive evidence."[38] Because the women most likely to be raped were lower class and powerless, they were unlikely to be vindicated in court. It was a vicious cycle.

At the root of the low prosecution and conviction rates in rape cases in Pennsylvania—as elsewhere—was a society wedded to patriarchal and deferential patterns. By its very nature hierarchical society imposed silence on a range of legitimate and illegitimate coercion. Coercive relationships, sexual or otherwise, have a history of their own, which has only recently begun to be probed seriously by scholars.[39] These scholars have found that because the consequences were greater for all concerned in sexual matters, sexual intimidation and exploitation fostered a deeper silence from both victim and victimizer than did other forms of forced behavior. The mechanisms for perpetuating silence in these instances were as varied as they were resourceful.

The renowned 1718 criminal revisions, coming as they did on the eve of a dramatic population spurt that flooded the colony with often dissolute and violent people, gave weight to conventional—and hierarchical—practices. Observers bemoaned crime perpetrated by newcomers, although only the Philadelphia Quaker, Isaac Norris, mentioned rape specifically.[40] During this burgeoning diversity and unruliness, the 1718 reforms gave greater rein to traditional English assumptions and practices inside and outside the colony's tribunals, including questions governed by hierarchical forms. And these included suppressing complaints of rape. Until patriarchal elements eroded and deferential practices declined after 1750 in Pennsylvania, the silence so integral to hierarchical society persisted.

There is evidence, then, for a darker portrait, one with deeper shadows than those offered by conventional sources. Rape is a variety of aggression and it bears upon its frequency to know that aggressive behavior in general was common in Pennsylvania. The rates of homicide and assault and battery were, in fact, exorbitant and surprising in a society leavened with nonviolent peoples and touted as a "peaceable kingdom."[41] That too is part of the collective portrait of sexual assaults.

A third depiction of Pennsylvania rape comes from materials offering clearer glimpses into thinking about gender, sexuality and their relationship to rape prosecutions. Generally speaking, a society's criminal law reflects traditional assumptions about deviant behavior and the priorities of the people living within that community. But as standards change, modifications are made in conventional sanctions and enforcement is tightened, or the laws are ignored both by those governed by them and those designated to enforce them. We have looked at prosecutorial configurations in Pennsylvania and at alterations in the statute law pertaining to rape. An examination of the thinking behind the evolution of the law and prosecution patterns is now in order. And that includes changing attitudes toward male and female sexuality and about the use of coercion in sexual relations. For this we turn to the public print media: newspapers, almanacs, magazines, and works of fiction.[42]

In the second half of the eighteenth century, images of women began to change discernibly and with the American Revolution the changes accelerated.[43] The altered or new conceptions had consequences for gender relations, including sexual relations and rape.[44] The quarters from which the new images emerged were diverse. At the most rarefied level, the philosophical literature of the Enlightenment promoted some limited rethinking of gender and relationships. The quasi-philosophical literature of republicanism, famous for influencing the political leaders of the Revolution, expanded its reach to engage women's roles in domestic and public life and women's natural talents. At the opposite end of the scale, the lower end culturally speaking, the print media consisted of commercial prints like almanacs, with their humor, doggerel, and aphorism. The topic of this popular and common literature was often women and men's treatment of them.

Compounding all the changes that emerged from this varied literature was the practical experience of men and women in the Revolutionary war. War stimulated greater independence for men, women, and youths.[45] War weakened parental control and patriarchy; higher rates of premarital conception than at any time since settlement reflected such independence.[46] War increased women's exposure to life outside the home and demanded of them an assertiveness and growth that peacetime rarely had. In the realm of higher culture, new ideas and expectations about women were part of what has been labeled the "cult of sensibility" that emerged late in the century. At the core of this cult was the belief that individuals could and should feel the pain of those in distress and that one's sympathy for the pain of people exhibited the strong character of the sentient man or women, and not their weakness.[47] Expressions of the new sensibility appeared in the press promoting humane treatment of the blind and the deaf, the poor, Negroes, and animals.[48] Such compassion also extended to unfortunate women, including those seduced and abandoned, unwed, and mothers of illegitimate offspring.[49]

Republican ideology complemented the concept of sensibility and expanded public discourse on the role of women in American society. Historians Linda Kerber, Mary Beth Norton, Jan Lewis, and Cathy N.

Davidson have described models for women that included especially the republican wife, mother, educator, and nurturer.[50] Philadelphia magazines brimmed with articles for and about women, treating courtship, marriage, family, and the republic. But important for the topic of sexual relations and rape, the literature also treated male behavior. It encouraged and praised men who were virtuous, honorable, discreet, tender, and giving. It upbraided the "vile seducer," an obvious expression of opprobrium for those who ignored the weak, unfortunate, and powerless. When listened to, men's natural sensibility could alert them to the distress they caused the women they seduced and the children they sired, both of whom they abandoned.[51] Their natural faculties could curb their mean sexual impulses. And as for those who had deviated and fallen, they could be rehabilitated and recovered.[52]

The voices of enlightenment, sensibility, and republicanism, however, were not the only ones in the marketplace of images and ideas in the new nation. There were other images of male and female nature and conduct abroad which did not complement the preceding ones. Indeed, some were irreconcilably different from them. Historian Claire Lyons found such images and ideas even before the Revolution and asserts that they constituted "a turning point in the history of sexuality." Beginning in 1759, Lyons discovered in popular literature and behavior in Philadelphia, "the emergence of a full blown urban pleasure culture." Most significantly for the history of rape, she finds that the new depiction of women clearly supplied men with invitation for sex without consent.[53]

In the new literature, Lyons argues, women become lustful. Although lust had earlier been part of their gender stereotype, in the 1760s the attention paid it was enlarged. More significantly, women's lust was touted in public and treated as an object for pleasure rather than for reprehension and moral lessons. Women longed for the attention of men and sexual experiences, the press said, but they longed covertly, behind a demure façade. In this depiction, the difference between women's passivity and their lust was critical to the commission of sexual assault. Knowing, as the popular literature told men, that what women really desired was sexual relations and that they only appeared disinterested, the need for permission to initiate seduction faded. A woman's presumptive wishes were not violated when a man proceeded, and if she did protest against his advances he could extrapolate that that too was not really her speaking. The *Universal American Almanac* rhymed in 1763:

The Stallion and the Bull now rampant grow,
And maids to Silence turn their modest No;
Which shews the Heart's consenting to the Bliss;
And serves for Answer just as well as yes.[54]

According to Lyons, "The accentuation of the sexual temptress side of female sexuality in the 1760s served to make a man's sexual involvement with women less his responsibility."[55]

In ascribing lust to women, the literature did not make exceptions for younger girls. In 1761, one almanac described the conscious sexual desire even in fourteen-year-olds: "At fourteen years young females are contriving tricks to tempt ye," it printed.[56] Among the seven young victims of rape identified in Pennsylvania, the oldest was twelve. Whether male readers were attentive to the two-year difference between the conniving fourteen-year-olds in the press and the real twelve-year-old victim is problematical, but the girls would have been better off had the press helped them enjoy privacy as well as their likely innocence.

In the rush of new ideas and images and in spite of their confidence in the malleability of human nature, when weighed and balanced most commentators came to expect the worst of men in sexual matters. The "coxcomb," "reptile," "seducer," "flatterer," "deceiver," "flirt," "fop," and "brute," overbore the philanthropist, the sensitive, the empathetic, and the helper. Ultimately, authors in the new nation saw men as ambitious, designing, tyrannical, even evil when it came to sexual relations.[57] The physically abusive husband was the second most prominent theme in contemporary periodicals.[58] Seemingly, domination and oppression were part of men's nature.[59]

If anything, the judicial record confirms the grimmer appraisal of gender relations. For all the touting of new ideas of male and female sexuality, and for all the progressive law reforms of 1786 and 1794, Pennsylvanians hardly changed their attitudes regarding rape. Women remained distrustful of male prosecutors in rape cases. Nor did they feel confident that male jurors understood their victimization any better than had earlier jurymen. The statement of a rape victim at the beginning of the nineteenth century that, "I thought that nothing could be done, as my father was away . . . I did not know if I went to a Justice, he wd take notice of it" echoed the sentiments of women in similar predicaments before the Revolution.[60]

After the Revolution men who raped demonstrated no discernible reformed attitudes toward women or repentance for their behavior. In the 1785 gang rape of Barbara Whitmore (or Witmer), Timothy Cockley and five other Lancaster County yeomen took turns with Whitmore of Donegal Township who was fifteen and inebriated. The men told the court they thought "a good fuck would make her a woman."[61]

Male jurors and judges continued to be suspicious of women bringing rape charges and voted to prosecute and convict only with the greatest reluctance. Sexual assaults on black women were studiously ignored or quickly dismissed, as in the John Shaffer trial. As Bradford admitted as late as 1793, only women of prominent families and those with powerful fathers or husbands could be assured that their complaints would be taken seriously. And jurors continued to acquit in rape cases "against positive and uncontradicted evidence." Even the enlightened Bradford assumed that rape did "not announce any irreclaimable corruption," and that "much of its atrocity resides in the imagination and is the creature of opinion."[62] In the end, conviction rates were virtually identical for the years before and after 1775 (36.3 percent versus 36.8 percent).

Only in the prosecution of black males is a shift in priorities relating to rape observable. Despite the characterization of African American males as lustful and likely rapists, only eight black males were convicted of rape in Pennsylvania prior to the nineteenth century, and three (four if one accepts Negro James in 1736) of those received reprieves or commutations of their sentences. Only five cases against black men—four rapes and an attempted rape—surface in the dockets after the Revolution. As for black women being assaulted by either black or white males, they had little motivation to seek prosecution and even less chance of successfully doing so. William Bradford observed that jurors considered the rape of black female slaves "so lightly" that they "w[ould] not let the victim herself testify."[63]

But these meager numbers on black convictions for rape do not reveal the full story of African Americans and rape offenses. Only seven executions for rape in all Pennsylvania can be confirmed.[64] Yet four of those were black men and a fifth may have been. This is a significant number in a population where blacks never constituted more than 5 percent of the total. All executions of black men occurred after the passage of the Gradual Abolition Act set in motion the enlargement of the state's free black population.[65] White Pennsylvanians were uneasy with the growing number of free blacks among them and they showed it by convicting in rape cases. White Pennsylvanians were generally no more concerned with rape after 1780 than before, except in those cases where the victims of alleged black rapists were white.[66]

Though citizens wrote to newspapers to rail against the mounting crime of the 1780s and 1790s, they never mentioned rape specifically among their concerns. When legislators debated the renovation of their criminal code in 1786 and 1794, no one stood to point to rape as a growing evil, or argued that the public reform its attitude respecting rape. Despite their increasing openness about male and female sexuality, they remained as quiet on the subject of criminal rape as had previous generations. It would take another two hundred years before the silence was broken and the attitudes that encouraged and sustained it were seriously challenged.

NOTES

1. Donald Veale, *The Popular Movement for Law Reform, 1650–1660* (Oxford: Oxford University Press, 1970); S. E. Prall, *The Agitation for Law Reform during the Puritan Revolution* (The Hague: Martinus Nijhoff, 1966).

2. Craig W. Horle, *The Quakers and the English Legal System, 1660–1688* (Philadelphia: University of Pennsylvania Press, 1988).

3. Jack D. Marietta and G. S. Rowe, *Law, Liberty, and License: Crime and Its Resolution in Pennsylvania, 1682–1801* (tentative title, forthcoming), chapter 2.

4. *Charter to William Penn and Laws of the Province of Pennsylvania* (Harrisburg, Pa.: T. Fenn and Co., 1879), 91–103, 107–116. (Hereafter cited as *Charter and Laws*.)

5. Ibid., 133, 144–145; Jean R. Soderlund, ed., *William Penn and the Founding of Pennsylvania, 1680–1684: A Documentary History* (Philadelphia: University of Pennsylvania Press, 1983), 95–183.

6. Kathryn Preyer, "Penal Measures in the American Colonies: An Overview," *American Journal of Legal History* 26 (1982): 336.

7. *Charter and Laws*, 107–116.

8. The literature on this issue is large and growing. See Mary Maples Dunn, "Saints and Sisters: Congregational and Quaker Women in the Early Colonial Period," in Janet Wilson James, ed., *Women in American Religion* (Philadelphia: University of Pennsylvania Press, 1980), 596; Mary Maples Dunn, "Latest Light on Women of Light," in Elisabeth Potts Brown and Janet Lindman, eds., *Witness for Change: Quaker Women over Three Centuries* (New Brunswick: Rutgers University Press, 1989), 73–74; Patricia Bonomi, *Under the Cope of*

Heaven: Religion, Society and Politics in Colonial America (New York: Oxford University Press, 1986), 105–115; Phyllis Mack, *Visionary Women: Ecstatic Prophecy in Seventeenth-Century England* (Berkeley: University of California Press, 1992), 236–261; Karin A. Wulf, 'My Dear Liberty': Quaker Spinsterhood and Female Autonomy in Eighteenth-Century Pennsylvania," in Larry D. Eldridge, ed., *Women and Freedom in Early America* (New York: New York University Press, 1997), esp. 85–86.

9. Marietta and Rowe, *Law, Liberty, and License,* chapter 2; Christopher Seglem, "A Legal History of Early Pennsylvania, 1681–1701" (Unpublished Senior Thesis, Princeton University, 1968); Preyer, "Penal Measures in the American Colonies," 336.

10. *Charter and Laws,* 110. The 1682 statutes also recognized the possibility of coerced incest for which the punishment was the same as for rape. Samuel Hazard, ed., *Annals of Pennsylvania* (Philadelphia: Hazard and Mitchell, 1850), 622. Hazard reprints the 1682 laws. The incest provision permitted the state to punish both partners if equally culpable.

11. Craig W. Horle, ed., *Records of the Courts of Sussex County, Delaware, 1677–1710* 2 vols. (Philadelphia: University of Pennsylvania Press, 1991), 1:358; *Records of the Courts of Chester County* (Philadelphia: Patterson and White, 1910), 328.

12. *Bucks County Court Records* (Meadville, Pa.: Tribune Publishing Company, 1943), 75.

13. *Records of the Courts of Chester County,* 163, 289–90.

14. Horle, *Records of Sussex County,* I, 17; *Minutes of the Provincial Council of Pennsylvania,* 16 vols. (Harrisburg, Pa.: J. Severns, 1851–53), 1:589; 2:11. Also see Joseph J. Kelley, Jr., *Pennsylvania: The Colonial Years, 1681–1776* (Garden City, N.Y.: Doubleday, 1980), 107.

15. James T. Mitchell and Henry Flanders, comps., *Statutes at Large of Pennsylvania, 1682–1809,* 18 vols. (Harrisburg, Pa.: Clarence M. Busch, 1908, 1915), 2:7–8, 489. (Hereafter cited as *Statutes at Large.*)

16. *The Earliest Printed Laws of Pennsylvania, 1681–1713,* rep. (Wilmington, Del: M. Grazier, 1978), 68–69; *Statutes at Large,* 2:233–36; Paul Crawford, "A Footnote on Courts for Trial of Negroes in Colonial Pennsylvania," *Journal of Black Studies* 5 (1974): esp. 167–185.

17. *Statutes at Large,* vol. 2, 489–497; Herbert K. Fitzroy, "The Punishment of Crime in Provincial Pennsylvania," *Pennsylvania Magazine of History and Biography* 60 (1936): 250.

18. Lawrence H. Gipson, *Crime and Its Punishment in Provincial Pennsylvania* (Bethlehem, Pa.: Lehigh University Press, 1935), 7.

19. *Statutes at Large,* vol. 3, 199–214.

20. Norris to Joseph Pike, 28 8 mo., 1728, Isaac Norris Letterbook,

1719–56, 515–516, Historical Society of Pennsylvania (hereafter cited as HSP), Philadelphia.

21. *Statutes at Large*, vol. 12, 280–290.

22. *Statutes at Large*, vol. 10, 67–73; G. S. Rowe, "Black Offenders, Criminal Courts, and Philadelphia Society in the Late Eighteenth Century," *Journal of Social History* 22 (1989): esp. 685–688.

23. *The Trial of Alice Clifton* (Philadelphia: Oswald, 1787), esp. 1, 9–10, 12–13. For petitions to save her life, including one from the judges, see April 1787, Clemency Records, 1775–90, RG–26, Pennsylvania Museum and Historical Commission, Harrisburg, reel 39.

24. Oyer and Terminer Dockets: Philadelphia, February 18, 1788; *Independent Gazetteer*, February 19, 1788.

25. William Bradford, *An Enquiry How Far the Punishment of Death Is Necessary in Pennsylvania* (Philadelphia: Dobson, 1793), 30.

26. *Statutes at Large*, vol. 15, 180–181.

27. Bradford estimated that Pennsylvania had a higher incidence of rape than Scotland. *An Enquiry*, 30.

28. In the case of attempted rape, between 1682 and 1793 and 1794 and 1801, the indictment rate declined by 7.3 percent and the conviction rate by 4.2 percent. Again, this is evidence of greater tolerance for sexual aggression.

29. Examination of Mary Gordon, December 26, 1754; Examination of Elizabeth Scott, April 28, 1755, Chester County Quarter-Sessions Papers, Chester County Archives, West Chester, Pennsylvania.

30. Examination of Ann Babb, November 23, 1792, ibid.

31. Examinations of Thomas Pryor and Silas Pryor, August 13, 1722; Examination of Thomas Browne, August 10, 1722; Recognizance for Thomas and Silas Pryor, August 1722.

32. Scholars have found the same pattern elsewhere in early America. See Bradley Chapin, *Criminal Justice in Colonial America, 1606–1660* (Athens, Ga.: University of Georgia Press, 1983), 126; Barbara S. Lindermann, "'To Ravish and Carnally Know': Rape in Eighteenth-Century Massachusetts," *Signs* 10 (1985–86): 81–82.

33. Francois La Rochefoucauld-Liancourt, *Travels through the United States of North America* (London: A. Baldwin, 1799), 2:396.

34. Bradford, *An Enquiry*, 29–30.

35. An excellent survey of the "dark figure" that bedevils historians of crime is offered by Cornelia Hughes Dayton, *Women before the Bar: Gender, Law, and Society in Connecticut, 1639–1789* (Chapel Hill: University of North Carolina Press, 1995), chapter 5.

36. Dayton, *Women before the Bar*, 262, discusses this phenomenon, as does Mary E. Odem, "Cultural Representations and Social Contexts of Rape in the

Early Twentieth Century," in Michael A. Bellesiles, ed., *Lethal Imagination: Violence and Brutality in American History* (New York: New York University Press, 1999), 353, 358.

37. *Carlisle Gazette,* July 30, 1788; Oyer and Terminer Dockets: Franklin County, July 8, 1788; Gottlieb Mittelberger, *Journey to Pennsylvania,* edited by Oscar Handlin and John Clive (Cambridge, Mass.: Harvard University Press, 1960), 38–39, 75; Marietta and Rowe, *Law, Liberty, and License,* chapter 12.

38. *The Columbian Museum, or Universal Assylum* (Philadelphia), January 1793, 44; Bradford, *An Enquiry,* 29–30.

39. For a discussion of this phenomenon, see Sharon Block, "Lines of Color, Sex and Service: Comparative Sexual Coercion in Early America," in Martha Hodes, ed., *Sex, Love, Race: Crossing Boundaries in North American History* (New York: New York University Press, 1999), 141ff.

40. See supra, note 20.

41. This theme is illustrated in Jack Marietta and G. S. Rowe, "Violent Crime, Victims, and Society in Pennsylvania, 1682–1800," *Explorations in Early American Culture* (a supplemental issue of the *Pennsylvania History: A Journal of Mid-Atlantic Studies)* 66 (1999): 24–54.

42. See Janet Wilson James, *Changing Ideas about Women in the United States, 1776–1825* (New York: Garland, 1981); Herbert Ross Brown, *The Sentimental Novel in America, 1789–1860* (New York: Pageant Books, repr. 1959); Dayton, *Women before the Bar.*

43. "The Deserted Infant," *Philadelphia Minerva* (December 16, 1797).

44. Changes in the law had repercussions for rape prosecutions. Note, "A Tract on the Unreasonableness of the Laws of England in Regard to Wives," *Columbian Magazine, or Monthly Miscellanies* (Philadelphia), January 1788, February 1788, 22–27, 61–65, which alludes to American law as well. The articles continued in the March (126–129), April (186–190), and May (243–246) issues. Also see, "A Historical View of the Criminal Law of Pennsylvania." *Philadelphia Monthly Magazine or, Universal Repository* (Philadelphia): January 1798, 42–45, February 1798, 94–97.

45. Jay Fliegelman, *Prodigals and Pilgrims: The American Revolution against Patriarchal Authority, 1750–1800* (Cambridge: Cambridge University Press, 1982); Jan Lewis, *The Pursuit of Happiness: Family and Values in Jefferson's Virginia* (Cambridge: Cambridge University Press, 1983); Edwin G. Burrows and Michael Wallace, "The American Revolution: The Ideology and Psychology of National Liberation," *Perspectives in American History* 6 (1972): 167–306; Winthrop D. Jordan, "Familial Politics: Thomas Paine and the Killing of the King, 1776," *Journal of American History* 60 (1973): 294–308.

46. Daniel Scott Smith and Michael S. Hindus, "Premarital Pregnancy in America, 1660–1971," *Journal of Interdisciplinary History* 5 (1975): 537–570; Susan

E. Klepp, *Philadelphia in Transition: A Demographic History of the City and Its Occupational Groups, 1720–1820* (New York: Garland, 1989), 62–137.

47. See especially, Rodney Hessinger, "'Insidious Murders of Female Innocence': The Representations of Masculinity in the Seduction Tales of the Late Eighteenth Century," in Merril D. Smith, ed., *Sex and Sexuality in Early America* (New York: New York University Press, 1998), esp. 263, 265.

48. "The Deserted Infant". See also "A Plea for the Indigent Blind," *Philadelphia Minerva* (March 7, 1795, December 19, 1795); "The Slave," ibid., November 7, 1795; "History respecting the Distresses of the Poor," *American Monthly Review* 2 (September 1795): 395–396;

49. See "The Reformer," *Philadelphia Minerva* (December 19, 1795); *Pennsylvania Magazine* (March 1775): 114; "Reflections on Scandal," *The Dessert to the True American* (Philadelphia), February 16, 1799; *American Museum of Repository* (January 1787): 59–61.

50. Mary Beth Norton, *Liberty's Daughters: The Revolutionary Experience of American Women, 1750–1800* (New York: Oxford University Press, 1980); Mary Beth Norton, "The Evolution of White Woman's Experience in Early America," *American Historical Review* 89 (1984): 615; Linda Kerber, *Women of the Republic: Intellect and Ideology in Revolutionary America* (Chapel Hill: University of North Carolina Press, 1980); Jan Lewis, "The Republican Wife: Virtue and Seduction in the Early Republic," *William and Mary Quarterly* 44 (1987): 689–721; Claire Anna Lyons, "Sex among the 'Rabble': Gender Transitions in the Age of Revolution, 1750–1830" (Ph.D. dissertation: Yale University, 1996), 87–88, 90, 106–107, 115, 139–40.

51. "The Deserted Infant".

52. Norton, *Liberty's Daughters*; Kerber, *Women of the Republic*; Davidson, *Revolution of the Word: The Rise of the Novel in America* (New York: Oxford University Press, 1986); Lewis, "The Republican Wife," esp. 696; Hessinger, "'Insidious Murders of Female Innocence,'" esp. 263, 265; "Letter of a Reformed Libertine," *The American Museum, or Universal Magazine* (Philadelphia), October 1790: 163–64; "On the Choice of a Husband," *Columbian Magazine, or Monthly Miscellany* (February 1788): 65–70; *A Faithful Narrative of Elizabeth Wilson* (Philadelphia: n.p., 1786); Henry D. Biddle, ed. *Extracts from the Journal of Elizabeth Drinker, from 1759 to 1807* (Philadelphia: W.F. Fell and Co., 1889), 299; "On the Power of Love," *Ladies Magazine* (November 1792): 255–56; "Scheme for Increasing the Power of the FAIR SEX," ibid., (June 1792): 22–24; *American Museum, or Repository* (Philadelphia), July 1788, 17; *Columbian Magazine* (November 1792): 303.

53. Lyons, "Sex among the 'Rabble.'" 87–88, 90, 106–107, 115, 139–140

54. Andrew Aguecheek, *The Universal American Almanac . . . for . . . 1764* (Philadelphia: Steuart, 1763), quoted in Lyons, 109.

55. Lyons, "Sex among the 'Rabble,'" 115.

56. "The Maids of PHILADELPHIA Petition," *in Father Abraham's Almanac . . . for the Year . . . 1762* (Philadelphia: Stewart, 1761), quoted in ibid., 92.

57. Lewis, "The Republican Wife," esp. 709–716; *The American Museum, or Repository* (July 1788): 17; "Hints for Young Married Women," ibid. (September 1789): 198–200.

58. Hessinger, "Insidious Murderers," p. 272, quoting Mildred Doyle, "Sentimentalism in American Periodicals, 1741–1800" (Ph.D. dissertation, New York University, 1941), 50–55.

59. Hessinger, "Insidious Murderers," esp. 263, 265, 272, 276; Lewis, "The Republican Wife," 719–721.

60. Quoted in Block, "Lines of Color, Sex and Service," 156.

61. Clemency Records, May 29, 1786, Pennsylvania Museum and Historical Commision, Harrisburg, reel 39; Yeates Papers: Legal Papers, folder 4, May–June 1786, Historical Society of Pennsylvania, Philadelphia.

62. Bradford, *An Enquiry*, 29.

63. *The Columbian Museum, or Universal Assylum* (Philadelphia), January 1793, 44.

64. Dockets indicate that Cumberland County's James Paxton (1783) and Philadelphia County's Frances Courtney (1785) were convicted of rape and sentenced to be hanged, yet no evidence of the resolution in those two cases has been uncovered.

65. Gary B. Nash, "Forging Freedom: The Emancipation Experience in the Northern Seaports, 1775–1820." in Gary B. Nash, ed., *Race, Class, and Politics* (Urbana, Ill.: University of Illinois Press, 1986), 284, 288, 301, 307.

66. For evidence that racial tension increased with the Gradual Abolition Act and the increase in black population in Philadelphia, see Rowe, "Black Offenders," 697–709; Nash, "Forging Freedom," 288; Kenneth and Anna Roberts, eds., *Moreau de St. Mery's American Journey, 1793–1798* (Garden City, N.Y.: Doubleday, 1947), 291, 302–303, 309.

6

"The Law Should Be Her Protector"

The Criminal Prosecution of Rape in Upper Canada,
1791–1850

Patrick J. Connor

IN THE SPRING of 1793 Colonel John Graves Simcoe, the first Lieutenant Governor of Upper Canada, issued a proclamation in which he
reminded the colonists of their "indispensable duty . . . to suppress all
Vice, Profaneness and Immorality," lest the province suffer "the Divine
Vengeance [of] Almighty God." The proclamation was published in the
colony's only newspaper, and Simcoe further ordered that it "be Pub-
lickly read in all Courts of Justice [and] . . . immediately after Divine Service, in all places of Public Worship." But while the proclamation
stressed the administration's concern for the promotion of virtue and
raised the specter of eternal damnation, Simcoe's pronouncements carried a more secular message, ordering laws against various offenses "to
be strictly put into Execution in every part of the Province" and urging
"Peace Officers and Constables, Judges, Justices and Magistrates" to
"exert themselves [in] putting the Laws against Crimes and Offences
into execution."[1]

An analysis of Upper Canadian court records reveals the extent to
which colonial officials did in fact exert themselves in the prosecution
of one particular crime, that of rape. A close reading of trial reports and
related accounts allows for an examination of the process by which rape
was discovered, reported, and prosecuted, and the difficulties inherent
for women in such an undertaking. The stories told by women, and the
men who raped them, reveal that Upper Canadians regarded rape as a
serious crime deserving of serious punishment. It was a crime that not

only saw a woman violated, but also relations between the sexes disrupted, and well-understood modes of community interaction thrown into disarray. Attitudes toward rape and its victims grew less sympathetic as the nineteenth century progressed. But in the first sixty years of the colony's existence, Upper Canadian women, backed by supportive kin and community networks, made use of a sympathetic legal system through which they were able to vigorously, and often successfully, assert their demands for sexual autonomy and personal safety.

Rape has traditionally been one of the most underreported of all crimes, and modern researchers estimate that there are perhaps as many as twenty unreported cases for every recorded prosecution.[2] The difficulty of estimating the true extent of sexual violence is particularly evident in Upper Canada. The colony was overwhelmingly rural in nature, economically dependant upon mixed agriculture, home production, and small-scale, local exchange networks. Settlement was sparse, communication awkward, and travel on the province's poor roads notoriously difficult. Consequently, the often arduous conditions of pioneer settlement affected routine enforcement of laws and the reporting of crime. Local magistrates, the most visible symbols of state power and the most basic form of law enforcement, were scarce and frequently difficult for the average settler to locate.[3] Once found, a magistrate might also have to be convinced that it was worth his time and expense to interfere in what sometimes turned out to be violent intracommunity disputes.[4] For large blocks of settlers of French Canadian, Scottish, German, or Native background, cultural differences—particularly those of language—could pose further difficulties in the detection and prosecution of crime. Although the province developed rapidly through the first half of the nineteenth century, many isolated areas retained a "frontier mentality," with their worldview focused inward on the family, the domestic farm, and the small, tight-knit circle of close neighbors.[5]

As if physical and cultural barriers were not enough, those who did manage to make use of the colony's legal system found themselves facing a judicial apparatus that frequently resembled a combination of the splendor and majesty integral to the English high court, and one of the many traveling circuses that so often advertised in local newspapers.[6] Commentators noted that court sessions overwhelmingly attracted the supporters of the accused, and hissing, comments from the gallery, and even full-fledged brawls were not unknown.[7] Architectural plans of the colony's early courthouses also reveal them to be rudimentary and purely functional spaces, with the principals of the case seated almost amongst the often hostile spectators.[8] Moreover, whatever their degree of formality, Upper Canadian courts, with their judge and associate judges, clerks, bailiffs, and recorders, were entirely dominated by men. For a woman who attempted to prosecute a charge of rape in such a setting, a trial could indeed be called a second assault.

In spite of these difficulties, between 1791—when Upper Canada was established as a separate political and legal entity—and 1850, a total of 104 women left some record of their experiences as the victims of sexual assault. For the historian, the difficulty of recovering their voices is enormous. Countless rapes, of course, were never reported at all, and of the 104 for which some record exists, sources are often fragmentary or frustratingly vague. While Upper Canadian newspapers delighted in regaling their readers with the minutia of grisly murders—especially American ones—rape was rarely the subject of their reporting. When the topic was mentioned, it was often limited to the brief acknowledgment of a successful prosecution and exemplary punishment. Legal records offer a somewhat more detailed view, but here too the gaps are large and information sketchy. Depositions taken before magistrates are almost entirely nonexistent, and the official minutes of court sessions offer little more than the names of those involved and a record of the trial's outcome.

For a more detailed description of events, it is necessary to turn to the benchbooks of the province's judges. These notebooks, kept during the trial, provide a verbatim transcript of testimony offered by prosecution and defense witnesses, as well as the judge's remarks and his charge to the jury. Even here, it should be noted, benchbooks survive in large part for only two of the colony's nineteen judges active in the first half of the nineteenth century. Once convicted, rapists frequently petitioned the Lieutenant Governor for mitigation of their sentences, and these petitions, as well as similar ones from the victims asking that a pardon *not* be granted, also offer details of the crime not found elsewhere. Reliance on such sources necessarily results in a somewhat patchwork result: a victim without a name or a verdict with no apparent sentence. Nevertheless, a careful reading of what remains provides enough evidence to reconstruct the experience of rape in Upper Canada, to retell the stories of the women and men involved, and to assess how these stories were understood both by the participants and by the community at large.

As a British colony, Upper Canadian rape laws were identical to those in force in England, the provincial House of Assembly having authorized the wholesale adoption of English criminal law as it stood in 1792. Colonial prosecutions were thus undertaken under the authority of 18 Eliz. I. c.7, a 1576 statute which declared rape to be a felony, punishable by death. The application of this statute was relatively straightforward, with Toronto attorney W. C. Keele, author of a magistrate's manual in wide use in Upper Canada, declaring that rape "signifies the carnal knowledge of a woman, forcibly and against her will."[9] While English jurists spilt much ink throughout the eighteenth century attempting to interpret this definition, the law in Upper Canada seems to have operated on a less strict evidentiary basis. The belief, prevalent in England, that if a woman became pregnant she could not have been raped, was dismissed by Keele as a "philosophy [which] may be very well doubted of," while the statutory requirement for the emission of seed was rarely, if ever, observed in the province.[10] At his March 1837, trial, Mary Ann Bullock stated simply that Patrick Fitzpatrick "had done what he wanted before he let her go."[11] In the summer of 1843, Courtland Travise was prosecuted for the rape of Susan Ann Still, with the court hearing testimony that "he remained in witness till satisfied,"[12] while at another trial later that same year, Julia Ann Wright merely declared that her assailant had "effected his purpose."[13] Such statements were good enough for a jury, which promptly convicted in each case, believing that penetration was in itself evidence of emission.

If the law was key in constructing definitions of rape, no less important were the impressions of the victims themselves. Rape is by its very nature a secretive crime, and women's testimony necessarily plays a central role. Instructing potential jurors, W. C. Keele wrote that a victim's credibility depended upon whether she "be of good fame; if she *presently* discovered the offence and made pursuit after the offender; shewed circumstances and signs of injury; if the place where the offence was committed was *remote* from habitation, [and] if the offender *fled* for it." If such testimony could be corroborated by others, so much the better. "On the other hand," Keele continued, "if she concealed her injury for any length of time, after she had the opportunity to complain; if the place where the offence was alleged to have been committed was *near* to inhabitants . . . and she made no outcry when the offence was perpetrated," jurors were to "carry a strong presumption, that the testimony is false or feigned." Overall, jurors were reminded that although rape was "a most detestable crime," they should not be "transported with indignation at the heinousness of the offence," but should instead pay close attention to the testimony and arrive at a verdict on the basis of evidence rather than outraged feelings.[14] Keele's fear that juries might be "transported with indignation" was not an idle one. Widespread property ownership meant that Upper Canadian juries were composed of a far more representative cross section of the (male) community than was the case in England, and if they felt a wrong had been done, they would often convict with little regard for legal hairsplitting.

Upper Canadian women were not always able to convince a jury of their claims. A woman *knew* when she had been raped, but many no doubt remained silent, ashamed of what had happened or fearful of further violence should they speak out. Those who refused to remain silent sought out other women for help, support, and advice. The unique sexual nature of the crime made turning to a female relative, friend, or neighbor seem an obvious choice, and seeking assistance from such quarters also highlights the female-centered social networks in which most Upper Canadian women moved.[15] The notion of female solidarity in the face of a sexual attack, however, should not be overstated, for just as many victims turned to men for aid, often appealing to a husband, father, or brother.

What mattered more than the gender of the listener was who was available close at hand, who was likely to be sympathetic, and who could most effectively set the wheels of justice in motion. Margaret Talbot testified in 1841 that "the first she spoke of the ravishment was to her husband . . . but she did not tell the women."[16] Fourteen-year-old Emma Sagerman, who was raped in a Windsor tavern, immediately told her brother, who was apparently so unconcerned by the news that he went back to sleep. Hearing the news the next morning, however, her father immediately "took steps in the matter" and sought a warrant for the arrest of his daughter's attacker.[17] But if some women could rely on quick and sympathetic action from those to whom they turned for help, others were not so fortunate, as illustrated by the experience of Julia Ann Wright. Raped by her hired farmhand one morning in 1843, she testified that she was afraid to tell her husband of the attack, and only spoke out once she had been raped a second time.[18] Her case, and others like it, are stark reminders that for many women the stigma of rape deprived them of the support they otherwise expected, even from their own families.

Upper Canada had no public prosecutor, and for much of its history no formal system of policing. Consequently, how a rape was dealt with was left largely to the discretion of the victim and her family. There is slight evidence that compensation of some sort occasionally settled the matter, while at the other extreme, Margaret Talbot, mentioned above, turned down the offer of a friend to stab her assailant to death. Some women, however, followed the example of Hannah Smith, who, only hours after she was raped in 1797 and in spite of the rapist's threats to kill her, sought out a nearby magistrate and filed a formal complaint. Her deposition described her assault in excruciating detail, telling how she had been interrupted while on a household errand, carried to "a rogering place . . . in the thick woods" where she had been "very much hurt and abused."[19] Other accounts, like that of Cornwall spinster Ann Bills, were more formalistic, merely stating that Farquhar MacDonnell "violently and feloniously did ravish and carnally know . . . against the will of her the said Ann Bills, and against the form of the statute in such case."[20]

The laying of a formal complaint was a collaborative effort between the victim and the magistrate. Whether making the complaint alone, or, as was the case with many women, with the support of a male family member, the victim engaged in a process of negotiation in the magistrate's parlor, as she told the details of her story and the magistrate decided whether the case was truly one which had "offended the statute" and how this could best be expressed in the necessary legal terms. Once made, the deposition would be passed on to a grand jury, which would send the case to trial.[21]

Some women, probably on the advice of magistrates, chose to describe their assault as an attempted rape. Although many women who prosecuted in this manner had doubtless experienced much more than just an attempt, such a charge may have represented a necessary compromise. Unlike in England, which had removed the death penalty for rape in 1841, the crime remained a capital offense in Canada well into the twentieth century. As John Beattie has noted, jurors in any capital case are notoriously reluctant to convict, and seeking a conviction for attempted rape might have represented a way for the prosecution to increase their odds of success.[22] If such a strategy was at work in Upper Canada, it seems to have been successful, although only moderately so. Of the fifty men who were charged with rape between 1791 and 1850, and for whom a verdict is known, twenty-seven, or 54 percent, were found guilty as charged, while 30 percent were found not guilty, and 10 percent were convicted of a lesser charge. The conviction rate in forty cases of assault with intent to rape was only slightly higher, at 60 percent, with 23 percent being acquitted and 18 percent being found guilty of a lesser charge. While legal historian Constance Backhouse has called guilty verdicts "atypical," declaring that "prosecutions for rape in Ontario rarely resulted in convictions in the nineteenth century," this was clearly not the case before the midcentury mark.[23]

If the charge of attempted rape was a way of avoiding the possibility of a jury hesitant to send a defendant to the gallows, such cases may also have been simply easier to prosecute. More successful rape prosecutions were often those involving children, or in which the victims were severely injured or raped by several men in succession. Cases of attempted rape required no proof of penetration, and with a lower burden of proof, were often the favored method of proceeding in cases with weak evidence or those that relied solely on the uncorroborated testimony of the victim. Such cases, however, had their own drawbacks, for while a woman may have been quite sure of her assailant's intent, her attacker could argue the case was one of common assault, and it was not always possible to convince a jury otherwise.

A charge of attempted rape also reminds us of the serious stigma associated with the crime throughout the nineteenth century, and the fact that although a woman may have desired justice, she may not have been willing to admit that she had been raped. Ruth Trufflemier told a neighbor that Jack York, a black slave belonging to a local merchant, had broken into her home, "treated her with great violence," and "entered her body." When the case finally went to trial in 1800, however, she testified that she had been unconscious and could remember nothing of the attack itself.[24] Similarly unwilling to testify that she had been raped, Jane Lambert successfully prosecuted soldier William Newbury for robbery later the same year, claiming that he had stolen a piece of her dress in the woods. After sentencing Newbury to death, Judge William Dummer Powell commented in a letter to the Lt. Governor that "the evidence respecting the robbery from her person had been concocted . . . to avoid the detail of the real crime, which was certainly an attempt to force her."[25] This assessment put to paper what was probably already understood by Lambert's neighbors, and emphasized the fact that even with a sympathetic jury, identifying oneself in a public courtroom as the victim of rape could be a difficult task with often unpleasant social consequences. Little had changed by midcentury, when a St. Catharines newspaper reported the parents of a rape victim "fairly begging to have the case kept out of print" and condemned rival newspapers which published the names as "panderers to, and caterers for, a depraved public taste" in scandal.[26]

But in spite of the potential for scandal and the myriad difficulties inherent in mounting a court case, women were no strangers to Upper Canadian courts. In criminal actions, women, most often prosecuting other women and men for simple assault, initiated approximately 11 percent of prosecutions at the Quarter Sessions level.[27] Women were also frequent participants in civil business, appearing regularly in court to relinquish their dower rights in land transfers, to claim military pensions, and to undertake other such administrative business. The seriousness with which women treated their experiences in court is also reflected in the manner in which their complaints were handled by magistrates. These men presided over the district Courts of Quarter Sessions, which had authority to try all noncapital crimes. Rape was not in their purview, but in theory they were able to try cases of assault with intent to commit rape. In all but two instances of attempted rape, however, magistrates considered the cases serious enough to refer them to the Superior Court of King's Bench for trial. Local magistrates may have merely been making awkward cases disappear, not wishing to preside over problematic trials potentially involving acquaintances and neighbors.

Whatever the reason for being referred to a higher court, doing so ensured that would-be rapists would be tried and sentenced by itinerant provincial judges with no connection to the community, and who would have no hesitation imposing harsh punishments. In deciding whether or not to believe a victim's story, the ultimate legal determination of whether a rape had occurred was the responsibility of the jury, but women exercised a fair degree of control over the handling of their own cases. Perhaps most important was the framing of the charge itself. A criminal charge of rape was fundamentally different from a civil action undertaken on a woman's behalf by her husband or father. The cases discussed here are not those featuring scheming seducers or unfulfilled marriage proposals, but are those involving the forcible and often violent assault of a woman against her will.

It is impossible to speak of a "typical" rape victim, for they were young and old, urban and rural, married and single, and from a variety of ethnic backgrounds. In terms of social standing, the women who were raped in Upper Canada ranged from domestic servants and farm help, to women like Margaret Ann Bultan, the wife of a man whose occupation is listed simply as "capitalist."[28] There is little to distinguish these women from the rest of the province's inhabitants, for they shared little more than their gender and the experience of violation. The single commonality that does emerge is the seemingly disproportionate number of victims who were very young: one-fifth of reported cases involved girls who were under the age of sixteen.[29] Such a trend, although startling, was by no means unique to Upper Canada. In her study of New York City cases in a similar time period, Marybeth Arnold has found that fully one-third of prosecuted rapes involved children under the age of fourteen, and in both places society reserved a special outrage for attacks on children.[30] Anna Clark has identified particular difficulties surrounding the prosecution of men who raped children. Very young witnesses sometimes lacked credibility, and due to their age and lack of sexual experience, often had no words with which to properly describe the attack.[31] This caution over children's testimony is evident in Upper Canada, where reports often made a point of stressing that young victims fully understood the nature of a criminal trial, and that they "did not appear to have been tutored by anyone."[32] Far from being a hindrance, however, the youth of the victim was often a favorable variable in a prosecution. Lacking a language of sex, young victims were able to avoid issues of reputation or consent, and instead stress the violence of the attack and the physical injuries sustained. Such factors worked in favor of the prosecution, and of the sixteen men tried for sexually assaulting women under sixteen, only four were acquitted. Well into the twentieth century, as Karen Dubinsky has shown, "assaults against children were treated far more seriously than assaults against adult women."[33]

The majority of Upper Canadian women did not lack the necessary vocabulary with which to explain rape, and their appearance in court provided them an opportunity to give a clear account of their experiences in their own words. Such accounts reveal rape to be an incident that could occur at almost any time and in almost any place, as a woman went about her daily activities. The intrusion of rape into daily activities is well illustrated by the experience of Julia Ann Wright, who was thrown to the floor by her hired hand as she sat knitting in her parlor.[34] Lois Thomas of Elizabethtown was returning to her father's farm one evening in November 1833, when she was overtaken and assaulted by Nixea Walker. She was just one of several women who were attacked while walking on deserted country roads.[35] Women's participation in the household economy could also place them in positions of vulnerability. Picking berries—a task often carried out by young women working alone—could be especially dangerous. Such was the case for Vashty Waterhouse, who was picking strawberries "on the Plains near Brantford" in 1831 when she was approached by John Standish. He spoke to her and departed, but returned an hour later and raped her.[36] Whether engaged in agrarian production, walking in one's immediate neighborhood, or even working inside the family home, there were few areas in which a woman was immune from potential attack.

The isolation of Upper Canada's farming communities, and indeed the overwhelmingly rural nature of the province as a whole, explains why the majority of rape cases occurred in rural settings. Nevertheless, it is startling that, with the exception of two cases each in Hamilton and Kingston, and one each in London and Toronto, *all* the rapes examined in this study took place outside an urban setting. Anna Clark has suggested that by the early nineteenth century rape in England was often used as a means of controlling the behavior of working-class women, especially in public places. Only those women who closely followed middle-class expectations of modesty, chastity, speech, and public decorum could expect any serious effort to be made to prosecute their rapists.[37] The relative absence of sexual assault cases in Upper Canadian cities may have reflected this ideology, and it is possible that women raped in the urban environment encountered difficulties in mounting a successful prosecution, unlike their rural counterparts. Questions of a rape victim's reputation and her social status may have created an atmosphere in which urban women, especially those who did not follow middle-class prescriptions of feminine behavior, were discouraged from pursuing their cases in court. Although rural communities were tighter knit and lacked the anonymity of the city, female prosecutors would have benefited from a lifetime of face-to-face interaction with their neighbors.

But while middle-class English concepts of propriety, and especially female morality, certainly existed in Upper Canada, it would be a mistake to assume that the colony had wholly adopted the attitudes of the mother country in this sphere.[38] Becoming the victim of a rapist was a real possibility for any woman, but there is no evidence that the province's elites, or the province's men, wielded this threat as a means of regulating women's public behavior.[39] Perhaps the most compelling argument against such an idea lies in the location of reported rapes. While the majority of sexual assaults took place on farms, in fields, and in other rural areas, a substantial minority occurred in taverns. Many such cases involved excessive drink, but this should not obscure the much larger role played by taverns in Upper Canadian society. They provided food and lodgings for travelers, served as labor exchanges, and provided a meeting space for patriotic, literary, and other such groups. As polling places, taverns were at the center of every Upper Canadian election and, in the early years of the colony's development, they provided a place for town meetings and even court sittings. Taverns in Upper Canada were thus more than mere places to take a drink; they were major sites of general sociability and ones that very much included women.[40]

Nonetheless, as a site of community interaction, taverns were also sites of sexual danger for women. An anonymous writer traveling between Bytown [Ottawa] and Kingston in 1830 recalled stopping at a roadside inn, where his traveling companion,

> under the predominating effects of gin, . . . or some other potent spell entered the breakfast parlour when the maid was arranging the table. Her fresh complexion and ruby lip attracted his attention, and he commenced a chase with the desire of submitting to the sense of feeling what appeared so tempting to the sight. From this rude attack the fair one defended herself with the Tea Tray . . . and was rescued from her perilous situation by the abrupt entry of the Hoste with the bill which procured a diversion of hostilities in her favour.[41]

Fourteen-year-old Sarah O'Meara was not so lucky. One rainy night in September 1845, while working as a serving girl at Mrs. Gray's tavern outside London, she was chased into the barn by a soldier named John English, who raped her, despite her screams and attempts to defend herself with a shoemaker's knife.[42] For female patrons, as well as employees, the tavern presented dangers. Hugh Kearney and his daughter Margaret were traveling home two days before Christmas 1838, when they stopped for the night at the inn owned by Daniel Tiers of Springfield. While the father was drinking at the bar, Henry Cole entered the daughter's room and offered her ten dollars for a kiss. When she refused, he threw her down and "abused her greatly." A rape was only averted when her father and his drinking companions, hearing the commotion, returned to the room and attacked Cole.[43] The experience of Margaret Kearney was a fairly common one, and important for what it and similar cases reveal about women's experience of rape in Upper Canada. At the ensuing trial, the defense attempted to smear Margaret Kearney's reputation, but this attack centered on the fact that she was Catholic. No one even questioned what an eleven-year-old girl was doing in a tavern at night, and Henry Cole was easily convicted of attempted rape.[44]

Margaret Kearney may have largely avoided an attack on her reputation due to her age. Certainly, she was spared the sort of questioning endured by women in other jurisdictions, or which became increasingly common in late-nineteenth-century Canada, in which the victim's behavior seemed on trial as much as the accused rapist's. Trial transcripts reveal that Upper Canadian women were rarely questioned in this manner, and that evidence of their character played at most a secondary role. Women who had been raped in taverns were asked if they had been drinking, but when the question was answered—invariably in the negative—the defense moved on. Questions concerning the victim's mode of dress, common even in modern rape trials, were entirely absent from Upper Canadian cases. As in the case of Margaret Kearney, questions about a woman's character were often unrelated to her sexual or moral behavior, but focused on whether she was hardworking, temperate, and a generally respectable member of the community. The court was less concerned with a victim's sexual history or reputation for modesty than it was in simply determining whether it could give "credit to her testimony."[45]

Despite the court's general lack of interest in a woman's sexual past, truly egregious sexual behavior could influence a woman's credibility on the stand. For example, Frances Burgess was unable to secure a conviction against Abel Conat for attempted rape in 1841. The court heard several hours of testimony in which details were exposed about her extramarital relations with several men—including her accused rapist—as well as illegitimate children, and sleeping arrangements that could only be described as irregular. The Attorney General abandoned the prosecution partway through the case, no doubt convinced that Burgess possessed no credibility as a witness.[46]

In spite of the Attorney General's frustration over his less than reputable witness, there were few all-out attacks on the character of the rape victim in Upper Canada. As the Kingston *British Whig* noted in 1835, "the bad character of a woman ought to be no reason that she should be without the protection of the law; for once establish that maxim, and every woman of doubtful reputation will be assaulted with impunity."[47] Judges were quick to limit testimony about the victim's reputation when in their view it was not materially related to the facts of the case. Nor were victims the only ones subjected to scrutiny over character, for just as often the court heard that the defendant's character was in some way lacking. At the 1839 trial of Ethan Card, the court heard much speculation about his reputation, including the fact that he "does not bear a good character for chastity."[48] Along the same lines, a would-be rapist named Tisdale had to defend himself from charges that he was "a notorious nuisance in the neighbourhood in which he resides for his propensities for the feminine gender."[49] A history of sexual immorality was important, and could often sway the jury one way or another, but it was seldom definitive. Chauncey Skinner introduced evidence that Mary Richie, who accused him of rape in 1829, was "a person of most abandoned character, and one altogether likely to prefer such a charge from inclines very different from a wish to bring to justice the perpetrator of such a crime." In spite of such damaging testimony, Skinner was convicted by the jury, and was sentenced to death.[50]

In 1849, the Kingston *British Whig* reported on the trial of Allan McInnis for the rape of Euphemia Brown. The newspaper commented that "great effort was made to shake the testimony of the girl, but without success."[51] Such efforts included questions about Brown's reputation and character, but this did not—and could not—represent the entire defense strategy. Clearly, defense lawyers understood that in Upper Canada, attacking a victim's reputation promised only limited success. The case of "Jean Marie" of Brockville is an illuminating one. She was a prostitute, described as "a Girl of ill-fame, and an inmate . . . of a Bagnio in this town." In 1834 she swore out a complaint that she had been raped by Jonas Jones, a member of the local elite. The charge was dismissed when she admitted that she had made up the story at the behest of Orange Order leader Ogle Gowan, in an attempt to ruin the reputation of Jones, his political rival.

Nonetheless, it is clear that in Upper Canada, a charge of rape was considered serious enough to ruin a man's career and reputation (if not end his life) and that even if such a charge came from a known prostitute it would not be considered to be without merit.[52] By the late nineteenth century, however, testimony concerning a rape victim's character would come to dominate the trial procedure. This was seldom the case in Upper Canada, where even a prostitute expected, and could possibly even receive, a sympathetic hearing from a jury. Legal writer W. C. Keele echoed this sentiment, declaring, "nor is it any excuse [for rape] that the woman is a common prostitute; for she is still under the protection of the law."[53]

Rape trials were speedy affairs in Upper Canada, none lasting more than a day and most disposed of in an hour or two. Defending her character was an element, albeit a minor one, of a woman's experience in court, but the majority of her testimony centered on describing for the jury the details of her rape. These narratives were clearly informed by the statute and, in addition to details of time and place, stress the victim's lack of consent and the resistance she made to the attack. The court repeatedly heard that the victim had "refused," that "she made all the resistance she could," or "resisted as much as she was able." Women "screamed" and "tried to holler," but although only two of the rapists are reported to have used a weapon, victims were unable to prevent themselves from being "thrown down on the floor" or being "dragged into the woods" by the side of the road.[54] Of all the elements that made up women's narratives of rape, it was violence that played the central role.

Garthine Walker has found that when rape victims in early modern England told their stories, like those in Upper Canada, they chose to emphasize violence and personal injury.[55] Framing the incident as a sexual crime, rather than a violent one, was potentially dangerous, for it might shift the trial's focus from the rapist's attack to the victim's sexual reputation. That women in Upper Canada were largely able to avoid sustained attacks on their reputation is perhaps an indication of the success of this approach. Another explanation for the emphasis on violence and injury in the court's records may be related to women's economic position in Upper Canada. Whether farmwives or tavern help, all the women examined in this study worked, and most made vital contributions to the household economy. When eighteen-year-old Euphemia Brown prosecuted her rapist in 1849, she made little overt reference to the sexual aspect of the crime. Instead, the court heard how after the rape she was "much bruised," "half-dead," and was "three weeks recovering."[56] Tavern keeper Mary Lee also testified that after the rape she experienced at the hands of Jacob Block, she "was about dead." She "had been confined for three months" as a result of her injuries, and "afterwards could hardly get up."[57] Brown and Lee were not alone in bemoaning the loss of good health, rather than the loss of virtue. In this regard, the women of Upper Canada may have shared concerns with the women of early national New York City studied by Marybeth Arnold, who noted that "a physical injury or a pregnancy sustained in a sexual assault could incapacitate them for work and destroy the precarious sustenance they had managed to eke out."[58]

With testimony relating to physical injury dominating Upper Canadian rape trials, the testimony of medical professionals could be of crucial importance. Particularly when the victim was a child, doctors confirmed cases of sexual assault and provided evidence of injuries sustained. The same role was often played by midwives, who "spoke from professional knowledge and experience" to draw similar conclusions for the court.[59] Such a commonsense basis for their knowledge seemed quite adequate for the jury. Neither were the statements of midwives challenged by physicians in cases where both were called to testify. The role of medical professionals in Upper Canadian rape trials differs sharply from that detailed by Anna Clark, who found that in early Victorian England doctors' testimony was more useful to the defense than for the prosecution, and that their moralistic pronouncements couched as scientific discourse often served to silence victims of rape.[60] In Upper Canada, unlike in England, doctors' pronouncements did not prevent women from defining rape for themselves. Although medical professionals played an important role, particularly in cases involving children, it was a peripheral one, and there is no evidence that they were actively defining sexual assault. The courts accepted a woman's characterization of rape. Summing up the attempted rape case of Alexander Greig for the jury in 1834, Chief Justice John Beverly Robinson noted that the victim "did in direct terms swear that she *believed* his intention was to proceed to the extremity of violence."[61] Although he further stated that the jury "might properly doubt whether she was correct in this opinion," he did not question—nor did any other judge of this period—a woman's right to bring a charge based solely on her own belief that she had been raped.

The testimony offered by women attempting to prosecute their rapists provides details not only of the circumstances of the crime, but also of the way in which women understood and responded to rape.

These women were by definition victims, but the cases examined here show this to be only one aspect of their identities. When physical resistance to their assailants failed, they turned to the legal system as a means of asserting their claim to personal safety and sexual autonomy. These claims were contested—sometimes successfully—by defendants who frequently had very different views on what constituted proper sexual behavior. Nevertheless, the court provided Upper Canadian women with a public forum for expressing their strong views on what they considered acceptable sexual conduct.

The men accused of rape in Upper Canada were as varied as their victims, and it is equally difficult to generalize about them. Nevertheless, even the most cursory glance at the list of defendants reveals a startlingly disproportionate number of soldiers. Upper Canadians lived in perpetual fear of American invasion, and throughout its history the province was garrisoned by British regular troops. Soldiers were thus a common sight in Upper Canada, and residents generally appreciated their presence.[62] But the men who guarded the colony were largely drawn from the age group statistically most likely to commit rape,[63] and it should come as no surprise that the violent, often alcoholic, homosocial world of the army barrack posed significant threats to the province's women. Commenting in 1800 on soldier and convicted rapist William Newburry, Judge William Dummer Powell remarked on "his depravity and want of a proper education" and noted that he was "a young man of bad character [who] was, I am told, enlisted out of the gaol."[64] It is possible that soldiers' status as single men, far from home, and without the ties of family and community simply made it easier to successfully prosecute them, but colonists were often convinced that soldiers inherently posed a special danger to local women. Writing in his diary in 1847, Marcus Gunn noted that his cousin Helen had been "assaulted by two Brutal British soldiers" and commented that it was "an instance of the danger of keeping together a hord of ignorant men."[65]

The presence of soldier-rapists in the community presented particular problems to prosecuting victims. As Marcus Gunn noted, he went to town the morning after the attack on his cousin "and obtained faculty to identify the two soldiers who assaulted Helen last night, but could not."[66] Gunn and his cousin found that soldiers in uniform simply all looked alike, and were notoriously difficult to identify. This fact was also realized by Brigit Stokes, who was attacked by members of the 81st

Regiment in 1846, but admitted "all three soldiers were dressed alike" and she could not pick out the one who had attempted to rape her.[67] It is perhaps an illustration of the hostility felt by local residents toward soldiers and the threats they posed to local women that in spite of Stokes's admitted inability to identify the prisoner as the man who had attacked her, the jury convicted him anyway. But it was not just local residents who found such behavior intolerable. "The Commander of the soldiers" at London aided Marcus Gunn in his unsuccessful identification attempt,[68] while the 1843 case of Jane Edgar saw three members of the regiment stationed at Hamilton testify against one of their fellow soldiers on behalf of the prosecution.[69]

The soldier as rapist was not an uncommon phenomenon in Upper Canada, but what is notable is his status as an outsider in the community. Other than those who were victimized by soldiers, few women in the colony were raped by strangers. Indeed, there were very few true strangers in the closed agricultural communities of Upper Canada. A woman might not know her attacker's name, but she often recognized his face. He might be the man from the next farm, a local hired laborer, or perhaps had even attended the same school or church as the victim. Mrs. Scott was returning home from Kingston in her wagon one morning in 1850 when she gave a lift to a local farmer, "a resident of the same neighbourhood." While on the road home, he "begged she would favour him with a kiss" and then "attempted some further liberties."[70] Witnesses frequently testified at trial that the families of the victim and accused had known each other for years, sometimes even decades. This familiarity highlights the vulnerable position of women in the province, and certainly accounts for the large number of women who were attacked in places where they believed themselves to be safe.[71]

Previous familiarity between victim and accused could also complicate matters when prosecuting a rape case. It was relatively easy to convict a stranger, but the task could be made significantly more difficult if evidence could be introduced pointing to a previous relationship between the individuals concerned. Allan McInnis attempted to counter Effy Brown's charge of rape by calling witnesses who recalled seeing the two of them kissing at a schoolyard frolic years before.[72] His strategy was not successful, but had the jury believed that Brown's rape had actually occurred within the context of an ongoing courtship, as the defense implied, McInnis might very well have been acquitted. Such was the case for Landon Henry, who was able to escape a rape conviction in 1832 by showing not only that he had been in a sexual relationship with Hannah Wheat for the past two years, but that she had also had a child by him.[73] Premarital sex was not uncommon in rural Upper Canada, and it was generally tolerated if it took place within the confines of an established courtship in which the participants were expected to eventually wed.[74] Such attitudes allowed women in Upper Canada a great deal more sexual freedom than their daughters or granddaughters could expect in later nineteenth-century Canada. But it was a mixed blessing, for it afforded women little protection against unwanted advances from current, and even former, suitors.

It is difficult to say with certainty how Upper Canadian attitudes about sexual behavior influenced attitudes toward rape. In spite of Lt. Governor Simcoe's earnest proclamation against immorality, contemporary travelers claimed that the province was "the most wicked and dissipated of any part of America."[75] In 1834 Belleville resident William Hutton "was quite shocked at the depravity of young people generally . . . the tone of morals is low, low indeed, and almost frightening me for my children."[76] Newspapers occasionally reported on the presence of "rowdies" and the fact that it was "not safe for a female to walk the streets alone after nightfall."[77] Nevertheless, it was not until the 1840s and the rise of a self-conscious and aggressively activist middle class that the courts began seeing large numbers of prostitution, vagrancy, and moral offenses. Even then, this remained a predominantly urban phenomenon.[78] In the countryside, sometime resident E. A. Talbot wrote, one could find "females who are destitute of virtue, as much respected, and as likely to make respectable alliances in the world, as if they were not merely its proud possessors, but its chaste and attentive guardians." Indeed, he continued, "an unmarried female with a baby in her arms is as much respected and as little obnoxious to public animadversion, as she would be, had she preserved her virtue with a Vestal's fidelity."[79]

In spite of such a free and easy approach to sex, the character of the libertine seems to have been largely absent from the Upper Canadian scene. Described by Anna Clark as a misogynist, sexually violent aristocrat, governed by "uncontrollable passions," the libertine regarded any woman not under the protection of a father or husband as fair game, and would even boast about seducing other men's wives or daughters.[80] That such attitudes were unacceptable in the colony was discovered by John White, the provincial Attorney General, who was shot dead in a duel after spreading rumors that he had seduced the wife of a colleague.[81] The casual Upper Canadian attitude toward sex did *not* extend to the elite world within which John White moved.

But even for the working classes, there were boundaries, one of which clearly involved the willing consent of one's partner. That these boundaries were understood differently by men and women is clear, for just under one quarter of the men charged with rape asked for the woman's consent at the outset. That after politely requesting a kiss or asking permission to get into bed, they would proceed to violently rape their victims, points to a belief by some men that consent may have required a certain amount of "persuasion." For the women who ultimately laid charges, this was clearly *not* the case.[82]

It is extremely difficult to draw conclusions about men's attitudes toward rape, for of all the men prosecuted for this crime in Upper Canada, not a single one took the stand in his own defense. Indeed, just under half the defendants called no witnesses whatsoever to testify on their behalf, relying instead on a mere cross-examination of the prosecution's witnesses. The absence of any serious defense on the part of the accused may in part be explained by the fact that in this period, the Attorney General undertook prosecutions personally. The accused rapist who chose to match wits with the Attorney General was a foolish man indeed, and many may have hoped to escape a guilty verdict by remaining silent themselves and simply attempting to discredit the stories of prosecution witnesses. As a strategy, it was not a particularly good one. Of those who did mount a defense, two-thirds were found guilty, while those who called no witnesses of their own were convicted in 73 percent of cases.

The importance of a good defense, especially in cases where a guilty verdict could mean execution, was recognized by defendants, for while only 52 percent of the accused in attempted rape cases made a defense, this rose to 74 percent in trials dealing with actual rape. Those men charged after 1836 could have taken advantage of the newly proclaimed Felon's Counsel Act, which allowed the accused the assistance of a lawyer to sum up his case to the jury. In practice, this seems to have made little difference. William Brass was "ably defended" in 1837 by John A. Macdonald—later to become Canada's first Prime Minister— yet despite Macdonald's "ingenious" efforts, the jury convicted Brass in less than half an hour.[83] The presence of lawyers in the courtroom may have been rather more beneficial to the victims, who at least no longer had to experience the ordeal of being cross-examined by the very man who was accused of raping them.

The punishment for rape in Upper Canada was death by hanging, and although many were convicted, few were actually hanged. The Lieutenant Governor could, at his discretion, grant a pardon to a convicted felon, and while accused rapists were silent at their trials, they frequently included an explanation of their actions as part of their petition for a pardon. Men occasionally complained that they had been the victim of mistaken identity, or that the rape victim's testimony should not have been believed due to her poor character. Some even swore that they believed consent had been obtained. Most invoked transparent excuses that, while failing to impress the Lieutenant Governor, reveal much about their attitudes toward rape. After being convicted for attempting to rape Margaret Kearney in 1838, Henry Cole felt "compelled to confess that having been intoxicated on the occasion alluded to, he may have done some act" which gave the impression of sexual assault, but he further argued for "the impossibility of his having entertained even an intention of committing a rape, when it is considered that it is alleged to have taken place in a public house, within a few feet of a number of individuals, and upon a child under the immediate protection of her father."[84]

Another defense strategy, used both in petitions as well as at trial, was to raise the specter of a false accusation. Upper Canadian jurist W. C. Keele, repeating earlier writers, noted that rape was "an accusation easily to be made, and hard to be proved, and harder to be defended by the party accused, though never so innocent," and this was doubtless a dictum with which most accused were familiar.[85] Trial witnesses were often questioned at length about whether there had been any quarrels between the families of the prosecutor and the accused, and the possibility that a charge of rape might be a false one was exploited by the defense. Elias Anderson was acquitted in 1838 when he was able to produce witnesses who had seen the victim's father visit him in jail, and overheard threats to "have his neck" if Anderson did not sign over a large tract of land.[86] Similarly, testimony at the trial of Ethan Card a year later reveals that Mary Switzer had concocted the charge of rape in an attempt to take revenge on the defendant. Since Switzer was seeking revenge for an earlier rape by Card which, all agreed, actually *did* happen, the jury convicted anyway.[87] Such initiative on the part of the jury was commonplace, but what is startling is the lack of direction from the trial judge in such cases. Perhaps Justice Macaulay was content to trust the instincts of the jurors, agreeing with the Kingston *British Whig*, which expressed surprise at an 1835 rape acquittal, but admitted, "as the jury were mostly from the part of the country in which both parties reside, it is not unlikely that they knew more of the matter than appeared in open court."[88]

False charges, mistaken identification, and imagined consent were all used, sometimes successfully, to escape rape convictions. But once a conviction had been secured, such arguments in a petition for pardon carried little weight. The Lieutenant Governor was not a court of appeal, but rather a dispenser of royal mercy. Most petitioners understood this well, and in their petitions they admitted the justice of their conviction and simply begged for the chance of a reprieve. Their convictions were painted as an aberration in an otherwise exemplary life, and friends and neighbors were called upon to speak to the petitioner's previously unblemished character. Indeed, a good character was the key to securing a pardon, and as such the Lieutenant Governor and his staff, aided by reports from the trial judge and local magistrates, closely examined the convict's habits. If a woman's character played only a peripheral role in influencing the outcome of the trial, a man's reputation could well make the difference between whether he would live or die.

Many of the petitions submitted by convicted rapists are formulaic and repetitive, echoing arguments also found in petitions submitted by those convicted of other types of crime. Appeals such as that made by John Turnbull in 1826 lead the reader to question whether the petitioner fully understood the nature of the crime for which he had been convicted. After being found guilty of attempting to rape Elizabeth Welsh in Asphodel Township, Turnbull argued for a pardon by reminding the Lieutenant Governor that he had a wife and child and, as "no person is now with them, they are greatly in want of your Petitioner's protection."[89] Such incongruity was not lost on the Lieutenant Governor, who denied his request. The position of the state on such matters had been clearly articulated in 1820, when Robert McIntyre, a Kingston soldier, was hanged for the rape of Nancy Dick. Although McIntyre had submitted a petition for pardon that even included the support of his victim, Chief Justice William Dummer Powell recommended the execution proceed as planned as an example "to protect from similar outrage the Persons and habitations of that numerous class of females whose Occupations retain them alone in their houses the greatest part of their Time, in absence of their Husbands, fathers, and Brothers."[90]

Such a clear statement of official views concerning rape and its punishment is rare in Upper Canada, but a similar case almost two decades later reveals a remarkable consistency. Convicted of raping nine-year-old Mary Ann Bullock in 1837, Patrick Fitzpatrick petitioned for a pardon "On account of his previous good character [,] from the consideration of how easy the crime may be charged, and how hard it is to be disproved," and finally, "On account of the disproportion of the punishment to the crime, which, however heinous, the petitioners are of opinion ought not to be punished with death." While on most petitions the head of state simply wrote "granted" or "not granted," in this case the government took the unprecedented step of responding to Fitzpatrick's plea point-by-point in the provincial press. The Lieutenant Governor refused to overturn the decision of the jury, and closed by noting that as the victim "was not strong enough to protect her[self,] it was deemed necessary that the law should be her protector." "Considering the inestimable advantages which society derives by this protection," he expressed his "deepest regret" at being unable to "extend to Patrick Fitzpatrick the Royal Mercy." The newspaper declared "the reasonings contained in this reply are unanswerable," and Fitzpatrick was hanged at Sandwich on 9 October 1837.[91]

The government's decision to publicly justify the execution of Fitzpatrick is a curious one, and raises important questions about Upper Canadian attitudes toward rape, and the extent to which the community at large shared this official view. The fact that Fitzpatrick was able to collect the signatures of many of his neighbors, including that of Colonel John Prince, the local Member of Parliament, seems to indicate a widespread consensus that execution was too harsh a penalty for rape. Other cases mentioned earlier in this essay show a similar trend. Twenty of his neighbors, as well as nine magistrates and several militia officers, signed Henry Cole's petition.[92] Dennis Russell's petition was signed by ten magistrates, a schoolmaster, and the commanding officer of Russell's militia unit,[93] while Chauncey Skinner managed to receive support from 106 "Sundry inhabitants of the Township of Whitby."[94] The support that many of these men were able to garner in their pleas for clemency also highlight the dilemma faced by a woman who was prosecuting not only a rapist, but also a neighbor.

It is this status as neighbor which allows for an alternative reading of the petitions for pardon. Upper Canada had no poor law, and support for the indigent was dependant upon informal charity. A husband or father who was executed or subjected to a lengthy imprisonment would place a burden on the entire community for the support of their families. This eventuality was especially feared by magistrates, who would have had to draw on limited district funds for the provision of assistance.[95] An ongoing drain of limited resources was probably uppermost in the minds of six Cornwall magistrates who signed a petition in favor of George Burns in 1826. They argued that he had already served one year of a seven-year sentence for attempted rape in their small district gaol and that it seemed enough. Whether they meant enough punishment, or enough of an expense, is left unsaid.[96] While John Turnbull may have displayed an uncommon degree of insensitivity by arguing for his release on the basis of having a wife and family in need of his protection, on another level, this argument shows he was quite attuned to the priorities of the magistrates who agreed to sign his petition. More than this, he attempted—albeit unsuccessfully—to tailor his own situation to fit a larger discourse on the role of men and the state in the protection of the colony's women.[97]

In spite of occasional grumbling over sentences, rape was considered a serious crime in Upper Canada, and was harshly punished. Although most convicted rapists had their death sentences commuted, this reflects a general distaste for executions rather than any feeling that rapists were deserving of leniency. In a larger context, of the 394 men and women sentenced to death in Upper Canada for all crimes between 1791 and 1841, only 88 were actually executed.[98] For those who escaped the gallows, punishment was nevertheless harsh, and was meant to be exemplary. Those pardoned could still expect to be transported or, after 1835, spend prolonged terms in Kingston Penitentiary. While a rape conviction required that a death sentence at least be pronounced, judges routinely sentenced those convicted for attempted rape to lengthy prison terms or fines far in excess of those assessed on other criminals. In 1834, a jury found Alexander Greig, charged with attempted rape, guilty of simple assault. The Chief Justice sentenced him to pay the enormous fine of 50 pounds and to stay in jail until it was paid.[99]

While harsh sentences were the rule, they generally reflect elite attitudes toward crime. But there is also evidence that ordinary community members shared such attitudes. Petitions for pardon were common—and were invariably filed with very negative comments from the presiding judge. Rape, however, was one of the few crimes in which petitions were *not* signed by members of the convicting jury, and which also generated counterpetitions—appeals from the community that a rapist *not* be released from jail. John Standish had been sentenced to death for rape in 1831, and quickly set about petitioning for royal mercy. His appeal arrived at Government House in September. Five weeks later it was followed by a petition from Vashty Waterhouse, his victim, who expressed her "unfeigned satisfaction" at the idea of Standish being pardoned, but nevertheless urged that he be transported. As long as he was in Upper Canada, she argued, she and her husband did "not consider themselves safe from personal injury, nor their property from danger of being destroyed." The administration apparently took Waterhouse's fears to heart. Standish was left to languish in the Hamilton gaol, without an answer to his own petition, for sixteen months. He was the only prisoner who was not released when the province suffered a cholera epidemic in 1832. He was ultimately transported to a penal colony in Bermuda, where the likelihood of him revenging himself on his prosecutor dimmed next to his chances of contracting malaria.[100]

Standish's case is but the most egregious of several in which community members urged even harsher punishments, officials deliberately delayed news of pardons, or convicts unable to pay high fines remained imprisoned for months or even years. A rape conviction was considered so distasteful that support could not always even be counted on from one's own family. Convicted of an attempted rape, a man named Tisdale petitioned for release from jail, but was unsuccessful when his own father informed the Lieutenant Governor that he was "well pleased that he should remain where he is" and "had no objection if he had been sent to the Penitentiary."[101]

Community sanction could also be expressed outside official channels. Several rape cases allude to the possibility—not pursued in these instances—of vigilante justice.[102] An 1822 incident in Kingston is uncommonly revealing. Accused of abusing—although not specifically raping—his wife, "a certain man" was approached by about twenty of his neighbors who, with their faces blackened to avoid recognition, "tore [him] from his horse and mounted him on a rail, carrying him by force upwards of a mile, thereby bruising and injuring him very materially."[103] Such instances rarely entered the official record, but nevertheless represented a manner in which justice of a sort might be served, and community outrage expressed.

More common were extrajudicial financial settlements. Many cases offer details of defendants who offered cash payments to victims if only prosecutions would be abandoned. Although there are several fairly obvious attempts to bribe both prosecutors and prosecution witnesses to remain silent, many also seem to represent a serious effort to arrive at some sort of settlement. Nancy Dick attempted to halt the execution of the man who raped her in 1820 by petitioning the Lieutenant Governor with news that Robert McIntyre had "attoned" for his crime.[104] Although Anna Clark has linked such payments to a corrupt English justice system,[105] a cash settlement may have seemed far more useful to a victim of rape, and done much more to preserve community harmony, than seeing her assailant "launched into eternity."

Rape cases in Upper Canada involved much more than a victim and an assailant. Issues of reputation, one's standing in the community, and understandings of often class-based codes of sexual behavior ensured that such cases were very much rooted in the problems and preoccupations of the larger society. Race played as much of a role in the way Upper Canadians understood rape as did class and gender. In 1868, Prime Minister John A. Macdonald commented on the necessity of retaining capital punishment for rape "on account of the frequency of rape committed by negroes. They are," he continued, "very prone to felonious assaults on white women."[106] But if Macdonald was expressing a widely held prejudice, it was a newly formed one. In the years up to 1850, the connection between black men and rape—so frequently made in the United States—is notable only for its absence.[107]

But while race was rarely an overt issue in Upper Canadian rape cases, there were nevertheless occasions when the racial element of a sexual assault threatened to disrupt the social harmony not just of the local community, but of the province as a whole. Such was the case of Carlisle Hammond, a white settler who fled the province after committing "a gross outrage upon an Indian woman in the Township of Alnwick." Native-settler relations, delicate at the best of times, were further strained by the event, which prompted a speech by John Sunday, a Mississauga chief. He reminded listeners of the promise made between Upper Canadian natives and the British government "to live like brothers . . . and not do one another any hurt" and questioned whether that promise had been kept. Indians often met white women on the roads in the woods without harming them, he noted, further stating: "I might do like white man, but I [do] not." Such behavior could not be expected to continue, Sunday warned, so long as white men could attack Indian women and go unpunished. Obviously hoping to restore cordial relations, the Lieutenant Governor immediately proclaimed a 50 pound reward for the capture of Hammond.[108]

The specter of an Indian uprising as the result of a rape is an extreme and unlikely scenario, but it nevertheless illustrates the extent to which issues of sexual violence influenced, and were influenced by, the communities in which they occurred. Within such communities, men were expected to protect women—particularly the women of their household—from unwanted advances and sexual danger. In the absence of such protection, Upper Canadian women could rely on the colony's criminal justice system, if not to protect them then at least to address the wrong done to them by their attackers. Mounting a prosecution was not a painless affair, and the colony's courts were themselves infused with a paternalistic ethos, but by and large women were able to prosecute men who raped, within a legal system that took their complaints seriously and made prosecution relatively simple.

NOTES

The research for this work was funded in part by a Doctoral Fellowship from the Social Sciences and Humanities Research Council of Canada. I would also like to thank Bettina Bradbury, Lykke de la Cour, Janet Miron, and Peter Oliver for their comments on an earlier draft of this essay.

1. *Upper Canada Gazette*, 18 April 1793.

2. Susan Brownmiller, *Against Our Will: Men, Women and Rape* (New York: Simon and Schuster, 1975), 175.

3. On the rarity of magistrates and the incompetence of those who did act, see *Niagara Gleaner*, 23 August 1823; *Colonial Advocate*, 21 March 1833; *St. Thomas Liberal*, 22 August 1833; *Canadian Emigrant*, 19 July 1834; *Kingston Spectator*, 23 July 1835; *Bytown Gazette*, 21 March 1838 and 19 July 1840. Hundreds of petitions from settlers begging for the appointment of local magistrates, can be found in the National Archives, RG 5, A–1, *Upper Canada Sundries* (hereafter: *Sundries*).

4. Susan Lewthwaite, "Violence, Law, and Community in Rural Upper Canada," in Jim Phillips, Tina Loo, and Susan Lewthwaite, eds., *Crime and Crim-*

inal Justice: Essays in the History of Canadian Law, vol. 5 (Toronto: University of Toronto Press, 1994). See also *Colonial Advocate*, 26 September 1833.

5. For an excellent analysis of the lives of ordinary women in Upper Canada, and especially their physical and social isolation, see Jane Errington, *Wives and Mothers, School Mistresses and Scullery Maids: Working Women in Upper Canada, 1790–1840* (Toronto: University of Toronto Press, 1995).

6. Douglas Hay, "Property, Authority and the Criminal Law," in Douglas Hay et al., eds., *Albion's Fatal Tree: Crime and Society in Eighteenth-Century England* (New York: Pantheon Press, 1975), esp. 26–31. For a particularly evocative description, from a slightly later date, of Upper Canadian courts and their spectators, see Paul Craven, "Law and Ideology: The Toronto Police Court, 1850–80," in David H. Flaherty, ed., *Essays in the History of Canadian Law*, vol. 2 (Toronto: University of Toronto Press, 1983).

7. *Brockville Gazette*, 21 May 1840; Lorne Pierce, *William Kirby: The Portrait of a Tory Loyalist* (Toronto: Macmillan, 1929), 42; P. J. R. King, "'Illiterate Plebeians, Easily Misled': Jury Composition, Experience, and Behaviour in Essex, 1735–1815," in J. S. Cockburn and Thomas A. Green, eds., *Twelve Good Men and True: The Criminal Trial Jury in England, 1200–1800* (Princeton: Princeton University Press, 1988), 298.

8. *Sundries*, 127544; Kenneth W. McKay, *The Court Houses of a Century* (St. Thomas, Ont.: Elgin Historical and Scientific Institute, 1901); Marian MacRae and Anthony Adamson, *Cornerstones of Order: Courthouses and Town Halls of Ontario, 1784–1914* (Toronto: University of Toronto Press, 1982).

9. W. C. Keele, *The Provincial Justice*, 2ᵈ ed. (Toronto: H. and W. Roswell, 1843), 516–21.

10. Ibid. On the difficulty of obtaining a conviction, in English cases, without proof of ejaculation, see Anna Clark, *Women's Silence, Men's Violence: Sexual Assault in England, 1770–1845* (London: Pandora, 1987), 55, 61–63.

11. *Sundries*, [Judge] Archibald McLean to Lt. Governor, 26 September 1837, 98163.

12. Archives of Ontario, RG 22, 390–91, Benchbooks of James Buchanan Macaulay (hereafter: Macaulay's Benchbooks). Gore District Assizes, 27 September 1843.

13. Macaulay's Benchbooks, Newcastle District Assizes, Spring 1844.

14. Keele, *Provincial Justice*, 518. Much of Keele's commentary on rape seems to have been lifted directly from earlier English sources. Cf. Constance Backhouse, "Nineteenth-Century Canadian Rape Law, 1800–92" in Flaherty, ed., *Essays in the History of Canadian Law*, vol. 2, 202–3.

15. Marybeth Hamilton Arnold, "'The Life of a Citizen in the Hands of a Woman': Sexual Assault in New York City, 1790–1820," in Kathy Peiss and Christina Simmons, eds., *Passion and Power: Sexuality in History* (Philadelphia: Temple University Press, 1989), 148.

16. Macaulay's Benchbooks, Talbot District Assizes, 6 May 1841.

17. Macaulay's Benchbooks, Western District Assizes, May 1846.

18. Macaulay's Benchbooks, Newcastle District Assizes, Spring 1844.

19. Archives of Ontario, RG 22–94, Home District General Quarter Sessions of the Peace, Misc. Filings, 1797.

20. Archives of Ontario, RG 22–49, Cornwall General Quarter Sessions of the Peace, Misc. Filings, 1794–96.

21. A grand jury could reject the indictment as frivolous, or lacking the requisite evidence for a conviction. In Upper Canada, however, they generally seemed willing to let a jury decide, and surviving records show they no-billed only two indictments for rape or attempted rape.

22. John Beattie, *Crime and the Courts in England, 1660–1800* (Oxford: Oxford University Press, 1986), 423–30.

23. Constance Backhouse, *Petticoats and Prejudice: Women and the Law in Nineteenth-Century Ontario* (Toronto: Women's Press, 1991), 99.

24. For an excellent analysis of this case, see Robert Fraser, "Jack York," in the *Dictionary of Canadian Biography*, vol. 4, (Toronto: University of Toronto Press, 1979).

25. *Sundries*, W. D. Powell to Lt. Governor, 8 August 1800, 443.

26. St. Catherines *Daily Times*, 8 July 1858.

27. This figure is based on my own analysis of the Home District Quarter Sessions (Upper Canada's largest and most populous district) between 1793 and 1841.

28. John Beverly Robinson's Benchbooks, Home District Assizes, Spring 1834.

29. Twenty-one of 104 cases. I have included an incest case for which the grand jury was unable to indict, lamenting the lack of any law applying to such circumstances. Although the age of the victim is not specified, it is almost certain that she was a child. See *Kingston Chronicle*, 12 November 1845.

30. Arnold, "The Life of a Citizen in the Hands of a Woman," 42–44.

31. Clark, *Women's Silence, Men's Violence*, 42. See also Garthine Walker, "Rereading Rape and Sexual Violence in Early Modern England," *Gender and History* 10 no. 1 (April 1998): 7.

32. See, for example, the prosecution of Dennis Russell for the rape of an unidentified nine-year-old girl in *Sundries*, [Judge] L. P. Sherwood to Lt. Governor, 15 September 1828, 49922. Also see the prosecution of William Brass for the rape of eight-year-old Mary Ann Dempsey, in *Kingston Chronicle*, 11 October 1837.

33. Karen Dubinsky, *Improper Advances: Rape and Heterosexual Conflict in Ontario, 1880–1929* (Chicago: University of Chicago Press, 1993), 23.

34. Macaulay's Benchbooks, Newcastle District Assizes, Spring 1844.

35. Macaulay's Benchbooks, Jonestown District Assizes, 8 August 1833.

See also ibid., Sandwich Assizes, 30 July 1832; Niagara District Assizes, October 1843.

36. There is a large amount of material relating to this case, including petitions to the Lt. Governor from both Standish and Waterhouse. See *Sundries,* 62203, 62208–18, 65511–17, 67504–24; Minutes of the Court of King's Bench, Gore District, 1831. Picking berries continued to be a dangerous occupation for women into the twentieth century, as illustrated by Dubinsky, *Improper Advances,* 38. For more such cases in Upper Canada, see *Dundas Weekly Post,* 18 August 1835, and Macaulay's Benchbooks, Colbourne District Assizes, October 1849; Gore District Assizes, 27 September 1843.

37. Clark, *Women's Silence, Men's Violence,* 110.

38. The best of many examples of middle-class Englishwomen shocked by Upper Canadian attitudes toward class and gender relations is Susannah Moodie, *Roughing It in the Bush* (London: Richard Bentley, 1854).

39. While there is no evidence of such a conspiracy in Upper Canada, an excellent article by Carolyn Strange shows that this had changed by the early twentieth century. See her "Patriarchy Modified: The Criminal Prosecution of Rape in York County, Ontario, 1880–1930," in Phillips, Loo, and Lewthwaite, *Crime and Criminal Justice.*

40. Indeed, many Upper Canadian taverns were owned and operated by women. There has been little work on the role of the tavern in Upper Canada, but a forthcoming University of Toronto Ph.D. dissertation by Julia Roberts promises to fill this gap.

41. Edwin Welch, ed., Anonymous (A. J. Christie?), *Yankies and Loyalists: A Trip from Bytown to Kingston in February 1830* (Ottawa: Bytown Museum, 1979), 12.

42. Macaulay's Benchbooks, London District Assizes, May 1846.

43. *Kingston Spectator,* 4 July 1839; *Sundries,* Case of Henry Cole, 117141–42, 117860–63, 122048–71; Macaulay's Benchbooks, Home District Assizes, July 1839.

44. For other cases in which women's presence in taverns is treated in such a matter-of-fact way, see *Sundries,* [Judge] L. P. Sherwood to Lt. Governor, 31 December 1833, 74589–92, 74714–17; Macaulay's Benchbooks, Western District Assizes, May 1846, and Wellington District Assizes, May 1846.

45. It should be kept in mind that issues of "character" were always key elements in any trial before the advent of modern forensic evidence.

46. Macaulay's Benchbooks, Home District Assizes, October 1841. With enough credibility, a victim's uncorroborated testimony was occasionally enough to secure a conviction. See *Sundries,* John Turnbull to Lt. Governor, 12 January 1826, 40532; Kingston *British Whig,* 3 August 1850.

47. Kingston *British Whig,* 12 August 1835, commenting on the attempted rape of Margaret Fair.

48. Macaulay's Benchbooks, Prince Edward District Assizes, Fall 1839.

49. *Sundries*, B. Biddell, M.P. to Lt. Governor, n.d., 139046–48.

50. Robinson's Benchbooks, Home District Assizes, 21 October 1829; *Sundries*, 54088–91, 55090–92, 55771–73. Skinner was pardoned for this rape but he was hanged for murder in June 1840, demonstrating that however bad Mary Richie's character was, his was far worse. For other cases where a jury convicted in spite of testimony concerning the victim's bad character, see Macaulay's Benchbooks, Newcastle District Assizes, Spring 1844, and April 1842.

51. Kingston *British Whig*, 3 November 1849. For details of this case, see Macaulay's Benchbooks, Colbourne District Assizes, October 1849.

52. *Sundries*, Ogle R. Gowan to Lt. Governor, 10 February 1834, 75362–64. Ironically, Gowan's own political career came to a halt in 1861 when he was charged with criminal assault for his sexual relations with a twelve-year-old Toronto girl. See Donald H. Akenson, *The Orangeman: The Life and Times of Ogle Gowan* (Toronto: James Lorimer, 1986), 155–56, 295–307.

53. Keele, *Provincial Justice*, 517. For a later nineteenth-century case involving the rape of a prostitute, with a decidedly unsympathetic jury, see Backhouse, *Petticoats and Prejudice*, 81–101.

54. Statements such as the ones quoted here occur repeatedly in the trial transcripts.

55. Walker, "Rereading Rape and Sexual Violence," 8. See also Clark, *Women's Silence, Men's Violence*, 55.

56. Macaulay's Benchbooks, Colbourne District Assizes, October 1849.

57. Macaulay's Benchbooks, Wellington District Assizes, May 1846.

58. Arnold, "Life of a Citizen in the Hands of a Woman," 47.

59. For cases involving midwives and doctors, see *Sundries*, [Judge] Archibald McLean to Lt. Governor, 26 September 1837, 98159–72; [Judge] Jonas Jones to Lt. Governor, 31 October 1837, 98350–61; Macaulay's Benchbooks, Gore District Assizes, September 1843; Home District Assizes, 23 October 1838. For doctors' unwillingness to testify for the defense, see Macaulay's Benchbooks, London District Assizes, May 1846.

60. Clark, *Women's Silence, Men's Violence*, 5.

61. Robinson's Benchbooks, Home District Assizes, Spring 1834. Emphasis in original.

62. For a view of the convivial relations between residents of London and the local troops, see in particular Robin S. Harris and Terry G. Harris, eds., *The Eldon House Diaries: Five Women's Views of the Nineteenth Century* (Toronto: University of Toronto Press, 1994), passim. For evidence of a less hospitable relationship, see *Kingston Gazette*, 15 and 29 March 1817; 5 April, 1817. One's relationship with the local military establishment seems to have been very much dependent on one's class status and—as is obvious from these cases—on one's gender.

63. Brownmiller, *Against Our Will*, 176, 182. Precise ages are not always given for Upper Canadian rapists, but most were young men, a few only teenagers. The exception seems to have been those charged with raping small children. For rape by soldiers in general, see also Brownmiller, *Against Our Will*, 31ff.

64. *Sundries*, W. D. Powell to Lt. Governor, 8 August 1800, 443–45.

65. Archives of Ontario, MU 1182–86, Marcus Gunn Diary, 29 January 1847.

66. Ibid., 30 January 1847.

67. Macaulay's Benchbooks, London District Assizes, May 1846.

68. Gunn Diary, 30 January 1847.

69. Macaulay's Benchbooks, Gore District Assizes, 27 September 1843.

70. Kingston *British Whig*, 3 August 1850. She gave him "a slap in the chops," turned the wagon back to Kingston, and had him arrested. He was fined ten shillings plus costs.

71. This trend (which continues to the present day) was also found by Arnold, "Life of a Citizen," 38.

72. Macaulay's Benchbooks, Colbourne District Assizes, October 1849. Brown responded, "he only kissed like a neighbour-boy, not like a lover."

73. Macaulay's Benchbooks, Sandwich Assizes, 30 July 1832.

74. There is little work on Upper Canadian sexual behavior. Peter Ward, *Courtship, Love, and Marriage in Nineteenth-Century English Canada* (Montreal and Kingston, McGill/Queen's University Press, 1990), is useful, although it largely neglects the rural working class and leans toward the later nineteenth century. A more accurate picture of Upper Canada would probably be gained from John Gillis, *For Better, for Worse: British Marriages, 1600 to the Present* (Oxford: Oxford University Press, 1985), esp. 126–30.

75. Cited in John Carroll, *Case and His Contemporaries* (Toronto: William Briggs, 1877), vol. 1, 182.

76. Gerald E. Boyce, ed., *Hutton of Hastings: The Life and Letters of William Hutton, 1801–1861* (Belleville: Mika Publishing, 1972), 14.

77. *Bathurst Courier*, 10 December 1852.

78. John Weaver, "Crime, Public Order, and Repression: The Gore District in Upheaval, 1832–1851," *Ontario History* 78, no. 3 (September 1986).

79. E. A. Talbot, *Five Year's Residence in the Canadas* (London: Longman, Hurst Rees, Orme Brown and Green, 1824), vol. 2, 38–40. While Talbot is doubtless exaggerating for effect, it is interesting to note the experience of unwed mothers who were the victims of rape in Upper Canada. By the turn of the century, Dubinsky notes that charges were dismissed "in every case in which the woman was found to have had illegitimate children." Yet several such women in Upper Canada were able to see their rape prosecutions through to a conviction. See Dubinsky's *Improper Advances*, 27, and Macaulay's Benchbooks, Newcastle District Assizes, 27 April 1842.

80. Clark, *Women's Silence, Men's Violence*, 23–24.

81. The best description of this affair is found in Katherine M. J. McKenna, *A Life of Propriety: Anne Murray Powell and Her Family, 1755–1849* (Montreal and Kingston: McGill/Queen's University Press, 1994), 70–72.

82. Transcripts reveal twenty-one cases where men asked permission before raping, although the actual number is certainly higher. See also Arnold, "Life of a Citizen," 39.

83. Kingston *Chronicle*, 11 October 1837. Brass was hanged at Kingston.

84. *Sundries*, Henry Cole to Lt. Governor, 8 June 1839, 122057.

85. Keele, *Provincial Justice*, 518.

86. Macaulay's Benchbooks, Home District Assizes, October 1838.

87. Macaulay's Benchbooks, Prince Edward District Assizes, Fall 1839. A similar case was tried by Macaulay at the Wellington District Assizes, May 1846.

88. Kingston *British Whig*, 12 August 1835.

89. *Sundries*, John Turnbull to Lt. Governor, 12 January 1826, 40532.

90. *Sundries*, W. D. Powell to Lt. Governor, 22 September 1820, 24195–99, 24224–25.

91. *Sundries*, 98159–72, 98245–55. The reply to Fitzpatrick's petition was published verbatim in various papers, including the *Bytown Gazette*, 29 November 1837.

92. *Sundries*, Inhabitants of the Township of Toronto to Lt. Governor, March 1840, 132260–62.

93. *Sundries*, Dennis Russell to Lt. Governor, 9 September 1828, 49920–26, 50291.

94. *Sundries*, Inhabitants of the Township of Whitby to Lt. Governor, 4 November 1829, 54088–91.

95. David Murray, "The Cold Hand of Charity: The Court of Quarter Sessions and Poor Relief in the Niagara District, 1828–1841," in W. W. Pru and B. Wright, eds., *Canadian Perspectives on Law and Society* (Ottawa: Carleton University Press, 1988).

96. *Sundries*, Six magistrates to Lt. Governor, 28 January 1826, 40707–8. Burns was also sentenced to stand in the pillory. See also Assize Minute Books, Eastern District, 9 August 1825. Due to its expense, imprisonment for more than ninety days was extremely rare in Upper Canada, until the establishment of Kingston Penitentiary in 1835.

97. This was a common, and often successful, argument. See *St. Catherines Journal*, 30 September 1829.

98. At least three rapists were hanged. Records are incomplete in many cases, and I suspect several more shared this fate. The overall number of pardoned and executed felons is drawn from research for my dissertation in progress on royal mercy in Upper Canada.

99. Robinson's Benchbooks, Home District Assizes, Spring 1834. Average fines for simple assault were generally well under twenty shillings.

100. *Sundries*, John and Vashty Waterhouse to Lt. Governor, 17 October 1831, 62203–17, 65511–17, 67505–7, 67822–5.

101. *Sundries*, B. Biddell, M. P. to Lt. Governor, n.d., 139046–48. It also seems likely that Allan McInnis, convicted of rape in 1849, was turned in by his own father. See Macaulay's Benchbooks, Colbourne District Assizes, October 1849.

102. Threats are detailed in many trial transcripts. See also *Kingston Spectator*, 5 October 1835.

103. *Sundries*, [Judge] D'arcy Boulton to Lt. Governor, 10 October 1822, 29985; Petition of Master and Journeymen Shoemakers of Kingston to Lt. Governor, 1 October 1822, 29900–02.

104. Regrettably, Nancy Dick's petition has been lost. It is commented upon in W. D. Powell's Circuit Report. See *Sundries*, W. D. Powell to Lt. Governor, 18 September 1820, 24195–99, 24224–25. See also Macaulay's Benchbooks, Midland District Assizes, July 1833.

105. Clark, *Women's Silence, Men's Violence*, 21–22. The Upper Canadian justice system had its failings, but the rampant corruption described by Clark had no counterpart in the colony.

106. Cited in Backhouse, *Petticoats and Prejudice*, 98. Between 1791 and 1850, only four black men were prosecuted for rape in the province. All four were convicted, but none had any trouble gaining large numbers of signatures on their petitions for pardon. Indeed, in 1836 Andrew Patterson submitted a plea for clemency supported by 136 of his white neighbors, the highest number of supporters for any rapist. See *Sundries*, Inhabitants of the District of Gore to Lt. Governor, n.d., 92041, 92643–46. "Since the Lt. Gov wished to Aavoid casualties," Patterson ultimately received five years in Kingston Penitentiary.

107. Recent work has shown that even in the United States, the linkage between race and rape emerged only following the Civil War. See Diane Miller Sommerville, "The Rape Myth in the Old South Reconsidered," *Journal of Southern History* 61, no. 3 (August 1995): 485; Daniel A. Cohen, "Social Injustice, Sexual Violence, Spiritual Transcendence: Constructions of Interracial Rape in Early American Crime Literature, 1767–1817," *William and Mary Quarterly* 56, no. 3 (July 1999): 496.

108. *Peterborough Despatch*, 4 March 1847. Sunday claimed that no Indian had ever raped a white woman, but only two months later an Indian was the one to commit an "infamous outrage." See *Peterborough Despatch*, 6 May 1847. For more on rewards for rapists, see *Sundries*, W. B. Jarvis to Lt. Governor, 27 August 1831, 61751–54; *Colonial Advocate*, 18 August 1831.

7

"I Was Very Much Wounded"

Rape Law, Children, and the Antebellum South

Diane Miller Sommerville

THE AMERICAN FAMILY has received a great deal of attention from historians in the last few decades, and more than a few of these works have yielded important historical markers about the development and makeup of families in the nineteenth century. We are told, for example, that a dramatic reconceptualization of childhood unfolded in the wake of important social, religious, and economic transformations. Children, it would seem, were no longer viewed as vessels of original sin or merely miniature adults, but rather as unique individuals with different needs than adults. A greater sensitivity to and appreciation for children occurred in the context of an increasing sentimentalization of family after the American Revolution.[1] But while some nineteenth-century children were adored, coddled, and even glorified, others were not. As Christine Stansell has shown, the increased commercialization and industrialization of the urban northeast required many families to send their children out to work merely to subsist, in the process exposing young children to street crime, vagrancy, and sexual exploitation.[2] Neither did slave children receive the doting attention of parents, as pointed out by Wilma King in her aptly titled work, *Stolen Childhood*.[3] Clearly, claims of idealized notions of childhood have to be qualified and need to take race and class into account.

The universality of the nostalgic view of childhood innocence becomes virtually untenable when confronted with the nation's child rape laws, revealing an apparent contradiction between ideology, the law, and behavior. In most states, only children nine and under were protected from sexual predators, regardless of consent. Children ten and older, however, were treated as adults, meaning that unless evidence of force had been established, there was a presumption of consensual sex. Moreover, even in antebellum cases where young children did bring charges of rape, courts, both local and appellate, sometimes sided with the alleged or convicted rapists. The evidence presented in this essay begs the question, how a society that maintained idealistic views about the sweetness and innocence of childhood could be so unmoved at times by the sexual assault of little girls? While elite white southerners demonstrated considerable emotional attachment to their own children, at times they, as individuals and through institutions, failed to offer the same sorts of protections and sensitivity to children of the middling or poorer sort. The explanation, I contend, is a complicated one, but one rooted in class difference and misogyny, as well as paternalism.

The setting for this study, the antebellum rural South, stands in contrast to previously published works on nineteenth-century childhood on a couple of fronts. First, very few works have been published solely on the role of childhood in the antebellum South. Most of what we know about southerners and childhood comes to us in the context of the larger subject of family or legal history. And most historians of family and childhood in the South—Jan Lewis, Jane Turner Censer, and Daniel Blake Smith, for example—have tended to focus on affluent planter families.[4] Even fewer studies examine the more nuanced subject of sexuality and childhood.

Furthermore, most of what we know about childhood and sexuality in the antebellum years, specifically sexual assault, comes from a few studies of one northern city, New York.[5] This essay, by contrast, seeks to explore how antebellum southerners viewed childhood and sexuality through the evidence provided by rape law and child rape cases. By examining these cases, it is possible to consider how the institution of slavery, as well as the factors of race and class, shaped the way white southerners viewed rape and children in the rural, slaveholding South. Finally, a study of child rape cases should reveal the extent to which idealized notions about the innocence of children were applied in antebellum southern society.

The definition of rape throughout antebellum America turned on the use of force and the lack of consent. When rapists used or threatened to use force, crafters of the law imagined that many women, for their own safety, willingly submitted to the act. The legal requirements for rape, however, were not always so easily determined. For example, some men stood accused of administering drugs to facilitate sex with unwilling women. Still other men impersonated the husbands of their victims under cover of darkness. Many courts felt bound by the letter of the law, and ruled that such cases fell outside the definition of rape, as determined by lawmakers.[6]

Another problematic area for antebellum courts hearing rape cases involved accusers too young to be considered women. Prosecution for the rape of children did not depend on proof of force, as in the case of adult women, since it was felt that children were unable to understand and therefore give informed consent. Moreover, children were believed incapable of good judgment and discretion when it came to sexual relations. Children "lacked the instinctive intelligence to comprehend the nature and consequences of this atrocious act," noted Judge Joseph Henry Lumpkin of the Georgia Supreme Court.[7] Consent of the child, then, became an irrelevant factor in child rape cases.

Carnal abuse of an infant, as sexual intercourse with an underage child was known, had been a crime under common law throughout British colonial America.[8] After the Revolution, most southern lawmakers enacted legislation that established an age threshold in rape cases, below which force did not need to be proven and consent was irrelevant. But communities throughout the South were not uniform or always specific in establishing the legal definition of a child. The age of consent was typically ten years of age but varied from state to state and over time. By the Civil War, only Virginia, Missouri, and Kentucky had raised the age of consent to twelve.[9] Arkansas maintained no specific age requirement, but recognized the onset of puberty as the age of consent.[10] In addition, Tennessee and Mississippi, curiously, maintained two different ages of consent on the basis of race. Both states established ten as the age of consent in cases of white males accused of statutory rape, but a higher age of twelve for cases in which the rapist was a slave (Mississippi later raised this to age fourteen). Though the motive for the statutory disparity is not explicit, one can imagine that lawmakers sought to be more diligent in the policing of the sexual relations of young girls with slaves than with white men. In practice, then, an eleven-year-old white girl from Tennessee would have been deemed legally incapable of understanding consent in the context of sexual relations with a slave, but perfectly capable and hence responsible for having sexual relations with a white male.[11] The racial double standard in the definition of statutory rape grew even wider when in 1857 the Mississippi legislature raised the age of consent in the slave statute to fourteen.[12]

Race obviously played a much greater role in the crafting of statutory rape laws in the antebellum South than elsewhere in the nation. Most salient of the racial differences was the uneven punishment for those convicted of the crime of child rape. In Arkansas, Mississippi, Tennessee, Texas, and Virginia slaves found guilty of having carnal knowledge with white female children could receive the death penalty, while white men were to serve penitentiary sentences ranging from five to twenty-one years.[13] Missouri punished white offenders with a minimum prison term of five years whereas slaves were to be castrated.[14] In both Carolinas, by contrast, white and slave men convicted of statutory rape would be condemned to death.[15]

A few states even appear to have explicitly established statutory rape as a crime for whites but not for slaves. However, it seems clear that legislators meant the states' rape statutes to encompass underage sexual relations as well. A number of southern states, such as Alabama, for instance, punished whites found guilty of having sex with girls under age ten with a term of life imprisonment, the exact punishment held out for the rape of females over age ten. Since slaves, and free blacks for that matter, suffered the death penalty for the rape and attempted rape of white women, it seems logical to assume that legislators believed slaves were covered under the existing legislation.[16] Similarly, Georgia courts could punish white men having unlawful sex with girls under age ten with solitary confinement up to six months, or hard labor for ten to twenty years. Slaves guilty of the rape or attempted rape of a white female suffered death.[17] Kentucky appears to have retained a distinction between the "rape . . . of an infant under the age of twelve years," which was punishable by death when committed by whites, and "carnally knowing a white girl under the age of ten years," a lesser offense, presumably because no force was employed, which warranted a prison term of ten to twenty years. The earliest rape statutes in Kentucky did not specify the race of the victim; however, by 1852, reflecting that state's deeper commitment to the institution of slavery, legislation became race specific.[18]

Despite the rather unambiguous criteria established by state legislatures for underage sexual assault, gray areas abounded and stymied some judges. Both appellate and local courts at times struggled with the murky middle ground of biological age and consent, reflecting some confusion about age, consent, and coerced sex. In 1850, for example, the Supreme Court of Arkansas heard a case brought on appeal, following the conviction of a slave named Charles, found guilty of assault with intent to ravish. Not only the age of the victim, but the level of her maturity was also deemed of material interest to the high court. Witnesses testified that the accuser, Almyra Combs, was about thirteen or fourteen years of age, "not a woman," and had "not attained the age of puberty," that state's criterion for statutory rape. Combs had been sleeping with six other girls in the same room when the defendant allegedly entered, grabbed her by the shoulder, and tried to turn her over, presumably to have sex with her. A startled Combs grabbed the intruder, discovering that it was a partially dressed man.(Combs delicately explained that she "found the portion of the undressed person to be that portion of which I cannot decently speak.") Charles, who had apparently been hired out to Michael Summerron, explained to his master that he had merely tried to summon Mr. Summerron because of his belief that there was an intruder in the barn. It had all been a case of mistaken identity.[19]

Charles's attorney zeroed in on a technicality, an apparent loophole in the law. He argued that white men found guilty of "carnally knowing or abusing unlawfully, any female child under the age of puberty," the statute upon which Charles's indictment was based, faced a prison term.[20] Section nine of the same law modified the punishments for African Americans, substituting death sentences for prison terms. But here Charles's attorney saw a possible legislative oversight. The provision for blacks read that "if such negro or mulatto shall attempt to commit any of such offenses, although he may not succeed, on a white *woman*, he shall suffer death."[21] The accuser, not yet having reached puberty, was therefore not a woman and hence fell outside the purview of this legislation. The high court, however, interpreted the statute more broadly, ruling that the law intended to embrace young girls incapable of consent, and thus rejected the defense argument. Nonetheless, the court was persuaded that the accused had not used force, in fact had no intention of using force, hoping instead to have sexual relations with Combs while she slept, which was not a crime, let alone a capital offense. The high court found in favor of Charles.[22]

A Louisiana slave whose lawyer made a similar pitch was not as successful in his 1844 appeal. The slave had been sentenced to die for attempting to rape a six-year-old white girl. Citing a definition of

"woman" as being ten years or older, his attorney argued that the accuser was too young to have been raped. The Louisiana high court,
however, was not swayed and upheld the conviction.[23]

The Tennessee Supreme Court heard a similar appeal in 1842, but
decided very differently from the Louisiana court. Defense counsel for
Sydney argued that "a female infant only six years of age is not a
woman within a statute which makes it a felony . . . for a slave to make
an assault with an intent to commit rape on a 'free white woman.'" The
rape law for slaves encompassed only women. And while an 1829
statute made it a felony to have carnal knowledge with a child under
age ten, the legislature had neglected to take children into account
when crafting the assault with intent to commit a rape provision. The
Tennessee legislature passed legislation while the case was making its
way through the appeals process designed to "include all and every
white female" in cases where slaves attempted to rape white females.
The legislation came too late, however. The high court ruled that Sydney could not be convicted under the new law as he had been charged
with attempted rape before the law was expanded. Since there "is a
manifest distinction taken between a woman and a female child," and
Sydney's victim was not a woman, his alleged crime was not an in-
dictable offense and he could not be found guilty.[24]

It is possible that local officials whose responsibility it was to make
indictments were confused about age, consent, and sexual assault statues. In another Tennessee case, local officials in 1829 levied two charges
against a white man, one for rape, the other for carnal knowledge with
a female under the age of ten. The uncertainty of a child's age, coupled
with a lack of understanding of the nuances of sexual assault law, may
have prompted the justice of the peace in this case to cover all bases. The
defendant, who was convicted of the rape charge, protested, but to no
avail. In the ruling, the court decided that the strategy of filing more
than one charge in a single indictment was appropriate.[25]

Occasionally, the confusion about age and sexual assault carried
over into rulings on who was capable of committing a rape. In 1864,
the North Carolina Supreme Court heard the case of Sam, a fourteen-
year-old slave charged with the rape of a four-year-old white girl.
Sam's defense argued that he had not yet reached puberty and thus
could not commit rape. The jurists agreed. Citing English common
and case law, they sided with legal precedent, which established that
boys who had not yet reached puberty were not believed physically

capable of committing rape. The court acknowledged, however, that "a large portion of our population is of races from more southern latitudes than that from which our common law comes" and who reach puberty at an earlier age. The court consequently urged the lawmakers of the state to consider lowering the age for which boys, especially slave boys, would be accountable for rape to below age fourteen.[26]

Because most of the published appellate opinions from which the above cases are culled fail to give detailed descriptions of the female accusers, few inferences about such markers as class and status can be accurately deduced. By examining the local records of trials in smaller southern communities, however, much can be learned about the way conditions of economic standing, geographic proximity, and reputation shaped the development and outcomes of these cases. The vast majority of contacts that male slaves would likely have had with white females would be with the wives, daughters, and nieces of slave masters, those who lived or visited in the same quarters. At first glance children of the planter class may seem to have been obvious targets for a slave with an eye toward convenient and vulnerable victims. The spheres of slave and master brought each other into frequent contact; chances were good that a slave bent on sexual assault would happen upon a master's daughter or visiting niece in some desolate recesses of the plantation, farm, or nearby surroundings. Furthermore, sexual assault of a master's daughter might release pent-up hostility and rage locked inside a male slave. What better way to exact retribution?

Despite opportunity and motivation, however, according to extant sources, slaves rarely assaulted young members of the master's family, perhaps out of fear of the consequences. Only seldom did members of the elite bring charges of rape or attempted rape against their slaves. But on the few occasions that they did, local courts generally exacted the harshest punishment available.

One such illustration is the rape case of Dick, a Southampton County, Virginia, slave owned by Charles and Jane Briggs. On Halloween in 1808, Jane Briggs shooed her four-year-old daughter, Sally, out of the house so that her husband, who had not slept well the previous night, could rest peacefully. About two hours later Jane Briggs heard her young daughter crying. She sent an older daughter, Polly, to investigate. As Polly opened the door, there stood Dick holding Sally. The child's legs and feet were covered with blood. Polly shouted, "Good Lord, Mama! Sally is ruin'd!" Jane Briggs, though, could find no apparent wound, despite Dick's explanation that Sally had fallen.[27] After a fair amount of coaxing by her mother, Sally Briggs reluctantly revealed that Dick had hurt her and threatened to kill her. Reassured by her mother, Sally led her mother to where she claimed Dick had hurt her. Sally charged that Dick had laid her on a log, covered her mouth, then "tore her with his fingers." The log appeared wet to Jane Briggs, as if it had been recently washed, although a few droplets of blood were discernible. Sally then directed her mother to the spot where she said Dick made her wait while he fetched some water to wash her up. Jane Briggs kicked up some sand and found a "good deal of blood" underneath. Sally then threw her arms around her mother's neck and cried, "Oh! Mama, you don't know how I was hurt." She further recounted that Dick had grabbed a chunk of wood and threatened her if she told anyone of the assault.[28]

As enraged as Sally's father surely must have been upon learning that one of his own slaves had sexually violated his four-year-old daughter, he successfully restrained any impulse he might have felt to defend his and his daughter's honor and seek personal retribution. Briggs would have also been painfully aware that the cost of exacting private retribution through lynching would have been high indeed. While the state would have partially compensated him for a duly convicted, condemned slave, Briggs would have received nothing for a slave executed extralegally.[29] Whatever Briggs's motive, he allowed the court to decide Dick's fate.

There is no evidence that Sally herself testified; as a young child she would not have been permitted to swear an oath. Her mother, however, did recount what Sally had told her. Several of Briggs's other slaves also testified that Dick seemed to have been obsessed with the young girl for quite some time. Davey, a slave about sixteen or seventeen years of age, reported that Dick had fantasized aloud about having sex with the young Sally. Dick told Davey that "after doing of it to her once or twice that he could do it to her at any time he pleased afterward, that she would be big enough." Davey also overhead Dick try to entice the young girl with the promise of a red apple.[30]

Another teenage slave, Sam, also testified that over the summer Dick had confided to him that he planned to have sexual intercourse with Sally "two or three times if she would not be large enough." Celia, another of Briggs's slaves, likewise recalled that she had overheard Dick ask "Miss Sally" if she wanted to be his wife and "the child said yes." None of these three slaves, though they had reason to suspect that Dick might try to sexually assault young Sally, ever reported their observations to their master or mistress.[31] Dick was found guilty and executed.[32]

A slave such as Dick, accused of sexually assaulting his master's young daughter, had very little hope of reprieve. In the eyes of the law and white society, he had committed two of the most egregious transgressions imaginable: the rape or attempted rape of a white child, and the rape or attempted rape of a member of his master's family. Master and slave inhabited the same physical space. Living in such close proximity required tremendous trust in one's bondsmen. A severe breach by a slave, such as the sexual assault of a member of the master's family, jeopardized the very linchpin of the institution of slavery and required severe retribution. For these reasons, in most cases in which slaves were found guilty of sexually assaulting girls of the master class, reprieves and/or pardons were not generally forthcoming, as they sometimes were when the young accuser was not wealthy.

Antebellum Virginia communities, courts, and elected officials vigorously prosecuted and punished slaves accused of raping or attempting to rape young white girls, especially those related to a slave master. There are a couple of notable exceptions, however, in which the convicted slaves escaped death sentences. These exceptions, admittedly atypical, warrant consideration, for they suggest that sometimes the courts considered other factors in adjudicating the final outcome, even though slaves believed to have been guilty of sexually assaulting a master's young female relative were usually treated harshly. A Henrico County, Virginia, court ruled in 1860 that Patrick had indeed attempted to have carnal knowledge of his master's niece. Nonetheless, the jury spared his life. Patrick belonged to Charles Vest, but resided and worked at the home of Dr. N. A. "Gus" Vest, Charles's son. We know little about Patrick, except that he was probably somewhat old and crippled—he was frequently referred to as "Old Uncle Patrick."[33]

As witnesses recounted for the court, it was a night in late November, when the Vest household had long since retired for the night. Dr. and Mrs. Vest were asleep in their bedchamber. Two young girls slept upstairs. One, Lelia Wingfield, was the eleven-year-old niece of the Vests and had been staying with them for several months in order to attend school. The other girl, Adelaide Kidd, aged twelve years, was a boarder. The two shared the same bed.[34]

Not long after Mrs. Vest had retired, she was awakened by noise she assumed was made by an intruder entering the house. She heard someone open the outer door, then crash into the opened door of a nearby medicine chest. Alarmed, she awakened her husband who, seemingly annoyed at being awakened, said it must have been the dog. "I told him the dog could not open the door," his wife sarcastically testified, obviously perturbed by her husband's indifference. A few minutes later, screams from upstairs pierced the darkness. Reflecting continued insensitivity, the doctor sent a servant to investigate the cause of the disturbance. The Vests' niece, Lelia Wingfield, was quite shaken. She asserted that "Old Uncle Patrick" had entered her room. But her uncle still dismissed the commotion as the antics of the family dog. Although Lelia continued to insist it had been Patrick, Vest wrote it off as a bad dream. Later, when she was alone with her aunt and out of earshot of her uncle, Lelia confided that a hand placed under her "drawers" had startled her. Dazed by slumber, she assumed it had to be the hand of her bedmate. "I asked Addie what on earth she was doing." She then touched the hand that was probing her undergarments and discovered a large, rough hand obviously not belonging to her bedmate. Lelia screamed, and the intruder quickly jerked his hand away. She rolled over and through the ample light from the moon could see that it was "Old Uncle Patrick." He shook his fist at her threateningly, warning her to be quiet. When pressed by both family members and the court, Lelia positively identified Patrick as her assailant.[35]

Circumstances all but ensured a guilty verdict in the case of the Commonwealth against Patrick. Throughout the trial, the character of Patrick's accuser was never challenged. Lelia Wingfield's blood ties to Patrick's master no doubt lent her credibility. Aside from Lelia's integrity and social status, other factors seemed to warrant a guilty verdict. Foremost, there was never any question about the identity of the perpetrator. Despite these factors, however, the court decided on sale and transportation, not death, as the appropriate punishment for this slave convicted of the attempted rape of his master's niece.[36]

What would account for this leniency? The defense offered no evidence undermining the credibility of Lelia Wingfield. There was no testimony about illicit sexual behavior of the prosecutrix that when offered up in slave rape trials of white women proved highly effective in securing reprieves for convicted slave rapists.[37] Lelia's uncle's behavior—his predisposition to disbelieve his niece—might have established the tenor of the trial, planting doubt in the minds of jurors. Vest, for whatever reason, seemed quite reluctant to believe that Patrick would have made such an unwanted, salacious attack. Perhaps years of loyal service may have made Vest all too willing to view his niece's accusation as misguided and mistaken, though not malicious.

More nefarious motives undergirded the accusation by John Burgess that his slave, twenty-year-old George, had raped his young daughter. In 1832, the Henry County, Virginia, slave was tried, found guilty of rape, and sentenced to hang on the basis of the father's allegation. Shortly thereafter, the Commonwealth's own attorney filed a motion with the same court summoning John Burgess to answer allegations that he had perjured himself during testimony in the trial of George. Burgess, it came to light, had had George severely whipped, possibly rather excessively, for playing the fiddle and dancing. Someone, possibly a neighbor, inquired into the reason for George's whipping. Burgess lied, saying that George was being whipped for the rape of his daughter. While the face-saving ploy may have made a severe beating of a slave palatable to community members, it created additional problems for Burgess, who was forced to continue the lie, bring the matter before authorities, and now stood to lose his slave property through state execution. But if he admitted lying while under oath, he risked prosecution for perjury. While the truth was eventually discovered and George spared a wrongful execution, the conviction was not entirely set aside. Under the circumstances, George was transported instead of hanged. Perhaps this official action was intended to punish Burgess more than George. It is also important to note that the local court convicted George for the rape of Burgess's daughter on what had to have been flimsy evidence, suggesting that accusations of slave rape made by members of the slaveholding class were taken very seriously.[38]

On a few occasions white communities became so outraged by news of a slave raping the female relative of a slave owner that lynch mobs formed, a relatively rare occurrence against slaves in the antebellum era. Mobs were most likely to form when it appeared that the authorities were dealing with the suspect too evenhandedly. For instance, James Thornton's slave was believed to be responsible for the 1855 rape and murder of Thornton's fourteen-year-old daughter. Alabama officials, fearing mob violence, granted a change of venue, but to no avail. A group of enraged citizens seized the alleged rapist from jail, chained him to a stake on the site where the murder was believed to have been committed, and burned him alive in full view of two to three thousand blacks and an untold number of whites.[39]

Of course, lynch mobs could also threaten when the children of non-slaveholders accused slaves of rape. U. B. Phillips cited an instance of a Deep South mob seizing a black man charged with sexually assaulting a white girl. The incident occurred in Georgia in 1851. The Columbus *Sentinel* reported that a "negro man" had attempted to rape a "little girl." After a "fair" trial, an "intelligent" jury rendered a guilty verdict. Despite the conviction, some community members continued to believe in the innocence of the man. That group began a campaign to secure a pardon for him and circulated a petition that was "very numerously signed." The petition was forwarded to the governor of Georgia who granted a full pardon. By the time news of the pardon reached the community, substantial crowds had already gathered in anticipation of the execution. The mob refused to disperse and eventually overpowered the sheriff, seized the "unfortunate culprit," and hanged him.[40]

Mobs threatened in other slave-child rape cases as well. The mother of twelve-year-old Lucy Dallas Beazley, who had charged a Virginia slave with rape in 1856, threatened to have him shot if he were not found guilty and hanged.[41] And in 1858, an Alabama slave was alleged to have raped a girl aged eleven or twelve. He was arrested but was seized from the jail by a vengeful mob before he could be tried. The crowd intended to burn the slave at the stake and was in the act of "applying the torch" when some of those present objected, stating that such an action "would not be in keeping with the custom of an enlightened and civilized community." He was then hanged from a nearby tree.[42]

The alleged rape of non-slaveholding children by slaves was far less likely to evoke either extralegal violence or swift, harsh official responses. Such cases differed from elite incidents in another respect. The accusations of slaves raping the children of the non-slaveholding were much more numerous. Moreover, the outcomes of those trials were much more ambiguous and unpredictable, suggesting that these female children were less likely to receive sympathy and support than the children of the privileged class. To be sure, many were prosecuted to the fullest extent of the law.

Typical is the 1822 case of a Wood County, Virginia, slave who was convicted and hanged for having carnal knowledge of a six-year-old white girl. The court transcript contains the testimony of a single eyewitness, James Rickman, who happened upon the assault while he was hunting turkeys. He saw the head of Jack, the accused, at first mistaking him for a turkey. Realizing his mistake, Rickman then observed that the slave was lying on top of a young girl. When pressed, he could not swear that actual penetration had taken place. Nor did he observe any evidence of semen on or near the girl's body. Proof of ejaculation, of course, aided in the corroboration of establishing rape. Evidence of seminal emission was not a required component of Virginia rape law, although some local judges could have operated under the incorrect assumption that it was required.[43] What Rickman did see, however, were the "privates of the prisoner exposed and his pantaloons unbuttoned." He also observed the accused "endeavor to open the private parts of the child." He added that Jack was "spitting up on his penis apparently in the act of preparing it." The court found Jack guilty of carnally knowing and abusing Barbara Carpenter. Consequently, he was hanged.[44]

Dinwiddie, a slave belonging to John Lamb of Sussex County, Virginia, suffered the same fate in 1826 for attempting an assault on thirteen-year-old Mary Jane Holloway, who was walking home with her younger sister and cousin.[45] According to testimony, a black male followed the three, passed them, and feigned to be cutting brush with a knife. He then tried to catch Jane Judkins, Holloway's cousin, but she escaped. He caught Mary Jane Holloway instead. The other two girls escaped and ran for help. Holloway testified that Dinwiddie laid her down in the woods,"pulled up her clothes, pulled down his breaches and got upon her." He made her "kiss him twice and take hold of his black thing," all the while brandishing a knife near her throat. Dinwiddie was charged with attempting to rape Mary Jane Holloway, although it is not clear whether he actually consummated his assault. It is possible that Holloway might have been too embarrassed to testify about such details as penetration and/or ejaculation. Given strict Victorian taboos and sensibilities that forbade discussions about sexuality and sex acts, even privately among family members and friends, a reluctance to graphically describe an act of sexual violation publicly and before strangers seems reasonable. And without testimony acknowledging the requisite penetration, attempted rape was the only crime with which Dinwiddie could be charged. Even so Dinwiddie was executed, apparently without any interference from community or slaveholder.[46]

The circumstances of some alleged assaults shed light on why a disproportionate number of non-slaveholding girls brought forth charges of rape against slaves. Many of the non-slaveholding child victims of sexual assault were attacked while walking along public roads or other poorly traveled areas. Children in the nineteenth-century South, as in many rural cultures, typically provided invaluable service to their families by running errands that often required traveling unaccompanied or with other children to remote or distant places. Isolation then made these children likely prey for sex offenders of all races. In contrast, female members of the elite class were far less likely to be sent on such errands alone or accompanied by other children.

One such errand cost young Sally Hudgins of Cumberland County, Virginia, her life. The Hudgins family found their ten-year-old daughter dead in a pool of water near a spring one summer day in 1826. Sally Hudgins had been sent there to fetch a jar of milk. At first, her father, William Hudgins, thought his daughter must have been struck by lightning. Further investigation revealed, however, that her clothes had been pulled over her head, intimating a sexual assault. Various deponents testified that Sally Hudgins had been severely beaten; her shoulder, throat, and thighs were black from bruises, indicating the child must have put up a struggle.[47]

For unstated reasons, suspicion quickly fell upon Charles, a slave owned by Robert Austin. One community member described him as "the vilest negro in the neighbourhood." Even Charles's mistress, Judith Austin, suspected him. He had been "roguish" and "frequently offended the neighbours." Likewise, her husband called Charles a rogue who would steal "any little thing." Charles's demeanor, his reputation for incalcitrance, and "his looks" had convinced Judith Austin that he had murdered the Hudgins girl.[48]

More substantive evidence was offered by Ginsey Hudgins, the deceased's sister, and a female Hudgins slave, who reported they had been pelted by "clods" earlier in the day near the spring where Sally was murdered. Both believed they had been hurled by Charles, who was lying near the corner of the fence nearby.[49] Eventually Charles confessed to the crime, explaining he had been "plaguing" Sally Hudgins and was afraid that she would tell her parents, who would have him whipped. Charles made no mention of any sexual motives for the attack, which principals had deduced from the bruises on her inner thighs and from the position of her clothes that had been pulled above her head. Charles was found guilty of murder and hanged.[50]

An isolated locale was the site of an alleged attack on a white schoolgirl by a slave in Buckingham County, Virginia, in 1856. Late one September afternoon, Mary Harris had been on her way home from school when, she claimed, she and a younger sister encountered a black male driving a wagon near the local sawmill. He later reappeared, about one-quarter mile from her home, grabbed Mary, dragged her into the woods where he beat her about the head with a stick and attempted to rape her.[51] Her younger sister ran off to get some help.[52] The assailant, whom Mary identified as the slave Jesse, left the Harris girl and fled into the woods, but not before Mary had put up a good struggle against her violent attacker. Harris's mother described the many scratches on Mary's face as well as bruises and cuts on her head.[53] Despite testimony vouching for Jesse's politeness and general obedience to white people, he was hanged.[54]

Soon after Mary Harris's purported assault in 1856, twelve-year-old Lucy Dallas Beazley of Spotsylvania County also claimed to have been attacked by a slave known as Anderson while returning from a visit to her grandmother's one afternoon. Like Mary Harris, Lucy Beazley had been traveling on a road when attacked, about one mile from home. A younger sister also accompanied her.[55]

Like most of the other young complainants, Lucy Beazley reported having been severely beaten, a factor that seems likely to have weighed heavily among jury members deciding this and other child rape cases. Use of force by the assailant all but ruled out the accuser's consent, if it were in question. And as in other cases in which young girls claimed to have been attacked, Beazley struggled, resisting the assailant's advances "as long as she could stand." Her attacker threatened to kill her if she cried out, claiming to have a pistol in his pocket. In the end, help did not come in time. "He threw me down and pulled up my clothes and . . . he penetrated my body with his peanis [*sic*]." The court found Anderson the slave guilty and sentenced him to hang.[56]

What followed was a bewildering whirlwind of activity that seems to have been orchestrated by Anderson's owner, William Goodwin, and spawned by posttrial disclosures that the purported attack had not played out exactly as Lucy Beazley claimed. Such confusion and contradictions were not uncommon when the accuser was quite young, as in Beasley's case. The new revelations cast doubt on Beazley family testimony that, for one, Anderson had completed the rape, and two, that Lucy had been hurt in the attack as she claimed. After the trial, Lucy Beazley's uncle, Atwell Cornwall [?], purportedly confided to someone named Joseph Sanford that the errant slave had not actually accomplished the rape of his niece. Four days later, Sanford's wife, Agnes, revealed to officials that prior to the trial, Clementina Beazley, the accuser's mother, had told her that the slave had attempted to commit a rape upon her daughter, but had not succeeded. Lucy Beazley, present during this conversation, did not deny her mother's version of the attack. Anderson's owner, William Goodwin, also swore out an affidavit stating that his father had requested that the girl be examined for evidence of a rape, but that none had been performed. And yet another citizen reported that Lucy's grandmother's husband, Isaac Cornwall [?] claimed there were no marks about Lucy's neck, as had been claimed in court.[57]

Confusion about whether or not the act of rape had been consummated permeated the proceedings as well as the discussion that followed. A child's confusion over the nature of the assault, ignorance of sexuality, and reticence over publicly testifying about a sexual assault may account all, or in part, for such uncertainty. And proof of seminal emission, evidence of penetration, as observed in this exchange, mattered in the eyes of the law because without it, the accused would be guilty of nothing more than an attempt.[58] No doubt, especially in the cases of children or young girls, much of the confusion about whether a rape had been completed stemmed from ignorance of or embarrassment about sexual relations.

Elizabeth Smith's testimony against a slave for rape sheds some light on this state of confusion about what constituted rape. Smith, described by some as a "very simple weak woman," contradicted herself in testimony in the 1819 rape trial of Dennis. Dennis was charged with rape although Smith testified that he "did not enter her body." Dennis's attorney, clearly exasperated with the contradictory testimony, asked of Smith, "In plain english, did he fuck you[?]" Smith answered that he had, that he had "done as he pleased, Rogered her and got off, after satisfying himself."[59]

Proof of ejaculation during a rape received much attention for nonlegal reasons as well. In the nineteenth-century South, a patriarchal, racist society, a raped woman or girl constituted damaged goods. Evidence of consummation would have had profound and long-lasting social and personal consequences for a victim of rape. If ejaculation had taken place, the rape victim may have been seen as "polluted, especially when the assailant was a black man," and therefore tainted for the rest of her life. Anna Clark's study of rape in nineteenth-century England informs us about the burden Lucy Beazley and her family would have been saddled with for the rest of her life. Clark observes that men "seemed to view ejaculation as a physical pollution or despoilation of a woman, rendering her damaged property forever."

It is understandable, then, that family members might have urged their young daughters to deny that ejaculation had taken place, helping us to understand the nature of the conflicting and contradictory versions recounted by Beazley family members. Lucy's mother telling neighbors the rape had not been consummated, but telling the court it had, may reflect the family's ambivalence at wanting justice for the sexual violation of Lucy but knowing that it was likely to cost ostracism by the community, and ultimately a low probability of marriage for Lucy.[60] Despite the obvious harm to Lucy's reputation, Lucy's mother, Clementina, testified that she had no doubt her daughter had been raped and "very much wounded." Lucy buttressed her mother's testimony with unequivocal affirmation that the act had taken place. He "penetrated my body with his peanis [*sic*]. I was very much wounded."[61]

Whether or not Anderson actually consummated the act of rape upon Lucy Beazley made little practical difference in the eyes of Virginia's slave law. A slave convicted of either the rape or attempted rape of a white female faced the death penalty. Clearly, though, Anderson's master, William Goodwin, understood that if Anderson had any chance of a reprieve, doubt about the consummation of the rape would have to be cultivated.[62]

Like many girls in the rural South, Lucy Beazley, accompanied only by a younger sister, proved to be an easy target for any man bent on taking sex by force or coercion. Opportunity—in this case, Lucy's traveling on an isolated road—appears to have played an important role in shaping the circumstances of sexual assault of southern white women and girls. In all likelihood, Anderson, if he were guilty of the crime alleged, simply took advantage of the vulnerability of a young girl. Would he have attacked had Lucy been much older? Did her youthfulness make her a more attractive target? Was she purposefully targeted because she was not an elite member of white society? Were some slaves, like other members of society, simply pedophiles? Or were slave attacks of girls merely random acts?

Trying to assess a rapist's motives and modus operandi is tricky business even in contemporary cases.[63] Looking back a hundred and fifty years and imagining what a rapist might have been thinking seems all the more futile and elusive. Nonetheless, by exploring why some slaves seem to have targeted female children, most particularly those of the poorer and middling classes, we can learn something about what nineteenth-century southerners, black and white, thought about sexual violence, childhood, and sexuality as well as conventions of gender and class.

If slaves viewed young girls as easy prey—physically weak, easily manipulated—and less credible witnesses, the number of such girls who reported their crimes, bringing them to the attention of the courts, must have come as a surprise to their attackers. When threatened with death or physical violence, some girls remained quiet and compliant, but usually only for a short time. Eventually, they seem to have confided in someone close to them who often took the first step in lodging a formal complaint. Moreover, we know from court depositions that many if not most of these young girls, despite their youth, fought back, either physically or by reporting their assault to others.[64]

Some slaves might have hoped to capitalize on a perception that young girls, as children, were less credible accusers than adult females. Given the serious consequences in a slave rape case, courts did seem intent on establishing the credibility of girl accusers by carefully scrutinizing their testimony. Eleven-year-old Rosanna Green's prior history of making mischief and "telling tales" made her accusation of rape against the slave Gabriel seem less than truthful and was probably crucial in the slave's eventual pardon. In the case of four-year-old Sally Briggs, even her own mother at one point asked her "if what she had said was not a story." Ultimately, the integrity of Lucy Dallas Beazley was also impeached, although not sufficiently or timely enough to spare the life of her alleged rapist. And recall that eleven-year-old Lelia Wingfield's own uncle doubted her accusations that "Old Uncle Patrick" had entered her bedroom as she claimed.[65] It would seem, then, if these examples are any indication, that white southerners were not necessarily inclined to take the word of a young accuser, given the serious nature of the assault, without some sort of independent corroboration or interrogation of the veracity of the accuser. Assumptions about the innate innocence of children seem not to have applied here.

The youthfulness of some of these victims also jeopardized the successful prosecution of the sexual assault cases in another way. Law proscribed the sworn testimony of those too young to comprehend the notion of swearing an oath. However, the crime of rape is rarely witnessed by anyone other than the victim herself. Consequently, state attorneys often had to rely on the second-hand testimony of a mother or older sibling, which may not have had the impact on a jury that the testimony of the victim herself would have had. In addition, assuming they were old enough to testify in court, child accusers typically made poor witnesses because their lack of experience and knowledge about sexual relations and anatomy often yielded vague, unspecific, even contradictory testimony about the assault and thus provided defense attorneys with ammunition for cross-examination.

Moreover, when female children accused black men of sexual assault, their reputations might be scrutinized for evidence of debauchery and deceit, just as readily as adult accusers. Indeed, mere blood ties to an adult female might be enough to throw doubt on a child's claim of rape.[66] Although a Frederick County, Virginia, court found free black Tasco Thompson guilty of the attempted rape of eleven-year-old Mary Jane Stevens, the jury penned an appeal for leniency on the grounds that the girl's mother "had long entertained negroes." The jury reasoned that Thompson had "repaired to the house of Mrs. Stevens in the belief that she would cheerfully submit to his embraces, as she doubtless had often done before, but finding her absent he probably supposed his embraces would be equally agreeable to her daughter."[67] Hence, a black man could purposefully target a female child for sexual assault, knowing that any one or more of these factors might allow him to escape prosecution or punishment, though admittedly the risk was high.

It is difficult to estimate what percentage of slave rape victims were children. Since the specific age of an accuser in a rape case is not always stipulated in court, it is difficult to identify accusers by precise age. Still, data drawn from Virginia cases of slave rape or attempted rape from 1800 to 1860 reveal a relatively small percentage of white girls who levied charges of rape against slaves. Of the 123 instances in which white females swore out complaints against slaves for sex crimes, only eleven were identified as girls thirteen or younger, roughly 8 percent.[68] That statistic seems low by both regional and chronological comparisons. However, given that rape trials of young girls frequently revealed that their attackers either threatened or bribed them into remaining silent, a low level of reporting is not unexpected. We cannot know how many children actually came forward with experiences of sexual assault, but certainly many children kept their attacks secret out of fear.

The low incidence of reported sexual assaults of white girl children also fails to speak to the frequency of child molestation by acquaintances and family members.[69] Finally, it is entirely possible that black child molesters targeted slave children, which would also have gone unreported to authorities.

When compared to sexual assaults in New York City from 1790 to 1820, the number of child sexual assaults in the antebellum South still seems quite low. Marybeth Hamilton Arnold found that fully one-third of the 48 cases of sexual assault brought before the New York County Court of General Sessions involved girls under the age of fourteen. Similarly, Christine Stansell found that in a random sample of 101 rape cases in New York City between 1820 and 1860, 26 involved complainants under the age of sixteen years, or roughly one-quarter. Of these, 19 were under twelve years of age. A very recent study of New York City in the early twentieth century yields similar results. Stephen Robertson, in looking at select sexual assault cases from 1886 to 1921, finds that about 26 percent of all rape cases involved children as the accusers.[70]

What might account for such a wide disparity between the incidence of child rape in New York City and a single southern state? Arnold argues that children in the urban working-class culture of New York City were saddled with tremendous adult responsibilities that at times blurred sexual boundaries as well.[71] Stansell also grounds part of her explanation in aspects of the burgeoning urban, commercial environment, namely, the transition of working-class men's understanding of class from an essentially masculine entity to a heterosexual one, an outgrowth of which was a new code of sexual behavior that was more abusive and exploitative of all females, including young ones.[72]

Clearly the rural antebellum south did not reflect the urban, cultural milieu of New York City of the same era. The socioeconomic and ethnic factors that thrust countless young girls into the streets of New York did not exist in the South. Poor and middling children living in a rural culture nonetheless performed essential chores that made them vulnerable to attacks at times. They were frequently called upon to fetch water, gather eggs, pick berries, or run a message to a neighbor, all of which potentially placed them alone or with other children in secluded spots. In short, young girls or children in rural areas may have been attacked simply because they were accessible and unprotected. Children of the poorer to middling classes, moreover, would have been even more vulnerable, simply because elite children in slaveholding families would not have been performing such mundane tasks. But only additional studies will determine whether or not the low incidence of reported child rape in the antebellum South accurately reflected the extent of the crime.

While most cases of slave rape of female children resulted in death sentences for the convicted rapists, the evidence suggests that white communities seriously deliberated such cases and did not axiomatically find the accused slave rapists of children guilty. Sometimes, for example, juries found ways around finding a slave guilty of raping a child by settling instead on a lesser offense. A Georgia slave went on trial in 1849 for the rape of a white four-year-old girl. The jury ultimately found insufficient evidence on the charge of assault with intent to rape, settling instead on assault and battery, which, when committed upon a white person was nonetheless a capital offense.[73]

Sometimes even slaves who were convicted of sexually assaulting girls found themselves the recipients of rather lenient sentences, suggesting that even though southerners tended to come down hard on child rapists, there were exceptions. In Louisiana, a special tribunal found a slave named David guilty of assault with intent to commit rape of a white girl under ten years of age. He was ordered to receive two hundred lashes and a sentence of ten years of hard labor in prison—hardly a mild punishment, but a far cry from execution.[74] And as far back as 1724, a slave from Spotsylvania County, Virginia, was convicted of the attempted rape and buggery of a four-year-old white girl only to receive rather minimal corporal punishment: twenty-one lashes, one-half hour standing at the pillory, and the severe cropping of both ears.[75]

Young girls also learned that, as with adult female accusers, whiteness did not necessarily shield them from official or community scrutiny. Despite the seriousness with which white officials and residents appear to have viewed child rape, youthfulness did not completely render girl children immune from charges of improper sexual conduct. As with white women who accused slaves of sexual assault, a girl's low status in the community was inextricably linked to notions of depravity and debauchery. The case of the servant girl, Rosanna Green, demonstrates that ample sympathy among certain whites for a slave charged with the attempted rape of a white girl could be effectively mobilized to spare his life. In the process, interclass and intraracial antipathy was bared.

Rosanna Green complained to a slave woman on Good Friday in 1829 that forty-year-old Gabriel had attempted to have his way with her. Rosanna had been sent by Mrs. Kincer, her mistress, to look for eggs in the hayloft of the barn. There, Green claimed, Gabriel grabbed her, covered her mouth, and carried her to the end of the barn where he attempted to have sex with her.[76]

Few good things were said by anyone about the character and integrity of Rosanna Green, an eleven-year-old orphaned servant girl who lived in Wythe County, Virginia, with the family of Peter Kincer. Neighbors, slaves, and Gabriel's owner, Kincer, rallied to defend slave Gabriel from Rosanna's charge of attempted rape. Rachel, the slave to whom Rosanna had complained about Gabriel's behavior, testified that the servant girl had appeared angry at the time, but afterward was in good humor. Rachel also reported having heard rumors that Green had "behaved badly with a black boy in the neighborhood." Another slave, Milly, swore that Green had a reputation for "telling stories" and "making mischief," which seriously jeopardized the credibility of her testimony.[77]

White neighbors and Rosanna's own master and mistress, whom she had learned to call mother and father, also derided her character. Both Catharine and Peter Kincer claimed that Green was practically incapable of telling the truth. Neighbor Joseph Atkins considered Green a girl of "bad character on account of telling lies." He also reported as fact the charge that she had had sex with a six-year-old "negro boy" from the neighborhood.[78]

In fact, the lone advocate for Rosanna Green was an uncle, William Mingle, who had taken out the warrant against Gabriel on Rosanna's behalf. Although his deposition contains no information about Green herself, Mingle did divulge a rift his actions had caused with his sister-in-law, Catharine Kincer. Kincer resented Mingle's interference in what she no doubt regarded as a personal, not a community, matter.[79]

The court found Gabriel guilty, but extenuating circumstances led the court, no doubt persuaded by the barrage of defamatory testimony against the eleven-year-old girl, to recommend leniency. This decision provoked outrage in at least one white citizen of Wythe County, prompting him to complain to the governor, and thereby demonstrating that sympathy for the slave was by no means universal. In a letter to the governor urging the executive to disregard pleas for leniency for Gabriel, the convicted rapist, Alexander Smyth wrote:

> I think it right to say, that I apprehend him [Gabriel, the slave] a proper subject to be made an example, and that an example is required. It is not many years since a man suffered emasculation for an attempt on his mistress; and a few days since a youth received 120 lashes from his master for an attempt on a girl. This fellow seems to be 40, and is notorious as a thief.[80]

Enclosed with the letter was a newspaper clipping that conveyed sympathy for the orphan girl. "[H]ad her father been living, or, had she have had any natural protector, who had reaked [*sic*] the vengeance due to such an offence, in the blood of the perpetrator, we could never have consented to his punishment for the offence."[81] In other words, male kin would have sought personal justice through revenge and not allowed the girl to be vilified in the local court.

Likewise, we can infer that the author of the letter perceived class bias in the adjudication process. Had Rosanna Green not been a servant girl, the outcome might have been substantially different. In the end, Smyth's appeal went unheeded, the slave's life was spared, and he was sold and transported out of Virginia.[82] The Kincers had succeeded in saving their slave's life, but lost his services nonetheless. Based upon their testimony, we can imagine that they were quite perturbed at the loss of a good, sturdy slave merely on the say-so of a disreputable, troublesome child who was more replaceable than her alleged assailant. The attempted sexual assault of a white child by a slave in the antebellum South, at least in this case, did not seem to some to warrant the death of the slave.

Sometimes the mere association of girls with deviant female family members was enough to taint them as well. Victoria Bynum documents the white-on-white rape case of a fifteen-year-old North Carolina boy convicted of raping of a young girl. Over a hundred and twenty Guilford County residents signed a petition to that state's governor soliciting a pardon for the teenage boy on the grounds that the "mother of the victim was of bad character and her daughter . . . [was] completely under her domination."[83] Similar disdain was shown for the mother of Mary Jane Stevens, the eleven-year-old Virginian who in 1833 charged

a free black man with attempted rape. Because her mother had con-
sorted with blacks, both she and her mother "yielded their claims to the
protection of the law."[84]

The sympathy displayed for the black assailants of Rosanna Green
and Mary Jane Stevens, however significant, was not typical in the antebellum South. The rape of children or child molestation seems to have
been perceived as especially heinous, whether committed by black or
white men. White men, too, occasionally were sentenced to die for raping children.[85] There are several antebellum cases in which white men
were officially charged with sexually assaulting young girls. For example, in 1810 William Dick, a Virginia laborer from Monroe County and
himself the father of three, was convicted of raping Nancy Maddy, a
child between the ages of ten and twelve. Dick received a stiff eighteen-
year solitary confinement sentence, nearly the most severe penalty allowed by law. Despite the stiff sentence, however, the governor pardoned Dick in January 1824, four years prior to the end of his sentence.
Ironically, as despicable as the rape must have been viewed, as is evidenced from the sentence, several petitions expressed great sympathy
for Dick's plight, including apparently members of the Maddy clan
who acknowledged that although they "view this crime with the utmost horror," they were willing to forgive.[86]

Importantly, white men in Virginia, unlike slaves, usually did not
face the death penalty for the rape or attempted rape of girls. Some
southern states, however, did hold out death sentences for white
rapists of children. Through published appellate decisions we are
made aware of several cases of whites who were sentenced to death
after their conviction for the rape of underage females. The earliest
nineteenth-century case appeared in South Carolina in 1813 when
Francis LeBlanc was convicted of raping a seven-year-old girl in his
barber shop one August afternoon. The child refrained from telling
anyone for several days until her mother noticed blood on her underclothes. A medical examination not only confirmed the assault but
also revealed that the young girl had contracted the "same disease"
as the defendant had been suffering from, probably venereal disease.
LeBlanc's appeal proved unsuccessful. The South Carolina jurists refused to "rescue him from the punishment he so justly deserves."[87]
Quite possibly, the jury believed LeBlanc to be especially depraved
because he had been infected with a sexually transmitted disease,
made all the more heinous when he infected a young girl.

Two residents of North Carolina were likewise convicted of raping children in the mid-1800s. Both of them were sentenced to hang. A Cumberland County courtroom was the stage for the rape trial of Alfred Terry, also known as Alfred Goings. Terry was charged with raping seven-year-old Mary M. Cook.[88] Several years later, in 1844, Jesse Farmer, a Bertie County laborer, was convicted of raping Mary Ann Taylor, a ten-year-old girl.[89] Both convictions were upheld; both men presumably received the death penalty.

White southerners at the local level, then, typically displayed the utmost abhorrence for perpetrators of child rape, regardless of the race of the accused, as manifested in the very harsh sentences handed down. Courts were especially tough on the accused when there was evidence of violence used to effect the rapes. In a highly paternalistic society, the question of whom to protect was usually settled on the side of the white female child. Both black and white men convicted of raping white girls could and sometimes did suffer death for their purported offenses. Moreover, the rape trials of children were characterized by a higher degree of consensus about the accused's guilt than in any other kind of sexual assault case. Still, slaves convicted of sexually assaulting female children faced death much more frequently than white men.

As a rule, the rape of white children was viewed as particularly heinous and generally not tolerated by antebellum southern communities. But what of cases in which the accusers were African American girls? Did they fall outside the protection of the law, as most scholars have claimed? Admittedly, there are very few cases in which slave children (or women for that matter) officially brought charges of rape against either a black or white man. Most scholars have assumed that African American females were not protected by rape legislation.[90] Indeed, their unique status as both property and human beings problematized the issue of sexual assault. How could property be sexually violated? Historians have also been well aware that masters and their sons probably represented the greatest sexual threat to their female slaves. Since a master's consent and/or intercession would have been necessary to file charges of rape, the absurdity of masters seeking redress for the slaves they had violated is readily apparent. Moreover, the rape of a white female—an unmarried daughter, for example—unquestionably damaged the girl's reputation, leaving a patriarch with a daughter who might never marry because she was considered damaged goods and creating a real lifelong burden for her family.

The rape of a slave child, however, posed no similar risk or threat to a white patriarch, unless of course the rape was accompanied by significant violence. In fact, in older girls, rapes could result in pregnancies that would actually benefit the master. Nor would masters have the incentive to subject male slaves to trials for the rape of slave females. The punishment of any slave would directly affect the condition and value of his property. So there was little incentive for a master to seek redress from the courts. In all probability, when made aware of the sexual assault of slave girls, masters took matters into their own hands, if they acted at all.

Conditions and circumstances of bondage, then, virtually precluded slave females from seeking the protection of the white courts from sexual assault. Nevertheless, it would be inaccurate to say, as most legal and southern historians have, that African American females were not regarded as rapeable in the eyes of the law. Invariably, most cite the 1859 Mississippi case of the slave George who was tried and convicted for raping a slave girl. Ironically, it was George's defense attorney, not the white prosecutor, who argued that the "crime of rape does not exist in this State between African slaves." He reasoned that the "regulations of law, as to the white race, on the subject of sexual intercourse, do not and cannot, for obvious reasons, apply to slaves; . . . the violation of a female slave by a male slave would be a mere assault and battery." The defendant's counsel went on to cite Mississippi statute law that made the slave rape of white women a capital offense. In short, counsel asserted, there was no provision under common or statutory law that made the rape of slave women or girls an offense, let alone a capital one. The high court concurred.[91]

But the harsh, antiseptic tone of the appellate case of George should not be the only consideration shaping our understanding of rape law and female slaves. Several overlooked aspects of the case suggest that not all white Mississippians would have agreed with the high court's finding. First, someone had to have been motivated to bring the charge to the attention of local law officials—perhaps the master of the young victim, or possibly an outraged neighbor. The published record simply is not forthcoming with this type of information. A white person learned of the assault and appealed to local officials to file charges against the alleged rapist, George. Second, some justice of the peace or magistrate took the complaint seriously enough not to dismiss it out of hand and followed through with issuing a warrant. Third—and this fact is often overlooked—an all-white Mississippi jury found the slave guilty of raping the slave girl! Apparently, white neighbors who sat in judgment of George believed the young slave child capable of being raped, the law notwithstanding.[92]

Furthermore, and this point has in fact been made, the case appears to have prompted state lawmakers into action. Before the end of that year, the Mississippi legislature passed a law making the actual or attempted rape by a "negro or mulatto" on a female "negro or mulatto, under twelve years of age" punishable with death or whipping, as determined by the jury. Neighboring Georgia soon followed suit by amending its rape law to embrace slave women. Punishment for a white man raping a white female was two to twenty years in the penitentiary; for the rape of a female of color, fine and imprisonment, "at the discretion of the court."[93] The racial disparity in punishment is glaring and irrefutable. But in crafting the statute, the Mississippi and Georgia lawmakers were conceding that slave females were owed some element of legal protection from sexual violation.

Though quite scarce, there are cases of white men charged with raping slave girls. One Tennessee slave girl's owner brought charges of rape against James Keyton, a white man. The grand jury handed down an indictment in the case, although he was eventually acquitted. Still, it is instructive to recognize that some members of the white community—the girl's master, the magistrate or justice of the peace, a grand jury—responded to a charge of rape of a slave girl just as they would have done had a white girl claimed to have been raped.[94] Perhaps some had been appalled by the blatant use of force in the attack. Or it is possible that enslaved children may have been considered, in a very loose sense, part of the paternalistic household and a master may have felt compelled to seek redress for reasons of personal honor. Only with more dogged research in the local court records will we be able to determine the extent to which slave children were accorded legal protection from white or black sexual predators.

One Virginia case of the rape of an African American child that aroused a tremendous amount of anger and emotion was that of Ned, the property of Walter Mills of Fredericksburg, Virginia. Ned was over sixty years of age and worked as a sexton at a cemetery in Fredericksburg. He went on trial in the spring of 1859 for raping two children, a six-year-old African American girl, Betty Gordon, and her friend, nine-year-old Eunice Thompson, a white child. According to

Betty Gordon's testimony, Ned lured her into the cemetery with the promise of flowers. There, he gave her something sweet to drink. Ned told her it would do her good. He then raped her. She deposed, "He pulled down his clothes. He hurt me. He put his paenis [sic] against me. He tried to put it in my body. I do not know whether he did get it in or not. It hurt me very badly."[95]

Ned alternately held out threats and rewards in an attempt to secure Betty's silence about the assault. He threatened to dig a hole and put her in it. He also said he would eat her, and that he would cut off her head with a nearby sickle. But he also promised to buy her some biscuits. The combination of threats and bribes proved very effective, and Betty kept their secret—for a time.[96]

No doubt a terrified Betty did her best to avoid Ned, a nearly impossible task, since her aunt sent her to fetch water from a spring near the cemetery two or three times a day. A few days after the alleged rape, on a Saturday afternoon Betty encountered Ned again. This time she was with her nine-year-old white friend, Eunice Thompson. Perhaps Betty had brought her friend with her intentionally, mistakenly thinking Ned would not dare bother her if she were not alone. But Ned was undaunted by the presence of a second child, a white one at that. Once again, he successfully lured the two children into the cemetery with the promise of flowers. Once in, he locked the gate behind them. He took the girls behind the vault where he threw Betty down on the ground and began raping her. Eunice stood close by, afraid to move, for Ned had again threatened to kill the girls with the sickle. After assaulting Betty, he turned to Eunice and raped her. Eunice described her assault in much the same way that Betty had.[97]

Neither girl reported the attack to family members for several days. Betty Gordon's aunt, Virginia Gordon, became concerned when Betty spent most of Sunday lying down. It wasn't until Tuesday that Betty finally divulged to her aunt what Ned had done to her. Upon examination, Virginia Gordon found her niece's genitalia very bruised and irritated. The very next morning the outraged aunt went looking for Ned in the cemetery, demanding to know what he had done to "her little girl." Ned denied hurting Betty.[98]

At about the same time Betty was divulging her horrible secret to her aunt, the Thompson household was also unraveling the story of the assault. Eunice had revealed the secret to an older sister, who in turn reported the incident to Jane Thompson, the child's mother. Like Betty's aunt, Thompson's first impulse was to confront Ned personally with the accusation. Unable to enter the locked gates of the cemetery, Jane Thompson swore out a warrant for Ned's arrest.[99] Two arrest warrants were issued against Ned on May 19, 1856, one for the rape of Eunice Thompson, a white girl, and a second for the rape of Betty Gordon, "a negro female child." He was tried on June 9 and sentenced to die. The hanging took place on August 5, 1859. It was the first execution in Fredericksburg in fifty years.[100]

Neither the court records, nor the local newspaper mentioned anything of the commotion the crime incited in the town of Fredericksburg. Only indirectly do we learn of the town's agitation. Governor Henry A. Wise received a letter from a P. F. Howard Wise praising the work of Richard Beach, whose title and occupation are unclear, but who may have been the sheriff. Apparently, acting in some official capacity, Beach had "returned with the convict Ned . . . in spite of the most violent opposition and threatening indications of personal violence." Beach found a mob gathered outside the jail angrily declaring that "the negro should never be brought off alive" and that Ned deserved to be shot.[101]

Since Ned had been sentenced to hang, the mob's threat is a bit curious. Community members may have been irked by a delay in meting out justice. The warrants for Ned's arrest had been sworn out in May. He was arraigned, tried, and found guilty in the first two weeks of June. But his execution was not scheduled until August 5. Perhaps the townspeople simply had grown weary of waiting. Nor is there any evidence to suggest that anyone, Ned's owner included, was working to get Ned a reprieve, a circumstance that sometimes triggered mob intervention. In the end, however, the threat of vigilantism abated and Ned was hanged.[102]

Fredericksburg's emotional, vigilante response to the rape of two small children, one white, one black, is what some works have incorrectly characterized as the "usual" response to accusations of black rape of whites.[103] More often than not, however, charges of black rape, even of white children, made their way calmly through antebellum courts. Eugene Genovese correctly observed that "the extent to which the law, rather than the mobs, dealt with slave criminals appeared nowhere so starkly as in the response to rape cases."[104] It was, however, cases involving the alleged sexual assault of children that most frequently brought a community to the brink of vigilante justice, as witnessed in Fredericksburg, Virginia, in 1859.

The cases of slaves accused of raping or attempting to rape white girls share some of the same characteristics as those involving white adult female accusers.[105] Typically, the cases proceeded through the legal system without threat of vigilante violence. In the process of the trials, slaves were accorded certain rights: the right to appeal, the right to interrogate an accuser, and the right to present defense witnesses. There are a few exceptional cases of lynch mobs that intervened when a slave was suspected of raping a white child, but these were relatively rare.

As in cases in which women accused slaves of rape, class mattered a great deal. For one, the absence of privilege in the lives of poorer white children exposed them to circumstances that made them more vulnerable to attack. Unable to rely on servants to perform chores, middling and poor folk frequently used young girls to run errands, either alone or with small children, thus providing attackers of both races with greater opportunities to assault them.

Second, like female adult rape cases, child rape cases sometimes served as channels for class and gender prejudice. White girls, especially those of the poorer classes, risked having their lives scrutinized for evidence of illicit behavior, sexual or otherwise. White girls, like adult white women, were judged within a culture steeped in grave suspicion of women. Misogyny was not blinded by any romantic notions of youthful innocence.

The behavior of white southerners in these cases reveals a gap between an ideology that idealized children and the actual means by which children were protected. Elite white southerners romanticized children; yet the statutory law recognized only girls under age ten as incapable of granting consent to sex. Local courts also at times rigorously interrogated the testimony of young girls in a manner that belies the sentimentalization of children. Poor and middling families sent their young children off on errands of great distances—and of great danger. The halting protection accorded some children who brought forth charges of sexual assault seems in part to reflect the limited nature of sentimental ideas about childhood. The ideology simply had not evenly permeated all aspects of southern antebellum society, namely the law.

Race also figured very prominently in the way these child rape cases played out. African American men were more likely to be sentenced to death for the sexual assault of white girls, though a smattering of white men appear to have been hanged as a result of child rape.

Convicted slaves ran a much higher chance of dying for their alleged offense against children than when charged with raping women, apparently reflecting a general trend in the antebellum South to punish child sex offenders more harshly than rapists of women. Although this essay focuses exclusively on the South, as compared with studies of antebellum New York, it appears that southern communities dealt more harshly with child rapists, black and white. This can only be a tentative, qualified assertion, however. The recent work of Mary Block, for example, which looks primarily at appellate law, finds that southern jurists frequently overturned the convictions of child rapists, both black and white. In fact, she describes a very unchivalrous record among high southern courts, calling into question the umbrella of protection white men claimed to have held up for women and children.[106]

Intriguing here is the apparent way in which paternalism manifests itself in the high court decisions. If we think of the paternalism of appellate judges as a form of humanitarianism, we see that it does not apply equally to (male) slaves, whom we (rightly) think of as the most oppressed people in southern society, and poor (female) children. In fact, the decisions underscore just how powerless and neglected these white female children must have been.

Furthermore, the relatively harsh sentences handed down to slaves convicted of sexually assaulting white girls at the local level should not diminish the importance of the deliberations that courts and other legal officers entered into during these cases. In this highly paternalistic society, judges were ever mindful of the need to utilize the law as a social arm of protection. But whom to protect, slaves or young white girls? White men, individually and through the institutions they created and represented, took seriously their responsibility to manage their charges and to fairly adjudicate conflicts that emerged—in this case, sexual transgressions.

At times the balance between protecting slaves (from unfounded accusations of rape) and white children (from black sexual predators) proved difficult, yielding some apparent ambivalence and even contradictions in court decisions and community debates. The courts—judges and juries—seem to have understood that the stakes were too high to take the word of a mere child at face value without interrogation. A vengeful, manipulative mother could too easily instigate charges of rape by a daughter in order to exact compensation from a wealthy slaveholder. Or less nefariously, a child may simply have been confused by or may have misinterpreted an innocuous display of affection. Either way, the scrutiny and sometimes ill-treatment of white children levying charges of black rape reflects, and does not contradict, the paternalistic ethos of the South.

NOTES

I would like to express my gratitude to Mary Block, Jan Lewis, and Merril Smith for the assistance they provided in the writing of this essay. For a fuller and more expanded version, see chapter 2 in my *Rape, Race, and Community in the Nineteenth-Century South* (Chapel Hill: University of North Carolina Press, forthcoming, 2002.)

1. The landmark work in the history of childhood is Philippe Aries, *Centuries of Childhood: A Social History of Family Life* (New York: Random House, 1965). A spate of works on family followed, including Jay Fliegelman, *Prodigals and Pilgrims: The American Revolution against Patriarchal Authority, 1750–1800* (New York: Cambridge University Press, 1982); Daniel Blake Smith, *Inside the Great House: Planter Family Life in Eighteenth-Century Chesapeake* Society (Ithaca: Cornell University Press, 1980); Philip Greven, *The Protestant Temperament: Patterns of Childrearing, Religious Experience and the Self in Early America* (New York: Alfred A. Knopf, 1977); Jan Lewis, *Pursuit of Happiness: Family and Values in Jefferson's Virginia* (New York: Cambridge University Press, 1977); Jane Turner Censer, *North Carolina Planters and Their Children, 1800–1860* (Baton Rouge: Louisiana State University Press, 1984), 16–41.
2. Christine Stansell, *City of Women: Sex and Class in New York, 1789–1860* (New York: Alfred A. Knopf, 1986).
3. Wilma King, *Stolen Childhood: Slave Youth in Nineteenth-Century America* (Bloomington: Indiana University Press, 1995).
4. Lewis, *Pursuit of Happiness.* Peter Bardaglio touches upon child custody and adoption in the antebellum South in *Reconstructing the Household: Families, Sex, the Law in the Nineteenth-Century South* (Chapel Hill: University of North Carolina Press, 1995), chapter 3. James Marten's work has looked at the impact of the Civil War on Confederate fathers, in "Fatherhood and the Confederacy: Southern Soldiers and Their Children," *Journal of Southern History* 68, no. 2 (May 1997): 269–292; Censer, *North Carolina Planters and Their Children*; Smith, *Inside the Great House*; and, Wilma King's recent work, *Stolen Childhood*, is an important addition to our understanding of childhood in slavery; however, no one has taken her lead by looking at childhood outside slavery.
5. Stansell, *City of Women.*
6. See Diane Miller Sommerville, "The Rape Myth Reconsidered: The

Intersection of Race, Class, and Gender in the American South, 1800–1877" (Ph.D. dissertation, Rutgers University, 1995), 112–115.

7. *Stephen, a slave v. State*, 11 Ga. 238 (1852). On this case and the legal definition of rape, also see Thomas D. Morris, *Southern Slavery and the Law, 1619 to 1860* (Chapel Hill: University of North Carolina Press, 1996), 304.

8. On British law and the age of consent, see Sir Matthew Hale, *The History of the Pleas of the Crown*, ed. George Wilson (London: E. Rider, Little-Britain, 1800), vol. 2, 627, and Leigh Bienen, "Rape I," *Women's Rights Law Reporter* 3 (1976): 45, 49. On early American law and its reliance on British common law, see Wilcomb E. Washburn, "Law and Authority in Colonial Virginia," in *Law and Authority in Colonial America*, ed. George Athen Bilias (New York: Dover, 1970), 117–118; Kermit Hall, *The Magic Mirror* (New York: Oxford University Press, 1989), 5–6, 31; Lawrence M. Friedman, *A History of American Law*, 2d ed. (New York: Simon and Schuster, 1986), 33–37, 102–115. On the difference between rape and carnal knowledge in English common law, see Mary Block, "'An Accusation Easily to Be Made': A History of Rape Law in Nineteenth-Century State Appellate Courts, 1800–1870" (Master's thesis, University of Louisville, 1992), 17–18. On colonial America's adaptation of British common law on rape and carnal knowledge, see also Block, "An Accusation Easily to Be Made," 24–29. I concede that legal scholars and jurists alike may take issue with my interchangeable use of "carnal knowledge" with rape and would rightly point out the technical difference; however, in nineteenth-century law the distinction was often blurred. I use the two here to mean essentially the same thing, largely to make a more readable text.

9. States that established the age of consent at ten were: Alabama, *Laws* (1840), ch. 3, sec. 17, p. 124; Allen H. Bush, comp., *A Digest of the Statute Law of Florida* (Tallahassee, 1872), ch. 43, sec. 41, p. 217; Georgia, *Laws* (1811), sec. 61, p. 44; Lewis Mayer, Louis C. Fischer, and E. J. D. Cross, comps., *Revised Code of Maryland* (Baltimore, 1879), tit. 27, art. 72, sec. 14, p. 787; William L. Sharkey, William L. Harris, and Henry T. Ellett, comps., *Revised Code of the State of Mississippi* (Jackson, 1857), sec. 46, art. 218, p. 608; William Scott, William B. Napton, James W. Morrow, and William C. Jones, comps., *Revised Statutes of the State of Missouri* (St. Louis, 1844–45), ch. 47, art. 2, sec. 26, p. 348; Frederick Nash, James Iredell, and William H. Battle, comps., *The Revised Statutes of the State of North Carolina* (Raleigh, 1837), v. 1, ch. 34, art. 5, p. 192; Benjamin James, comp., *A Digest of the Laws of South Carolina* (Columbia, 1822), Act of 1792, p. 87; R. L. Caruthers and A. O. P. Nicholson, comps., *A Compilation of the Statutes of Tennessee* (Nashville, 1836), Act of 1829, ch. 23, sec. 15, p. 29; Williamson S. Oldham and George W. White, comps., *A Digest of the General Statute Laws of the State of Texas* (Austin, 1859), tit. 17, ch. 6, art. 523, p. 523, Act of 1856. Virginia initially established ten as the age of consent, in Joseph Tate, comp., *Digest of the Laws of Virginia* (Richmond, 1823), sec. 11, 3, p. 127, but raised it to twelve in *Acts of the*

Virginia General Assembly (1847), tit. 2, ch. 3, sec. 15, p. 97. Kentucky initially established the age of consent at ten years. William Littell, comp., *The Statute Law of the State of Kentucky* (Frankfort, 1810), Act of 1801, 2:469 8, then raised it to age twelve in 1813. Littell, comp., *The Statute Law of the State of Kentucky* (Frankfort, 1819), 5:50, ch. 73, 4. Missouri raised its age of consent from ten to twelve in 1856. See Charles H. Hardin, *The Revised Statutes of the State of Missouri* (Jefferson City: James Lusk, 1856), 1:564, secs. 27 and 28. Louisiana and Georgia relied upon common law to prosecute, which established age ten as the age of discretion. In Louisiana's black codes, white girls as well as women were included in its rape statute. *Laws* (1818), p. 18.

10. E. H. English, comp., *A Digest of the Statutes of Arkansas* (Little Rock, 1848), ch. 51, art. 4, sec. 4, p. 380. Arkansas revised the code to read age ten after the Civil War, *Chapters of the Digest of Arkansas Approved November 17, 1868* (Little Rock: Price and Barton, 1869), ch. 2, sec. 4, p. 217. A later statute digest, however, appears to reinstate "puberty": Edward W. Gantt, comp., *Digest of the Statutes of Arkansas* (Little Rock, 1874), ch. 42, art. 8, sec. 1303, p. 333.

11. Mississippi laws (June 1822), sec. 55, p. 198 (slaves, age twelve); Mississippi laws (1839), tit. III, sec. 22, p. 116 ("every Person," presumably meaning whites, age ten); Return J. Meigs and William F. Cooper, comps., *The Code of Tennessee* (Nashville, 1858), art. III, sec. 4614, p. 830 (whites, age ten); Return J. Meigs and William F. Cooper, comps., *The Code of Tennessee* (Nashville, 1858), art. III, sec. 2625, pt. 7, p. 509 (slaves, age twelve).

12. Sharkey, Harris, and Ellett, *Mississippi Revised Code*, (Jackson, 1857), ch. 33, sec. 11, art. 58, p. 248.

13. Arkansas statutes (1838), sec. 4, p. 122 (five to twenty-one years for whites); Josiah Gould, comp., *A Digest of the Statutes of Arkansas* (Little Rock, 1858), ch. 51, art. IV, sec. 9 (death for slaves); John W. Harris, Oliver C. Hartley, and James Wille Willie, comps., *Penal Code of Texas* (Galveston, 1857), ch. VI, art. 529, p. 103 (whites, five to fifteen years); Harris, Hartley, and Willie, comps., *Penal Code of Texas* (Galveston, 1857) tit. III, ch. II, art. 819, p. 163 (slaves, death); Harris, Hartley, and Willie, comps., *Penal Code of Texas*, (Galveston, 1857), tit. III, ch. II, art. 824, p. 164 (Free blacks, death or one year to life); Meigs and Cooper, comps., *Code of Tennessee* (Nashville, 1858), pt. IV, tit. I, ch. 2, art. III, see c. 4611, p. 830 (whites, ten to twenty-one years); Meigs and Cooper, comps., *Code of Tennessee* (Nashville, 1858), ch. 3, art. III, sec. 2625, 7 (slaves, death for having sexual intercourse with a free white female under age twelve); B. W. Leigh, comp., *The Revised Code of the Laws of Virginia* (Richmond, 1819), vol. I, sec. 3, p. 585 (whites, one to ten years); Virginia General Assembly (1847–48), tit. II, ch. 13, sec. 1, p. 126 (free blacks and slaves, death or five to twenty years). Although Florida appears not to have made statutory rape criminal until after the Civil War, it almost certainly relied on common law to prosecute it. Rape of a white child resulted in the same sentence as that of a woman, namely, death for slaves.

Leslie A. Thompson, comp., *A Manual or Digest of the Statute Law of the State of Florida* (Tallahassee, 1847), tit. IV, ch. 1, sec. 1, p. 6. In 1872, Florida passed a statutory rape law setting the age of consent at ten and establishing death or life imprisonment as punishment. Bush, comp., *A Digest of the Statute Law of Florida* (Tallahassee, 1872), ch. 43, sec. 41, p. 217.

14. Missouri included in its definition of rape having carnal knowledge of a female under age ten, punishable, like forcible rape, by five to ten years in prison. Scott, Napton, Morrow, and Jones, *Revised Statutes of Missouri* (St. Louis, 1844–45), ch. 47, art. II, sec. 26, p. 348. For slaves, see A. A. King, comp., *Revised Statutes of Missouri* (St. Louis, 1835), art. II, 28, p. 171 (castration).

15. Bartholomew Moore, Asa Biggs, and Rodman, comps., *Revised Code* of *North Carolina* (Boston, 1855), ch. 34, sec. 5, p. 203 (whites, death); Moore, Biggs, Rodman, comps., *Revised Code* of *North Carolina* (Boston, 1855), ch. 107, sec. 44 (slaves, death); James, comp., *Digest of the Laws of South Carolina* (Columbia, 1822), p. 87 (whites, death without benefit of clergy); Thomas Cooper and David J. McCord, eds., *The Statutes at Large of South Carolina* (Columbia, 1843), vol. 9, no. 2893, p. 258 (slaves, death without benefit of clergy for assault and battery on a white woman with intent to commit a rape). There does not appear to have been a specific slave code criminalizing sex with a child; however, the language in the statute intended for whites was so universal that it would appear to have applied to nonwhites as well.

16. Alabama sessions laws 24:1 (1830), General Assembly, 12th session, p. 13 passed January 13, 1831, and John J. Ormond, Arthur P. Bagby, and George Goldthwaite, comps., *Code of Alabama* (Montgomery, 1852), tit. 1, ch. 2, art. 10, 3307, p. 594 (slaves and free blacks, death for rape and attempted rape); Ormond, Bagby, and Goldthwaite, comps., *Code of Alabama* (Montgomery, 1852), tit. 1, ch. II, art. II, sec. 3091, p. 562 (whites, life imprisonment).

17. Georgia session laws (1811), "An Act to Ameliorate the Criminal Code" (December 14, 1811), ch. 60, p. 44 (whites); Georgia acts (1816), sec. 1, p. 15 (slaves).

18. Kentucky acts (1801), ch. 67, sec. 7 and 8, p. 120 (age of consent at ten, ten to twenty-one years); Kentucky acts (1802, Act of December 22, 1802, ch. 53, p. 116 (slaves, death for rape); Littell, comp., *The Statute Law of Kentucky* (Frankfort, 1819) 5:50, ch. 73, 4 (age of consent raised to age twelve).

19. William McK. Ball and Sam C. Roane, comps., *Revised Statutes of Arkansas* (Boston, 1838), sec. 4, p. 122; *Charles v. State of Arkansas* (July term, 1850), 390–410.

20. English, comp., *A Digest of the Statutes of Arkansas* (Little Rock, 1848), ch. 51, art. IV, sec. 4, p. 330.

21. Ibid., sec. 9, p. 331. Italics mine.

22. *Charles v. State of Arkansas* (July term, 1850). Inexplicably, the court did

not consider Almyra Combs's underage status, not yet having attained puberty, in deciding the issue of force and lack of it in this case.

23. *The State v. Bill* (February 1844). See also Judith Kelleher Schafer, *Slavery, the Civil Law, and the Supreme Court of Louisiana* (Baton Rouge: Louisiana State University Press, 1994), 86.

24. *Sydney v. the State* (3 Humphreys), 22. Tenn. 465 (1842). See also Arthur Howington, "The Treatment of Slaves and Free Blacks in the State and Local Courts of Tennessee" (Ph.D. dissertation, Vanderbilt University, 1982), 186.

25. *Wright v. State*, 4 Hum., 194, as cited in James M. Quarles, *Criminal Code of Tennessee* (Nashville: Tavel, Eastman, and Howell, 1874), p. 818.

26. *State of North Carolina v. Sam* (1 Winst. 300), 183. On the age requirements for rapists, see Bienen, "Rape I," 46, 49–50; and Block, "An Accusation Easily to Be Made," 29–30.

27. Trial of November 19, 1808, box 157 (October–December 11, 1808), Letters Received (hereafter LR), Virginia Executive Papers (hereafter VEP), Library of Virginia, Richmond (hereafter LOV). Bertram Wyatt-Brown also discusses this incident in *Southern Honor: Ethics and Behavior in the Old* South (New York: Oxford University Press, 1982), 387–388.

28. Trial of November 19, 1808, box 157 (October–December 11, 1808), LR, VEP, LOV.

29. In 1840, long after this case, the Virginia legislature modified its compensation policy so that the value of the condemned slave would be adjusted to market value with the purchaser's knowledge of the slave's offense. Va. *Acts*, 1839–40, pp. 51–52.

30. Ibid.

31. Ibid.

32. Condemned Slaves (hereafter CS) Executed, 1808, Auditor of Public Accounts (hereafter APA), LOV.

33. September–December 1860, box 472, Pardon Papers (hereafter PP), LR, VEP, LOV.

34. Ibid.

35. Ibid.

36. Official notation, Ibid.

37. See, for example, Sommerville, "The Rape Myth Reconsidered"; Dianne Miller Sommerville, "The Rape Myth in the Old South Reconsidered," *Journal of Southern History* 61 (August 1995): 481–518; Diane Miller Sommerville, "Rape, Race, and Castration in Slave Law in the Colonial and Early South," in *The Devil's Lane: Sex and Race in the Early South*, ed. Catherine Clinton and Michele Gillespie (New York: Oxford University Press, 1997): 74–89; Martha Hodes, *White Women, Black Men: Illicit Sex in the Nineteenth-Century South* (New Haven: Yale University Press, 1997), chapter 3.

38. Henry County Court Minute Book (1820–49), July 9, 1832, August 14, 1832, pp. 183, 187 (microfilm reel no. 23); CS Transported, 1832; Bonds for Transportation, 1806–39, LOV.

39. James B. Sellers, *Slavery in Alabama* (University, Ala.: University of Alabama Press, 1950; rpt. 1964), 253.

40. Columbus (Ga.) *Sentinel*, reprinted in the August (Ga.) *Chronicle*, August 17, 1851, as cited by Ulrich B. Phillips, *American Negro Slavery: A Survey of the Supply, Employment and Control of Negro Labor as Determined by the Plantation Regime* (New York: D. Appleton and Co., 1918; rpt. Baton Rouge: Louisiana State University Press, 1966), 461–462. Although the quotation does not make explicit the "negro" man's status, I have to rely on Phillips's keen researching skills to assume he was a slave, since this account is included in Phillips's chapter on slave crime. Nor does the account yield any information about the status of the young girl.

41. October 1856, VEP, LOV.

42. New Orleans (La.) *Bee*, October 9, 1858.

43. November 1–30, 1822 folder, box 274 (October 1–December 11, 1822), LR, VEP, LOV. Virginia rape statutes appear not to have required proof of seminal emission. A footnote to an 1819 statute states that penetration, not emission, is evidence of rape and cites Virginia and British case law (*Commonwealth v. Thomas*, 1 Va. Cas. 307; *Rex v. Cox*, Moo. C.C.R. 337; *Rex v. Reckspear*, ibid., 342; *Rex v. Cousins*, 6 C. and P. 351) and British statute, 9 *Geo. IV*, c. 31, sec. 18. Act of February 8, 1819–January 1, 1820, *Digest of the Laws of Virginia* (Tate, 1841), p. 212. A Virginia statute of 1861 explains the legal logic behind the modification:

> The statute of 9 Geo. IV, ch. 31, sec. 17, after reciting that upon the trials for the crimes of buggery and of rape, and of carnally abusing girls under certain ages, offenders frequently escaped by reason of the difficulty of the proof required of the completion of those crimes, enacts that it shall not be necessary, in any of those cases, to prove the actual emission of seed in order to constitute a carnal knowledge, but that the carnal knowledge shall be deemed complete, upon proof of penetration only.

Digest of Laws of a Criminal Nature (Matthews, 1861), ch. XV, sec. 15, p. 118, fn. 8. See also Block, "An Accusation Easily to Be Made," 33.

44. November 1–30, 1822 folder, box 274 (October 1–December 11, 1822), LR, VEP; CS Executed, 1823, LOV.

45. Since the accuser in this case was over the age of ten, the prosecution would have had to establish the use of force by the defendant.

46. Trial of July 6, 1826, box 294 (May 21–July 31, 1826), VEP; CS Executed, 1826, LOV.

47. Trial of July 15, 1826, box 294 (May 21–July 1826), VEP, LOV.

48. Ibid.

49. Ibid.

50. Official notation, ibid.

51. As in the case of Dinwiddie (1826), it is unclear why the charge was attempted rape. There is no mention of anyone or anything scaring the accused slave, Jesse, off before he could rape Mary. Nor is there any testimony pertaining to penetration or ejaculation, which often accompanied such trial records. It may very well be that the young girl was reluctant to testify about the details of her assault and settled on the attempted rape charge to avoid public embarrassment.

52. September 1856, LR, VEP, LOV.

53. Ibid.

54. Ibid.; Cash Journal (hereinafter CJ), LOV.

55. October 1856, LR, VEP, LOV.

56. Ibid.

57. Sworn affidavits of Agnes Sanford, November 1, 1856; Joseph Sanford, October 28, 1856; William M. B. Goodwin, November 3, 1856, all located in October 1856, LR, VEP, LOV.

58. See note 43.

59. June 24–30, 1819 folder, box 254 (June 1819), LR, VEP, LOV; and Schwarz, *Twice Condemned*, 206.

60. On the importance of reputation and its relationship to marriage to white southern females, see Kirsten Fischer, "'False, Feigned, and Scandalous Words': Sexual Slander and Racial Ideology among Whites in Colonial North Carolina," in Clinton and Gillespie, *Devil's Lane*, 139–153.

61. Sworn testimony of Clementina Beazley and Lucy Dallas Beazley, October 6, 1856, Spotsylvania County Court, October 1856, LR, VEP, LOV.

62. Letters of October 28, 1856 and November 1, 1856 from Robert Dabney, clerk of court of Spotsylvania County, October 1856, LR, VEP, LOV.

63. By exploring rapists' motives, I realize I run the risk of acknowledging the guilt of at least some of those African American men on trial for sexually assaulting young white girls. However I think it is fair to say that such assaults did occur from time to time.

64. Violence by the attacker as well as resistance by the rape victim was established in Marybeth Hamilton Arnold's study of New York City as well. See "'The Life of a Citizen in the Hands of a Woman': Sexual Assault in New York City, 1790–1820," in *Passion and Power: Sexuality in History*, ed. Kathy Peiss and Christina Simmons (Philadelphia: Temple University Press, 1989), 45–47.

65. June 1–20, 1829 folder, box 311 (May 1–July 20, 1829), LR, VEP; box 157, October–December 11, 1808, VEP; October 1856, LR, VEP; September–December 1860, box 472, PP, LR, VEP, LOV.

66. This continued to be the case well into the twentieth century. See

Stephen Murray Robertson, "Sexuality through the Prism of Age: Modern Culture and Sexual Violence in New York City, 1880–1950" (Ph.D. disssertation, Rutgers University, 1998), 72.

67. October 18, 1833, LR, VEP, as quoted in James Hugo Johnston, *Race Relations in Virginia and Miscegenation in the South, 1776–1860* (Amherst: University of Massachusetts Press, 1870), 263. This document could not be located at the Library of Virginia as cited by Johnston. Also see *Thompson v. Commonwealth of Virginia*, 4 Leigh 652 (1833); and Frederick County Superior Court Order Book, 1831–1835, entries for May 22, 23, June 10, 1833, pp. 208, 210, LOV (and microfilm reel no. 100). No documentation that verifies the outcome of Thompson's appeal has been found. However, his name does not appear on lists of blacks executed or transported in the early 1830s.

68. Sommerville, "The Rape Myth Reconsidered," 185–186.

69. I have only come across one antebellum southern case of a white man raping his own daughter, in this case, a thirteen-year-old stepdaughter. See Sommerville, "The Rape Myth Reconsidered," 271–272.

70. Robertson, "Sexuality through the Prism of Age," 50.

71. Arnold, "The Life of a Citizen in the Hands of a Woman," 42.

72. Stansell, *City of Women*, 101, 278n33.

73. *Alfred, a slave, v. State of Georgia* (March 1849).

74. Schafer, *Slavery, the Civil Law, and the Supreme Court of Louisiana*, 86.

75. Trial of Cesear, November 18, 1724, Spotsylvania County Court Order Book (1724–30), p. 37 (microfilm reel no. 43), LOV.

76. June 1–20, 1829 folder, box 311 (May 1–July 20, 1829), LR, VEP, LOV.

77. Ibid.

78. Ibid.

79. Ibid.

80. June 21–30, 1829 folder, ibid.

81. Ibid.

82. September 1829 entry, 1806–39 folder, Bonds for Transportation; CS 1829 Transported; and August 7, 1829 entry, "A List of Slaves and Free persons of color received into the Penitentiary of Virginia for sale and transportation from the 25th June 1816 to 1st February 1842" (hereafter referred to as 1816 "List") in CS, LOV.

83. Petition to Governor Clark, August 23, 1861, Governor's Papers, Clark, and Governor's Letter Books, p. 80, NCDAH, as quoted in Victoria E. Bynum, *Unruly Women: The Politics of Social and Sexual Control* (Chapel Hill: University of North Carolina Press, 1992), 118.

84. October 18, 1833, LR, VEP, as quoted in Johnston, *Race Relations in Virginia and Miscegenation in the South*, 263.

85. On free African Americans accused of sexually assaulting children, see

chapter 5 in my book, *Rape, Race, and Community in the Nineteenth-Century South* (Chapel Hill: University of North Carolina Press, forthcoming 2002).

86. September 11–20, 1810 folder, box 168 (August–September 1810), VEP, LOV. Petition with fifty signatures, n.d., ibid. The law under which Dick was prosecuted held that the term of imprisonment for a convicted [white] rapist was ten to twenty-one years. Samuel Shepherd, ed., *Statutes at Large for Virginia from October Session 1792, to December Session 1806, Inclusive*, 3 vols., 1835–36, rpt. (New York: AMS Inc., 1970), vol. 2, ch. 2, sec. 4, p. 6 (Act of December 15, 1796).

87. *State v. LeBlanc*, 1 Tread. Const. 354 (1813), pp. 105–106. South Carolina lacked a penitentiary until after the Civil War. As a result, many more crimes were capital, even for whites, than any other southern state. Michael P. Hindus, *Prison and Plantation: Crime, Justice, and Authority in Massachusetts and South Carolina* (Chapel Hill: University of North Carolina Press, 1980), 210–249.

88. *State v. Alfred Goings, alias Alfred Terry*, 20 N.C. 289 (1838), pp. 229–230.

89. March 19, 22, 23, September 16, 1844, Bertie County Superior Court Minutes, 1828–57; *State v. Farmer*, 26 N.C. 224 (1844), pp. 173–175. In 1867, Franklin Smith (no race given) was convicted and sentenced to die for raping a girl under ten years of age. *State v. Franklin Smith* (June term, 1867), v. 61, pp. 304–305. On the other end of the spectrum, a white Missouri man received a mere three years in prison for the attempted rape of a nine-year-old girl. *McComas v. State*, 11 Mo. 116 (1847).

90. Relying almost exclusively on statutory law and not on court records, most scholars claim that the sexual assault of a black female was not a capital offense, let alone a crime in some states. Block, "An Accusation Easily to Be Made," 37; Judith Kelleher Schafer, "The Long Arm of the Law: Slave Criminals and the Supreme Court in Antebellum Louisiana," *Tulane Law Review* 60 (June 1986), 1256 and 1265; Schafer, *Slavery, the Civil Law, and the Supreme Court of Louisiana*, 85; Susan Brownmiller, *Against Our Will: Men, Women, and Rape* (New York: Simon and Schuster, 1975), 162; Catherine Clinton, "Bloody Terrain: Freedwomen, Sexuality and Violence during Reconstruction," *Georgia Historical Quarterly* 76 (Summer 1992), 315; Catherine Clinton, "'Southern Dishonor': Flesh, Blood, Race, and Bondage," in Carol Bleser, ed., *In Joy and Sorrow: Women, Family, and Marriage in the Victorian South, 1830–1900* (New York: Oxford University Press, 1991), 65; Deborah Gray White, *Ar'n't I a Woman? Female Slaves in the Plantation South* (New York: W. W. Norton, 1985), 152; Karen A. Getman, "Sexual Control in the Slaveholding South: The Implementation and Maintenance of a Racial Caste System," *Harvard Women's Law Journal* 7 (Spring 1984), 135; Thomas R. R. Cobb, *An Inquiry into the Law of Negro Slavery in the United States of America* (1858; New York, Negro Universities Press, 1968), 99; John D'Emilio and Estelle Freedman, *Intimate Matters: A History of Sexuality in America* (New York: Harper and Row, 1988), 101.

91. *George v. State*, 37 Miss. 316 (1859). For historians' treatments of this particular case, consult Bardaglio, *Reconstructing the Household*, 67–68; Morris, *Southern Slavery and the Law*, 51; White, *Ar'n't I a Woman?* 152; Clinton, "Bloody Terrain," 315; Clinton, "Southern Dishonor," 66; Mark Tushnet, "The American Law of Slavery, 1810–1860: A Study in the Persistence of Legal Autonomy," *Law and Society Review* 10 (Fall 1975): 120, 133–134. On rape and slave women more generally, see Peter Kolchin, *American Slavery, 1619–1877* (New York: Hill and Wang, 1993), 124–125; Margaret A. Burnham, "An Impossible Marriage: Slave Law and Family Law," *Law and Inequality* 5 (July 1987), 199; Clinton, "Southern Dishonor," 57–58, 65–66; Melton A. McLaurin, *Celia, A Slave: A True Story of Violence and Retribution in Antebellum Missouri* (Athens: University of Georgia Press, 1991); Darlene Clark Hine, "Rape and the Inner Lives of Black Women in the Midwest," 912–913; Harriet A. Jacobs, *Incidents in the Life of a Slave Girl Written by Herself*, ed. Jean Fagan Yellin (Cambridge: Harvard University Press, 1987).

92. Other cases of slaves indicted for the rape of female slaves include *Commonwealth v. Kitt*, May 29, 1778, and *Commonwealth v. Kitt*, July 29, 1783, Westmoreland County Order Book, 1776–86, LOV, as quoted in Morris, *Southern Slavery and the Law*, 306. In 1797 a slave was hanged for the murder of a woman identified as a mulatto. See Schwarz, *Twice Condemned*, 207; Morris, *Southern Slavery and the Law*, 306.

93. "An act to punish negroes, and mulattoes, for rape or an attempt to rape," December 13, 1859, ch. 62, sec. 1, p. 102 (Mississippi law); Clark, Cobb, and Irwin , comps., *Code of Georgia*, tit. I, div., IV, 4248–49, p. 824 (Georgia law).

94. Shelby County, Circuit Court Minutes, January 1855, pp. 400–401, 425–427, 428, as cited in Howington, "The Treatment of Slaves and Free Blacks in the State and Local Courts of Tennessee," 114.

95. Depositions of various witnesses, n.d., but trial of Ned, June 9, 1859, City of Fredericksburg Court Records, Fredericksburg Circuit Court House, Fredericksburg, Virginia. My thanks to Barry L. McGhee for making these documents available to me.

96. Ibid.

97. Ibid.

98. Ibid.

99. Ibid.

100. Arrest warrants made out for Ned for the rapes of Eunice Thompson and Betty Gordon, May 17, 1859, by order of Hugh Scott, justice of the peace, ibid. The arrest warrant sworn out for a "negro" girl seems to refute blanket assertions that females of color could not be raped in the eyes of the law. Fredericksburg (Va.) *News*, June 14, 1859, p. 2.

101. Undated letter but received August 29, 1859, VEP. The purpose of the letter was to request a commendation for Beach.

102. Schwarz, *Twice Condemned*, 292–293, and CJ, LOV.

103. Typical is the characterization by James B. Sellers. "Most heinous of all crimes a Negro might commit was rape or attempted rape. No other crime aroused as much passion and thirst for revenge." James B. Sellers, *Slavery in Alabama* (1950; University, Al.: University of Alabama Press, 1964), 252–253. He later qualifies this statement by acknowledging that despite the excitement it aroused, "usually the law took its course and citizens abided by its decision." Ibid., 253. See also Kenneth Stampp, *Peculiar Institution: Slavery in the Ante-Bellum South* (New York: Alfred A. Knopf, 1956), 190–191. Of course in this double child rape in Fredericksburg, blacks could very well have participated in the mob as well as incensed whites.

104. Eugene D. Genovese, *Roll, Jordan, Roll: The World the Slaves Made* (New York: Random House, 1975), 33. See also Thomas D. Morris, "Slaves and the Rules of Evidence," *Chicago-Kent Law Review* 68 (1993), 1210–1211.

105. See, for example, Sommerville, "Rape Myth in the Old South Reconsidered"; Sommerville, "Rape, Race, and Castration in Slave Law in the Colonial South"; Hodes, *White Women, Black Men*.

106. Mary Block, "'An Accusation Easily to Be Made': A History of Rape Law in Nineteenth-century America," Ph.D. dissertation in progress (University of Kentucky, expected 2001).

8

"A Most Detestable Crime"

Character, Consent, and Corroboration in Vermont's Rape Law, 1850–1920

Hal Goldman

MANY HISTORIANS AND scholars have been highly critical of the role played by American courts in creating and enforcing American law.[1] They have argued that common law courts treated female complainants more like criminals than victims. Women who complained of sexual assault had their reputations dragged through the mud, were accused of inviting the assault by their dress or behavior, or were simply not believed. The law encouraged this kind of treatment by imposing special evidentiary requirements on rape prosecutions that did not apply to other kinds of violent crimes. As a result, rape law promoted highly gendered models of proper and improper sexual behavior for men and women. The values both reflected and reinforced a sexual double standard discouraging and even punishing women who transgressed the bounds of female modesty, while excusing or even promoting male sexual promiscuity and aggression. Some have argued that the courts did not take women's sexual safety seriously at all. Judges and juries either did not view women's need for protection as important or sought to use rape as a means to dominate women through the use of sexual terror practiced with impunity. As a result, the law offered little protection to women from sexual assault or offered it selectively, protecting middle-class women or girls to the exclusion of members of the working class, ethnic minorities, or women with immodest reputations.

Though some of the work making these arguments has relied on local studies, most has been based on national surveys of appellate decisions in rape cases.[2] While these studies are helpful in exploring the broad contours of a criminal matter like rape, they are to a great extent ahistorical because no person living in the nineteenth or early twentieth centuries ever experienced the law in the way these works present it. Rape law was the product of an almost exclusively local and state process. State judges and legislators, and local juries were responsible for the definition of the law and its application. This resulted in wide variation from state to state. If we want to understand how rape law really worked on real people, we must study it in the way it acted on them, that is, as a local and state phenomenon.

This study of rape law in Vermont draws on the statutes passed by the state legislature, the appellate decisions of the Vermont Supreme Court, and the records of four of the state's county courts. That examination reveals a far more nuanced interplay of law, sex, and gender than earlier work has led us to understand and reveals the significant variations that existed even between neighboring states such as Massachusetts and New York.

Under Vermont law, a rape occurred when a man had sexual intercourse with a woman by force and without her consent.[3] The simplicity of the prohibition was deceptive. For rape, while the most serious sexual offense, also posed the greatest evidentiary difficulties for both the prosecution and the defense. Rape rarely occurred in the presence of a third party. Thus, corroboration was difficult. Evidence was often lacking in an unwitnessed rape, and such physical evidence as there might be—torn clothing, bruises, body fluids—did not in and of itself prove the elements of the crime. Unlike adultery, for example, it was not enough merely to show that intercourse had taken place in order to prove the criminal act. This was because the question of whether or not the crime had taken place was contingent upon the mental understanding of the alleged victim. Had force been used to accomplish the intercourse? Had it been accomplished without her consent? Resolution of these issues typically depended entirely upon the perceptions of the woman. As a result, rape cases, more than other sexual infractions such as seduction, bastardy, adultery, or statutory rape, were for the most part decided by the jury's weighing of the testimony of the alleged victim (usually referred to as the "prosecutrix").

Typically, to prove an unwitnessed rape, the state had to put the woman on the stand to testify.[4] A defendant without an alibi had two choices: argue that he had not had sexual relations with the woman or claim that the sex was consensual. Either way, the woman's credibility often lay at the heart of the case, and in the nineteenth century credibility depended on character. But how was character to be assessed? What role, if any, could past sexual behavior play in that assessment?

CHARACTER

Those who would be witnesses in Vermont's eighteenth- and nineteenth-century courts faced a raft of exclusions and challenges to their credibility based on beliefs and assumptions that are now alien to us. Some were excluded because they had an interest in the case. Thus, plaintiffs and defendants in civil cases could not testify because the temptation to lie on their own behalf was deemed too great to trust their testimony.[5] Criminal defendants could not be compelled to testify against themselves, of course, but they could not voluntarily testify on their own behalf either until 1866.[6] Others were excluded because of social policy considerations. The sanctity of the marital relationship outweighed the search for truth. Therefore, husbands and wives could not testify for or against each other in any civil or criminal proceeding.[7] Those who did not believe in God could not testify. Nor could people who had been convicted of treason, any felony, or any crime involving dishonesty. These latter two disabilities were removed in 1851, but those who had been convicted of crimes involving perjury were still prohibited from testifying, and those whose past crimes had involved moral turpitude could have their credibility impeached as a result.[8]

In addition to these exclusions and grounds for challenging credibility, Vermont courts also allowed lawyers to attack witnesses in civil and criminal cases based on their reputation for honesty. In general, though, nineteenth-century law carefully limited the admission of character evidence in civil and criminal trials.

In criminal cases including rape, reputation evidence could be used to impeach a witness (including the alleged victim or the defendant if he chose to testify). In general, lawyers could impeach the testimony of a witness only through the use of evidence of their general reputation for honesty. The lawyer would place someone on the stand who lived in the witness's community and ask him or her about the witness's general reputation for truth-telling. These witnesses could not make reference to specific acts by the impeached witness nor express their own opinion. All they could do was testify as to what they believed the general reputation of the witness was for truth-telling in the community.[9]

Lawyers in some civil or criminal cases sought to attack the sexual reputation of a witness or party in order to impeach credibility, but such efforts were generally prohibited by the Vermont Supreme Court. During the 1830s and 1840s, the Court held, for example, that a woman's history as a prostitute could not be used to impeach her credibility in civil or criminal cases. In so ruling, the Court expressly rejected—as it had done in bastardy cases—Massachusetts's holdings which were to the contrary. In an 1835 prosecution for assault and battery, for example, the Supreme Court upheld the trial court's refusal to permit the defendant to impeach two of the state's witnesses by introducing his own witnesses who would testify that they were common prostitutes. The Court repeated the rule that only evidence of a general reputation for truth-telling was admissible. It acknowledged that the practice of most vices tended to "impair the moral sense, and weaken the force of the obligation to speak or act with due regard to truth," and it likened prostitution to intemperance or thieving in this respect. But the Court noted that if such behaviors did lead to dishonesty, it was easy enough to limit the testimony to the effect of such vice on the witness's general reputation for truth-telling without having to delve into the cause of such reputation. The Court asserted that to do otherwise would introduce a new rule of evidence, and it was unprepared to take such a step, that "would be entirely new in our courts of justice, dangerous, and [in] some cases slanderous, and no equivalent benefit would be derived from permitting such an inquiry."[10]

Because the testimony of the alleged victim was so crucial in most rape cases, defense lawyers were particularly keen to impeach the credibility of the woman. To do so they often sought to introduce evidence about the woman's sexual morality. But they came up against the law's general prohibition of such evidence as a means of gauging credibility. As a result, Vermont's judges were repeatedly called upon to determine the nature of evidence the state and the defendant could enter about women who charged rape. In attempting to resolve these disputes, judges found themselves facing a dilemma. On the one hand, the limited evidence available in most rape trials and the importance of the woman's testimony was a strong temptation to permit the admission of character evidence. On the other hand, it seemed unfair to the alleged victim to judge the credibility of her allegations based on behavior prior to and sometimes even following the alleged rape. Some judges were well aware that such evidence could be used to punish a victim, both by humiliating her and preventing the conviction of her rapist. Perhaps most importantly for Vermont's conservative judges, its introduction ran contrary to the general rules governing the admissibility of character evidence.

In the middle of the nineteenth century, Vermont's Supreme Court began to sort out the question of character evidence with regard to the prosecutrix. The question that arose in rape cases was this: to what extent could her testimony be impeached by questions concerning her moral character? Could one simply inquire of her general moral reputation? Or could one delve further, either by putting her past sexual behavior into question or even by inquiring about past specific sexual encounters with other men?

The Court's first decision on the matter was *State v. Johnson*, an 1855 prosecution against Levi Johnson for rape and incest committed on his sixteen-year-old daughter Sarah. This was the first reported rape case of any kind in Vermont. The state alleged that Johnson had had sex with Sarah at least three times and that she had gotten pregnant as a result. On cross-examination, Johnson's lawyers had asked Sarah whether she had had sex with other men, naming them and specifying the particular times and places. These occurrences were alleged to have taken place both before and after the time she claimed her father had raped her and before she became pregnant. The trial judge had refused to allow the cross-examination. In reversing the trial court, Supreme Court Judge Pierpont Isham, writing for the two-judge majority, ruled that a defendant could not introduce evidence of the woman's past sexual experiences with other men. However, if the state put the prosecutrix on the stand, which it typically had to do in order to prove the case, the defendant, on cross-examination, could inquire about her sexual experiences. Judge Isham based the opinion on his interpretation of several English cases which had considered the matter. Since consent was a purely mental act, in determining whether it took place or not one could inquire into a woman's previous habits. If she was moral, then consent to the act would be "inconsistent with her previous life, and repugnant to all her moral feelings." But if she was immoral, then consent would be "the natural result of her mind . . . and rebut the inference or necessity of actual violence." This called into doubt the credibility of her claim that she had consented because of her past habits. While Isham's opinion held that a woman could be asked these questions if she testified, he did not claim that she could be made to answer them. If an affirmative answer would subject her to prosecution for engaging in adulterous acts, for example, she had a right to claim the privilege against self-incrimination.[11]

Judge Isham's opinion drew a strong dissent from fellow judge Milo Bennett. Bennett absolutely rejected the proposition that past immoral acts should be used to discredit the testimony of a prosecutrix. While he agreed with the proposition that a general reputation for lack of chastity was admissible in rape cases, he denied that specific past bad acts could be used. In the first place, it was contrary to authority. Simon Greenleaf's influential treatise on evidence had made clear that such specific evidence of immorality could not be used. Instead, the defendant could only rely on general reputation evidence of immorality. Second, Bennett was troubled by the logic and morality of the leap from one illicit action to the next.

> A general want of chastity may furnish a basis for a presumption that the illicit connection was by consent, and thus it becomes material to the issue. But no such presumption should be allowed to arise from a particular instance of an illicit connection with another person. Presumptions cannot rest upon mere suggestion or surmise. They must have some ground to stand upon, some facts upon which they can arise.

Bennett's criticism was more than a critique of Isham's faulty logic. It reflected a view of human nature influenced by his known evangelical view of redemption:

> Though we may concede, so far as our moral convictions are concerned, to use the language of JUDGE COWEN, that "one who has already started on the road to prostitution, would be less reluctant to pursue her course, than one who still remained at her home of innocence," yet courts of justice cannot act upon evidence addressed simply to their moral convictions. . . . [W]hy should we presume that a female continues in a voluntary course of lewdness, because she has had, at some previous time a sexual connection with some other man. If the law will not allow such evidence to be the basis of a presumption, it should not be received.[12]

Bennett lost this battle. But he waged a guerilla war on the decision in a way typical of mid-nineteenth century jurists—he wrote a treatise. Nineteenth-century jurists who opposed the ideological direction of the state or federal courts wrote law treatises in an effort to sway legal opinion to their side. These authors sought to exploit the fact that many lawyers and judges had limited access to reported decisions or little inclination to do legal research. By authoring a treatise and directing it at these individuals and particularly at students or young lawyers, they could hope to inculcate their values into the next generation.[13] Bennett's *Vermont Justice* (1864) became one of the most widely used legal authorities in the state during the second half of the nineteenth century.[14] Though marketed as a guide to Vermont's nonlawyer justices of the peace, both its title page and Bennett's preface made explicit his hope that it would be used by the junior members of the bar. Its contents went beyond matters strictly within the jurisdiction of justices of the peace— in short, it was Bennett's attempt to have a lasting influence on the law.

Thus it comes as no surprise that Bennett would attempt to undo the Supreme Court's ruling on evidence in rape cases set down on the Johnson decision nine years before. In the section on rape, Bennett ignored the Johnson ruling, arguing, based on citation to Greenleaf, that:

> The respondent may give in evidence the general bad character of the female, for want of chastity, as furnishing a basis for a presumption that the illicit connection was by consent; but we apprehend the true rule is, that no such presumption can arise from a particular instance of prior illicit connection with another person, other than the accused.[15]

Furthermore, any woman could be raped, regardless of her station in life or her reputation: "It is no defence that she was a common strumpet, if a rape was actually committed upon her." That is, the law did not immunize men against rape charges when their victim had a bad reputation for chastity. Rather, that reputation went to her credibility in determining "if a rape was actually committed upon her."[16]

The influence of Bennett's treatise was reflected almost immediately in the case of *State v. Reed* (1867). Amaretta Marcott claimed that Albert Reed had raped her. Reed, thirty-three and a farm laborer, was the Marcotts' neighbor. On cross-examination Reed's lawyers asked Amaretta if she knew one Eleazer Harwood, a conductor on the railroad. She had denied knowing him, but offered that she might have seen him. Reed's lawyer then asked her whether she had had sex with Harwood the previous spring when he walked her home along the railroad track. The state objected and the trial judge, James Barrett, upheld the objection. The defendant then entered general evidence that Marcott's character for chastity was bad and the state gave evidence that she had a good reputation for chastity. Reed was convicted.

On appeal, the state cited Bennett's treatise and argued that *Johnson* was bad law. According to the state's brief, *Johnson* was "rejected by a large majority of the profession of this state, as a wide departure from the ancient land marks of the law; in fact a perversion of the principles that have received approval of the best legal minds in the past and present."

The Court's defensiveness over its opinion in *Johnson* was obvious. Judge Benjamin H. Steele noted that it had been the result of a divided court and was legally questionable, but felt he could not overrule so recent a decision. "Before the decision was made the question was, at least, debatable both upon reason and authority, and it was perhaps more important that the point should be settled, than how it was settled."

Nonetheless, Steele justified the admission of the sexual experience evidence on the grounds that such evidence was extremely valuable to the defendant in the case before it. "The jury would be less ready to conclude that a woman who had once improperly yielded afterwards properly resisted, than they would if she had been a woman of unquestioned virtue." The Court held that the matter of the admissibility of such evidence was now settled in the state of Vermont. Tried again, Reed was found guilty a second time. He appealed again, and his case was continued for four years before the prosecutor finally entered a nolle prosequi.[17]

The Court's decision on this issue was one of the few in which Vermont law was potentially more hostile to women than that of other states in matters concerning sex and sexual injury. In bastardy cases and on the question of the effect of prostitution on a witness's credibility, Vermont tended to be more accommodating toward female complainants and witnesses then other states. But on the question of past reputation, Vermont was distinct from its New England neighbors. Both Massachusetts and New Hampshire had declared that only evidence of general reputation for chastity could be introduced to impeach the credibility of an alleged victim on matters of consent. Both cited Greenleaf for the proposition, and neither decision displayed any of the agonized soul-searching of the Vermont cases.[18]

Despite the Court's decisions in *Johnson* and *Reed*, resistance continued. In an appeal from an adultery prosecution in 1876, Judge Hoyt Wheeler stated that in a rape case evidence of prior sexual intercourse with the defendant was admissible, but "evidence of like acts of intercourse between her and other men is not."[19] In his notes to the second edition of the annotated reports of the Vermont Supreme Court, published in 1890, editor Charles L. Williams observed that the rule in *Johnson* had been approved in *State v. Reed*, but then went on to state the contrary rule promoted by Greenleaf and Bennett that specific acts with others were inadmissible and that a woman's "general reputation for chastity in the community before the alleged rape is all that can be shown." Williams cited Nevada, Alabama, and Michigan cases in support.[20]

In 1894 Judge Russell Taft had refused to permit a rape defendant to introduce evidence that the alleged victim had had intercourse with another man. Mary Gilman, a fourteen-year-old servant girl, was living in the home of George Hollenbeck when, she claimed, she was raped by Hollenbeck's brother Eddie. Eddie, aged twenty-six, was a brass finisher. He and his wife had been staying temporarily with George. Hollenbeck's lawyer cross-examined Mary, asking whether at the time she claimed to have been raped, she had had intercourse with a man named Billett. Upon objection, Judge Taft excluded the question. Hollenbeck was convicted. On appeal, Judge Henry R. Start held that the question had been proper, citing *Johnson* and *Reed* for support. He noted that the prosecutrix was normally the only witness on the question of consent, and therefore it was vital for the defendant to be able to discredit her testimony. Retried, Hollenbeck was again convicted and sentenced to ten years.[21]

Though they differed about the nature of the sexual reputation evidence that could be admitted in rape cases, all the jurists agreed that the alleged victim's sexual reputation was fair game if she testified. This was a departure from the general rules of evidence which normally allowed only a witness's general reputation for honesty to be admitted. The unself-consciousness with which they accepted this departure is worth thinking about. In no other criminal or quasi-criminal case was such evidence permitted. In bastardy and assault cases, the Court repeatedly held that such evidence was inadmissible and that only general reputation for truth could be used to impeach witnesses who had not been convicted of committing crimes involving moral turpitude. Just two years after *Hollenbeck*, for example, the same Supreme Court ruled that a murder defendant could not impeach witnesses for the state (a husband and wife) by cross-examining them about their operation of a brothel. In *State v. Fournier* (1896) the Court cited the long line of cases discussed above and held that only a witness's general reputation for truth could be tested. None of the judges dissented from the opinion, including Judge Start who had written the opinion in *Hollenbeck* allowing such evidence (and more) in rape cases.[22]

Why then did jurists so easily accept the departure from the general rules of evidence when it came to rape cases? Some men mistrusted women, believing that rape was an easy charge for a woman to make and extremely hard for a defendant to disprove.[23] Sexually promiscuous women were seen as particularly untrustworthy, and given the morality of the times, it would be surprising if they were not so perceived.

As a result, the Supreme Court permitted a woman's reputation for chastity, as well as past specific acts of sexual immorality, to be used against her if she testified. This was an exception applied only to rape cases and was not permitted even in other criminal and civil cases of a sexual nature where there were female witnesses or victims. Technically, its use in rape cases was quite limited. The evidence was admitted solely to impeach the alleged victim on the question of consent and only if she testified. Because the crime's existence rested on the woman's perceptions, and successful prosecution depended on her testimony, her credibility was all-important on the issue of consent. The rule was not intended to immunize men from the risk of prosecution by raping unchaste women. The limited purposes for which such evidence was to be admitted might seem like a distinction without a difference, however. The admission of sexual reputation evidence might well prejudice a conservative, all-male jury against the female victim, since Vermonters were intolerant of nonmarital sexual activity.

If the woman's sexual reputation could be called into question, could the sexual reputation of the male defendant be used against him as well? The law permitted a limited use of character evidence if the defendant chose to testify. Evidence that a testifying defendant had been previously convicted of a crime involving perjury or moral turpitude could be introduced as a means of impeaching him. This included past convictions for sexual assault.[24] And prosecutors sought to introduce character evidence (including sexual character evidence) every chance they got—regardless of its legality.

Thus in *State v. Gile* (1918), a statutory rape prosecution, the state sought to introduce evidence that the defendant had had an illicit relationship with another woman. On objection, the prosecutor argued that the testimony was to be used only to fix a particular date in the mind of the complainant. The Court warned the prosecutor to focus solely on the "intimacies" committed with the complainant herself, but the prosecutor's next question specifically named the other woman anyway. The state also examined a witness about the defendant's general reputation for morality in the community (rather than his reputation for honesty). The witness responded that it was bad. The defendant was convicted and raised the admission of this character evidence on appeal. The Supreme Court recited it without comment and upheld the conviction. Gile was sentenced to three to five years in the state prison.[25]

There is no question that the exception to the general rule regarding character evidence reflected gender conceptions. If a woman had engaged in sex with one man in the past, some judges at least believed that it was likely that she would consent to do it with another man in the future. But even these judges refused to extend this exception beyond rape cases. Only in cases where consent was an issue was this evidence permitted. Thus, in statutory rape cases where consent was not an issue, the Supreme Court refused to permit cross-examination of the girl victims on issues of past sexual activity, except where such evidence showed that another person had committed the act in question.[26]

What effect did the Court's jurisprudence actually have on rape prosecutions? It is difficult to know how many women never came forward because they feared having their past sexual experiences aired in court. We also do not know how many cases were not prosecuted by the state because of this issue, or how many men might have been acquitted after the alleged victim had been impeached by the use of such testimony. But I do not believe that jurists, in allowing such evidence, were motivated by any desire to make it easier for Vermont men to rape women and girls. We know that in some cases admission of this evidence did not prevent convictions. For example, in the *Reed* and *Hollenbeck* prosecutions discussed above, after ruling that the defendant had a right to ask the alleged victim if she had had sex with another man the

Supreme Court remanded the cases for a new trial. As we have seen in both cases, the defendants were again convicted. Furthermore, at the same time that the Court was carving out its exception to the character evidence rule, it also developed a parallel line of decisions. These rulings placed men on notice that it was the woman's perception of events that mattered in a rape prosecution rather than their own.

CONSENT AND THE FEMALE PERSPECTIVE

Vermont society in general and its courts and juries in particular had little tolerance for anyone who engaged in sexual deviance, violence, or self-help.[27] Instead it valued the rule of law, communal peace, and the right to be left alone. At the same time that the courts were carving out an exception to the rules of evidence that applied only to women in rape cases when consent was at issue, other cases carefully defined the right of a woman to control male access to her body. These decisions made it clear that a determination of whether a woman's legal rights had been violated depended on her perceptions of events rather than those of the male defendant.

Four years after the *Johnson* case was decided in 1856, John Hartigan was tried for the rape of Orilla Vincent. Orilla, aged twenty-one, had been a servant in the home of the Rockwell family. Hartigan, aged thirty, was their newly hired hand. One Sunday morning while the Rockwells were at church, Hartigan came in and started flirting with Orilla. He propositioned her, asking if she wanted to have a baby. She told him she would not have one for $300. Hartigan grabbed her, pushed her against a flour barrel, then forced her to the floor, and raped her. After thirty minutes, Hartigan got up and left. Orilla then locked the door. Hartigan went around to a window, but she told him that if tried to come in, she would tell Rockwell. Later, he begged her not to tell what had happened, offering to pay her money and give her a silk scarf. She testified that she would not take his money and he threw it on the floor. She later gave the money—twenty-five cents—to Mrs. Rockwell.

Rockwell testified that Orilla was silent at first about the incident, but once she asked her what was wrong, Orilla told her what had happened and showed her marks and bruises from the assault. Orilla was described as being "a woman of good health and strength, of medium size." Hartigan was described as being "of medium size, and apparent strength." Two doctors testified that as Orilla had described the assault "it was practically impossible that sexual connection or penetration could have taken place," presumably because she should have been able to physically frustrate Hartigan's attempt.

Hartigan faced two counts in the case, one for rape, the other for attempted rape. The trial judge, John Pierpoint, instructed the jury on the law of rape, then turned to the second count for attempt. He told the jury that if they found that Vincent had resisted Hartigan's attempt for a time, "but ultimately yielded," it could find him guilty of the second count for attempt, even if it found that she had later consented to the intercourse. Based on this instruction, and perhaps on the testimony of the doctors concerning the likelihood of actual penetration, the jury acquitted Hartigan of the rape, but found him guilty of attempt.

On appeal, Hartigan's lawyers argued that if Vincent had consented to the later intercourse, that consent "related back" to retroactively condone the initial assault. Judge Loyal C. Kellogg rejected this argument. Writing for the Court, he held that a woman could never retroactively consent to a sexual assault, not even if she later forgave her attacker. "It has never been regarded as a legal excuse for the consummated offence that the woman consented after the fact, and we regard this principle as being applicable to the case of an assault with an intent to commit a rape as well as to the higher offence." If Hartigan had used force against Orilla Vincent with the intent to rape her, he had committed a criminal act. It did not matter if she had later consented to the sexual intercourse. He had no right to assault her in the first place. The Court upheld the conviction and remanded the case for sentencing.[28]

There are several ways to read *Hartigan*. On the one hand, the notion that a woman could be sexually attacked, resist, and then end up consenting to intercourse is the bête noire of feminist rape critiques. This narrative of resistance followed by capitulation leaves women extremely vulnerable to sexual attack and serves as an excuse for men unwilling to take "no" for an answer. On the other hand, the *Hartigan* decision reflects a finely honed technical sense of the right to bodily autonomy. The legal schema imposed by the appellate court allowed a woman to control access to her body on a minute by minute, second by second basis. She could refuse and then consent or, as we will see, she could consent and then refuse. The issue of consent was dependent on the female's perspective, and men attacked women at their own peril. Even assuming that Orilla Vincent had had consensual sex with the hired hand, that had not immunized him from punishment for past bad acts—even those which led to the supposedly consensual sexual encounter.[29]

Fourteen years later, the Court was confronted with the mirror image of the facts of *Hartigan*. In *State v. Niles* (1874) the Court heard an appeal of the conviction of David Niles, aged fifty-five, for the rape of twelve-year-old Lillian Gray.[30] Gray was Niles's stepdaughter. She testified that she had left the house with Niles in late January and walked two miles with him up to a nearby sugar house. On the way, Niles told Lillian that they were going to have sex when they got to the sugar house. She testified that he made no threats nor used any violence toward her. Lillian explained that when they got to the sugar house, Niles took off her underclothes, put her on some boards, and climbed on top of her. She tried to get away from him, but he held her down. She made no outcry. After fifteen minutes they walked to a nearby village where he bought her a dress. They then returned home. On the way, Niles threatened her and told her not to tell anyone about what had happened. Several months later, Lillian's mother left Niles and took Lillian with her to the home of a friend. The friend, a Mrs. Ladd, who was characterized as "unfriendly" toward Niles, asked Lillian if she had been abused by him, and Lillian told her that she had. She told Ladd that she had not told anyone because Niles had threatened to kill her and her mother if she did. Medical testimony showed that Lillian had had sex, probably more than once.

The trial judge, Jonathan Ross, charged the jury that if Lillian had consented to the sexual act, but then withdrew her consent after it had begun, and the defendant thereafter forcibly continued it, knowing she objected, it was still rape. The jury then convicted Niles of rape.

On appeal, Niles's lawyer argued, among other things, that once she had consented, she could not then withdraw her permission in the middle of the act. "When a woman exposes her person, invites sexual intercourse, rouses a man's passions and allows him, in pursuance of such invitation, actually to penetrate her person, the mere fact that the animal passions which have been roused by her own act, refuse to submit to her commands—instantly to cease—has no resemblance to the high crime of rape." The state on the other hand argued that "rape implies violation of the woman's person; and it occurs at any time during the carnal intercourse when the woman withdraws her consent."

The Supreme Court agreed with the state. Judge Homer E. Royce held that there was no rule of universal application on the subject. Instead, the Court could take into account the physical strength of the alleged victim, her relationship to the defendant, and all the other circumstances disclosed by the evidence. Based on the facts of the case, Royce wrote that the trial judge's instruction was not in error and that Lillian's resistance and Niles's continued action rendered him guilty of rape. The Court reversed on other grounds.[31] On retrial, the prosecutor changed tactics and tried the married Niles for adultery instead. Found guilty, he was sentenced to four years in prison.[32]

The Court spoke again on this issue, this time in a decision stemming from a civil ravishment case which fell between *Hartigan* and *Niles* and was decided in 1872. The defendant, Royal Blodgett, worked for Charles Alexander and had been living with the family. Charles's daughter, Mary Alexander, aged fifteen, claimed that she had been sexually assaulted by Blodgett in her father's barn. Blodgett exposed himself to her, then grabbed her shoulders, and tried to lift her dress. Mary told him to "desist" and that if he did not she would tell her father. A few days later, while her parents were out, Blodgett told her he wanted to do the same thing to her again. He chased her around the kitchen, held her, exposed himself, and again tried to lift her clothes. Mary told her mother who told her father. Blodgett continued to work and live in the household for another year before being fired. He went to work for a business rival of Alexander's, and it was then that Charles Alexander brought suit against Blodgett for the assault on his daughter. Blodgett denied that the assaults had ever taken place.

After the evidence had been presented, the trial judge, the same Judge Ross who would instruct the jury in the *Niles* case two years later, charged the jury on the law of assault and battery. In the case of the first incident in the barn, Ross told the jurors that if Blodgett had merely exposed himself and "went towards her, supposing it was in accordance with her wishes, and laid hands on her supposing it was not against her wishes and desire, that would not amount to any assault there." As for the second incident in the kitchen Ross instructed the jurors that:

> when he pursued her, (which would evidently indicate that she didn't desire him to come near her and take hold of her,) if he did take hold of her, it would amount evidently to an assault and battery. On the second occasion if he exposed himself, and she knew what his desire was,

and he went towards her, and she did *not* flee from him, and evidently gave him license, perhaps it would be virtual consent. (emphasis in the original)

The jury then returned a verdict for the defendant and Alexander appealed.

Judge Hoyt H. Wheeler began his opinion with a ringing endorsement of the right of persons to be free from fear of an assault. "The plaintiff had a right to absolute security against any attempt to violate her person," he wrote, and "any invasion of that right was unlawful, and if proceeded with so far as to interfere with her person was actionable." Though the trial judge had correctly stated the law for assaults generally, according to Wheeler, he had failed to take into account the sexual nature of the case before him. Wheeler focused on that part of Judge Ross's instruction that so long as the defendant thought Mary desired his attentions, his exposing himself, coming toward her, and putting his hands on her could not be an assault and battery. He rejected this, noting that for a "virtuous woman or girl" there could be no more grievous personal injury than what the defendant attempted to do to her and what mattered was not what Royal Blodgett thought, but what Mary Alexander perceived.

What he supposed about her wishes or desires would make it none the less an assault unless she directly gave him the right to suppose so. He had no right to make any attempt in that direction without her express and direct consent, and that too first had to be obtained. If he proceeded at all without such free and full consent, it was at his own risk. Furthermore, she had no obligation to flee from him in order to sustain her claim since she might stay without consenting "and if she did so it should not be taken against her." The Court reversed the defense verdict and returned the case to the trial court.[33]

Rounding out the Court's jurisprudence on the issue of male intent in sexual assault cases was an 1890 decision, *State v. Hanlon*. James Hanlon had been charged with the attempted rape of Anna Thompson. He claimed intoxication as a defense, testifying that he had been so drunk at the time that he had no memory of the events in question. As a result, he argued that he could not have formed the requisite mental intent necessary to commit a criminal act. State courts were split as to whether intoxication was a valid defense to a criminal act. Vermont, a dry state since 1852, had little tolerance for this defense, and the Court ruled in

1878 that voluntary intoxication was not a defense to a crime.[34] The trial judge refused to instruct the jurors that intoxication was a defense and in fact told them affirmatively that if Hanlon was drunk, it made no difference. Instead, the jury was to focus on what Hanlon did and said at the time of the assault to determine what his intent had been, rather than what might have been in his mind. The jury convicted. The Supreme Court, on appeal, upheld the trial court, noting that both the victim and the others present at the time of the assault all agreed as to what had taken place.[35]

CORROBORATION

While some legal rulings might appear to have worked a hardship on rape complainants at first glance, sometimes the opposite was true. Take, for example, another exception to the general rules of evidence, which at least one judge believed applied to rape cases—corroboration. In *State v. Bedard* (1892), a Supreme Court judge stated for the first (and only) time that a man could not be convicted for rape solely on the testimony of the woman. Judge Loveland Munson, taking a page from Matthew Hale, noted that rape complaints were "easily simulated" and that proof of the complaint was received "in disregard of the general rules of evidence, because of the peculiar nature of the charge, and of the suspicion with which the law regards the testimony of the prosecutrix."

Judge Munson's statement was not supported by any authority, and I can find no precedent for it in any Vermont materials which preceded the decision. In fact, Vermont judges imposed the corroboration requirement only in criminal cases where the state relied solely on the testimony of an accomplice or particeps criminis (such as the partner in an adultery case). But even that was not law, but simply a rule of practice, and one not closely adhered to at that.[36] At first glance such special requirements (and the attitude reflected by them) might lead one to believe that this new line of reasoning would work a hardship on alleged rape victims and prosecutors—after all, Munson's rule seemed to conceive of the female complainant as an accomplice to a crime rather than as an alleged victim.

But instead of using the law to shield rape defendants, it was a sword in the hands of the state. For in making the statements as he did,

Judge Munson was justifying the introduction of state's evidence harmful to the defendant, and not normally permitted. In *Bedard* the trial court had allowed the state to show that while returning home after the alleged assault, the woman cried continuously. Judge Munson, citing the special need for corroboration, upheld the admission of such evidence in order to bolster the state's case. Furthermore, evidence of a woman's physical or mental distress following the alleged assault could be used to explain "what might otherwise be deemed a suspicious delay in making complaint." The Supreme Court upheld Bedard's conviction and sentenced him to ten years in prison.[37]

Just as the Court's belief that consent was hard to prove had allowed exceptions to the general rules governing the admission of character evidence, the corroboration handicap meant that courts allowed prosecution evidence which was generally inadmissible in other criminal cases. For example, the courts allowed testimony by witnesses who said that the woman had complained to them of being assaulted and had named the assailant. This was a clear exception to the hearsay rule—one which aided prosecutors and harmed defendants. Challenged repeatedly, the Court upheld the admission of such evidence each time, finally declaring in 1918 that the matter was settled for good.[38] And lastly, despite Judge Munson's belief that corroboration was required, defendants were convicted solely on the uncorroborated testimony of women and girls and continued to be despite Munson's ruling.[39]

CONCLUSION

At the same time the courts were carving out a gendered exception to the rules of evidence permitting specific sexual character evidence to refute a claim of consent, they also created another line of precedent making it clear that in Vermont the question of civil and criminal culpability for sexual assaults depended on the female's perspective. The courts rejected attempts by defense lawyers (and some trial judges) to create a subjective male-centered standard for determining consent. Men were not permitted to escape punishment because they "thought" the woman had consented. Instead, they were on notice that they had to be sensitive to the woman's desires, as she perceived them, at all times—not just before the act—but during it as well. And it did not matter if they were mentally impaired by alcohol either. It was their actions that mattered and the effect of those actions on women, not what they thought the woman wanted.

While one opinion late in the period under study asserted that a man could not be convicted solely on the testimony of the victim, the effect of that opinion actually worked a hardship on the defendant rather than the victim, since it was used to justify the admission of state's evidence not normally admitted in criminal cases. Furthermore, later Supreme Court decisions did not adhere to this rule even when raised by defendants appealing their convictions.

It is difficult to assess the impact of character evidence, woman-centered perceptions of sexual assault, and corroboration requirements on efforts to enforce rape laws. We can never know how many rapes actually took place as compared to those prosecuted. Thus we cannot know how many women refused to bring such charges because they feared being cross-examined about past actions. Nor can we know whether a woman's past history may have influenced grand juries or prosecutors not to go forward with a prosecution because of the prosecutrix's past history, nor how many men were acquitted because juries believed that their accusers were immoral, untrustworthy, or not worth protecting. But there is evidence that male Vermonters took the crime seriously.

A survey of every sexual assault case brought in four central Vermont counties between 1794 and 1920 demonstrates high rates of conviction and imprisonment.[40] These data compare favorably to other serious but nonsexual violent crimes, such as murder and attempted murder (see Table 8.1). The only significant difference between sexual assault cases and these other violent crimes was the rate at which state's attorneys chose not to prosecute. Twenty-two percent of sexual assault cases were not ultimately pursued by prosecutors—a rate identical to the nonprosecution rate in simple assault cases, but about twice the rate of more serious crimes like homicide and attempted murder (see Table 8.2). This may reflect the greater evidentiary difficulties posed by a rape case as well as the effect of the admissibility of sexual character evidence in consent cases.

Anecdotally we also know that Vermonters extended the protection of rape law to a wide variety of women who fell outside the mold of traditional Victorian respectability. Examples include Mary Josephs, a Syrian immigrant who found herself in rural Windsor County far from her new home in Burlington. Josephs had numerous strikes against her as a foreigner, stranger, non-English speaker, and peddler. Kate Bowen was a divorced mother of three boys living with her elderly father. She suffered from nervous prostration, did not immediately report the assault, and stayed in the house for fifteen minutes following the attack while a friend waited outside. She never explained this oddity. Mabel Fairbanks was young, deaf, and working class, and evidence was admitted that she had a reputation for sexual immorality. Her parents were separated and lived in local hotels. As a young, non-English-speaking French Canadian, Mary Pratt was at the bottom of Vermont's social pecking order. She and her fiancé told a story of a gang rape by local men which contained many troubling inconsistencies.

The defendants in all four cases advanced plausible defenses to the charges against them. Hostile juries could easily have decided that the high burden of proof required in a criminal case had not been met in all these prosecutions. But they chose instead to convict in all four.[41]

Neither the particular jurisprudence that developed in Vermont, nor its application by local judges and juries was inevitable. One need only look across the border to New York State to see how differently each state could treat an allegation of rape. That state was relentlessly hostile to female accusers. Whereas Vermont had discarded the ancient requirements of outcry and immediate reporting as prerequisites for bringing a rape charge soon after independence in 1777, New York required them throughout the study period. New York also required female victims to make the utmost resistance to their attackers, failing which they were deemed, as a matter of law, to have consented to the intercourse. Victims who had not reported the rape immediately were not permitted to explain the delay. In cases where there was no corroboration the jury had to acquit the defendant as a matter of law. This requirement was by statute. And evidence that a woman had told another person of the assault was not considered corroborative for purposes of the statute. New York also wrote a marital rape exclusion into its statute law.[42]

There is no doubt that Vermont's law was the product of an exclusively male legal system which viewed the world through a highly gendered lens. A significant number of women who made allegations of rape and attempted rape did not see their alleged attacker convicted or even tried. Yet for all that, the system seems to have made an attempt to balance the needs of men and women and apply the law in a way which was reasonable and fair, and it ended up sending many men to prison for violating the integrity of female bodies. The system reflected the gendered assumptions of the time, but also acknowledged the tensions inherent in the rape charge. It did so without sending a message that rape would be tolerated, that women were fair game for men who wanted what was not theirs to take, or that men who attacked women of unconventional social status or morality were immune from prosecution.

The evolution of rape law occurred within a complex local dynamic. Rape law developed within the interstices created by the tug and pull of various local (that is, state) institutions: the appellate court, the legislature, trial courts, and juries. This process was unique to each state. This fact and the existence of important differences between various jurisdictions demonstrates the benefits (and necessity) of studying the law of sexual regulation in the nineteenth and early twentieth century as a state rather than as a national phenomenon.

Table 8.1
Outcomes of Cases Going to Trial or Verdict[1]

Cause	Total	Guilty	Guilty (Jury)	Guilty (Plea)	Not Guilty	Avr. Sent.	Avr. Fine
Rape	52[2]	34 (65%)[3]	25 (48%)	9 (17%)	14 (27%)	8.6 years[4]	n.a.
Homicide	84[5]	56 (67%)[6]	42 (50%)	14 (17%)	27 (32%)	n.a.	n.a.
Att. Rape	59[7]	51 (86%)[8]	34 (58%)	16 (28%)	7 (12%)	4.6 years[9]	$37/88[10]
Att. Murder	138[11]	123 (89%)[12]	60 (43%)	63 (46%)	14 (10%)	5.4 years[13]	$73/81[14]
Sex. Assault	33[15]	31 (94%)	8 (24%)	23 (70%)	2 (6%)	2.0 years[16]	$75

[1] Data cover Orange County (1794–1920); Windsor County (1790–1920); Addison County (1827–1920); Rutland County (1839–1920).
[2] This figure includes 3 cases ending in hung juries and 1 case *nolle prossed* during trial.
[3] Includes 4 verdicts for attempted rape and 1 for simple assault.
[4] N = 25. Average sentence for a rape conviction (8.6 years) and for attempt (7.6 years).
[5] One case ended in a hung jury.
[6] Includes convictions for first- and second-degree murder, manslaughter, and assault.
[7] One case was *nolle prossed* during trial.
[8] Includes 15 verdicts for assault.
[9] N = 30. Average sentence for an attempted rape conviction (4.6 years) and for assault (3.25).
[10] The first figure is the average fine in attempted rape verdicts (n = 9); the second is for assault verdicts (n = 9).
[11] One case resulted in a hung jury.
[12] Includes 59 verdicts for attempted murder and 64 for assault.
[13] N = 83. The average sentence for an attempted murder conviction (5.4 years) and for assault (1.6 years).
[14] The first figure is the average fine for attempted murder verdict (n = 15); the second is for (n = 27).
[15] Includes 29 cases for lewdness and 4 for assault.
[16] N = 18.

Table 8.2

Comparative Non-Prosecution Rates in the Four Counties[1]

Cause	Total	To Verdict	Nolle Prossed	Other[2]
Sexual Assault[3]	209	146 (70%)	47 (22%)	16 (8%)
Homicide	69	58 (84%)	8 (12%)	3 (4%)
Att. Murder	111	91 (82%)	11 (10%)	9 (8%)
Simple Assault	470	341 (73%)	103 (22%)	26 (6%)

[1] Windsor County (1851–1920); Orange County (1880–1920); Addison County (1883–1920); Rutland County (1893–1920).
[2] Includes cases not carried forward by the court and defaults.
[3] The records do not permit distinctions between cases of rape, attempted rape, statutory rape, and attempted statutory rape in calculating nonprosecution rates. This category combines the figures from all of the causes of action.

NOTES

1. This essay is part of a larger comprehensive study of law, sex, and the courts in Vermont between 1777 and 1920. For a greatly expanded examination of rape and other sexual causes of action, see Harold A. Goldman, "'He Had No Right': Sex, Law, and the Courts in Vermont, 1777–1920" (Ph.D. dissertation, University of Massachusetts, Amherst, 2000).

2. Frequently cited authors are Susan Brownmiller, *Against Our Will: Men, Women, and Rape* (New York: Simon and Schuster, 1975); Catharine MacKinnon, "Feminism, Marxism, Method and State: Toward Feminist Jurisprudence," *Signs* 8 (Summer 1983): 635–658; Catharine MacKinnon, "Reflections on Sex Equality under Law," *Yale Law Journal* 100 (1991): 1281–1328; and Susan Estrich, "Rape," *Yale Law Journal* 95 (1986): 1087–1184. Historical studies making such arguments include Lyle Koehler, *A Search for Power: The "Weaker Sex" in Seventeenth-Century New England* (Urbana: University of Illinois Press, 1980); Marybeth Hamilton Arnold, "'The Life of a Citizen in the Hands of a Woman': Sexual Assault in New York City, 1790–1820," in Kathy Peiss and Christina Simmons, eds., *Passion and Power: Sexuality in History* (Philadelphia: Temple University Press, 1989); Terry L. Chapman, "Sex Crimes in the West, 1890–1920," *Alberta History* 35 (Fall 1987): 6–18; Constance Backhouse, *Petticoats and Prejudice: Women and Law in Nineteenth Century Canada* (Toronto: Women's Press, 1991).

3. "If any person shall ravish and carnally know a female of the age of eleven years or more, by force and against her will." 1849 Vt. Acts 7.

4. "Usually the prosecutrix is the only witness upon the question of whether the act was by force and against her will, and without her testimony no conviction can be expected. It is all important to the respondent that he discredit her testimony, and usually his only means of doing this is by cross-examination. If he cannot cross-examine the prosecutrix with a view to discrediting her story,

he is deprived of the substantial benefits of a cross-examination." *State v. Hollenbeck*, 67 Vt. 34, 37 (1894).

5. This disability was removed by statute in 1852. 1852 Vt. Acts 13.

6. Vermont Constitution, chap. I, art. 10 (1793); 1866 Vt. Acts 40.

7. Subject to exceptions Vermonters retain the right to prevent their spouses from testifying as to confidential statements made between them in criminal cases or in civil cases in which the husband and wife are not adverse parties. Vt. R. Evid. 504.

8. The religious and criminal conviction disabilities were removed by statute in 1851. 1851 Vt. Acts 12. The Court did not define "moral turpitude" until 1963 in *State v. Fournier*, 123 Vt. 439, where it declared that such acts had to be "base or depraved" in addition to being criminal. Other authorities define moral turpitude as behavior "that gravely violates moral sentiment or accepted moral standards of a community." *Black's Law Dictionary*, (St. Paul: West Publishing, 1990) abridged 5th ed.(1983).

9. Milo L. Bennett, *The Vermont Justice* (Burlington, 1864), 343; Henry A. Harman, *The Vermont Justice and Public Officer* (Rutland: Tuttle Company, 1905), 366–369.

10. *State v. Smith*, 7 Vt. 141 (1835)(assault and battery); *Morse v. Pineo*, 4 Vt. 281 (1832) and *Spears v. Forrest*, 15 Vt. 435 (1843) (bastardy). The Massachusetts case was *Commonwealth v. Moore*, 3 Pick. (Mass.) 194 (1825).

11. *State v. Johnson*, 28 Vt. 512, 514 (1856). Consent would not have been an issue on the incest count, but incest was punished the same as adultery which allowed a maximum sentence of only five years (as opposed to twenty years for rape). 1797 Vt. Acts 9. On retrial, Johnson was acquitted by a jury. He was later tried that year for an assault on his wife, pleaded guilty, and was sentenced to four months in jail. *State v. Johnson*, Windsor County Court, Woodstock, Vermont, December 1860 Term, State Cases, vol. 1, 538, 596.

12. *State v. Johnson*, 519. On Bennett's evangelical outlook, see "Remarks at the Funeral of Milo Bennett," *Daily Free Press* (Burlington), 10 July 1868. My thanks to Crocker Bennett for this citation.

13. On the role of treatise writing during this period, see R. Kent Newmyer, *Supreme Court Justice Joseph Story: Statesman of the Old Republic* (Chapel Hill: University of North Carolina Press, 1985), 181–195.

14. S. Crocker Bennett II, "Judge Milo Bennett: Puritan in an Industrial Age," paper presented at a symposium of the Vermont Judicial Historical Society, Burlington, Vermont, June 1997, 18. Copy in the possession of the author.

15. Bennett, *The Vermont Justice*, 574–575.

16. This comported with Blackstone. "The civil [i.e. Continental] law seems to suppose a prostitute or common harlot incapable of any injuries of this kind: not allowing any punishment for violating the chastity of her, who had indeed no chastity at all, or at least hath no regard to it. But the law of England

does not judge so hardly of offenders, as to cut off all opportunity of retreat even from common strumpets, and to treat them as never capable of amendment. It therefore holds it to be felony to force even a concubine or harlot; because the woman may have forsaken that unlawful course of life." William Blackstone, *Commentaries on the Laws of England*, vol. 4 (Oxford, 1769), 213.

17. *State v. Reed*, 39 Vt. 417, 418–420 (1867); *State v. Reed*, Windsor County Court, May 1867 Term, Docket No. 233; *State v. Reed*, Windsor County Supreme Court, February 1871 Term, Docket no. 1.

18. *State v. Forshner*, 43 N.H. 89 (1861); *Commonwealth v. Harris*, 131 Mass. 336 (1881). The Harris decision consisted of only one paragraph.

19. *State v. Bridgman*, 49 Vt. 202 (1876).

20. Note to *State v. Johnson*, 28 Vt. 512 (1856) in Charles L. Williams, ed., *Reports of Cases Argued and Determined in the Supreme Court of Vermont* (Minneapolis, 1890).

21. *State v. Hollenbeck*, 67 Vt. 34 (1894); "Report of the Superintendent of the State Prison for 1895–1896," in *Vermont State Officers' Reports for 1895–1896* (Rutland, 1896), 31; *Records of the State Prison at Windsor*, vol. 4, p. 292, Special Collections, University of Vermont, Burlington, Vermont.

22. *State v. Fournier*, 68 Vt. 262 (1896).

23. Judges sometimes referenced Matthew Hale's comment, later quoted in Blackstone, that rape "is a most detestable crime, and therefore ought severely and impartially to be punished with death; but it must be remembered, that it is an accusation easy to be made, hard to be proved, but harder to be defended by the party accused, though innocent." *Blackstone*, vol. 4, 214–215. See for example, *State v. Bedard*, 65 Vt. 278 (1892) in this respect.

24. In *State v. Danforth*, a prosecution for rape, the state's attorney cross-examined the defendant on his prior conviction and imprisonment for attempted rape. The judge instructed the jury that the prior conviction could only be used in assessing the defendant's credibility rather than his propensity to commit the second rape. *State v. Danforth*, Windsor County Court, December 1894, Transcript of Trial. Copy located at Special Collections, University of Vermont, Burlington, Vermont.

25. *State v. Gile*, Vermont Reports Briefs, 93(2), no. 21 (1918), State Law Library, Montpelier, Vermont; *State v. Gile*, 93 Vt. 142 (1919); *Records of the State Prison*, vol. 9, p. 59.

26. Lawyers in statutory rape cases sought to raise the issue of past sexual activity as a test of general credibility. The Court refused to allow an expansion of the narrow rule it had created in adult rape cases where consent was at issue. *State v. Stimpson*, 78 Vt. 124 (1905).

27. "Self-help" means taking an action with legal consequences, whether legal or not—in effect taking the law into one's own hands. *Black's Law Dictionary*, Abridged 5th ed.

28. *State v. Hartigan*, 32 Vt. 607 (1860).

29. Hartigan himself did escape punishment in the end. Remanded back to the county court for sentencing, he was pardoned by the governor instead. *State v. Hartigan*, Addison County Court, Middlebury, Vermont, June 1860 Term, Docket no. 84.

30. At the time, the age of consent in Vermont was eleven. 1818 Vt. Acts 1.

31. *State v. Niles*, 47 Vt. 82 (1874). Vermont law allowed a witness to testify that the alleged victim had told her of the assault and named the perpetrator. The witness was not, however, permitted to give the name of the perpetrator or the particulars of the crime. Mrs. Ladd had done just that in *Niles* and this was the grounds for reversal.

32. For Niles's 1875 conviction for adultery, see "Report of the Superintendent of the State Prison for 1876," in *Vermont Legislative Documents and Official Reports* (Rutland, 1876), 15. Prosecutors sometimes hedged their bets and brought counts for both rape and adultery against defendants in the same prosecution. *State v. Shedrick*, Windsor County Court, December 1896 Term, State Cases, vol. 4, p. 286 (statutory rape and adultery); *State v. Sterlin*, Windsor County Court, May 1866 Term, Docket nos. 107–109 (rape, adultery, lewdness); *State v. Bridgman*, Windsor County Court, December 1857 Term, State Cases, vol. 1, p. 543–544 (rape and adultery).

33. *Alexander v. Blodgett*, 44 Vt. 476 (1872). The courts' emphasis on the issue of consent in Blodgett is odd, given the fact that the defendant denied the incidents had ever taken place. We do not have the transcript of this case, but it is possible that Blodgett argued consent as an alternative defense to non est factum. This may explain why the issue was raised at all.

34. *State v. Tatro*, 50 Vt. 483 (1878). *Tatro* was a prosecution for the axe murder of a woman, Alice Butler, by her husband's hired hand. An example of the Vermont courts' attitude toward alcohol is the 1890 sentence of John O'Neil of Whitehall, New York, to fifty-four years' imprisonment for mailing liquor into the state c.o.d. The U.S. Supreme Court upheld the sentence, mostly on federalism grounds. *State v. O'Neil*, 58 Vt. 140 (1885); aff'd 144 U.S. 323 (1892).

35. *State v. Hanlon*, 62 Vt. 334 (1890).

36. *State v. Potter*, 42 Vt. 495 (1869).

37. *State v. Bedard*, 65 Vt. 278 (1892); "Biennial Report of the Superintendent of the State Prison for 1893–1894," in *Vermont State Officers' Reports for 1893–1894* (Rutland, 1894), 28.

38. "Hearsay" is an out of court statement intended to prove the truth of the matter asserted. *Davis v. Fuller*, 12 Vt. 178 (1840); Harman, *The Vermont Justice and Public Officer*, 350. Vermont law permitted witnesses to testify that the woman or girl had reported an assault to them and to affirm that she had named an assailant. It did not permit the witness to name the man—but the alleged victim could do that. *State v. Carroll*, 67 Vt. 477 (1895); *State v. Niles*, 47 Vt. 82 (1874).

39. See, for example, *State v. Stimpson*, "Brief for State," 3, and "Certification of Appeal," 2; *Vermont Reports Briefs*, 78(1), no. 19 (1905), where the defense argued that there was no corroborating testimony. The Supreme Court never addressed this point in its opinion upholding the conviction. *State v. Stimpson*, 78 Vt. 124 (1905).

40. The four counties are Addison, Orange, Rutland, and Windsor. Court records document every cause of action in Orange and Windsor counties from the late eighteenth century to 1920. The Addison County Court record books become reliable in 1827 and Rutland County's records, supplemented with judgment files located at the courthouse, are reliable from 1838 onward.

41. *State v. Danforth*, Windsor County Court, December 1894 Term, Transcript of Trial; *State v. Buckman*, Windsor County Court, June 1901 Term, Transcript of Trial; *State v. Gauthier*, Windsor County Court, June 1904 Term, Transcript of Trial. Copies of transcripts are also located at Special Collections, University of Vermont, Burlington, Vermont. The facts of the Pratt rape were gleaned from several sources: *State v. Bedard*, 65 Vt. 278 (1892); *State v. Wilkins and Blow*, 66 Vt. 1 (1892); *State v. Bedard*, Vermont Reports Briefs, 65 (1), no. 42 (1892), State Law Library, Montpelier, Vermont. These and other cases are discussed in greater detail in Goldman, "He Had No Right," 268–285.

42. Vermont's original rape statute enacted in 1779 had required the woman to make an "out-cry" during the rape and bring her complaint immediately after the assault. These prerequisites were dropped from the law in 1791. Vermont never required utmost resistance as some other states did. Allen Soule, ed., *Laws of Vermont, 1777–1780*, vol. 12 of *State Papers of Vermont* (Montpelier: Secretary of State, 1964), 40–41; John A. Williams, ed., *Laws of Vermont, 1791–1795*, vol. 15 of *State Papers of Vermont* (Montpelier: Secretary of State, 1967), 20. New York cases: *People v. Morrison*, 1 Parker Cr. R. (N.Y.) 625 (1854); *Reynolds v. People*, 41 How. Prac.(N.Y.) 179 (1871); *People v. Dohring*, 59 N.Y. 374 (1874); *People v. Clark*, 3 N.Y. Cr. R. 280 (1885); *People v. Butler*, 66 N.Y.S. 851 (1900); *People v. Flaherty*, 162 N.Y. 532 (1900); *People v. Page*, 162 N.Y. 272 (1900); *People v. Carey*, 223 N.Y. 519 (1918); *People v. Meli*, 193 N.Y.S. 365 (1922).

9

"In the Marriage Bed Woman's Sex Has Been Enslaved and Abused"

Defining and Exposing Marital Rape in Late-Nineteenth-Century America

Jesse F. Battan

"FROM ONE END of the country to the other," argued *Woodhull and Claflin's Weekly* in 1871, "there comes up one great and mournful cry—the almost universal weakness of women."[1] The author of this editorial was only one of many who decried the deplorable condition of women's health throughout the last half of the nineteenth century. Drawing on her own experience as well as her contact with other women as she toured the "Free States" of the North and the West in the decade before the Civil War, Catherine Beecher, for example, came to the conclusion that there is "a terrible decay of female health all over the land." Listing the prevalence of a host of ailments plaguing women, ranging from nervous headaches, consumption, and neuralgia to pelvic disorders, general debility, and feebleness, Beecher demonstrated to her own satisfaction that the number of "sound and healthy" women of all classes, living in the countryside and in the cities, had declined appreciably in only one generation.[2]

Like Beecher, most nineteenth-century commentators identified this change as a recent phenomenon and blamed it on what they identified as the corrosive elements of modern civilization. In the hands of social critics and moral reformers, women's frail health became a symptom of the social, emotional, and physical changes they roundly condemned, such as the ingestion of "stimulating" food and beverages, the

lack of fresh air and exercise, the wearing of constricting undergarments essential to "fashionable" dress, and the general overstimulation
of the nervous system through contact with "improper" ideas, images,
and amusements.[3] Unlike most observers of this phenomenon, however, the editorial in *Woodhull and Claflin's Weekly* provided a different
etiology of the sudden emergence of the new maladies plaguing
women. The most obvious cause, it argued, was an increase in the use
of contraceptives as well as in efforts to terminate conceptions. This desire to avoid childbearing, however, was only a reflection of an even
more profound shift in women's sense of self: they were becoming increasingly resentful of their inability to say no to intercourse within
marriage. Women, in short, were beginning to feel that access to their
bodies should be "theirs to grant or refuse." The conflict between
women's desire for self-ownership and their subjection to "undesired
sexual relations" was generating an inner "antagonism" that was ultimately responsible for the destruction of their physical well-being.[4]

Recent work in women's history has explored the nineteenth century's preoccupation with the decline of women's health. Some scholars have argued that rather than reflecting changes in the actual physical condition of women, their claim of frail health was perhaps an
affectation adopted as a sign of delicacy and gentility.[5] Most historians, however, have taken women's complaints at face value. Edward
Shorter, for example, argues that the common descriptions of the pale
and physically weak Victorian woman indicate that she was suffering
from "iron-deficiency anemia" as well as a host of gynecological disorders—contracted pelvis, leukorrhea, perineal tears and fistulas,
uterine tumors, ovarian cysts, and endometriosis—that would have
made intercourse and pregnancy painful and encouraged women to
shy away from physical contact.[6] More to the point, some have maintained that women presented a frail demeanor in order to resist the
unwanted sexual attentions of their husbands and to avoid unwanted
pregnancies. Women's medical complaints, they argue, were a psychosomatic expression of their desire for sexual autonomy as well as
the anger and frustration they experienced when this was not forthcoming.[7] Supporting the conclusions reached by the author of the editorial in *Woodhull and Claflin's Weekly*, twentieth-century historians
have concluded that many of the illnesses women suffered were an
outgrowth of conflicts between husbands and wives over the issue of
sexual consent within marriage. This essay examines the emerging

struggle for women's sexual autonomy by focusing on the efforts of nineteenth-century sexual radicals known as the "Free Lovers." These reformers sought to reconstruct the sexual politics of domestic life by publishing the testimonies of wives who complained of marital sexual abuse. In the process, they richly documented the conflicts such treatment engendered.

By the 1820s, Victorian novelists, moralists, and clergymen had created sentimentalized images of the companionate marriage that portrayed private life as a utopian retreat from the lust and greed of the commercial economy.[8] In addition to providing women with a social identity and economic security, marriage was also described as the only institution that would protect the "true" pious and pure Victorian woman from the lascivious brutality of men in the marketplace. Throughout the nineteenth century, jurists, clergymen, and moral reformers argued that marriage was the essential precondition for the rise of civilization, and that both marriage and civilization ensured that woman's chastity would be cherished and protected.[9]

In the early nineteenth century this sentimental image of marriage and women's identity was accompanied by a corresponding preoccupation with sexual coercion in the public arena. In order to control male licentiousness, for example, nineteenth-century moral reformers campaigned for laws against seduction, prostitution, and sexual assaults.[10] Few of these reformers, however, were concerned with sexual coercion within marriage. This was true in part because of what legal scholars have referred to as the "marital rape exemption," which granted a husband immunity from prosecution even if he forced his wife to have sex against her will. This influential common law doctrine, expressed by the seventeenth-century English jurist Sir Matthew Hale, held that a wife's consent, once given at the altar, could not be rescinded. In legislative enactments and court opinions, rape was thus defined as "an act of sexual intercourse with a female not the wife of the perpetrator." As a Massachusetts Supreme Court opinion bluntly stated in 1857, "A man cannot commit a rape on his own wife." Clearly, the doctrine of "implied consent" argued that once married, wives lost their right to refuse their husbands' sexual advances.[11] Moreover, many women internalized the belief, maintained by friends and family as well as by medical, legal, and religious authorities, that it is a wife's duty to sexually cohabit with her husband regardless of her desires. Law and ideology thus mitigated against resistance, and shame and reticence discouraged disclosure. As a result, unless it was accompanied by extraordinary acts of violence, marital rape was almost invisible in Victorian America, since it seldom found its way into public discourse, private correspondence, the dockets of criminal courts, or the transcripts of divorce trials.[12]

By the 1840s, however, some temperance workers, abolitionists, social purity crusaders, and advocates for women's rights extended their concern with sexual coercion to include the relationship between husband and wife. Comparing the gap between the sentimental, companionate ideal and the everyday realities of mundane marriages, they argued that while marriage protected women from sexual predators in the public sphere it subjected wives to the unregulated appetites of their husbands.[13] Drawing on the sexual ideology of the radical Enlightenment and the abolitionist movement, these reformers used terms like "prostitution" and "slavery" to describe the emotional condition and the legal position of the married woman.[14] The image of marriage as prostitution, like the image of marriage as slavery, centered around the issue of sexual consent within marriage itself. Both became potent metaphors for those who extended their critique of unrestrained male desire expressed in the relationships between master and slave, procurer and prostitute, and seducer and victim to include that of husband and wife.

For the most part, however, this critique was limited by several factors. Like those who sought to end extrafamilial forms of sexual coercion—seduction, prostitution, and "white slavery"—most reformers who attempted to reconstruct the sexual politics of married life were unwilling to attack the institution itself. The vast majority of moral reformers, purity crusaders, temperance workers, and women's rights advocates insisted that alcohol or unrestrained male sexuality were the primary causes of marital sexual abuse.[15] Even though these reformers promoted the idea of sexual self-ownership or "voluntary motherhood," which served as the basis for their critiques of the sexual authority of husbands, they essentially sought to strengthen marriage by bringing it into line with the companionate ideal. For example, the feminist-abolitionist Sarah Grimke railed against the "horrors of forced maternity"—her euphemistic reference to marital rape—and celebrated women's sexual and political autonomy, but she was quick to defend herself against critics who argued that this would lead to the abolition of marriage. The goal of her efforts, she maintained, was "to purify and exalt the marriage relation," and she advised those who had not found such "true" marriage to endure their fate and "bear in quiet home seclusion, the heart withering consequences" of their own mistakes.[16]

A second characteristic of mainstream reformers' critique of marital sexual abuse was its extreme reticence. While many complained that a wife was often forced to submit to her husband's unwanted advances because she did not have the right to control her body, few openly explored, in speeches or in print, the experiences of women who suffered from marital sexual abuse.[17] This was in part the result of their unwillingness to violate the Comstock Act, which after 1873 was used to punish public discussions of sexual topics.[18] It also reflected the power of Victorian notions of propriety and decorum. "Women keep silence upon many points, not breathing their thoughts to their dearest friends," wrote Matilda Gage in 1868, "because of their inner reticence, a quality they possess greatly in excess of men."[19] Unlike their vivid portrayals of the sufferings endured by prostitutes and slaves, the descriptions of domestic sexual abuse written by these reformers were filled with euphemisms and vague references to the condition being described. As an editorial in the conservative *Woman's Journal* argued in 1871: "If the secrets back of the early deaths of young wives and mothers, which are appalling in numbers, could be revealed—and we are hastening to a time when there will be an unveiling of these secrets, which we shrink to contemplate—it would be seen that we are mildly hinting at perpetually enacted tragedies, secret, social and domestic, which are enough to sadden angels."[20]

There were other reformers, however, less timid than the editors of the *Woman's Journal*, who did not wait until some future time to unveil the secrets of nineteenth-century marriages. The most consistent and outspoken critique of marital sexual abuse in the late nineteenth century was created by a loose coalition of sexual reformers, the Free Lovers. Contrary to Victorian characterizations of the Free Lovers as advocates of irresponsible promiscuity, they sought to bring "reason, knowledge and continence" to play in the regulation of human sexuality and to bring a higher state of order and responsibility to the sexual lives of men and women.[21] Moreover, the central goal of Free Love was not to grant "more freedom for men to gratify their sensual natures," as Lois Waisbrooker argued in 1891. In contrast, the reforms they sought would grant a wife the right to say *no* to her husband and create emotional and sexual relationships that would be based on mutual consent and desire rather than on unilateral domination and conquest. Free Love, according to Francis Barry, was based on the "theoretical and practical recognition of woman's absolute right to self-ownership."[22]

While they also sought to curb the unrestrained desires of husbands, the Free Lovers differed fundamentally from most nineteenth-century marital reformers. First, they avoided the use of euphemisms. Unlike many feminists and social purity crusaders, who used such terms as "enforced motherhood" to describe marital sexual abuse, the Free Lovers boldly defined sexual assault within marriage as rape.[23] They also did more than hint at the sexual abuse suffered by wives. In an effort to eliminate it they openly challenged the reticence of Victorian culture and in their newspapers, pamphlets, and novels they exposed the various forms of sexual coercion—physical, economic, and psychological—they encountered. In their public speeches and writings they also cataloged a host of ills suffered by wives as a result, ranging from heartbreak, humiliation, and anger to nervous strain, physical debility, and death. Finally, while their attack on marital sexual abuse was profoundly influenced by the logic and language of feminist-abolitionists and temperance advocates before the Civil War and women's rights and neoabolitionist social purity crusaders after it, the Free Lovers identified marriage as the institution that legitimized sexual intercourse without consent. As a result, rather than reform marriage they sought to abolish it.

The Free Lovers could not have vilified the institution of marriage in more ardent terms. Marenda B. Randell, for example, described it as a "great cancerous growth upon the social structure" whose true nature has been discovered by those who had finally "probed its rottenness, . . . stirred its filthy waters," and uncovered a "deep, dark, foul, stagnant pool of semi-translucent corruption." Francis Barry, a lifelong crusader against marriage, described it as the "vilest thing in existence." As commonly practiced, marriage was a corrupt bargain that produced only "misery and degradation."[24] Sweeping in their condemnation of it, the Free Lovers were unanimous in their belief that "legal marriage" was the source of all "the misery, vice and crime" that plagued mankind.[25]

The Free Love critique of marriage was influenced by a variety of ideas and experiences. The antislavery experiences of many Free Lovers, for example, provided them with a rhetoric that was quickly tailored to their struggle with an institution they found to be more "degrading and damning" than the southern system of chattel slavery.[26] This influence is clearly demonstrated in their argument that marriage, like slavery, placed women in a condition of perpetual servitude. Stripped of its romantic trappings, they argued, the power relationship between husband and wife was identical to that of master and slave. Thomas L. Nichols insisted, for example, that the marriage ceremony sanctioned a husband's legal ownership of the mind and body of his wife. At the core of the institution was the "absolute right of one human being to control the life of another," sanctioning the most nefarious form of enslavement. Marriage laws, asserted Rachel Campbell, were created by men to ensure their control over women. Their primary aim was to "protect each man from the encroachments of all other men and insure him the peaceful possession of the woman he claimed," and had little to do with the protection of the rights and welfare of women and children. Sensitive to the consequences of absolute and arbitrary power in human relationships, Free Lovers such as Moses Harman argued that marriage, like slavery, rendered women powerless and placed them in a state of servile subjection to "man's caprice, passion and cruelty."[27]

The injustice that was at the heart of the institution of marriage lay not only in the husband's usurpation of his wife's right to political and economic self-determination. What was most devastating to the well-being of the wife was that matrimony granted her husband absolute control over her body and her sexual desires. "Marriage," Barry bluntly argued in 1857, "is a system of Prostitution." More importantly, he continued, it is also "a system of Rape." Within marriage, argued Mary Gove Nichols, women are "subjected to more amative abuse than any paid harlot." Wives, concurred Moses Hull, "for no other reason than because they are such, are compelled to yield their bodies to the 'animal passions' of their husbands" with little chance to defend themselves from such onslaughts of sensuality. As one supporter of the Free Love cause concluded: "Can a Czar have more absolute power over a subject than a man has over the genitals of his wife?"[28]

Of all the rights lost by wives within marriage, the Free Lovers argued that this "sexual slavery" was the most detrimental to the happiness and dignity of women. The husband's absolute control over the body of his wife unleashed his base, lustful desires.[29] "None can deny that custom, law and religion give the husband full control of his wife's person," asserted Lizzie M. Holmes, and as a result there was little "to prevent the occasional abuse of this power and consequent agony of sick, weak, lacerated wives." Moreover, Free Lovers such as Dagmar Mariager argued that the husband's "legal right to impose himself sexually upon his wife" undermined all her rights and "invites his imposition of every other conceivable form of abuse upon her, and compels her submission to it." Connecting the politics of public and private life, the Free Lovers identified the instrument of abuse—the penis—with a legal system that denied the rights of citizenship to women, and bemoaned the fate of the wife who suffered from the "abuse inflicted upon her by her husband's 'voting qualification.'"[30]

The Free Lovers did more than critique the institution of marriage. They also challenged a legal system and moral culture that strictly regulated the social geography of sexual conversations, restricting them to the private bedroom whispers of husbands and wives or to the restrained discourses of social elites. In their effort to expose and eliminate marital sexual abuse the Free Lovers rejected the claims made by physicians, clergymen, jurists, and moralists that they alone were empowered to discuss sexual issues in public and provided a powerful alternative voice in public sexual conversations.[31]

Because they were unhampered by Victorian reticence or the fear of portraying marriage in too negative a light, the Free Lovers are a valuable source for understanding the intimate experiences of American men and women in Victorian America. In order to "tear aside the veil that the Church and the Law have placed around wedlock" and expose the "pollution, the outrages, and the murders, thus sanctioned and protected," they were anxious to acquire a first-hand knowledge of the actual, everyday experiences of wives.[32] This was not an easy task, however, since most women fiercely guarded these secrets from the public eye. "Women are taught that it is a shame for them to tell these things," wrote Lois Waisbrooker in 1896, "so they are silent or only whisper their woes into the ears of some sympathizing friend."[33]

Often, the Free Lovers themselves provided the sympathetic ear to which many wives poured out their complaints of marital sexual abuse. Through conversations, private letters, and published correspondences the Free Lovers had access to what the abolitionist and sex reformer Stephen Pearl Andrews described as "a wonderful mass of 'confidences' and 'appeals'" from thousands of women which described in intimate detail the forms of sexual abuse suffered by nineteenth-century wives. Warren Chase, an itinerant reform lecturer made similar claims. "No one can travel in this country, and become acquainted with social life, and not find his pathway strewn with the wrecks of matrimonial misery," he wrote in 1866. "I have received hundreds of mournful histories in the last ten years,—some written, some printed, and some never to be written, nor hardly spoken aloud."[34] As confidants to "people of all ages" who sought to relate to them "the secret stories of their lives," the Free Lovers amassed ample evidence to support their claim that "force and rape reign[ed] triumphant in the marriage bed."[35]

Collecting this information, however, was only half the battle. The Free Lovers also sought to expose horrific examples of marital rape to "the gaze of an incredulous" public.[36] By publicizing these experiences they were attempting to communicate to wives that they were not alone. Rather than encourage them to endure such treatment, as reformers such as Sarah Grimke had done, their goal was to embolden women to assert their "dignity as human beings" and not suffer in "silence and pain."[37] Moreover, by bringing to light "what delicate women are compelled to suffer without redress at the hands of brutal, lustful husbands to whom the law binds them bodily without power to refuse," the Free Lovers attempted to transform isolated private experiences into personal and political action that would transform law, sentiment, and social custom.[38] To do this, they worked to bridge the gap between public and private life maintained by genteel codes of conduct and parade before the eyes of "respectable society" the aberrant forms of sexual behavior bred by a marriage system that provided a husband with "a legal license to rape at pleasure."[39]

Like the antislavery, temperance, and antiprostitution activists who drew on the "actual conditions" of those who suffered from abusive relationships in order to make their point, the Free Lovers knew that the detailed presentation of the "facts of real life" was a powerful tool in the hands of reformers.[40] "The 'abolitionists' found it necessary to report all the horrors of African slavery in order to create a sentiment sufficient to prevail against it," argued E. B. Foote, Jr., in 1893, "and the advocates of equality for woman will probably have to employ all the weapons at their command and paint the horrors of modern matrimony in their worst colors in order to make any telling impression on such minds as now see sanctity in its slavery." Through vivid descriptions of the pain suffered by sexually abused wives, the Free Lovers sought to transform public sentiment. "Public exposure" of the sexual cruelties experienced by wives, they defiantly proclaimed to their critics and censors, would perhaps offend public modesty. But it would also reshape society's view of the institution of marriage itself, which was an essential step toward the elimination of the abuses they described. "If such recitals help to open the eyes of men and women to see that a system cannot be wholly good that permits such outrages," concluded Moses Harman, "then our first object will be gained."[41]

Challenging the marital ideal celebrated in nineteenth-century sentimental literature, the Free Lovers instead argued that the laws of marriage created an environment that unleashed the worst in men. The sweet words and gracious manner that characterized the conduct of the young lover courting his heart's desire were quickly replaced by the vicious, demanding demeanor of the slaveholder once the marriage ceremony had been performed. Reflecting on her own "honeymoon," one of the central characters in a Free Love novel entitled *A Woman's Story Seldom Told*, recalled the anxiety and fear she felt as a result of this transformation. Left by her friends to the solitude of her wedding suite, she waited for the appearance of her husband of but a few short hours. Standing before a mirror she contemplated her "blushing, happy face," and admired her "white and pretty" shoulders that had been revealed where the straps of her wedding dress had fallen. Suddenly, her husband appeared. As she shyly peered through the "tresses of hair" that had shaded her eyes she looked up and saw "not the tender, reverential gaze of a *gentleman*, but the wild, eager glare of an unchained animal" who then lunged and grabbed her in a fit of unrestrained passion, crushing her with "a wild, terrible embrace."[42] Licentiousness and lust were not curbed by marriage, they concluded, but were inflamed by it.

Throughout the last half of the nineteenth century, the pages of Free Love newspapers and pamphlets were filled with accounts of the sexual brutality women faced at the hands of their husbands. The real-life examples of sexual abuse they described in the articles they wrote and the letters to the editor they published closely paralleled the terror, pain, and disgust experienced by the heroines in their novels, and were paraded before the eyes of the public as examples of "the hidden mysteries of the marriage institution."[43]

Physicians sympathetic to the feminist goals of the Free Lovers provided one important source of information on the sexual abuse suffered by nineteenth-century wives. While most women "would rather die than confess to *this* sort of abuse" from their husbands, observed Elmina Drake Slenker in 1890, a "doctor receives many confessions from his patients." A good example is provided by a Dr. W. G. Markland who sent Moses Harman, the editor of *Lucifer, Light-Bearer* a letter from a close female friend which described the experiences of a woman who had recently given birth. Because of the incompetence of her attending physicians she suffered lacerations and subsequently endured several painful operations to correct her condition. While she was recuperating from her latest experience under the surgeon's knife, Markland reported, her husband "forced himself into her bed and the stitches were torn from her healing flesh, leaving her in a worse condition than ever." Incensed by this behavior, Markland was even more irate that the wife had no legal recourse to punish her attacker. "Will you point to a law that will punish this brute?" he rhetorically asked his reader. "If a man stabs his wife to death with a knife," he continued, "does not the law hold him for murder?" But if he "murders her with his penis, what does the law do?"[44] Another physician, a Dr. Lydia Hunt King from Portland Oregon, also provided the readers of *Lucifer* with several of the cases of marital abuse she encountered in her practice. When one of her patients went into labor, for example, "her liege lord demanded his *marital rights* before going for the doctor." Another patient who resisted her husband's sexual demands soon after giving birth was forced to flee to the bed of her other children in order to "save herself," but was taken back to her marriage bed "at the point of a pistol."[45]

Specifically responding to such disclosures Dr. Richard V. O'Neill, writing from New York City, concluded that the incidents of marital sexual abuse reported in Free Love newspapers were "not at all uncommon." During his two decades as a physician he claimed to have encountered many wives who were murdered by selfish, lust-driven husbands. "It is a well known fact," he wrote, "that thousands of women are killed every year by sexual excesses forced on them." To support this assertion he gave specific examples of such abuse. "Mrs. M— of this city *died* of injuries caused by the brutal sexual connection of her husband, a few days after an operation had been performed for perineal laceration." He also described the condition of several wives who were "slowly dying" as a result of the excessive sexual demands made by their brutish husbands. Women such as this, who endured frequent and lengthy periods of such abuse, he concluded, faced "mental and physical destruction—the mad-house or a premature grave."[46]

In addition to physicians who gained the confidences of their patients, the Free Love newspaper published the letters of others who similarly described the drastic consequences of husbands who imposed themselves on unwilling wives. One reader, Jeremiah Hacker, wrote to Moses Harman and described his conversation with a man whose first two wives had eighteen children and several abortions between them. According to Hacker, he complained that "both his wives died young" because they were not strong enough to perform "the duties of wifehood." Contradicting the conclusions of this obtuse husband, Hacker argued that the death of the two women was caused by a marital system that denied women the right to say no to their husbands. These wives, he wrote, were murdered by "sexual abuse," which yearly sends "thousands" to their early graves.[47]

Warren Chase, who claimed to have encountered scores of women who had been sacrificed "on the altar of lust," provided a more detailed example of a husband who was able to sexually abuse his wife without any repercussions. The man in question, a self-righteous churchgoer who prided himself on his Christian virtues, boasted of his fidelity to his wife while he adamantly attacked those, such as the Free Lovers, who challenged the "marital rights of husbands." But Chase demonstrated the hypocrisy of this position. Five days after the birth of his first child he announced to his "slender" and "delicate" wife and her nurse that he was going to take his place beside her in their marriage bed. Aware of his true designs she resisted, "assuring him it would kill her." The nurse also warned that intercourse would weaken her health. "He of course conquered, as the wife had promised to obey, and both church and State said she must—and she did. He occupied the bed with her that night, and the consequence of which was a fever brought on by sexual abuse, followed by the death of the wife." Rather than face a prison sentence, within a short time after his wife's death this "stout and plethoric orthodox deacon" was out looking for another victim with the full support of the religious and legal authorities.[48]

One question that was repeatedly asked in response to such portrayals of domestic abuse was, why did these wives endure such treatment? The answer to this question is complex and provides insight into both the coercive aspects and the emotional dynamics of nineteenth-century marriages. As one woman argued, "No wife dreams of the tyrannical power she is under until she begins to assert her selfhood."[49] In support of this assertion, some described the violence a wife encountered that all but assured submission to her husband's will. One reader, for example, provided the case of a "fair, healthy young widow" who had married a "middle-aged man with a family of grown-up children, a farmer, as well off as need be, and of good repute." After seven years of marriage and two more children, she soon lost her health. "She knew that sexual intercourse caused her a great deal of pain, and she resolved to avoid it for a time, although her husband was not willing to be denied even one night." One morning, after she had refused his advances, "he became so enraged that he clutched her by the throat and held her, till her face was very purple and she ceased to struggle, and settled down like one dead." Frightened, he loosened his grasp of her neck and tried to revive her. While she soon regained her breath, her spirit had been broken and she finally gave in to him, "saying she might as well be killed one way as another."[50]

In addition to the coercive power of domestic violence, the experiences described in Free Love newspapers also revealed the power of community pressure that husbands could draw on to enforce their sexual prerogatives. In the 1850s, Lily White gave the example of one woman who "'refused her husband continuously,' for a time—after submitting to his nightly demands for several years, and suffering all she thought her duty in childbirth and otherwise." Angry at her refusal her husband, a well-respected man in his community, took the matter to his church council who decided that she should return to her husband's bed and "submit to the duties or requirements of the 'sacred institution.'" Realizing that resistance was futile, "she gave up in despair, and in a little over a year, was in such a condition, that the women who witnessed her extreme agony of body and mind, concluded she had borne more than was her duty; but the church did not reverse its decision, or deal with him for abusing his power." Because men rule in the church, the state, and the family, she concluded, women had little choice but to "suffer and die."[51]

Some wives were also reluctant to resist their spouses' sexual demands because of their sense that it was their "duty to yield obedience to their husbands."[52] Citing her own experiences as a guide, one wife wrote to Moses Harman and complained that she was incapable of restraining her husband from "asserting his 'marital rights.'" Married at the age of seventeen to a man she barely knew, her husband's insensitivity to her desires made her feel little but "loathing and horror" when he forced himself upon her. As a result, she confided,

I soon learned to despise him. For ten long weary years I endured a life of cruel outrages—thinking I was married I must submit and keep silent. You are my wife! was the answer I got when I ventured to remonstrate. Notwithstanding tears, cries, and agony, pleadings to God for death, and almost in my heart a murderer, I bore three children.[53]

Another woman related a conversation she had had with her mother soon after the death of her father, in which her mother complained that she "could never talk to him on any subject, or lie one moment in the morning, without his becoming excited." She submitted to his excessive demands, she revealed, "because I thought I was married, and ought. I thought it was woman's duty to submit to what I conceived man's right, and that what I had to suffer, others had, the wide world over." Looking back on a life of physical suffering and emotional disgust that resulted from the "force and violation" she experienced in her marriage bed, she confided to her daughter, "Oh! your father's death is such a relief."[54]

What is clear from such testimony is that wives endured abusive treatment because they felt they had no recourse. Women often felt excluded from the legal system or did not have the money to use it. And even if they had access to the courts, many were reluctant to reveal their experiences to "jeering lawyers, a cross examiner whose business it is to make the witness a liar, and the usual roomful of the curious."[55] Moreover, throughout most of the nineteenth century American courts paid little attention to wives' complaints of sexual abuse in divorce proceedings unless it was the result of malicious intent or accompanied by other forms of legally defined cruelty.[56] In addition, economic dependence, the fear of losing their children, the power of the church in women's lives, and the "disgrace, calumny, [and] persecution" that awaited wives who demanded their right to control their bodies, the Free Lovers concluded, explained why many women endured abusive relationships.[57]

In their descriptions of sexual abuse within marriage, then, the Free Lovers included all forms of coercion. Unlike the rape cases tried in the courts, the standard by which they defined marital rape had little to do with the amount of "physical compulsion" imposed by the husband or by the amount of "physical resistance" put forth by the wife. Francis Barry, for example, described rape as "imposing the sexual act upon a woman, or demanding sexual gratification, without exciting the reciprocal feeling on her part." Lack of desire on the part of the woman—single or married—was all that mattered.[58] Wives who submitted to their husbands out of a desire to "keep peace in the family," or out of fear "that refusal will alienate" their husbands' affections were as much the victims of marital rape as those who yielded to their husbands through violence and physical intimidation.[59]

For the Free Lovers, the pain and discomfort associated with intercourse, pregnancy, and childbirth have been women's constant companions throughout history. What was new was their unwillingness to submit without choice. And based on the conversations and observations, the Free Lovers concluded that it was the lack of consent that was destroying the physical and emotional health of American women. When a woman "voluntarily" endures physical pain and discomfort "for love or parentage," the anarchist Lizzie Holmes argued in the pages of *Lucifer* in 1891, "no man can be blamed or reproached." But when these are forced "upon her unwillingly—there lies the terror, the awful misery which no vividness of description can exaggerate."[60] In addition to the somatic illnesses women faced that were generated by the mistreatment of their reproductive systems, the Free Lovers also identified psychosomatic conditions shaped by the anger and disgust that wives were beginning to experience more intensely and in larger numbers than ever before. Imagine the feelings experienced by a wife, argued Lois Waisbrooker, whose protest against undesired intercourse are ignored, forcing her to yield "with every feeling of her soul repulsed and with a sense of degradation that nearly crushes the life out of her." In the "secret stories" described in the pages of Free Love newspapers, broken hearts, bred by humiliation and disappointment, as well as bodies broken by physical maladies associated with undesired marital intercourse, pregnancy, and parturition, took their toll on the well-being of America's women in nineteenth-century America.[61]

Throughout the nineteenth century critics of the Free Lovers were quick to deny their claims of the prevalence of marital sexual abuse in the Victorian bedroom. In 1854, for example, Adin Ballou argued that these sexual radicals "are prone to exaggerate the evils of dual marriage. They seem to think the best half of their battle is won, if they can only make these evils appear sufficiently dreadful. Accordingly they harp incessantly on this string."[62] As part of their project to eliminate marriage, the Free Lovers clearly had a stake in publicizing these incidents of abuse. They did not, however, make them up. In response to the frequently asked question, "Are these things true?" the Free Lovers were quick to argue that the experiences of marital rape they published occurred all too frequently. "I *know* both from oral confessions to me personally and written confessions of hundreds to me in letters, that these terrible tales are more than true," argued Elmina Slenker in 1890. "For twenty years or more I've been searching for these cases, and in confidence have received information enough to fill a volume." Priscilla Lawrence, writing from South Bend, Indiana, made similar claims. After some eight years traveling from town to town lecturing on the virtues of temperance and health reform, Lawrence reported that she had "been repeatedly made sick at heart by the private histories of wives and mothers. I have heard enough of their wrongs and abuses from the hands of husbands to cause the blood to curdle with horror at the recital."[63] Drawing on their own experiences as well as those of the women they encountered, the Free Lovers insisted that thousands if not millions of wives had been raped by "husbands who professed to love them, and promised to love them and be kind to them after marriage and then, when the knot was tied, falsified their promise and made them the victims of sexual abuse."[64]

Free Love periodicals were one of the few venues that gave voice to these women and described experiences that for the most part were hidden from public view in Victorian America. Lizzie Holmes, for example, described *Lucifer* as "the mouthpiece, almost the only mouthpiece in the world, of every poor, suffering defrauded, subjugated woman. Many know they suffer, and cry out in their misery, though not in the most grammatical of sentences." The "simple woman," she argued, knows "whether she wishes to become a mother or not," and her complaint when "she is forced into a relation disagreeable or painful to her" should be published and heeded. By publishing these experiences the Free Lovers gained a good deal of notoriety. Free Love editors, for example, frequently ran afoul of the Comstock Act. But through their well-publicized arrests, trials, and imprisonments they drew attention to the plight of abused wives. Even if some of their claims were apocryphal, their efforts nonetheless comforted these wives and provided them with the courage to publicly reveal their experiences rather than endure them in silence.

Charlotta Harman, for example, wrote that while she disagreed with her cousin Moses' stand on many issues, she supported his belief that the sexual abuse of wives was a common occurrence. "As a result of his publication of the experiences described in *Lucifer*," she argued, "some not quite so bad have been told me by poor helpless women" that read of them in his newspaper. Melissa Melhollin, from Blaine, Washington, made a similar observation in a letter to Moses Harman in which she ordered several copies of a back issue of *Lucifer, Light-Bearer*, containing an article—"Wanted: Protection from Our Husbands"—that had a profound impact on her. "I never dreamed," she wrote, "until I saw that article, that there was a place on *earth* where I might open my heart's bleeding fountain like that!" Before reading this article, she had only shared her unhappiness with her "Savior" in private prayer. But after reading of the experiences of women who were sexually abused by uncaring husbands she now sought to publicize them and spread the article's message that wives "ought to be the owners of [their] own bodies."[65]

Moreover, by identifying undesired marital sexual intercourse as rape they emboldened other wives to resist demanding husbands and insist on their right of sexual self-control. "Women with awaking pride and self-respect will not submit to the tyranny in the marriage relation they endured a century ago," argued Elizabeth Cady Stanton in 1870.

> They may be dragged into the courts, a spectacle to men and angels, there to be grossly questioned by vulgar, unfeeling lawyers; they may have their children torn from them, their virtue doubted, be compelled to earn their own bread in the garrets and cellars of the metropolis: but when they once understand that their affections are more holy and binding than man's laws, rather than live with men they loathe and abhor, they will sacrifice ease, luxury, respectability [and] trample creeds, codes and customs under their feet.

A reading of radical newspapers in the nineteenth century provides evidence that Stanton's claims were more than political rhetoric, reflecting fundamental changes in the sexual politics of private life.[66]

Rejecting the image of marriage maintained by sentimental literature, the Free Lovers challenged the portrayal of the home as a "haven in a heartless world." Suspicious of the unbridled power granted to husbands by the church and the state, they sought to destroy the invisible wall built around married life. This wall immunized marriage from the contractual ideology that regulated conduct in public life. "Because of the delicacy of the situation, the modesty of women, and their disposition to endure endless torment rather than expose their shame," argued Dr. E. B. Foote, Jr., "there is very little public exposure of the right side of married life, and so almost no public sentiment brought to bear in the way of curbing the propensity of sexual perverts to go as they please in the direction of self-destruction and wife-torture in the 'sanctity' of their home castles."

The Free Lovers were at the forefront of efforts to rectify this by peering into the privatized world of marriage and exposing "the disagreeable facts" of marital sexual abuse, not simply to "debate and dramatize," as A. James Hammerton has argued in his discussion of British marital reformers, "but to investigate, judge and regulate."[67] By breaching the barriers established by public opinion and legal authority to keep these experiences ineffable, unnamable, and private, the Free Lovers brought marital sexual abuse to popular awareness, and subsequently to the historical record. Moreover, by asking and answering the question, "Why are man-made statutes so inconsistent as to leave a wife unprotected against a husband rapist more than against a rapist not a husband?" the Free Lovers prefigured efforts by feminists in the last decades of the twentieth century to overturn the "marital rape" exemption and to provide wives with legal protection against the unwanted attentions of husbands as well as strangers.[68]

NOTES

1. Editorial, "The Prevalence of Female Diseases," *Woodhull and Claflin's Weekly*, November 11, 1871, 10.

2. Catherine E. Beecher, *Letters to the People on Health and Happiness* (New York: Harper and Brothers, 1855), 121, 124–127, 129–132. For twentieth-century comments on this phenomenon, see Ann Douglas Wood, "'The Fashionable Diseases': Women's Complaints and Their Treatment in Nineteenth-Century America," *Journal of Interdisciplinary History* 41 (Summer 1973): 25–52, especially 26, and Diane Price Herndl, *Invalid Women: Figuring Feminine Illness in American Fiction and Culture, 1840–1940* (Chapel Hill: University of North Carolina Press, 1993), 21–22.

3. Beecher, *Letters*, 162, 164–174, 176–178.

4. "The Prevalence of Female Diseases," 9.

5. Wood, "The Fashionable Diseases," 27, and Richard W. Wertz and Dorothy C. Wertz, *Lying-In: A History of Childbirth in America* (New York: Free Press, 1977), 111.

6. Edward Shorter, "Women's Diseases before 1900," in Mel Albin and

Dominick Cavallo, eds., *Family Life in America, 1620–2000* (St. James, N.Y.: Revisionary Press, 1981), 151–162.

7. Barbara Ehrenreich and Deirdre English, *For Her Own Good: One Hundred Fifty Years of the Experts' Advice to Women* (New York: Anchor Books, 1989), 136. See also Carroll Smith-Rosenberg, "The Hysterical Woman: Sex Roles and Role Conflict in Nineteenth-Century America," in Carroll Smith-Rosenberg, *Disorderly Conduct: Visions of Gender in Victorian America* (New York: Alfred A. Knopf, 1985), 197–216; Wertz and Wertz, *Lying-In*, 112–113; Barbara Berg, *The Remembered Gate: Origins of American Feminism: The Woman and the City, 1800–1860* (New York: Oxford University Press, 1978), 120; Barbara Leslie Epstein, *The Politics of Domesticity: Women, Evangelism, and Temperance in Nineteenth-Century America* (Middletown: Wesleyan University Press, 1981), 86; Herndl, *Invalid Women*, 28. On the growing view of pregnancy as a disease, see Jane Donegan, "'Safe-Delivered' But by Whom?" in Judith Walzer Leavitt, ed., *Women and Health in America* (Madison: University of Wisconsin Press, 1984), 302–317; Judith Walzer Leavitt, *Brought to Bed: Child-Bearing in America, 1750–1950* (New York: Oxford University Press, 1986), 20–28, 32–35; Shorter, "Women's Diseases," 162; Wertz and Wertz, *Lying-In*, 94, 109–110; Sylvia D. Hoffert, *Private Matters: American Attitudes toward Childbearing and Infant Nurture in the Urban North, 1800–1860* (Urbana: University of Illinois Press, 1989), 39–42, 63–64, 68–69; Jan Lewis and Kenneth A. Lockridge, "'Sally Has Been Sick': Pregnancy and Family Limitation among Virginia Gentry Women, 1780–1930," *Journal of Social History* 22, 1 (Fall 1988): 7–8, 12–13; Sally G. McMillen, *Motherhood in the Old South: Pregnancy, Childbirth, and Infant Rearing* (Baton Rouge: Louisiana State University Press, 1990), 84–93.

8. Herbert Ross Brown, *The Sentimental Novel in America, 1789–1860* (New York: Pageant Books, 1959), 282–322; Mary Kelley, *Private Woman, Public Stage: Literary Domesticity in Nineteenth-Century America* (New York: Oxford University Press, 1985), 259–276. For discussions on the emergence of this nineteenth-century "cult of domesticity," see Barbara Welter, "The Cult of True Womanhood: 1820–1860," *American Quarterly* 18, 2 (Summer 1966), part 1: 151–174; Kirk Jeffrey, "The Family as Utopian Retreat from the City: The Nineteenth-Century Contribution," in Sallie TeSelle, ed., *The Family, Communes, and Utopian Societies* (New York: Harper and Row, 1972), 21–41; Kathryn Kish Sklar, *Catherine Beecher: A Study in American Domesticity* (New York: W. W. Norton, 1976); Nancy F. Cott, *The Bonds of Womanhood* (New Haven: Yale University Press, 1977); Mary Ryan, *The Empire of the Mother: American Writing about Domesticity, 1830–1860* (New York: Haworth Press, 1982); and Maxine Van de Wetering, "The Popular Concept of 'Home' in Nineteenth-Century America," *Journal of American Studies* 18, 1 (April 1984): 5–28.

9. Cott, *Bonds of Womanhood*, 130–132; and Catherine E. Kelly, *In the New*

England Fashion: Reshaping Women's Lives in the Nineteenth Century (Ithaca: Cornell University Press, 1999), 140.

10. For efforts to enact laws that punished male seducers, see Mary Frances Berry, "Judging Morality: Sexual Behavior and Legal Consequences in the Late Nineteenth-Century South," Journal of American History, 78, 3 (December 1991): p 848–849; Smith-Rosenberg, Disorderly Conduct, 109–128; Barbara Hobson, Uneasy Virtue: The Politics of Prostitution and the American Reform Tradition (New York: Basic Books, 1987), 66–70; John D'Emilio and Estelle Freedman, Intimate Matters: A History of Sexuality in America (New York: Harper and Row, 1988), 144–145; and Pamela Haag, Consent: Sexual Rights and the Transformation of American Liberalism (Ithaca: Cornell University Press, 1999). On social purity and antiprostitution efforts to control male sexuality in the public arena, see David J. Pivar, Purity Crusade: Sexual Morality and Social Control, 1868–1900 (Westport, Conn.: Greenwood Press, 1972); Carroll Smith-Rosenberg, "Beauty, the Beast, and the Militant Woman: A Case Study in Sex Roles and Social Stress in Jacksonian America," in Carroll Smith-Rosenberg, Disorderly Conduct, 109–128; William Leach, True Love and Perfect Union: The Feminist Reform of Sex and Society (New York: Basic Books, 1980), 205–206; Ruth Rosen, The Lost Sisterhood: Prostitution in America, 1900–1918 (Baltimore, Md.: Johns Hopkins University Press, 1987), 8, 11–12, 54–56; Epstein, Politics of Domesticity, 126–128; Berg, Remembered Gate, 181, 183, 207–210, 212; Lori D. Ginzberg, Women and the Work of Benevolence: Morality, Politics, and Class in Nineteenth-Century United States (New Haven: Yale University Press, 1990), 20–23; and Jean V. Matthews, "Consciousness of Self and Consciousness of Sex in Antebellum Feminism," Journal of Women's History 5, 1 (Spring 1993): 72.

11. Sir Matthew Hale, The History of the Pleas of the Crown, 1736 ed., vol. 1 (Abingdon, Oxon: Professional Books Ltd., 1987), 629; Laws of New York, 1881, vol. 3, chapter 676, 66–67, quoted in Stephen Robertson, "Signs, Marks, and Private Parts: Doctors, Legal Discourses, and Evidence of Rape in the United States, 1823–1930," Journal of the History of Sexuality 8, 3 (January 1998): 373; Commonwealth v. Patrick Fogerty et al., Supreme Court of Massachusetts, 74 Mass. 489, 1857; and Linda Jackson, "Marital Rape: A Higher Standard Is in Order," William and Mary Journal of Women and the Law 1, 1 (Fall 1994): 183–216. See also D'Emilio and Freedman, Intimate Matters, 79; Elizabeth Pleck, Domestic Tyranny: The Making of Social Policy against Family Violence from Colonial Times to the Present (New York: Oxford University Press, 1987), 94; Peter W. Bardaglio, Reconstructing the Household: Families, Sex, and the Law in the Nineteenth-Century South (Chapel Hill: University of North Carolina Press, 1995), 200; "To Have and to Hold: The Marital Rape Exemption and the Fourteenth Amendment," Harvard Law Review 99, 6 (April 1986): 1255–1273; Diana E. H. Russell, Rape in Marriage, rev. ed. (Bloomington: Indiana University Press, 1990), 17; Rebecca M. Ryan,

"The Sex Right: A Legal History of the Marital Rape Exemption," *Law and Social Inquiry* 20, 4 (Fall 1995): 941–1001; Sara L. Zeigler, "Wifely Duties: Marriage, Labor, and the Common Law in Nineteenth-Century America," *Social Science History* 20, 1 (Spring 1996): 80–81; and Nancy Isenberg, *Sex and Citizenship in Antebellum America* (Chapel Hill: University of North Carolina Press, 1998), 162–167.

12. A. James Hammerton, *Cruelty and Companionship: Conflict in Nineteenth-Century Married Life* (London: Routledge, 1992), 108; Lucy Bland, "The Married Woman, the 'New Woman' and the Feminist: Sexual Politics of the 1890s," in Jane Rendall, ed., *Equal or Different: Women's Politics, 1800–1914* (New York: Basil Blackwell, 1987), 141–164.

13. Daniel Scott Smith, "Family Limitation, Sexual Control, and Domestic Feminism in Victorian America," in Mary S. Hartman and Lois Banner, eds., *Clio's Consciousness Raised: New Perspectives on the History of Women* (New York: Harper and Row, 1974), 123; Linda Gordon, *Woman's Body, Woman's Right: A Social History of Birth Control in America* (New York: Penguin Books, 1983), 95–115; Nancy F. Cott, "Passionlessness: An Interpretation of Victorian Sexual Ideology, 1790–1850," *Signs* 4, 2 (1978): 233–234; Leach, *True Love and Perfect Union*, 85–82; Epstein, *Politics of Domesticity*, 128; Pleck, *Domestic Tyranny*, 89–94; Karen Sanchez-Eppler, "Bodily Bonds: The Intersecting Rhetorics of Feminism and Abolition," in Shirley Samuels, ed., *The Culture of Sentiment: Race, Gender, and Sentimentality in Nineteenth-Century America* (New York: Oxford University Press, 1992), 92–114; Elizabeth B. Clark, "Matrimonial Bonds: Slavery and Divorce in Nineteenth-Century America," *Law and History Review* 8, 1 (Spring 1990): 34–35; idem., "'The Sacred Rights of the Weak': Pain, Sympathy, and the Culture of Individual Rights in Antebellum America," *Journal of American History* 82, 2 (September 1995): 463–464; and Isenberg, *Sex and Citizenship*, 158–159.

14. Mary Wollstonecraft, *Vindication of the Rights of Men, In a Letter to the Right Honorable Edmund Burke; Occasioned by His Reflections on the Revolution in France*, 2d ed. (London: J. Johnson, 1790), 45–46; Robert Dale Owen, "Independence of Women," *Free Enquirer*, September 9, 1829, 365; and Robert Dale Owen to Nicholas Trist, New York, February 23, 1831, quoted in Louis Martin Sears, "Some Correspondence of Robert Dale Owen," *The Mississippi Valley Historical Review*, 10, 3 (December 1923): 313. See also William Thompson and Anna Wheeler, *Appeal of One Half of the Human Race, Women, against the Pretensions of the Other Half, Men* (1825; rept. New York: Source Book Press, 1970), 64, 70; Barbara Taylor, *Eve and the New Jerusalem: Socialism and Feminism in the Nineteenth Century* (New York: Pantheon Books, 1983); Celia Morris, *Frances Wright: Rebel in America* (Urbana: University of Illinois Press, 1992), 156–157. On the feminist-abolitionist critique of marriage, see Ronald G. Walters, *The Antislavery Appeal: American Abolitionism after 1830* (New York: W. W. Norton, 1984), especially chapters 5 and 6; Gordon, *Woman's Body, Woman's Right*, 95–96, 109, 124; Eliza-

beth Glassman Hersh, *The Slavery of Sex: Feminist Abolitionists in America* (Urbana: University of Illinois Press, 1978), 9, 26, 196–199; Lewis Perry, "'Progress, Not Pleasure, Is Our Aim': The Sexual Advice of an Antebellum Radical," *Journal of Social History* 12, 3 (Spring 1979): 354–366; idem., *Childhood, Marriage, and Reform: Henry Clarke Wright, 1797–1870* (Chicago: University of Chicago Press, 1980), 183, 190, 196–203, 218–255; Peter F. Walker, *Moral Choices: Memory, Desire, and Imagination in Nineteenth-Century American Abolition* (Baton Rouge: Louisiana State University Press, 1978), 288–302; Clark, "Matrimonial Bonds"; and Chris Dixon, *Perfecting the Family: Antislavery Marriages in Nineteenth-Century America* (Amherst: University of Massachusetts Press, 1997), 216–227.

15. Ellen Carol Dubois and Linda Gordon argue that while "feminists occasionally organized against domestic violence, they did not make it the object of a sustained campaign, largely because they were unable to challenge the family politically. The focus on prostitution was a focus on extrafamilial violence." See their "Seeking Ecstasy on the Battlefield: Danger and Pleasure in Nineteenth-Century Feminist Sexual Thought," *Feminist Studies* 9, 1 (Spring 1983): 11.

16. Gerda Lerner, "Sarah M. Grimke's 'Sisters of Charity,'" *Signs*, 1, 1 (Autumn 1975): 254–255; Gerda Lerner, "Letters/Comments," *Signs*, 10, 4 (Summer 1985): 814; and Sarah Grimke, "Marriage," in Gerda Lerner, ed., *The Female Experience: An American Documentary* (Indianapolis, Ind.: Bobbs-Merrill, 1977), 92–93. See also A., "Marriage and Maternity," *The Revolution*, July 8, 1869, 4.

17. Grimke, "Marriage," 90; Hersh, *Slavery of Sex*, 65–67.

18. Elizabeth Pleck, "Feminist Responses to 'Crimes against Women,' 1868–1896," *Signs* 8, 3 (Spring 1983): 452, 457.

19. Matilda E. J. Gage, "Is Woman Her Own?" *The Revolution*, April 9, 1868, 15. Jerome Nadelhaft argues that, in spite of their call to illuminate the suffering of abused women within marriage, temperance workers were reluctant to explore this in depth. See his "Alcohol and Wife Abuse in Antebellum Male Temperance Literature," *Canadian Review of American Studies* 25, 1 (Winter 1995): 38, and idem., "Wife Torture: A Known Phenomenon in Nineteenth-Century America," *Journal of American Culture* 10, 3 (Fall 1987): 39–59.

20. Quoted in Editorial, "The Woman's Journal and Free Love," *Woodhull and Claflin's Weekly*, June 10, 1871, 10. The goal of the *Woman's Journal*, founded by Lucy Stone in 1870, was to cultivate a readership among "well-educated, as-yet-uncommitted club women, professionals, and writers." See Lee Jolliffe, "Women's Magazines in the 19th Century," *Journal of Popular Culture* 27, 4 (Spring 1994): 132. On the conservative nature of the *Woman's Journal*, see Pleck, "Feminist Responses," 458–459, and Lynne Masel-Walters, "A Burning Cloud by Day: The History and Content of the 'Woman's Journal,'" *Journalism History* 3, 4 (Winter 1976–77): 103–110.

21. Ezra Heywood, *Cupid's Yokes* (Princeton, Mass.: Co-Operative Publish-

ing Co., 1879), 19; Moses Harman, "The Main Issue," *Lucifer, Light-Bearer*, September 14, 1894, 2.

22. Lois Waisbrooker, "Free Love," *Lucifer, Light-Bearer*, April 3, 1891, 2; Francis Barry, "Crudities Criticised—No. 3," *Lucifer, Light-Bearer*, May 28, 1898, 167.

23. Epstein, *Politics of Domesticity*, 128; Lerner, "Sarah M. Grimke's 'Sisters of Charity,'" 254–255; Lerner, "Letters/Comments," 814.

24. Letter from Marenda B. Randell to James A. Clay (1/9/1855), reprinted in James A. Clay, *A Voice from the Prison; or Truths for the Multitudes, and Pearls for the Truthful* (Boston: Bela Marsh, 1856), 326; Francis Barry, "Correspondence," *The Word*, May 1882, 3; and Francis Barry, "Wife Holding," *The Word*, April 1877, 3.

25. Editorial, "The Relations of the Sexes," *Woodhull and Claflin's Weekly*, October 30, 1875, 5; Thomas Low Nichols and Mary S. Gove Nichols, *Marriage: Its History, Character, and Results* (Cincinnati: Valentine Nicholson and Co., 1854), 104.

26. J. H. Cook, "Correspondence," *The Word*, July 1882, 4.

27. Nichols and Nichols, *Marriage*, 115; Prodigal Daughter [Rachel Campbell], "The New Social Order," *Lucifer, Light-Bearer*, October 30, 1885, 3; Moses Harman, "Free Marriage and Free Divorce," *Kansas Liberal*, March 2, 1883, 3.

28. Francis Barry, "What Is Marriage?" *Social Revolutionist*, February 1857, 42–43; Nichols and Nichols, *Marriage*, 203; Moses Hull, "Letters to Mrs. E. B. Duffey," *Hull's Crucible*, June 24, 1876, 2; W. G. Markland, "Another 'Awful Letter,'" *Lucifer, Light-Bearer*, June 18, 1886, 3.

29. Sada Bailey Fowler, "The First Right," *Lucifer, Light-Bearer*, October 11, 1889, 2; Hulda L. Potter-Loomis, "Social Freedom, Part II," *Lucifer, Light-Bearer*, April 13, 1905, 282; Lizzie M. Holmes, "Lucifer's Critics," *Lucifer, Light-Bearer*, August 28, 1891, 3.

30. Dagmar Mariager, "Woman's Enslavement," *Lucifer, Light-Bearer*, February 14, 1890, 3; Flora Wardall-Fox, "Editor Lucifer," *Lucifer, Light-Bearer*, August 24, 1888, 4.

31. Jesse F. Battan, "'The Word Made Flesh': Language, Authority, and Sexual Desire in Late Nineteenth-Century America," *Journal of the History of Sexuality* 3, 2 (October 1992): 223–244.

32. Editorial [J. M. Peeples], "The Iniquities Uncovered in Marriage," *Universe*, October 23, 1869, 136.

33. Lois Waisbrooker, *My Century Plant* (Topeka, Kans.: Independent Publishing Co., 1896), 232–233. A good example of this in the general population can be found in the diary of Emily Gillespie, who only referred to her struggle for sexual autonomy with her husband in opaque terms. "I have written many things in my journal," she confided in its pages, "but the worst is a secret to be buried when I shall cease to be." See Judy Nolte Tensin, *"A Secret to Be Buried":*

The Diary and Life of Emily Hawley Gillespie, 1858–1888 (Iowa City: University of Iowa Press, 1993), 369.

34. Stephen Pearl Andrews,"Correspondence," *Woodhull and Claflin's Weekly* May 27, 1871, 6; idem., *Love, Marriage and the Condition of Women* (Weston, Mass.: M and S Press, 1975), 23–25; Warren Chase, *The Fugitive Wife: A Criticism on Marriage, Adultery and Divorce* (Boston: Bela Marsh, 1866), 104.

35. Sada Bailey Fowler, "Zeno's Criticisms Criticized," *Lucifer, Light-Bearer*, May 6, 1887, 3; Cora Corning, "The Other Side of the Picture," *Social Revolutionist*, July 1857, 25.

36. J. W. Towner, "Another Fact," *Social Revolutionist*, July 1857, 26.

37. Athelia, "Fowler's Lectures to Females," *Vanguard*, May 23, 1857, 94.

38. J. De Buchananne, "Demands of Liberalism," *Lucifer, Light-Bearer*, May 8, 1891, 4.

39. E. B. Foote, Jr., "Shall the Facts Be Told?" *Lucifer, Light-Bearer*, July 28, 1893, 2

40. Theodore Dwight Weld, *American Slavery as It Is: Testimony of a Thousand Witnesses* (1839; rept. New York: Arno Press, 1968), 7; Mrs. H. A. Richardson, "Dear Weekly," *Woodhull and Claflin's Weekly*, May 9, 1874, 13. See also Arthur Young Lloyd, *The Slavery Controversy, 1831–1860* (Chapel Hill: University of North Carolina Press, 1939), 71–77, 83–91; Myra C. Glenn, *Campaigns against Corporal Punishment: Prisoners, Sailors, Women, and Children in Antebellum America* (Albany, N.Y.: State University of New York Press, 1984), 63–83; Karen Halttunen, "Humanitarianism and the Pornography of Pain in Anglo-American Culture," *American Historical Review* (April 1995): 313, 325–326; Martin J. Wiener, "Market Culture, Reckless Passion, and the Victorian Reconstruction of Punishment," in Thomas L. Haskell and Richard F. Teichgraeber III, eds., *The Culture of the Market: Historical Essays*, (Cambridge: Cambridge University Press, 1993), 136–160; and Clark, "The Sacred Rights of the Weak," 463–64, 470–473.

41. Foote, "Shall the Facts Be Told?" 2; Moses Harman, "'Awful' Subject and Awful Words," *Lucifer, Light-Bearer*, June 18, 1886, 2.

42. May Huntley, "A Common Story Seldom Told," *Our New Humanity*, September 1895, 67–68.

43. Lily White, "Sexual Abuse in Marriage," *Social Revolutionist*, March 1857, 85. Those who provided readers with examples of marital rape came from a variety of social backgrounds. Those who confided to them their experiences were the wives of respected clergymen and businessmen as well as women married to poor men from the "slums." See, for example, Foote, "Shall the Facts Be Told?" 2.

44. Elmina Drake Slenker, "A Few Words of Comment," *Lucifer, Light-Bearer*, February 28, 1890, 2; W. G. Markland, "Another 'Awful Letter,'" *Lucifer, Light-Bearer*, June 18, 1886, 3.

45. Lois Waisbrooker, "For Truth and Justice," *Lucifer, Light-Bearer*, September 20, 1889, 1.

46. Richard V. O'Neill, M.D., "A Physician's Testimony," *Lucifer, Light-Bearer*, February 14, 1890, 3.

47. J. Hacker, "Save the Mothers—No. 2," *Lucifer, Light-Bearer*, November 9, 1894, 1.

48. Warren Chase, "Sacrifices to the Holy Marriage Institution," *Woodhull and Claflin's Weekly*, June 20, 1874, 4.

49. "A. C.," "Various Voices," *Lucifer, Light-Bearer*, June 17, 1899, 175.

50. White, "Sexual Abuse in Marriage," 85.

51. Ibid., 85.

52. Henri B. Armand, "Social Radicalism," *Lucifer, Light-Bearer*, July 24, 1885, 1, 3.

53. E. S., "Various Voices," *Lucifer, Light-Bearer*, December 16, 1899, 391.

54. Cora Corning, "The Other Side of the Picture," *Social Revolutionist*, July 1857, 25.

55. Voltairine de Cleyre, "Did Not Frighten Her," *Lucifer, Light-Bearer*, April 18, 1890, 3.

56. A nineteenth-century American wife had a difficult time securing a divorce based on the claim of "an excess of sexual intercourse." Unless her husband's unwanted advances were accompanied by other forms of physical cruelty that injured her health or were the result of her husband's conscious intent to harm her, American courts turned a deaf ear to her complaints. For examples of this, see *Winterburg v. Winterburg*, 52 Kan. 406 (1893); *Shaw v. Shaw*, 17 Conn. 189 (1845); *Melvin v. Melvin*, 58 New Hampshire 569 (1879); *Oxley v. Oxley*, 191 Pennsylvania 474 (1899); *Youngs v. Youngs*, 130 Illinois 230 (1889). See also Robert Griswold, "Sexual Cruelty and the Case for Divorce in Victorian America," *Signs*, 11, 3 (Spring 1986): 529–530.

57. Lizzie M. Holmes, "A Criticism Analyzed," *Lucifer, Light-Bearer*, August 26, 1892, 1; Waisbrooker, *My Century Plant*, 235.

58. Barry, "What Is Marriage?" 42–43.

59. Armand, "Social Radicalism," 1; Janet E. Runtz Ree, "Still They Come," *Lucifer, Light-Bearer*, January 11, 1889, 3.

60. Lizzie M. Holmes, "Lucifer's Critics," *Lucifer, Light-Bearer*, August 28, 1891, 3.

61. Waisbrooker, *My Century Plant*, 33; Warren Chase, "Conference of Spiritualists," *Woodhull and Claflin's Weekly*, September 6, 1873, 4–5; Fowler, "Zeno's Criticisms Criticized," 3.

62. Editorial response to Austin Kent, "Free Love," *Practical Christian*, December 16, 1854, 66.

63. Helen Rochester, "Questions to be Answered," *Lucifer, Light-Bearer*, September 26, 1890, 1; Elmina Drake Slenker, "A Few Words of Comment," *Lu-*

cifer, Light-Bearer, February 28, 1890, 2; and Priscilla R. Lawrence, "Mrs. Victoria C. Woodhull," *Woodhull and Claflin's Weekly*, August 2, 1873, 6.

64. Waisbrooker, "For Truth and Justice," 1.

65. Holmes, "Lucifer's Critics," 3; Charlotta Harman, "Cousin Moses," *Lucifer, Light-Bearer*, August 31, 1888, 4; Melissa Melhollin, "Comments on 'Wanted: Protection from Our Husbands,'" *Lucifer, Light-Bearer*, June 14, 1895, 2; Constancy, "Wanted: Protection from Our Husbands," *Lucifer, Light-Bearer*, May 24, 1895, 1.

66. Elizabeth Cady Stanton, "Anniversary of the National Woman Suffrage Association," *The Revolution*, May 19, 1870, 307. Nancy M. Theriot writes that the public denunciation of this problem indicates an unwillingness to put up with it, and argues that late-nineteenth-century American women were less likely to submit to unwanted demands than earlier generations of women. See Nancy M. Theriot, *The Biosocial Construction of Femininity: Mothers and Daughters in Nineteenth-Century America* (New York: Greenwood Press, 1988), 108, 109. A. James Hammerton attributes this change to the evolving power of the companionate marital ideal in the nineteenth century, which reshaped women's views on the ways in which they should be treated and made wives less likely to endure even nonviolent forms of sexual mistreatment. See A. James Hammerton, "Victorian Marriage and the Law of Matrimonial Cruelty," *Victorian Studies* 33, 2 (Winter 1990): 283. See also Jesse F. Battan, "The 'Rights' of Husbands and the 'Duties' of Wives: Power and Desire in the American Bedroom, 1850–1890," *Journal of Family History*, 24, 2 (April 1999): 165–186.

67. Foote, "Shall the Facts Be Told?" 2; Hammerton, *Cruelty and Companionship*, 163.

68. Charlotte C. Luce, "Crimes against Womanhood," *Lucifer*, November 1, 1889, 1; Hendrik Hartog, *Man and Wife in America: A History* (Cambridge: Harvard University Press, 2000), 306–308; and Ryan, "The Sex Right," 941–1001.

10

Race, Honor, Citizenship

The Massie Rape/Murder Case

Bonni Cermak

FOR MR. AND MRS. Eustace Bellinger it had been a relatively quiet Saturday evening in Honolulu. They had spent most of that night, September 12, 1931, playing cards with their neighbors, Mr. and Mrs. William Clark, and the Clarks' son, George. In the early morning hours, the small group of friends decided to venture out for a late night snack of fresh fish chowder at the nearby Kewalo Inn. Their excursion, however, was abruptly disrupted by a distraught young woman in a green evening gown desperately signaling for the car to stop. Obligingly, Mr. Bellinger pulled over to see what the trouble was about. The woman, her face bloody and bruised, asked the party, "Are you white people?"[1] Once she was assured that, yes, they were indeed white, she climbed in the car where she informed the Bellingers and the Clarks that she had been brutally attacked by a gang of Hawaiian men.[2]

This brief confrontation began a series of events which included two trials and a murder that has become better known as the "Massie Incident."[3] The young woman who stopped the Bellingers' car was Thalia Massie, the wife of Lieutenant Thomas Massie, a Naval Officer stationed at Pearl Harbor. According to Mrs. Massie's testimony, she had left a party at the Ala Wai Inn that night to get some fresh air. As she was walking down John Ena Road, four or five Hawaiian men jumped out of a car, forced her into the back seat, and drove her to an isolated area where they took turns alternately beating and raping her. The Honolulu police responded swiftly to Thalia Massie's accusations, and before the night was over, five men had been arrested for the assault: David Takai, Henry Chang, Horace Ida, Ben Ahakuelo, and Joseph Kahahawai.

The case against the men, however, was weak. The investigation conducted by the Honolulu police was careless, and much of the testimony regarding the incident was contradictory. After ninety-six hours of deliberation, the jury was unable to agree on a verdict and a mistrial was declared. Before a second trial could take place, one of the accused men, Joseph Kahahawai, was murdered. After police found Kahahawai's body rolled up and bundled on the floor of a rental car driven by Thalia Massie's mother, Grace Fortescue, they charged Fortescue, Thomas Massie, and two enlisted Navy men with the murder. All were brought to trial, where they were found guilty of all charges and sentenced to ten years each despite the best efforts of famed attorney Clarence Darrow, who had been hired to defend Thomas Massie. In the end, though, the prosecution's victory was fleeting. Hawaii's territorial Governor, Lawrence Judd, refused requests by both the United States Senate and military officials to pardon Massie, Fortescue, and the two enlisted men involved, but he unofficially sanctioned the "honor slaying" of Kahahawai by commuting their sentences to one hour in the Governor's office and exile from the island.

Like the more notorious 1931 Scottsboro case, in which nine black men were accused of raping two white women on a westbound train to Memphis, the Massie case provides an excellent opportunity to explore constructions of race, sexuality and citizenship during the interwar period.[4] In both cases the alleged sexual misconduct of nonwhites was used to reinforce racialized boundaries that protected the status and privilege of the white community. Of course, questions regarding the relationship between incidents of interracial sexual violence and race formation are not limited to these two cases. Recently, historians have begun to mine a rich vein of legal sources which allow scholars to begin to reconstruct the intimate connections between ideologies of race and sexuality. These studies have aptly demonstrated that campaigns to protect the sexual virtue of white women through both legal and extralegal means (such as lynching) effectively controlled the actions of both black men and white women. They have also shown how white men have claimed power and privilege through the rape of black women.[5]

Yet while studies like these offer an exciting initial examination of the historical relationship between race, sexuality, and citizenship, the scholarship on interracial sexual relations has been largely limited to studies of the South and the dynamics of black-white interactions. In order to more fully understand the ways in which both racial and sexual identities have been continuously constructed, dismantled, and reshaped, the narrative of interracial sexual assault needs to be retold and recentered to include Asians, Hispanics, and Native Americans as well as blacks and whites. In doing so we can begin to explore the ways in which sexual ideologies were employed in the construction of complex social hierarchies in which multiple racial groups competed for limited opportunities and positions of authority.[6]

In some ways, the events of the Massie case seemed to follow the model of legal lynching prevalent in the South during this period. By the late nineteenth century, women reformers had launched an effective campaign against extralegal racial violence as a barbaric practice which in fact undermined white masculinity. Yet in order to retain both their masculine honor and their position of authority within the social structure of the South, white men needed to be able to regulate and patrol racial and gender boundaries. As a result, as in the Massie Incident, white men began to increasingly rely on the legal system to avenge the violation of white male honor resulting from the sexual assault of white women by nonwhite men.[7]

While the Massie Incident certainly raised concerns about the maintenance of white male privilege similar to those raised in these southern cases, it also presented a more complicated scenario. First, in both trials the jury was racially mixed, whereas black defendants in the South faced all-white juries. Second, although the suspects were arrested solely on the basis of the testimony of Thalia Massie, the jury refused to convict the men based on her word alone. In contrast, in most interracial rape trials in the South the jury was willing to accept the alleged victim's testimony as proof of guilt even when presented with contradictory evidence. Finally, unlike in the South the Massie jury was willing to find a white man guilty of killing a nonwhite. Yet, despite all these deviations from the standard model of racist justice, the Massie case could hardly be considered a stand for racially blind justice. In the final analysis, Thomas Massie and Grace Fortescue did, after all, get away with murder.

The Massie case is particularly important for the unique glimpse it offers into the ways in which sexual and racial ideologies have been intimately connected to ideas of citizenship. In most, if not all, of the cases involving black men accused of raping white women there was de facto jury segregation. Guilty verdicts handed down by white male juries served to continually re-create existing racial and sexual boundaries. In Hawaii during the 1930s, however, racial boundaries were in flux as more Japanese, Chinese, and Filipino residents of the island became territorial citizens.

This essay examines the ways in which the Massie Incident was used as a site of public discourse on the nature of citizenship and its connections to ideologies of race and sexuality in Hawaii during the interwar period. By refusing to convict the five nonwhite men charged with assaulting Thalia Massie, the racially mixed jury sequestered in the first Massie trial sparked a controversy over whether citizens of color in Hawaii were capable of fulfilling their obligations as citizens. Both locally and nationwide, angry members of the white community pointed to the mistrial as an example of racialized groups' inability to adhere to white standards of sexual propriety. Similarly, a second racially mixed jury's guilty verdict in the case of Thomas Massie confirmed suspicions that both white masculine honor and white female respectability were at risk if nonwhites' participation as citizens went unregulated.

The distinctive characteristics of the Massie case were intimately tied to the unique circumstances surrounding Hawaii's incorporation into the United States and the varieties of citizenship status afforded its racially diverse population. The annexation of Hawaii in 1898 presented the United States with a peculiar set of problems regarding the precise form of government that would be imposed on the new territory. First, there was the question of who would be granted U.S. citizenship. Some decisions seemed easy. The smallest segment of Hawaii's population, the local whites, were automatically granted citizenship. Just as automatically, the majority of Hawaii's population, Chinese and Japanese immigrants who came to Hawaii to work as laborers on the islands' sugar plantations, were excluded from citizenship on the grounds that U.S. naturalization laws did not extend to Asians. The status of Hawaiians presented a more complicated dilemma. Hawaii's white elite argued that native Hawaiians were not sufficiently civilized to fulfill the duties of citizenship and, therefore, should not be accorded the full rights of citizens.[8] In doing so, they were appealing to a precedent set by Congress in its policies toward new territories in the wake of the Spanish-American war, Puerto Rico, and the Philippines. In both these possessions, the nonwhite native residents were granted less-than-citizen status based on racist assumptions that neither Puerto Ricans nor Filipinos were sufficiently civilized to self-govern their islands. Yet ultimately Congress decided that the decades of Anglo-Hawaiian interaction preceding Hawaii's annexation had a meritorious effect on the native population and they were indeed civilized. Consequently, the Organic Act of 1900, which dictated the terms of Hawaii's incorporation into the United States as a territory, granted native Hawaiians full citizenship.

Under the Organic Act voting privileges mirrored citizenship rights: that is, whites and Hawaiians could vote, but all "resident aliens" (a category of noncitizens that included Japanese, Chinese, and Filipinos and made up about three-fourths of Hawaii's population) could not. The Organic Act, however, could only deny the franchise to resident aliens of the first generation. The children of Asian immigrants were automatically granted citizenship of the United States under the principle of jus soli (birthright) if they were born on the islands. Within a generation then, the Organic Act would no longer be a useful legislative device for maintaining white privilege in Hawaii. As a result, the congressional decision to grant citizenship to native Hawaiians led to a rather uneasy coalition between local Hawaiians and the white haole elite. In effect, whites were able to maintain political control over the territory, despite the fact that the native Hawaiians constituted the majority of the voting population, by promising Hawaiians key government posts and positions of local authority. But this alliance, bolstered by a mutual suspicion and fear of Hawaii's numerous Japanese and Chinese population, was decidedly precarious. Both groups recognized the potential force of the Japanese and Chinese as a voting bloc once the children of the immigrants who had arrived in the early twentieth century came of age in the 1930s and 1940s.[9]

As a preemptive strike against the potential power of a large Japanese and Chinese citizenry, both Hawaiians and the haole elite urged Congress to postpone Hawaii's passage from annexed territory to U.S. state. Statehood represented a potential threat to Hawaii's status quo. If statehood was granted, the children of Asian immigrant laborers would soon be in a position to elect all of Hawaii's government officials. But if Hawaii remained a territory, the citizens of Hawaii would elect only a delegate to Congress and the members of the local legislature; other important posts in the territory's government would be filled by appointments made in Washington D.C. While the haole elite expected that their economic and social position would influence these political appointments, they were less confident about their ability to retain authority over a legally enfranchised nonwhite majority. Territorial status, therefore, seemed to be the much safer political option for Hawaii's white ruling elite and their Hawaiian political allies.[10]

By the time of the Massie Incident, the children of Asian immigrants had already shown their power to affect political decisions in the island, and the coalition between whites and native Hawaiians was starting to break down as Hawaiians began to form new political alliances with the new generation of enfranchised Asian citizens. By the 1930s, Honolulu was partitioned politically, socially, and economically along racial lines. Although the territorial government remained in the hands of the Republican haole elite, Hawaiian local politics were dominated by a Hawaiian-Democratic bloc that was more responsive to the needs of Hawaii's nonwhite residents than to the haole elite. In the years immediately preceding the assault of Thalia Massie, political conflict between the largely white Republican elite and the Hawaiian-Democratic element had reached a point of crisis. Reform Republicans had managed to oust the Democratic part-Hawaiian mayor, John H. Wilson, and replace him with their own candidate, Fred Wright. A key component in achieving this electoral coup was the support of high-ranking Navy and Army officers stationed in Honolulu. Although an impermanent class, military officials exercised a great deal of economic authority in Honolulu, and usually found themselves aligned with the interests of the leading haole elite. Yet the political ascendancy of the Reform Republicans was by no means assured. The Hawaiian-Democrats garnered a great deal of support from the local nonwhite community, including a majority of the Chinese, Japanese, and native Hawaiian urban population.[11]

The kidnapping, beating, and alleged rape of Thalia Massie served to further polarize the Hawaiian community. Immediately upon hearing of the attack, Admiral Yates Stirling Jr., commandant of the Pearl Harbor Navy Yard, demanded the arrest of Mrs. Massie's assailants, stating that "American men will not stand for violation of their women under any circumstances."[12] The Honolulu police, however, were unsure of exactly whom to arrest. When John McIntosh, Inspector of Detectives for the Honolulu police, questioned Thalia Massie only hours after the incident, she was unable to provide a description of her molesters other than that, based on their manner of speech, they were Hawaiian. The only other clue she could provide was a vague description of the car and a license plate number. There had been no other notable incidents that night except for a minor altercation between some young men driving home from a dance and a local Hawaiian woman, Agnes Peeples. Although the whole episode amounted to little more than a few scratches and hurt feelings, the policeman who took the report noted that the license plate number of the vehicle involved in the incident with Peeples was remarkably similar to that provided by Mrs. Massie. It seemed a logical assumption to connect the two events. By the end of the night the young men in the car—David Takai, Henry Chang, Horace Ida, Ben Ahakuelo, and Joseph Kahahawai—had been identified by Thalia Massie and arrested for the assault. Apparently, by the next day, Mrs. Massie was able to recognize the voices by the faces of her alleged assailants and to positively identify each of the suspects the police paraded before her.

In their support of Thalia Massie, the white community employed imagery that conflated ideas of race and class. In doing so, the lines between civilized and savage, and white and nonwhite were clearly and publicly demarcated. Just as the myth of the hypersexual black male was used in the South to affirm the status and position of white men, the rape of Thalia Massie was used as a metaphor by the local media to affirm ideologies of white privilege in Hawaii. The coverage of the assault in the city's two leading newspapers, the *Honolulu Advertiser* and the *Honolulu Star-Bulletin,* were clearly slanted in Thalia Massie's favor. The editors refused to provide the name of the victim, referring to Mrs. Massie as "a white woman of refinement and culture" in order to protect her anonymity.[13] The accused, on the other hand, were not offered the same discretion. The newspapers not only printed their names but also the criminal records of both Ahakuelo and Chang, who had previously been arrested for the rape of a young Chinese woman.[14]

Similarly, the alleged rape of Thalia Massie was used in more private venues to affirm and reassert white male authority. Within days of the attack, the President of Honolulu's Chamber of Commerce called a closed meeting with representatives of the Navy, Army, and twenty of the community's leading businessmen, including two former Governors, the City Attorney, the sheriff, and the Chief of Detectives. During the course of this meeting, the Army and Navy affirmed their position in support of Mrs. Massie, money was pledged to support the prosecution, and the editors of Honolulu's English-language newspapers were persuaded to "use their best efforts to correct gossip" aimed at inspiring sympathy for the defendants. Participants were assured by local officials that there was sufficient evidence to make a strong case against the accused.[15]

Support for Thalia Massie was clearly split along racial lines. While Honolulu's haole elite effectively circled the wagons in defense of Mrs. Massie, members of Hawaii's nonwhite community tended to doubt the veracity of Thalia Massie's story. According to Admiral Stirling in an exposé written for *True Detective Magazine*, the supporters of the accused attempted to malign Thalia Massie's moral character. Stirling recalled that "vile rumors were circulated about the victim of the bestial assault—by various members of the police department; by thoughtless persons of the 'tell me' persuasion; by friends of the accused."[16] Most likely, these "members of the police department" and "friends of the accused" were nonwhite members of Honolulu's community who found a common purpose in the defense of the accused men.Both the prosecution and the defense recognized the ways in which ideologies of race could potentially impact the trial. As a result, each attempted to build a jury sympathetic to their clients' cause. The prosecution attempted to avoid persons who were sympathetic toward Hawaii's nonwhite community. At the same time, the defense was wary of seating any jurists who displayed anti-Asian sentiments. In the end, the exclusively male jury selected to hear the case was composed of six whites, two Chinese, two Japanese, and one Hawaiian—which composition, as reported in the local press, was a satisfactory compromise for both sides.

Although finding an impartial jury was one of the many obstacles facing the two sides, there seemed to be little, if any, initial public concern regarding its multiracial composition. Community debate surrounding the trial focused more on the numerous conflicting testimonies regarding the events that night, the mistakes committed by the Honolulu police during the course of the investigation, and the rather improbable time line of events presented by the prosecution. Ultimately, the jury was also thwarted by these same issues. After almost four days of jury deliberation the case was declared a mistrial.[17]

The declaration of a mistrial would begin the reshaping of the Massie case into a debate on the nature of citizenship that would reach well beyond local politics and race relations to become part of a national discourse. The jury's refusal to hand down a guilty verdict cast doubt on the willingness of nonwhite men to protect white female virtue. In this rhetoric, the obligations of citizenship were directly tied to racial and sexual ideologies. For example, a flurry of newspaper columns in the aftermath of the trial lamented the treacherous living conditions for white women in Hawaii. In one editorial published in the *Honolulu Times*, Hawaii was described as a "paradise infested by the snake—a foul, slimy creature crawling through the streets and attacking the innocent and defenseless."[18]

Within a month of the trial, however, this inflammatory rhetoric erupted into more tangible forms of violence. On Saturday, December 12, one of the defendants, Horace Ida, was kidnapped and beaten by a gang of white men who repeatedly demanded a confession.[19] Ida was unable to identify any of his assailants, and no arrest was made in the incident. Only weeks later on Thursday, January 8, 1932 the Honolulu police responded to a call reporting that another defendant, Joseph Kahahawai, had been kidnapped. Before the department had the opportunity to even begin an official investigation, the suspected kidnappers had been almost inadvertently apprehended. Detective George Harbottle and policeman Tomas Kekua were out on regular patrol when a black Buick sedan sped past them, apparently headed for Diamond Head. A chase ensued, but the Buick was eventually overtaken and forced to pull over. In the back seat of the car was the body of Joseph Kahahawai, naked, shot through the heart, and rolled up in a canvas bundle. One woman and two men emerged from the front seat of the vehicle. The woman was Grace Fortescue, Thalia Massie's mother. One of the men was Thalia's husband, Thomas Massie, and the third was an enlisted Navy man, Ed Lord. Later a fourth suspect, Albert O. Jones, would also be arrested as an accomplice. All four suspects were subsequently charged with murder and, in a controversial move, turned over to the Naval authorities, ostensibly to keep them safe and away from the public eye.[20]

The death of Joseph Kahahawai was the inauspicious beginning of what could be considered part two of the Massie narrative, the murder trial of Thomas Massie and Grace Fortescue. All the racial tensions that had been building since the alleged rape of Thalia Massie suddenly exploded. Thomas Massie's actions served to transform the incident that had begun with the alleged assault of his wife from a notorious but rather sordid rape case set in an exotic locale to a topic of national interest. Essentially, the Massie Incident raised two disparate but interrelated questions. Were nonwhites capable of fulfilling their obligations as American citizens? And did Thomas Massie have the right to take extralegal measures against Kahahawai since, in his eyes, a multiracial jury had failed to defend his wife's honor legally? In the coming months both these questions were hotly contested not only in the courtroom but in the press and on the floor of the U.S. Senate.

The disparate reactions of the local Hawaiian and U.S. national press reflect the degree to which the Massie Incident challenged the white elites' place in Hawaii's social hierarchy. The haole elites were placed in the precarious position of having to simultaneously reassure fearful whites that Hawaii was a safe place for white women, while condemning Thomas Massie in order to pacify the local nonwhite electorate. As a result, the local papers in Honolulu responded to the news of Massie's actions with what can be characterized as restrained disapproval. The *Honolulu Star-Bulletin* warned the city's residents that "people who take the law into their own hands usually make a mess of it. . . . we have before us a horrible example of what hysteria and lack of balance will do."[21] The response to the murder of Kahahawai in the mainland newspapers was considerably more fervent in its condemnation of Hawaii's racial situation. For example, a typical story printed in the *New York American*, declared that:

> The situation in Hawaii is deplorable. It is an unsafe place for white women outside the small cities and towns. The roads go through jungles and in these remote places bands of degenerate natives lie in wait for white women to drive by. . . . the perpetrators of this crime against pure womanhood, against society and against civilization, were freed on bail after a disagreement of a jury of their kind.[22]

This type of rhetoric, which questioned Hawaii's local political leaders' ability to administer the islands, led to an investigation into the efficiency and competency of Hawaii's police force and judicial system. On January 11, 1932, the U.S. Senate adopted a resolution requesting that the Attorney General of the United States report on the administration and enforcement of criminal laws in the Territory of Hawaii to determine whether any changes needed to be made in Hawaii's 1900 Organic Act.[23] While this report was pending, the federal government began to initiate changes in Hawaii's criminal procedures. In early January, Oahu's first police commission was appointed by the Governor and a reorganization of the department was undertaken, despite some protests from local officials that a police commission controlled by the Governor would "emasculate the city government."[24] Concurrently, a special territorial legislative session was called and several laws were passed designed to bring the local situation under control, including an act changing the jury law so that the prosecution would have as many challenges as the defense and a new piece of legislation making the penalty for rape either life imprisonment or death.

Many in Honolulu's white community justified the murder of Kahahawai as an honor slaying. They argued that the verdict of a mistrial in the earlier case prevented Thomas Massie from claiming his white, masculine honor by punishing the men who had attacked his patriarchal authority through the alleged sexual assault on his wife. Thomas Massie, therefore, had no choice but to defend his honor through extralegal means once the judicial system had failed him. In fact, the grand jury (the majority of whom were white) initially refused to charge Massie with the crime. On January 22, 1932 the grand jury met to hear evidence on the kidnapping and killing of Joseph Kahahawai. After two days and twenty-six witnesses, the grand jury returned with a ruling of "no bill." The judge assigned to the case, Albert Christy, rejected the jury's decision, explaining that a grand jury was not required to determine guilt or innocence. Its only obligation, he stated, was to evaluate whether there was enough evidence to proceed with a trial, and in this case the presence of a dead body in the back of the suspect's car seemed sufficient proof that a crime had been committed.[25] Christy then dismissed the grand jury and asked that they reconvene the following week and render a new verdict. After a day of deliberation the jury returned to Christy asserting that they had been unable to reach an agreement. Once more, Judge Christy sent the grand jury back to review the evidence, admonishing them not to return without an indictment and explaining to them the potentially dire consequences if they refused to indict for the third time, given the preponderance of evidence against the accused. This time the jury returned within two hours with an indictment.

The same ideology of honor that came into play during Judge Christy's struggle to get the grand jury to indict formed the basis of Thomas Massie's defense. Massie's defense attorney, Clarence Darrow, was perhaps the country's most famous defense attorney at the time. His reputation was built in part on his zealous defense of the underdog.

Therefore, his decision to accept the Massie case may have provided the white community with further ammunition in its attempts to represent the murder of Kahahawai as an honor slaying. Darrow's plan of defense, in fact, supported this theory. His central argument throughout the trial was that Thomas Massie's actions were justifiable based on an unwritten "code of honor." According to this theory, whether the men accused of raping Thalia Massie were actually guilty was in some ways incidental. What was important was that Thomas Massie *believed* they were the men who had assaulted his wife. As a result, when the case ended in a mistrial, Massie went temporarily insane and committed the rash act of kidnapping Joseph Kahahawai in order to obtain a confession. The subsequent death of Kahahawai was, then, only an unfortunate consequence of Thomas Massie's unrestrained emotions.

Although Darrow avoided mentioning race, his defense of Thomas Massie was implicitly racialized. By portraying Kahahawai's murder as an honor slaying he was appealing not only to sexual but also to racial ideologies. Interracial sexual assault posed a threat to both patriarchal and racial authority. While the sanctity of white female virtue was certainly intimately connected to a man's ability to claim honor by protecting women under his immediate authority, white women's bodies were also symbols of larger social boundaries that privileged white males. The rape of white women by men of color was usually read as an attack and deliberate inversion of the dominate social and political hierarchy. Whether Darrow was consciously invoking the larger social metaphors of race associated with the term or not, his use of the specific ideology of honor had the effect of transforming the Massie case into a discourse on both masculine and racial authority.

Darrow, in fact, quickly discovered that he could not avoid the question of race. Although he told one reporter that he was convinced that the charges would "be tried on their merits and not on any line of prejudice, racial or otherwise,"[26] he also admitted that the examination of potential jurors had left him "struggling to fit his own thoughts to the complicated psychology of race."[27] Despite all his protests to the contrary, Darrow realized that race would be a mitigating factor in the trial as it was in his client's best interests to seat a predominately white jury who would be more sympathetic to Darrow's "honor slaying" defense strategy. In the end, the jury selected was, once again, multiracial, comprised of seven white men, one Portuguese, two Chinese, and three men who were at least part Hawaiian. Both Darrow and the state prosecutor, John Kelly, therefore began the trial acutely aware of the role race would play in the Massie murder case.

While Darrow's defense implicitly appealed to white racial ideologies, he studiously avoided referring to race during the trial for fear of antagonizing the nonwhite members of the jury. Kelly, on the other hand, made a two-pronged attack. First, he relied on the overwhelming strength of the physical evidence. Second, Kelly countered Darrow's ostensibly color-blind appeal to masculine honor by insisting that the murder was racially motivated. Massie was, in fact, defending his *white* male honor. Toward this effort, Kelly unhesitatingly raised the issue of race by asking Massie, who had been raised in the South, if he was "proud of being a Southerner," to which Darrow instantly objected, stating that he knew "what the prosecution's purpose was in asking that question."[28] For the next two weeks Kelly repeatedly attempted to bring the courtroom discourse back to race. In each instance, Darrow objected on the grounds that the trial was not about race but about human emotion and passion. In the end, however, the evidence was impossible for the jury to ignore, and it came back with a guilty verdict. While to some degree the jury was compelled by the evidence to deliver a guilty verdict, it did recommend the minimum sentence of ten years for each suspect.

A number a backroom deals ensured that Thomas Massie, Grace Fortescue, and their two enlisted henchmen would never serve time in prison. Within a day of the verdict a petition had been prepared asking Governor Lawrence Judd for executive clemency, which was granted without hesitation. Immediately after sentencing, the four convicted suspects were ushered into the Governor's office, where he handed each of them a document indicating that their individual sentences had been commuted to one hour. By noon, three days after the jury had handed down a guilty verdict, Thomas Massie, Grace Fortescue, Ed Lord, and Albert Jones were free to go, their debt to society having been paid.[29]

While the ordeal was over for the Massies, the repercussions of the entire Massie Incident were just coming to light. Both regionally and nationally, whites decried the Massie verdict. Senator Royal S. Copeland considered it "distressing beyond words that so cruel a verdict could be rendered in an American possession."[30] An editorial in the *San Francisco Examiner* charged that "the whole island should be promptly put under martial law. . . . until such drastic measures are taken, Hawaii is not a safe place for decent white women."[31] Even Clarence Darrow was now willing to make a statement regarding the case along racial lines. He asserted that "a jury of white men would have acquitted . . . there were Chinamen in the jury box, and Japanese, and Hawaiian and mixed bloods . . . [o]bviously they do not think as we do."[32]

Similar opinions were expressed in the *Report on Law Enforcement in the Hawaiian Islands* prepared by Assistant Attorney General Richardson. Richardson asserted that he believed that prosecution in criminal cases was hindered by racially mixed juries, particularly in "sex crimes due to different sexual standards involved."[33] The solution the Senate proposed was to place Hawaii under commission rule. Commission rule would solve several dilemmas, according to the report. First, it would offer the U.S. Navy and Army more political authority in the territory so as to ensure a "peaceable, loyal population."[34] Second, commission rule would reduce the tax rate by getting rid of an expensive, corrupt, and incompetent civil government. Third, it would eliminate the problems associated with political inefficiency and enable the federal government to wrest economic control away from the large sugar and pineapple interests. Most importantly, commission rule would solve the problems associated with:

> dealing with a strange polyglot people coming from sources affording governmental views wholly dissimilar to American governmental standards and principles[.] [The government] is fundamentally wrong in giving to such a population the broad rights of self-government, based, in perhaps the majority of cases on the accident of birth in the Territory, with the ultimate hope that the "inoculation" might "take" and the result be wholly favorable to the American principles of government and citizenship.[35]

Ultimately, it took another ten years for the United States to devise a settlement to the problems articulated by Attorney General Richardson, which was to place Hawaii under martial law.

Although it is too much to say that the Massie case led to the imposition of martial law in Hawaii, I would argue that the case did shape the contours of the debates that led to this "solution." The alleged rape of Thalia Massie, the murder of Kahahawai, and the two trials provided in essence the script for a national discourse on ideologies of race, sexuality, and citizenship at a time when Hawaii's relationship with the rest of the nation was being renegotiated. The rhetoric of an honor slaying cast Kahahawai's death in the familiar terms of racial barbarism and white civilization. In doing so, the Massie Incident provided a powerful narrative which was used to both justify white privilege on the islands and to question the citizenship status of Hawaii's nonwhites.

NOTES

1. Report of Pinkerton Detective Agency to Governor Lawrence Judd of Hawaii, October 5, 1932, Lawrence Judd Papers (hereafter LJP), Archives of Hawaii, Kekauluohi Building, Iolani Palace Grounds, Honolulu, 3.

2. Ibid.

3. To date, the most thorough scholarly examination of the Massie Incident is included in Pamela Haag's larger work on changing ideologies of sexual consent in the United States. Pamela Haag, *Consent: Sexual Rights and the Transformation of American Liberalism* (Ithaca: Cornell University Press, 1999).

4. For an excellent account of the Scottsboro trial, see James Goodman, *Stories of Scottsboro* (New York: Pantheon Books, 1994). For an earlier study, see Dan Carter, *Scottsboro: A Tragedy of the American South* (Baton Rouge: Louisiana State University Press, 1969).

5. On ideas of race and rape, see Jacquelyn Dowd Hall, "'The Mind That Burns in Each Body': Women, Rape, and Racial Violence," in *Powers of Desire: The Politics of Sexuality*, ed. Ann Snitow, Christine Stansell, and Sharon Thompson (New York: Monthly Review Press, 1983); Peter Bardaglio, "Rape and the Law in the Old South: Calculated to Excite Indignation in Every Heart," *Journal of Southern History* 60, 4 (1994): 749–772; Diane Miller Somerville, "The Rape Myth in the Old South Reconsidered," *Journal of Southern History* 61, 3 (1995): 481–518; Martha Elizabeth Hodes, *White Women, Black Men: Illicit Sex in the Nineteenth-Century South* (New Haven: Yale University Press, 1997); Laura Edwards, *Gendered Strife and Confusion: The Political Culture of Reconstruction* (Urbana: University of Illinois Press, 1997). For works that examine the rape of African American women by white men, see Deborah G. White's classic work, *Ain't I a Woman? Female Slaves in the Antebellum South* (New York: W. W. Norton, 1985). Also see Hannah Rosen, "'Not That Sort of Woman': Race, Gender, and Sexual Violence during the Memphis Riots of 1866," in *Sex, Love, and Race: Crossing Boundaries in North American History*, ed. Martha Hodes (New York: New York University Press, 1999). Finally, for a more recent analysis of the impact of race in criminal rape trials, see Gary LaFree, *Rape and Criminal Justice: The Social Construction of Sexual Assault* (Belmont, Calif.: Wadsworth Publishing, 1989).

6. For an excellent discussion of racial hierarchies, see Tomas Almaguer,

Racial Fault Lines: The Historical Origins of White Supremacy in California (Berkeley: University of California Press, 1994).

7. For a discussion on this transformation to "legal lynchings," see Eric Rise, "Race, Rape, and Radicalism: The Case of the Martinsville Seven, 1949–1951," *Journal of Southern History* 58, 3 (1992): 461–490; Walter Howard, "In the Shadow of Scottsboro: The 1937 Roberts Hinds Case," *Gulf Coast Historical Review* 4, 1 (1988): 64–81; Steve Lawson, David Colburn, and Darryl Paulson, "Groveland: Florida's Little Scottsboro," *Florida Historical Quarterly* 65, 1 (1986): 1–26.

8. For several excellent studies on immigration and citizenship, see Roger Smith, *Civic Ideals: Conflicting Visions of Citizenship in U.S. History* (New Heaven: Yale University Press, 1997), 430. See also, Peter Schuck and Roger M. Smith, *Citizenship without Consent: Illegal Aliens in the American Polity* (New Haven: Yale University Press, 1985); Judith Sklar, *American Citizenship: The Quest for Inclusion* (Cambridge: Harvard University Press, 1991).

9. Lawrence Fuchs, *Hawaiian Pono: A Social History* (New York: Harcourt Press, 1961).

10. Roger Bell, *Last among Equals: Hawaii Statehood and American Politics* (Honolulu: University of Hawaii, 1984), 33.

11. For an anecdotal account of the Massie trials I have relied on Theon Wright, *Rape in Paradise* (New York: Hawthorn Books, 1966). For an alternative narrative, see Peter Van Slingerland, *Something Terrible Has Happened* (New York: Harper and Row, 1966).

12. Lawrence W. Judd, *Lawrence W. Judd and Hawaii: An Autobiography* (New York: C.E. Tuttle, 1971), 186.

13. *Honolulu Star-Bulletin*, September 14, 1931, p. 1, Ala Moana Papers (hereafter AMP), Hawaiian Pacific Collection, Hamilton Library, University of Hawaii.

14. Both the *Honolulu Star-Bulletin* and the *Honolulu Advertiser* hastened to add that although the rape of the Chinese girl was further reason to doubt the men's protestations that they had not raped Mrs. Massie, the rape of the Chinese woman was in no way comparable to the crime perpetuated against Thalia Massie. According to the *Honolulu Advertiser*, in the first incident the "girl was a very willing participant with the six boys in what is vulgarly called a shag party." *Honolulu Advertiser*, September 14, 1931, 9 (AMP).

15. Walter F. Dillingham, "A Memorandum" (Honolulu: University of Hawaii, Unpublished Manuscript Collection, 1932), 4.

16. Yates Stirling, *True Detective Magazine*, February 1939, p. 13, AMP.

17. Wright, *Rape in Paradise*, 189.

18. *Honolulu Times*, December 12, 1931, AMP.

19. Wright, *Rape in Paradise*, 183.

20. Ibid.

21. *Honolulu Star-Bulletin,* January 9, 1932, AMP.

22. *New York American,* January 11, 1932, AMP.

23. *Law Enforcement in the Territory of Hawaii,* Document no.78, 72nd Congress, First Session, April 4, 1932.

24. Stirling, *True Detective Magazine,* 16.

25. Wright, *Rape in Paradise,* 204.

26. *Honolulu Star-Bulletin,* April 10, 1932, AMP.

27. Ibid., April 6, 1932.

28. Ibid., April 19, 1932.

29. Eighteen months after the end of the trial, the Massies divorced. Thalia Massie later committed suicide. After finishing his stint in the Navy, Thomas Massie led a quiet life out of the public eye. For more on the Massies after the trial, see Wright, *Rape in Paradise.*

30. *Honolulu Advertiser,* May 1, 1932, AMP.

31. *San Francisco Examiner,* January 12, 1932, AMP.

32. Masaji Marumoto, "The Ala Moana Case and the Massie-Fortescue Case Revisited," *University of Hawaii Law Review* 5, 2 (Winter 1983): 118–32.

33. Senate Committee on Territories and Insular Affairs, 72nd Congress (1st Session), *Law Enforcement in the Territory of Hawaii,* U.S. Government Printing office, Doc. 78, April 4, 1932, 22.

34. Ibid., 42.

35. Ibid., 43.

11

"Another Negro-Did-It Crime"

Black-on-White Rape and Protest in Virginia,
1945–1960

Lisa Lindquist Dorr

IN 1946, TWO white women in Portsmouth, Virginia, told police that
they were walking to a nighttime meeting when a car passed them. The
car stopped, and two black men, William Daniels and William Hayes,
got out and began to walk toward the women. The women fled and
called the police from a nearby home. Police arrested the two men, and
charged them with attempted rape. When the case came before a trial
justice, the two women conceded that the men had neither spoken to
them nor been close enough to touch them. The judge immediately dismissed the charges, saying, "It is the duty of the court not to let prejudice interfere with the administration of justice." When the black newspaper, the *Norfolk Journal and Guide*, first reported the case, it noted that
it "had all the earmarks of being another one of those notorious Negro-
did-it affairs."[1]

This was not the only time the black press used that phrase. The
Guide also used it in two cases in which white women eventually admitted that their charges of rape were false.[2] Unlike cases in which
women accused members of their own races of assault, white legal authorities usually accepted white women's accusations of rape against
black men, regardless of other evidence. Despite white women's apparent credibility in these cases, cases of black-on-white rape were more
contested than historians have acknowledged. As the case of William
Daniels and William Hayes suggests, white legal authorities did not
regard every encounter between black men and white women as a

potential rape. This essay explores the nexus of racism and sexism in Virginia's legal system, using cases of interracial rape to uncover the way rape victims, accused assailants, and the black and white communities shaped the legal process and negotiated the boundaries around interracial interaction after World War II.

After World War II, blacks were increasingly sensitized to racial injustices, and they frequently united to combat oppression. African Americans began to place the prosecution of black men for rape within the discourse of civil rights. Organized groups and the black press publicized the plight of black men accused of rape, and ridiculed whites for their intolerance of racial interaction. Changing ideas about women's sexuality aided these efforts, making white men more willing to believe that white women claimed rape to save their own reputations or hide their own indiscretions. White women, who previously had near-absolute power to accuse and convict black men of rape, saw that power limited as white men became distrustful, not of their willingness to accuse black men falsely, but rather of their willingness to accuse *any* man of rape at all. For black men, being accused of rape still placed them in serious legal jeopardy, and many faced long years in prison or the death sentence on the word of a white woman. But as white women faced scrutiny of their motives, characters, and truthfulness, black men received a small, but real, share in the gender privileges white men held in the legal system. White juries and white legal officials increasingly accepted black men's accounts of sexual interactions over those of white women, even in the face of seemingly corroborative evidence. Criminal prosecutions of rape in Virginia became a step less contaminated by racial prejudice, while white women who accused black men faced more of the obstacles other rape victims had always faced when seeking redress through the courts.

Any analysis of interracial rape cases in the postwar period makes sense only in light of the adjudication of earlier cases of interracial rape. Recent scholarship has shown that in the antebellum period, whites tolerated sexual relationships between white women and black men as long as they did not blur the connection between race and slavery through the birth of a "black" child to a white woman. Whites also considered the class status and sexual history of white women who accused black men of rape, deeming the assault of a poor or compromised woman to be a less serious crime. This toleration, according to the existing scholarship, ended during Reconstruction when whites conjoined freedmen's desire for political and economic rights with their presumed sexual desire for white women. Black men faced increasingly harsh punishment for being suspected of sexual misbehavior with white women, and many scholars have argued that by the twentieth century, black men faced near-certain death for being accused of any misbehavior toward or with a white woman.[3] The scholarship on lynching reinforces this point, as whites justified their use of extralegal violence by citing black men's alleged propensity to rape white women.[4] Studies of lynching, and of black-on-white rape cases which commanded considerable national attention, imply that whites demanded the lives of accused black men in cases of black-on-white rape.[5]

My analysis of rape cases from Virginia in the twentieth century, however, shows that lynchings or executions were not inevitable endings to charges of black-on-white assault. Although most accused black men were convicted, clemency petitions demonstrate that legal officials considered the class status and sexual history of the victim as mitigating factors which might merit a convicted man's release. These cases reveal a complicated world of interracial relationships that belied the mandates of segregation. Communities could overlook inappropriate racial interactions as long as their public, visible performance continued to conform to segregation's rules.[6] Rather than racial solidarity being the inevitable norm, these cases produced a multitude of cross-racial (and cross-gender) alliances. White men did not always leap to the defense of white women. Some white men chose to support their black tenants and laborers rather than their white neighbors. Some white men sided with black men against white women whose class or sexual history they found suspect. White women retained their status as innocent victim only as long as they followed the dictates of middle-class morality, even long after the juries' verdict. The black community also protested black men's treatment in the legal system, and exerted what power they could to protect accused black men.

That black men faced a trial rather than a lynch mob does not mean they received justice. Eighty-eight percent of arrested black men in Virginia were convicted of some crime, ranging from assault to robbery to rape, a considerably higher conviction rate than for most crimes, and higher than for white men accused of assaults against women. Nevertheless, between 1900 and 1945, considerations of the victim's class and reputation, rather than solely her whiteness, protected some black men from the full force of the law. Of the 220 black men accused by white women, 17 men were lynched (8 percent), 46 men were executed (23 percent of convicted men), 40 men (20 percent) received a sentence of five years or less, and 20 (10 percent) were acquitted. Governors also granted many convicted men conditional pardons long before they completed their sentences.[7]

Virginia law defined rape as carnal knowledge by force and against the will of the victim. It required that the victim resist her assailant to the limit of her ability. Failure to resist adequately at any time during the assault could be construed by the jury as consent.[8] Scholars have noted that the legal requirement of resistance was unnecessary in cases of black-on-white rape, the reasoning being that no white woman would consent to sexual relations with a black man. Courts encouraged juries to assume that any sexual relations between white women and black men inherently constituted rape. A judge in North Carolina in 1946 made this belief explicit in his instructions to the jury in a case of rape. He instructed the jury that there was no consent on the part of the white victim "because it was contrary to the training and natural instinct that she should permit a person of the opposite race to have sexual intercourse with her."[9] Like the resistance requirement, inquiries into the victim's reputation and sexual history also placed legal focus on the victim rather than on the actions of her assailant. Questions about character theoretically shed light on the issue of consent, under the assumption that if a woman had consented to intercourse in the past, she was more likely to do so in the future. They also spoke to her credibility as a witness.

Although evidence of resistance and character appeared less frequently in cases of black-on-white rape, legal officials did consider it relevant. Juries received instructions that the law still required white women to resist black men using "every means of faculty within the woman's power" throughout the assault. Failure to do so could be considered evidence of consent.[10] Attorneys in Virginia cases also publicly acknowledged that though questioning the character of a white rape victim was distasteful, it was nonetheless legitimate when a man's life was at stake.[11] One attorney prosecuting a black man made plain the role of character: "Of course I realize that the law does not permit a man to assault a lewd woman, at the same time her lewdness if it exists can always be shown by the defense in cases of this nature in order to affect the credibility of the testimony."[12] Questions of character remained legitimate parts of black-on-white rape trials in the twentieth century.

Despite evidence that white women who accused black men of rape faced some of the scrutiny other rape victims faced, they had other advantages. Like other southerners, Virginians' fear of the mythical black beast rapist colored their application of rape law. After Reconstruction, Virginia law placed sentencing in the hands of white, male jurors, thereby ensuring that although Virginia's criminal code appeared to be race neutral, it was biased in its application. Rape and attempted rape were both capital offenses, but no white man was executed for either crime. White male jurors usually accepted the testimony of a white woman over that of a black man. An attorney defending Lee Archer in 1913 stated that a white man told him that "he would believe [the victim's] statement against that of a dozen Negro witnesses . . . and he believed everybody else would do the same."[13] In a system of racial hierarchy, legal procedure and common custom privileged white accounts of black men's crimes, and black men were convicted accordingly. This does not mean that the convicted men were guilty. A few, some, many, or even most of the black men accused by white women may have been entirely innocent of the charges brought against them. But perceptions of black men's inevitable guilt accorded with white beliefs about black men's nature, the allure of white women, and the racial hierarchy, and therefore carried far more explanatory power than did narratives of black men's innocence.

The advent of an organized civil rights movement in the postwar period lessened these disadvantages. The prosecution of black-on-white rape cases aligned with the civil rights movement most directly in the Martinsville Seven case.[14] In 1949, seven black men were accused of gang-raping a white woman. They were convicted and sentenced to death. There was little doubt that the men committed the rape, and no procedural grounds for an appeal. The defense attorneys, in a new approach, argued that discrimination in the punishment of blacks in capital cases represented a violation of the equal protection clause. As evidence, the lawyers showed that since 1908 Virginia had executed forty-five men for rape or attempted rape in Virginia, every one of them black.[15] Such statistics demonstrated persistent racial discrimination in sentencing in Virginia, assertions that would be repeated throughout the South. The NAACP's appeal in the Martinsville Seven case ultimately failed. All seven men were executed in 1951. Nevertheless, the arguments of their lawyers had a profound impact on the way African Americans responded to charges of black-on-white rape in subsequent years. Arguing that racial discrimination in sentencing violated African Americans' right to equal protection placed rape cases squarely within the realm of civil rights.[16]

Pointing out racial disparities in punishment as a defense tactic rarely seemed to sway a judge or jury alone, but it did affect the advice that defense lawyers gave their clients. In 1959, Oliver Hill encouraged Sam Townes to plead guilty to charges of rape specifically to avoid the death penalty. Other black men received similar advice. Kenneth Weatherspoon, a naval man accused of raping a fifteen-year-old girl, pleaded guilty and refused to take the stand in his defense on the advice of his attorney, saying, "If I took the stand, I would have a chance of going to the electric chair." Weatherspoon received a life sentence.[17] The focus on racial disparity in punishment dovetailed with other efforts by the black community to secure their legal rights in the criminal justice system.

The presence of African Americans on juries was one way in which the black community sought to minimize racial disparities in punishment. Although the effect of having blacks serve on juries is difficult to determine, as news reports did not always state the racial composition of the jury and could not report how individual jurors voted, it appears that black jurors could prevent maximum sentences. Frasker Young, for example, was accused of rape by a white housewife in 1949. According to the *Richmond Afro-American*, Young's first trial ended in a mistrial. At his second trial, a jury of ten whites and two blacks convicted him and sentenced him to twenty-five years in prison, a substantial term but one considerably less than the life term or the death sentence they could have imposed.[18]

In only one case did the black press explicitly credit African Americans on the jury with altering the outcome of a trial. In 1951, Clifford Wulk, a white Marine officer, was accused of raping a six-teen-year-old black baby-sitter as he was taking her home. Despite his indictment, Wulk's trial was repeatedly delayed until the NAACP sent lawyers to act as special prosecutors. Wulk finally went on trial in June 1952. After two days of testimony, the jury of six whites and six blacks could not reach a verdict, splitting along racial lines. The *Richmond Afro-American* announced that the hung jury "mark[ed] the first time in Virginia's history that a jury has split down the middle along racial lines." It was, however, only a temporary victory. Six months later, the judge dismissed the charges against Wulk, citing doubts about the state's ability to win a conviction. Though the NAACP protested the decision and mass meetings occurred in Spotsylvania County, Wulk was never retried.[19]

Many black men accused by white women owed their freedom to the willingness of the African American community to support them. The case of Ruffin Junior Selby in 1953 illustrates the forms of protest that the African American community might muster. Selby was accused of murdering a Navy quartermaster, and raping his companion, a divorced white woman named Carmelia Cravedi.[20] Police arrested and charged Ruffin Junior Selby with rape, murder, and robbery after grilling him for almost two days.[21] Cravedi eventually identified Selby as the assailant, and her identification provided the only evidence of Selby's involvement in the crime. Despite the paucity of evidence against him, Selby still faced considerable legal jeopardy. Though the white press's coverage of the case avoided inflammatory racial rhetoric, the brutality of the crime alone could have turned the jury against him. The black community, after holding mass meetings to publicize his case, began a fund-raising campaign to hire legal counsel. Several of Selby's neighbors, both whites and blacks, mortgaged their homes and businesses to provide bail for his release. The black press continually published articles about his case, both on the success of the fund-raising efforts and the quality of the state's case against him.[22] It also published the various reasons Cravedi gave for why she and her date were parked at a well-known lover's lane so late at night, the implication being they had gone there for sex.

The protest of the black community criticized a legal system that put black men almost exclusively in the shadow of the electric chair. Most Virginians knew that rape and murder could be punished with death, and most were probably aware that, in the case of rape, juries reserved the death penalty for black men. For Ruffin Selby, justice prevailed. At Selby's trial for rape, the prosecution could produce little testimony, other than Carmelia Cravedi's shaky identification, that Selby was responsible for the crime. The jury, composed of eleven whites and one black, voted to acquit Selby after deliberating less than fifteen minutes. The courtroom erupted into applause when the jury announced its verdict.[23]

Selby benefited from the lack of evidence against him. But he needed competent legal help to ensure that the jury noted the prosecution's weak case. The funds raised by his supporters through the

NAACP provided him with the counsel of some of the best attorneys in the area. Activities in cases like Ruffin Selby's illustrate how organized activity could force the legal system to render a mode of justice to black men accused of assaulting white women.[24] Opposition to Selby's prosecution came from both blacks and whites. A mixed-race jury acquitted him, and an audience of both blacks and whites cheered his acquittal. It is also likely that citizens of both races contributed to his defense fund.

Mass meetings, defense funds, competent attorneys, and a jury that included African Americans helped to offset the disadvantages black men faced because of the racial configuration of the case. By the 1950s, black men were more likely to be acquitted of charges of raping white women, or to have the charges against them downgraded to lesser offenses. Certainly not every black man accused of a crime against a white woman benefited from these developments. Some black men received lengthy sentences for crimes, others pleaded guilty out of fear of the death penalty, and others received the death penalty from juries, a punishment never handed down to white men convicted of rape. But between 1945 and 1960, only five black men (8 percent) were executed. Indeed, of the fifty-nine men accused of some form of sexual misbehavior with a white woman, sixteen (27 percent) saw the charges against them dismissed, or were acquitted, three were committed to Central State Hospital, and eleven (19 percent) received a sentence of less than five years. Together, thirty, or slightly more than half, received little or no punishment. Compared to the years between 1900 and 1945, when 23 percent of convicted men were executed, and only 10 percent were acquitted, the postwar period represents significant change.

The efforts of the African American community and of civil rights organizations played a large role in changing some black men's experiences in the legal system, but these were not the only sources of change. New attitudes about white women's sexual nature encouraged whites to look with suspicion on women's charges of rape. By the 1950s, common views of female sexuality posited that women were not always in conscious control of their sexual desires. These beliefs took a pernicious form in the courtroom, and can be attributed to Freudian theories of criminology popular in the 1950s.

Freud advocated a theory of seduction in which young girls, harboring an aggressive sexuality, cloaked their own sexual desires in fantasies of seduction, projecting their desires onto others.[25] Freud himself did not apply this theory to rape, but his disciples superimposed these ideas on women's experience of rape. The most famous of these disciples, and the most frequently quoted, was Helene Deutsch, who wrote in the 1940s. She argued that women possessed an inherently masochistic sexual impulse. According to her theories, women required painful penetration in order to achieve sexual satisfaction. Fantasies of rape, and rape itself, were merely exaggerations of normal sexual relations for women. Deutsch's theories erased women as rape victims, arguing that the desire to be raped was a fundamental part of female sexuality.[26]

Ideas about women's alleged fantasies of rape became a common addition to legal treatises on rape prosecutions in the postwar period, and encouraged courts to be suspicious of all women's charges of rape. Legal theorists argued that despite a woman's apparent resistance, she may have subconsciously desired to be violated, thereby relieving her attacker of responsibility for his actions. One of the most famous authors on legal theory and evidence, Henry Wigmore, warned in the 1940s that women who charged rape often suffered from psychological disorders, which influenced them to bring false charges of rape against otherwise innocent men.[27] Similarly, many psychologists believed that women themselves did not know their own minds when it came to sexual activity. Women supposedly enjoyed being overpowered sexually, and often were attracted to, rather than repulsed by, aggressive men. Ultimately, according to one influential article in 1952, "[A] woman's need for sexual satisfaction may lead to the unconscious desire for forceful penetration, the coercion serving neatly to avoid the guilt feeling which might arise after willing participation." Charges of rape, they argued, frequently arose out of women's desire to avoid responsibility for their sexual activity.[28]

Most scholars of rape note the effect of Freudian theories on attitudes toward the victims of sexual violence, but they maintain that such attitudes prevailed primarily in cases of rape between people of the same race, or in cases in which the assailant and victim were acquainted.[29] Women, especially white women, who claimed to have been raped by black men supposedly escaped such suspicions. Helene Deutsch, however, in her theories of women's psychosis disagreed, arguing that white women were especially prone to fantasize about being raped by black men. She argued that claims of rape were "fantastic stories . . . produced by the masochistic yearnings of these women."[30]

An examination of the cases in the Virginia press from the 1950s shows that they fall somewhere between the extremes of Helene

Deutsch's rape fantasies and the carte blanche supposedly given to white women to accuse black men. Raising suspicions of white women's sexual activity prior to being assaulted by black men did not automatically result in black men's acquittal, though that did happen. But the appearance of impropriety cast a taint over a woman's charge of assault, and could result in a minor sentence for her assailant, if he was convicted.

Any suggestion of familiarity between white women and black men might be enough to acquit black men of charges filed against them. George Washington, charged with attempted rape in Richmond in 1949, was acquitted after the victim, who was separated from her husband, admitted that during the alleged assault Washington called her by her first name, even though she claimed he was a stranger to her.[31] Whites and white authorities were no longer shocked by evidence that white women might consent to sexual relations with black men. Leon Woodley stood trial for rape in Portsmouth, Virginia, in 1953. The victim claimed that Woodley had dragged her into a field and raped her. He claimed that she had approached him, asking about bus schedules, and then told him he could have sexual relations with her for five dollars. After two separate juries in two separate trials failed to reach a verdict in his case, the prosecution decided to dismiss all charges against him, and he was released. Though police reported that they saw Woodley's accuser emerging from the field "hysterical," Woodley's account had sufficient credibility to prevent his conviction.[32]

Philip Holley and Drexel Williams's experience in court six years later was similar. A white woman accused both men of raping her in 1959, after they dragged her from her car. The two men disputed her account, claiming instead that she had approached them looking for whiskey. After singing and dancing together for five hours, both men had consensual sexual relations with the woman. Philip Holley's trial ended in a hung jury. Charges were dismissed completely when a separate jury acquitted his companion, Drexel Williams. Both the white and the black press covered the case, and both printed Williams and Holley's claims that they had only had sex with the woman after a prolonged afternoon of drinking and dancing.[33]

Juries were less sympathetic to women who violated norms of proper behavior, and there is some evidence that black men were aware of this. John Clabon Taylor, one of the seven men convicted and executed in the Martinsville case in 1951, openly acknowledged the role of the victim's character when he warned the other men at the scene "that that was a Christian woman and it would cause us some trouble. . . . That if she was a drunk we might get by with it but I could tell from the way that she talked that she was a good woman."[34]

In other cases involving consensual relations between white women and black men, authorities held white women responsible along with black men. These cases demonstrate that legal authorities no longer labeled these interactions rape, but they continued to police interracial relationships. Charley Wallace was arrested "with Blonde in car," in a white neighborhood, with the woman's arms about Wallace's neck. Both Wallace and the "blonde," Elsie May Williams, posted $300 bonds for good behavior and submitted to medical tests to determine if they had venereal disease. Wallace claimed that he had never seen the woman before she opened the door of his car and asked for a ride. He could not explain why she had her arms about his neck, but he denied that they had been caught in a "love tryst."[35]

New ideas about women's sexual nature brought white women's experiences in rape trials closer to that of black women. Nonwhite women's claims of sexual exploitation had long been ignored because of the belief among whites that black women were innately hypersexual, which mirrored later Freudian arguments that all women desired to be raped. Throughout the twentieth century, legal officials, giving Virginia governors their opinions on requests for clemency in cases involving black women, often stated that they viewed any charge of rape by a black woman with suspicion. One prosecuting attorney wrote in 1933 regarding the case of William Watson, a black man convicted in 1926 of rape and sentenced to fifteen years in prison, "Cases like this among negroes are very difficult to get at the facts," as he believed Watson's case might merely involve a case of "rough wooing."[36] At the same time, the changes wrought by the civil rights movement brought black women's ability to seek legal redress a degree closer to that of white women. As the black community became increasingly vocal about the injustices black men faced in the legal system, they frequently compared black men's experiences to those of white men accused of assaulting black women. Their protest resulted in more trials for white men accused of assaulting black women, and a few convictions as well.

African Americans used several strategies to promote the equal treatment of accused rapists in the legal system regardless of race. The most direct form of action was protest. African Americans held mass meetings to pressure white law enforcement and legal officials to prosecute white men accused of rape. Lawyers from civil rights organizations observed the trials of white men accused of rape, or aided the Commonwealth in prosecuting cases. The black press promoted the good character of black victims, and criticized attempts by defense attorneys to capitalize on racist stereotypes of black women's sexual character. The black press also publicized cases in which African Americans physically and even violently resisted white men who attempted to harass black women. Whites joined in African Americans' complaints about white men's treatment of black women.[37] These activities did not guarantee that black women received justice in a court of law. To the contrary, many charges were dismissed or downgraded, and juries acquitted many white men. But the increase in the number of trials of white men for assaulting black women itself represented a step forward.

The black press reported cases in which black community members succeeded in pressuring white authorities to respond to black women's charges. In Amherst, Virginia, in 1948, a white man named Dudley raped a black woman described as "feeble-minded." Hearing of the assault, respected African American community members conducted their own investigation and turned their findings over to the Commonwealth's Attorney. As a result of their efforts, police arrested Dudley for rape, but the judge reduced the charges to assault and only fined Dudley $20 plus costs.[38] The case of Corbett A. Witt, a white man, appeared in the same paper reporting Dudley's case. Witt received a fine of $350 for raping a pregnant black married woman, though again the judge reduced the charge to assault.[39] The black newspaper headline, "Rape of Expectant Mother by White Farmer Draws $350 Fine" both announced the conviction, and criticized the minimal penalties white men paid.

No occupation placed black women in more danger than working in the homes of white men. Many black women accused white men of assaulting them while they were doing domestic work in white households, or—especially for young black girls—when white fathers were returning them home after a night of baby-sitting. Freddie Lancaster, for example, assaulted his housemaid while she was cleaning the bathroom, and then paid her for her housework. Though she waited five days to charge the man with assault, he was charged with rape.[40]

Civil rights groups intervened in these cases, but their efforts did not guarantee that black interests received more attention. In 1951, for example, Oliver Hill represented the victim of Oscar Hopkins, a white man accused of attempted rape. Though Hopkins admitted to having sexual relations with the seventeen-year-old girl at trial, he was acquitted.[41] The intervention of well-known black activists, regardless of the jury's verdict, sent a message to the white community and the legal system that the African American community considered legal redress for crimes against black women to be part of their quest for civil rights. The presence of such well-known men in the courtroom also exerted overt pressure on white officials to hold white men accountable for their actions.

The case against William Whitley in Isle of Wight County in 1950 provides a good example of community involvement in cases of white-on-black rape. Whitley, a recently married white man, was charged with rape in 1950. He appeared at the home of a black girl, and asked her parents if she could watch his elderly mother while he and his wife went to a movie. The parents agreed. Instead of taking her to his home, he drove around for two hours, finally stopping in a secluded patch of woods. He pulled a gun on her and raped her. He then returned her to her home. She reported the attack to her parents, and her father confronted Whitley. Whitley admitted the rape, saying he had "been looking at her" for a long time. The parents enlisted the help of Samuel Tucker, an NAACP attorney in Emporia to investigate the case, along with officials from the NAACP and the Negro Organization Society. Whitley was arrested and indicted as a result of the investigation. NAACP attorneys and activists also held a mass meeting to map strategy. According to the *Afro-American*, the case would probably have been hushed up had it not been for the intervention of the NAACP.[42]

Despite the efforts of the black community, Whitley's jury did not hold him accountable for his actions. Black citizens protested the all-white jury as African Americans represented a majority in the county. Black citizens also complained that white legal officials treated black witnesses without respect by refusing to use courtesy titles when addressing them. Though civil rights attorneys worked with the prosecution, they could do little more than "flinch" and "grit their teeth" when a white defense witness stated that "It's nothing strange for a colored girl to have an illegitimate child." Though there was no indication that the victim had had any previous sexual encounters, the defense maintained that the sexual intercourse between the victim and defendant was consensual. The prosecuting attorney did little to counter stereotypes about black women's nature, and the jury voted to acquit Whitley.[43]

Despite the concerted efforts of Virginia's African Americans and the support they received from local civil rights organizations, black women faced inordinate obstacles in having their charges of rape heard by the criminal justice system. Though the black press frequently covered these cases and gave voice to the anger of their readers, the white press usually ignored them. The white press's lack of interest reflects the disinterest of most whites. Though by the 1950s white men increasingly faced criminal trials when accused of rape by black women, only rarely did those trials result in a conviction, much less a significant sentence. Absolute numbers are difficult to obtain, as the black press did not always report trial outcomes. Of the thirty-six white men charged with assaults between 1945 and 1960, trial dispositions are only readily available for twenty-four.[44] Of those twenty-four, ten were acquitted outright at trial, and six saw the charges reduced to some form of assault and paid a fine. Only six received sentences of more than five years. Even a vocal and active civil rights movement could not ensure that black women had their day in court.

Interracial rape cases after World War II represent the shifting power that different groups could exert over the legal system. Previously, white women had considerable, though not absolute, power to force the conviction of the black men they accused of assault. Black men had little ability to convince juries that their sexual interactions with white women did not constitute criminal conduct. Only in pardon petitions did legal authorities reconsider those interactions, and grant convicted men conditional pardon. The black community had limited power to shape the legal process. However, after the start of an organized civil rights movement, they began to increase their influence over the legal system. Black men still faced considerable danger when accused of misbehavior by a white woman, and the distrust of rape victims by the legal system did not usually work to their benefit. But they were more likely to receive a minor sentence or be acquitted entirely. Part of their success stemmed from an increasing unwillingness on the part of white men to allow white women to accuse black men with impunity. Beliefs about white women's sexual nature and their supposed tendency to give voice to their rape fantasies could overshadow their whiteness when they accused black men. The scrutiny white women faced as the victims of black assailants moved them a step closer to the treatment black rape victims had always received.

The civil rights agitation that had contributed toward better legal protections for accused black men also carried benefits for black women. Though the white men they accused of assault were rarely convicted, they were more likely to be indicted and tried by a jury. Whites still viewed black women as inherently lascivious, and thus as unlikely victims. But the willingness of white authorities to arrest white men moved black women's treatment in the criminal justice system closer to that of white women. Both black and white women faced scrutiny of their characters when they accused a man of the other race of rape, and both groups faced disadvantages in a legal system controlled by white men who had sole power to arbitrate what interactions constituted criminal conduct. The disadvantages facing black women were greater than those facing white women, but beliefs about women's sexuality hindered all women in achieving vindication through the legal system.

NOTES

1. *Norfolk Journal and Guide*, October 12, 1946.

2. Norfolk *Journal and Guide*, October 26, 1946 and December 13, 1947.

3. See, for example, Leon Litwack, *Trouble in Mind: Black Southerners in the Age of Jim Crow* (New York: Pantheon, 1998), 344.

4. See Martha Hodes, *White Women, Black Men: Illicit Sex in the Nineteenth-Century South* (New Haven: Yale University Press, 1997); Diane Miller Sommerville, "The Rape Myth in the Old South Reconsidered: The Intersection of Race, Class, and Gender in the American South" (Ph.D. dissertation, Rutgers University, 1995).

5. Notable studies of lynching include Dominic J. Capeci, Jr., *The Lynching of Cleo Wright* (Lexington: University of Kentucky Press, 1998); W. Fitzhugh Brundage, *Lynching in the New South: Georgia and Virginia, 1880–1930* (Urbana: University of Illinois Press, 1993); James R. McGovern, *Anatomy of a Lynching: The Killing of Claud Neal* (Baton Rouge: Louisiana State University Press, 1982). Studies of famous rape cases include James Goodman, *Stories of Scottsboro: The Rape Case That Shocked America and Revived the Struggle for Equality* (New York: Pantheon, 1994); Eric W. Rise, *The Martinsville Seven: Race, Rape, and Capital Punishment* (Charlottesville: University Press of Virginia, 1995).

6. This analysis supports Grace Elizabeth Hale's arguments that segregation was primarily a performance of racial hierarchy. See Grace Elizabeth Hale,

Making Whiteness: The Culture of Segregation in the South, 1890–1940 (New York: Pantheon, 1998).

7. For an in-depth discussion of these issues, see Lisa Lindquist Dorr, "'Men, Even Negroes, Must Have Some Protection': Black-on-White Rape and Retribution in Twentieth-Century Virginia," *Journal of Southern History*, LXVI (November 2000): 711–48.

8. Virginia's law regarding rape was similar to that of other states. See Susan Estrich, *Real Rape* (Cambridge: Harvard University Press, 1986).

9. *State v. Thompson*, 227 NC (1946) 19, at 25.

10. *Commonwealth v. John Anderson*, Case File, December Term, 1938, Circuit Court of Loudoun County, Leesburg, Virginia.

11. Attorneys for both the prosecution and the defense supported this statement in the case of John Clements, tried and acquitted of rape in 1914. See the *Richmond Virginian*, June 18, 1914; the *Richmond Evening Journal*, June 18, 1914; and the *Richmond News-Leader*, June 18, 1914.

12. The attorney made this statement in the petition for conditional pardon for Wilson Allen, convicted in 1917. *Commonwealth v. Wilson Allen*, Petition for Conditional Pardon, Executive Papers, March 1–March 15, 1929, Box 510, the Library of Virginia.

13. *Commonwealth v. Lee Archer*, Bill of Exception #2, Princess Anne Circuit Court Papers, 1913, the Library of Virginia.

14. For an in-depth analysis of the Martinsville Seven case, see Rise, *The Martinsville Seven*.

15. Ibid., 102. These statistics would eventually become the basis for Donald H. Partington's article on rape and the death penalty in Virginia, which appeared in the *Washington and Lee Law Review* in 1965.

16. Rise makes this point specifically. See *The Martinsville Seven*, 4.

17. *Norfolk Virginian Pilot*, July 23, 1949; *Norfolk Journal and Guide*, July 30, 1949. *Commonwealth v. Kenneth Weatherspoon*, Common Law Order Book #75, 504, 573, Norfolk Corporation Court I, Norfolk, Virginia.

18. *Richmond Afro-American*, March 31, 1951. This article appeared after Young was convicted of a second count of rape, this time of a black girl. He received an additional fifteen-year sentence.

19. *Norfolk Journal and Guide*, September 20, 1952; *Richmond Afro-American*, September 20, 1952; *Norfolk Journal and Guide*, March 21, 1953; *Richmond Afro-American*, March 21, 1953.

20. Accounts of the crime appear in the *Norfolk Virginian-Pilot*, June 7, 1953, June 8, 1953, June 9, 1953, and June 10, 1953.

21. *Norfolk Virginian-Pilot*, June 22, 1953, June 23, 1953.

22. *Norfolk Journal and Guide*, June 27, 1953.

23. *Commonwealth v. Ruffin Junior Selby*, Common Law Order Book #25, esp. quote on p. 11, 12, 22. Circuit Court of Princess Anne County, Princess

Anne, Virginia. See also *Norfolk Virginian-Pilot*, October 2, 1953; *Norfolk Journal and Guide*, October 3, 1953; *Richmond Afro-American*, October 17, 1953.

24. This is not to suggest that the black community had not protested these cases effectively before 1945. Ida B. Wells pointed out the sexual politics of lynching as early as 1892, and the black press did publish articles on cases before 1945. Nevertheless, their protests were general, and when they did address specific cases, they were reluctant to appear as though they were questioning white women's testimony or condoning the crime of rape. The black press and the black community were much more willing to protest black men's treatment directly after World War II.

25. Peggy Reeves Sanday, *A Woman Scorned: Acquaintance Rape on Trial* (New York: Doubleday, 1996), 131. See Sigmund Freud, *Dora: An Analysis of a Case of Hysteria* (New York: Collier, 1963).

26. Helene Deutsch, *Psychology of Women* (New York: Grune and Stratton, 1944). Many other disciples of Freud disagreed with Deutch's analysis. Susan Brownmiller criticized Deutsch in *Against Her Will*, claiming that she offered all men an iron-clad defense for rape. See Susan Brownmiller, *Against Her Will: Men, Women, and Rape* (New York: Bantam, 1975), 252.

27. John Henry Wigmore, *A Treatise on the Anglo-American System of Evidence in Trials at Common Law, Vol. IIIA* (1940; rept. Boston: Little, Brown, 1974), 744, 737. See also Glanville Williams, "Corroboration—Sexual Cases," *Criminal Law Review* (October 1962): 662–671; and Note, "Corroborating Charges of Rape," *Columbia Law Review* 67 (1967): 1137–1138.

28. Note, "Forcible and Statutory Rape: An Exploration of the Operation and Objectives of the Consent Standard," *Yale Law Journal* 62 (December 1952): 52–68.

29. See, for example, Estrich, *Real Rape*, 32–33.

30. Deutsch, *Psychology of Women*, quoted in Brownmiller, *Against Her Will*, 252.

31. *Commonwealth v. George Washington*, Proceedings from Police Court Transcript, 8B9, Criminal Section Files, 1952–1963, Box "1959 A–Y," Richmond Hustings Court Papers, held at the Library of Virginia. The defense also asked the witness if her husband had accused her of being unfaithful. She answered that though he never accused her outright, he was extremely jealous, to the point of refusing to allow her to talk with bill collectors. Transcript, 14.

32. *Richmond Afro-American*, June 20, 1953; *Norfolk Journal and Guide*, June 20, 1953. *Commonwealth v. Leon Woodley*, Common Law Order Book #47, 34, 92, 105, 242, 292, Portsmouth Corporation Court, Portsmouth, Virginia.

33. *Norfolk Virginian-Pilot*, December 8, 1959, December 9, 1959, January 16, 1959; *Portsmouth Star*, January 17, 1960; *Norfolk Journal and Guide*, December 12, 1959. *Commonwealth v. Philip Holley*, Common Law Order Book #54, 354, 418,

421, 502; *Commonwealth v. Drexel Williams,* Common Law Order Book #54, 355, 410, 493, 494, Portsmouth Hustings Court, Portsmouth, Virginia.

34. Rise, *The Martinsville Seven,* 16. The quotation appeared in Taylor's statement. See *The Martinsville Seven,* 169n28.

35. *Richmond Afro-American,* December 12, 1953. The *Afro-American* frequently referred to whites as "blondes."

36. Letter from A. D. Watkins to Governor Pollard, March 20, 1933, *Commonwealth v. William Watson,* Petition for Conditional Pardon, March 21–April 4, 1933, Box 587, the Library of Virginia.

37. The *Richmond Afro-American,* for example, reported an incident in which a white couple intervened when two white men attempted to assault a black woman. After the two white men were fined $50 for being "persons of ill fame," the white woman criticized their meager punishment noting that two black men accused of assaulting a white woman would never have received such lenient sentences. "I don't think the verdict was fair at all," she stated. *Richmond Afro-American,* August 31, 1957, and September 7, 1957.

38. *Norfolk Journal and Guide,* October 16, 1948.

39. *Norfolk Journal and Guide,* October 16, 1948.

40. *Richmond Afro-American,* August 25, 1953, September 5, 1953.

41. *Richmond Afro-American,* August 25, 1951, September 8, 1951, September 29, 1951.

42. *Richmond Afro-American,* September 16, 1950.

43. *Richmond Afro-American,* November 25, 1950, November 21, 1950. Quotation on November 25, 1950.

44. I have located only two cases prior to 1945 in which white men were convicted for assaulting black women.

12

Sexual Coercion and Limited Choices

Their Link to Teen Pregnancy and Welfare

Robert Cherry

IN THE MOVIE *The Accused*, Jodie Foster played a working-class woman who engaged in risky behavior that led to her being gang-raped. She went to a bar and began playing pool and flirting with a man in an area where she was the only woman. While the movie indicated that the men were at fault, and looked realistically at the downside of contemporary sexual mores, it blamed women for putting themselves in compromising positions. When I showed the movie in one of my classes, nearly all my students blamed the Foster character. Their reactions seemed to be consistent with those of a broad section of the American public who felt that Mike Tyson was not solely responsible for the sexual assault on a young woman. After all, what should she have expected going up to his hotel room at 2 A.M.? What should the Foster character have expected when she went into the pool area scantily clad and flirted with a man? Similarly, many of my students were unforgiving of wives and girlfriends who stayed in abusive relationships.

My students' attitudes reflect their tendency not to acknowledge that poor and working-class women face much more constrained choices than they do. This lack of sensitivity to constrained choices often comes out most sharply when the behavior of poor black women is judged. During the 1980s, depression-like employment conditions within the black community increased their powerlessness. As a result, many of these women made risky choices to maintain relationships with men who may have brought crucially needed income into their households. Not surprisingly, they continued in abusive relationships

265

and engaged in unprotected sex that middle-class women of all races mistakenly believe could be avoided if only these poor women had not allowed themselves to be victims.

However, the strong economy of the last few years offers some hope for these vulnerable women. Tight labor markets after 1996 forced many employers to change their hiring decisions. They could no longer refuse to hire female household heads. This essay will summarize studies that document how these employment opportunities have begun to undermine long-held negative stereotypes and have begun to change the benefit-cost calculations that had previously trapped many poor women in abusive situations.

All individuals, not just vulnerable women, must make benefit-cost calculations that affect their personal safety. Individuals must judge how much money and time they should allocate to the prevention of household crimes. Allocations are made only as long as benefits outweigh the opportunity cost of alternative allocations. After some point, benefits from the purchase of additional safety devices are outweighed by their costs to households. Homeowners then refuse to make further allocations of time or money, even though safety would be increased. Households choose to go on vacations or do not obtain the *maximum* number of safety devices available, although these decisions increase the likelihood that they will suffer home losses. Similarly, in the labor market, individuals trade off safety for higher wages by accepting jobs that have higher accident rates, in return for compensating wage differentials.

More controversially, this benefit-cost model can be applied to individual decisions that put women at risk. Should women stop going unescorted to shopping malls, since there is a modest probability that they will be victims of carjackings or worse? Should women stop going unescorted to parties because there is some probability that they will be sexually assaulted? Just as individuals accept risks in their jobs and their homes, the benefit-cost model suggests that it is rational for women to accept some risk to their personal safety.

The benefit-cost model allows us to see that many personal safety decisions should be analyzed in a more consistent manner. Generally, people don't blame construction workers who are injured on their jobs or vacationing families when their homes are robbed. Similarly, in general women should not be blamed for the sexual assaults they suffer when they go unescorted to shopping malls, parties, or bars, nor for

their willingness under certain circumstances to continue in abusive relationships. Well-to-do households, for example, can reduce the risks
they face. As a female executive wrote,

> I understand how the women who were harassed and assaulted by a
> mob of men in Central Park must feel. That such terrifying attacks
> could take place in daylight in Central Park, with people all around,
> utterly shakes our sense of safety. Women learn early which streets are
> safe to walk on, when it's safe to be there and even how to walk. We
> accept that we must pay for our safety in the form of cabs and door-
> man buildings in more expensive neighborhoods.[1]

Although these women have the resources to reduce (but not completely eliminate) their risks, poor women, who cannot afford more expensive neighborhoods and must take public transportation instead of
cabs, do not. Due to the neighborhoods in which they are forced to live,
poor women must accept more risks when they are shopping, commuting, or socializing. As a result, poor women will experience more
crimes against their homes, more injuries at their jobs, and more physical and sexual assaults than better-off women with the same set of values. Since poverty has a strong racial dimension, it should not be surprising that black women disproportionately experience these hard-
ships. This has had important consequences for the childbearing,
welfare, and work decisions made by poor black women.

This benefit-cost model might also be helpful in explaining why,
after decades of continuous decline, the teenager birth rate began to rise
during the 1980s. In 1985, the birth rate for black women aged fifteen to
seventeen years old was 69.3 (per 1,000). This was almost triple the rate
of 24.4 for comparably aged white women, and only slightly lower than
the white rate for eighteen- and nineteen-year-old women. By 1989, the
rate for fifteen- to seventeen-year-old black women had increased by 18
percent to 81.9 percent; slightly more than the rate increase among black
women eighteen to nineteen years old. In contrast, the rates increased
by 15.2 and 3.6 percent for white women aged fifteen to seventeen and
eighteen to nineteen years old, respectively. Most troubling to some, 95
percent of these black births were to unwed mothers.[2]

Though they disagreed as to the underlying motives, both liberals
and conservatives agreed that young women, including those who
were poor and black, were not avoiding pregnancy. Conservatives like

Charles Murray[3] focused on the role of welfare in providing incentives for this "dysfunctional" behavior, while liberals emphasized how these women ignore the long-term adverse consequences of unwed motherhood. For example, liberal psychologists Ellen Freeman and Karl Rickels concluded:

> Like many teenagers, they did not get around to obtaining contraception, and they believed that pregnancy, because it had not yet happened, would not occur to them. More important, many of these disadvantaged teenagers did not believe that consequences of pregnancy, would negatively affect their lives. Although they did not "want" pregnancy, they had no strong motivation to avoid it, because they had no understanding that their lives would be any different.[4]

In the 1990s, however, new studies began to document the high level of sexual coercion all young women were experiencing. In a 1995 nationwide study, 23 percent of young women who became sexually active before they were fourteen years old characterized their first intercourse as involuntary, and another 14 percent indicated that, while voluntary, they didn't really want it.[5] Among those who became sexually active as fifteen- and sixteen-year-olds, rates were still appallingly high, though somewhat lower than for younger teens.[6] This contrasted with a mid-1980s survey that found much lower rates of involuntary intercourse among women younger than sixteen years old.[7] The 1995 survey found that the "unwantedness" of first intercourse increased as the age difference between the sexual partners increased. Among girls fifteen to seventeen years old, limited wantedness averaged 17 percent with a same-age male partner but grew to 44 percent when their partner was at least seven years older.

Clearly, becoming sexually active at a young age, whether it is by choice or not, increases the likelihood of experiencing an unintended pregnancy. But sexual coercion and unintended pregnancies are linked in other ways. First, after adjusting for age, the use of contraception was about 10 percentage points lower among young women who had a low degree of wantedness compared to those who had a high degree of wantedness. Second, young girls who had an involuntary first sexual intercourse tended to have significantly lower levels of protected sex in subsequent encounters.[8] A 1992 Washington state study found that young women who had experienced sexual abuse at some point in their lives were twice as likely not to have used contraception during their last intercourse than those who had not been abused. Almost one-half of those young women who became pregnant suffered sexual abuse compared to only 21 percent of those who were never pregnant.[9] Third, the use of contraception was particularly low when the male partner was substantially older. As a result, though men six years and older than their partners comprised only 6.7 percent of all partners of fifteen- to seventeen-year-olds, they comprised 19.7 percent of the partners of those who became pregnant.[10]

Coercion influenced the decision of pregnant women to abort or deliver. Among fifteen- to seventeen-year-olds, 49.6 percent chose to abort if the age difference of the partners was less than three years, 34.3 percent if the age difference was between three and five years, and 20.9 percent if it was at least six years. As a result, men who were at least six years older than their partners comprised 24 percent of all fathers.[11]

Young black women were particularly at risk for unwanted pregnancies. Studies consistently found that black women become sexually active at a much younger age than white women. Charles Barone and his associates estimated that 65 percent of black but only 11 percent of white female eighth graders were sexually active. These numbers may also reflect the greater degree of coercion experienced by young black women.[12] Another study found that the share of young black women who characterized their first intercourse experiences as involuntary was 37 percent higher for black than for white young women.[13] Overall, 30 percent of the first intercourse of young white women was either involuntary or not really wanted, whereas the share was 46 percent among young black women. These findings contrast with an earlier survey that reported the involuntary rate for young black women in the early 1980s as one-half the white rate.[14]

There are many theories why young African American women appear to experience more sexual coercion than young white women. On the basis of a five-year study he conducted in Philadelphia, conservative sociologist Elijah Anderson claimed that a subculture had developed in which young black males attempt to have "casual sex with as many women as possible, impregnating one or more, and getting them to 'have their baby' brings a boy the ultimate in esteem from his peers and makes him a man."[15] Consistent with this viewpoint, William Marsiglio found that after controlling for some socioeconomic differences, there was a much larger core of black young men than white young men who were positively affected by their partners' pregnancy.[16] Whether or not the coercion they experienced met the definition of rape, Frank Furstenberg and his associates feared that young black women were at risk for unwanted pregnancies because of their inability to "exercise contraceptive vigilance." They concluded that subcultural norms put enormous peer pressure on very young black men to be sexually active and this "has implications for females who are exposed in their early teens to sexually experienced and some have argued, sexually demanding partners."[17]

Sexual coercion within the black community has been a common theme throughout the last one hundred years. Southern racists used it to justify violence against black men during the Jim Crow era, Gunnar Myrdal claimed it reflected a lack of sexual mores among uneducated blacks, and black feminist writers Toni Morrison and Alice Walker have made the sexual abuse of black women by black men a central motif of the books they have written.[18] Unlike the southern racists, however, these other observers have argued that abusive behavior is not a distinctive cultural trait but reflects a response to powerlessness and vulnerability. In the view of these writers, many black men realize that they don't have much to offer and cannot really support their partner or their children. They are worried that women will leave them and therefore become extremely jealous, possessive, and violent to keep the women with them. Jody Raphael's book, *Saving Bernice*, in telling one woman's story, attempts to show why her partner feels so threatened by her attempts at self-sufficiency. In personal correspondence, Raphael noted, "I tried to tell it in such a way so that the reader, while abhorring and not condoning the violence and coercion that he used, would feel some sympathy toward his basic plight that fuels that violence."[19]

This sense of powerlessness was exacerbated by the collapse of black employment beginning in the early 1970s. Just as the ending of the Vietnam War was thrusting thousands of black GIs into the labor force, the economy began to fizzle. Unemployment rates for black men rose sharply, accelerated by the reduction of blue-collar employment opportunities in major urban centers. For example, between 1975 and 1989 the share of young black men in the Midwest employed in durable manufacturing fell from 40 to 12 percent due to the closing of older plants in central cities.[20]

When the economy suffered a severe recession during the early 1980s, official black unemployment rates rose to more than 20 percent for black men over twenty years old and over 40 percent for black teenagers. Even this understated the employment difficulties. During the 1980–82 recession, 21 percent of all black men between the ages of twenty and twenty-four who were out of school, had had *no* work experience in the previous year. This rate was triple the white rate (7.2 percent) and almost double what the black rate had been a decade earlier (12.8 percent).[21] However, this joblessness did not show up in official unemployment statistics because most of these young men did not meet the government criterion for job search, and so they were not considered part of the active labor force.

For many black men born around 1970, the mid-1980s was a troubling period. Their entire life's experience seemed to demonstrate that economic opportunities were diminishing. When they reached their teenage years, depression levels of unemployment only made them feel more powerless and that may have translated into becoming more coercive and violent in their sexual relationships. This might explain why beginning in the late 1980s an increasing number of young black women perceived their initial intercourse to be involuntary, and why their rate of unwanted intercourse grew higher than that of white women. It also might explain why the birth rate of fifteen- to seventeen-year-old black women increased relative to all other groups between 1985 and 1989.

The depression-like economic situation and the upsurge of violence also affected the decisions of young black women. Although coercive situations helped to cause an increase in unintended pregnancies, other pregnancies were deliberate, as some women began to believe that motherhood could enable them to leave an abusive family life. For example, at the Crittenton Center for young women in Los Angeles, Almonica recounted how she saw her mother set on fire and murdered by her stepfather during a drunken fight. At age sixteen, she got pregnant by a twenty-one-year-old man. "It was the only way out," she said. The Center's director, Yale Gancherov, stated, "The parents of these young women were violent, were drug abusers, and were sexually abusive. While privileged people can see a detriment in a teenager becoming a mother, these girls see it as a realistic improvement in their lives."[22]

Conservative politicians, however, frown on women choosing to become unwed mothers in order to go on welfare. They blame women for declining marriage rates and favor social policies that increase female willingness to marry. One such policy, known as Bridefare, was enacted by the Wisconsin legislature in 1994. It allowed the welfare department to raise the monthly benefit from $440 to $531 for recipients who married. Opposing it, Wisconsin state representative Gwendolyn Moore stated:

> The Bridefare program . . . may place battered women in more danger.
> . . . Aid to Families with Dependent Children (AFDC) has traditionally been one way that women could escape from abusive situations that were dangerous for them or their children. Let us not begin telling battered women that if they do not marry, they and their children will be thrust deeper into poverty.[23]

Liberal hostility to teenage motherhood was based in large part on the initial assessments of long-term studies. In 1972 Frank Furstenberg interviewed women who had become teen mothers six years earlier, and found that one-half had not completed high school, 70 percent had been on welfare, and many had a second child, increasing the likelihood that they would become welfare dependent. While two-thirds had married their child's father, only a small percentage remained married five years later.[24]

Researchers also believed that there were serious adverse health consequences associated with teenage childbearing. In 1960, among black women the infant mortality rate of children born to mothers fifteen to nineteen years old was 5 percent, but it was only 3.8 percent for those born to mothers twenty-five to thirty years old.[25] This bleak assessment of the consequences of teen childbearing was widely accepted and provided the backdrop for the National Research Council's 1987 report, *Risking the Future*.

When Frank Furstenberg and his associates did further follow-up interviews with the teen mothers in 1984, however, some of the adverse social consequences had disappeared. The share of teen mothers with less than a high school degree had declined from 49.2 percent in 1972 to 32.6 percent. They also found that welfare dependency was not as widespread as it appeared in 1972. In 1984, two-thirds of teen mothers had not been on welfare in any of the previous five years. Instead, most teen mothers had entered the workforce. The percentage employed increased from 45 percent in 1972—when their children were young—to 72 percent in 1983. These findings indicated that the adverse consequences were not as large as they had thought in 1972.[26] Studies also began to find that teen motherhood might have only a limited effect on lifetime earnings. In a study of teen mothers, Elaine McCrate surveyed twenty-eight-year-old black and white women living in poor Los Angeles neighborhoods. She grouped subjects into those who had a child when they were younger than eighteen years old and those who had not. Teen mothers did have lower educational attainment, and due to the weak job market they faced, black women had a lower rate of financial return from additional schooling than white women. Among black women, the wage rate of teen mothers was only 9 percent lower than nonteen mothers. In contrast, among white women delaying childbearing raised the wage rate 30 percent.[27] To isolate the effect of teen childbearing, Arline Geronimus and Sanders Korenman compared outcomes for sisters, one who became a teen mother to the other who did not. Using three different data sets, at age thirty teen mothers lived in households with annual family incomes about one-quarter less than their siblings who had not become teen mothers.[28]

By the early 1990s, there no longer was a consensus that teen childbearing was detrimental to infant survival in poor black communities. Given the devastating effects of joblessness, poverty, and the growing drug epidemic, delaying childbearing to their mid-twenties put poor black women at increased risk that they would enter pregnancies with adverse health conditions, such as hypertension and high blood lead levels. Delaying pregnancy increased the risk that these women would smoke or drink during pregnancy and decreased the likelihood that they would breastfeed their infants. As a result, delaying childbearing increased the risk of preterm birth, low birth weight, and neonatal deaths.[29]

Taken together, this more recent evidence indicated that the adverse economic consequences are not as severe or as pervasive as suggested by earlier assessments. As a result, teen childbearing is not necessarily an irrational decision, especially if support services are provided and health and safety issues are taken into account. Most importantly, government agencies should focus on improving the employment and earnings opportunities available to less-educated black women and reducing the sexual coercion and domestic violence they endure.

While teenage motherhood may allow some women to escape abusive families, it does not prevent abusive relationships. The Center for Impact Study found that among teenage black mothers who were on

welfare, 55 percent of the women had experienced some form of domestic violence from their partner in the past year; 23 percent had experienced severe physical aggression, 18 percent moderate physical
abuse, and 14 percent only verbal aggression.[30]

Most troubling, the vast majority of these teen mothers maintained a stable relationship with their abusers. Over four-fifths of
teen mothers had a boyfriend and the average duration of the relationship was 2.74 years. These young women often stayed in abusive
relationships because their boyfriends provided some financial support and/or presented a threat to their safety if the relationship was
terminated.[31] The financial support was, however, quite meager since
one-half of these men were high school dropouts, only 15 percent had
at least some college or trade school education, and only 48 percent
were currently employed.

Given the limited financial benefits provided, many of these young
men consciously sabotaged the efforts of these teen mothers to gain independence, taking steps such as attempting to father more children to
further limit the teen mothers' independence. Among those young
women who did not experience domestic violence, 28 percent experienced mild birth control sabotage and 3 percent experienced high sabotage. In contrast, among those women who experienced severe physical aggression, 50 percent experienced moderate birth control sabotage,
and 24 percent high sabotage.[32] Violent partners also sought to limit the
ability of teen mothers to gain additional education or outside employment. Among the teen mothers who were currently experiencing a severe level of domestic violence, 57 percent reported some form of sabotage of their employment and/or school efforts. In contrast, only 17 and
7 percent of those who experienced low levels of domestic violence or
no violence, respectively, reported employment and/or educational
sabotage.

These studies document the downside of patriarchal relationships
when women have limited choices. Due to rising incarceration rates,
there is a scarcity of black men available for marriage. For example, in
the Midwest in 1992, there were 20 percent more black women than
black men in the noninstitutionalized population.[33] Not surprisingly,
black welfare recipients realize that, given the shortage of available
men, women must accept male prerogatives. As one recipient told
Kathryn Edin, "There's a shortage of men so that they think, 'I can have

more than one woman. I'm gonna go around this one or that one, and I'm gonna have two or three of them.'"[34]

Many of these women feared that they would become their partner's personal slave, cooking his meals, cleaning his house, and doing his laundry. These women expected that their partners would feel free to spend money on personal leisure activities rather than on family necessities. As one respondent recounted: "I gave my child's father the money to go buy my son's Pampers. He went on some street with his cousin and they were down there partying, drinking, everything. He spent my son's Pamper money on partying."[35]

Unfortunately, the price that many of these vulnerable women paid for their relationship was domestic violence. From a wide variety of mid-1990s studies, Jody Raphael and Richard Tolman found that 15 to 20 percent of women on welfare experienced physical abuse during the most recent twelve months and about 60 percent had done so some time in their past. Current abuse was about 20 percent higher among recipients who were currently involved in a relationship with a man. In a New Jersey study, Raphael and Tolman found that "three times as many abused women as nonabused women (39.7% as compared with 12.9%) reported that their intimate partner actively prevents their participation in education and training."[36] Even if partners did not overtly sabotage their efforts, more abused recipients than nonabused recipients had symptoms of depression, which itself creates a barrier to sustaining employment or educational efforts.[37]

For a long time both conservative and liberal policy makers ignored this growing evidence. Joe Klein claimed:

> Conservatives are uncomfortable because it posits another victim class: girls who become pregnant aren't just amoral, premature tarts— they are prey. Who could support cutting off these children's benefits, as some Republicans have proposed? But liberals are also uncomfortable because the data are further proof that an intense social pathology—a culture of poverty—has overwhelmed the slums.[38]

This bleak picture was changed during the 1990s by the combination of welfare changes and economic expansion. Beginning in 1994, the federal government allowed states to experiment with various reforms; all focused on reducing the number of recipients. Building on these state experiments, in 1996 federal legislation enacted lifetime limits on the number of years welfare could be obtained. As a result, by 1999 the welfare population was halved.

The great fear was that welfare recipients would have extreme difficulty finding employment because of the negative stereotypes held by employers. In a study conducted during 1994 and 1995, seventy-eight white employers were interviewed concerning the difficulty they had finding qualified workers.[39] Almost one-half mentioned parenthood, family, or both when discussing female applicants, but rarely when discussing male applicants. The tendency to discuss motherhood was most prevalent when these employers discussed the hiring of black women, and, most importantly, one-third of the respondents referred to black women by using the image of the single mother. In contrast, only 12 percent of the respondents mentioned single motherhood when discussing either white women or women in general. In these firms, 20 percent of black but only 6 percent of white mothers were single householders. However, the use of this stereotype stigmatized all black mothers, including the 80 percent who were living with a spouse or partner.

Most employers believed that mothers, especially single black household heads, were employment risks because they would have to take time off to care for their children. Indeed, one employer lamented that because of federal laws he could no longer ask applicants if their children became sick, "Do you have someone who can take care of them?" However, surveys of these firms' employees found that employer perceptions were generally unfounded. Even though black women were disproportionately single householders, they had a lower rate of absenteeism or lateness due to concerns about child care than white mothers. Most notably, 30 to 40 percent of male employees indicated that over the previous year they had either been late, or had to change hours, or been absent because of child care responsibilities. Indeed, the white male rate was slightly higher than the black female rate.

How can employers maintain stereotypes that are inconsistent with their own experience? If one embraces a stereotype, it distorts the way observations are processed. When black mothers are absent, the employer might immediately project that regardless of the reason given, they must have been taking care of their children. When men are absent because of family responsibilities, it might be viewed as an exception, whereas when black women give this reason it confirms the stereotype.

As a result of welfare changes, between 1994 and 1999 the share of black women aged twenty-five to fifty-four in the labor force increased from 73 to 79 percent. Facing the racial stigma, employment difficulties arose, particularly in New York City where the economic boom was weakest. Owing to anemic job growth, the NYC employment rate of black women declined between 1994 and 1997, causing their unemployment rate to increase from 8.6 to 15.2 percent. However, throughout most of the nation, where tight labor markets were becoming the norm, it was no longer possible for most employers to engage in profiling. Between 1996 and 1999, the wage rate of young black men with no more than a high school education increased by more than double the white rate. Among those not in school, the employment rate rose from 56.6 to 61.4 percent, while the share of those working full-time rose from 43.4 to 53.4 percent.[40]

When firms began hiring former welfare recipients, it appeared that the traditional stereotypes were true. Sandra Danziger and her associates reported that many recipients lost their jobs because "they failed to understand the importance of punctuality, the seriousness of absenteeism, and resented or misunderstood the lines of authority and responsibility in the workplace."[41] Over time, however, it became clear that former recipients became valuable employees. In a large survey of major corporations, researchers found to their surprise that former recipients stayed on the job longer, with less turnover, than other employees. Robert Pear reported that Borg-Warner, Giant Food, Marriott International, Salomon Smith Barney, Sprint, United Airlines, United Parcel, and Xerox found that they retained a larger proportion of former recipients than other entry–level employees. Typical was United Airlines, where after one year, of the 760 recipients hired, 70 percent were retained whereas the retention rate for others hired at similar jobs was only 40 percent. At Giant Foods, 100 welfare recipients had been hired as cashiers, clerks, and assistants. The retention rate after ninety days was 79 percent, but it was only 50 percent for other employees in similar jobs.[42] A recent study of the Minnesota welfare-to-work policies also showed how successful the transition can be when labor markets are very tight. In little over two years, the program reduced poverty by 25 percent, and increased incomes by 15 percent.[43]

The Minnesota study also found an 18 percent decline in domestic violence. Undoubtedly, the strong employment growth of former recipients provided choices other than staying in abusive relationships. In addition, the Family Violence Option adopted by more than thirty states further increased the ability of vulnerable women to end abusive relationships. This option, which was part of the 1996 welfare reform act, requires each welfare recipient to be screened confidentially in order to: (1) identify victims of domestic violence; (2) provide referrals to services for victims; and (3) grant waivers from time limits. Ruth Brandwein and Diana Filiano found that the option has not been fully effective because assessments have sometimes been used to judge the truthfulness of the women's claims, and recipients fear that disclosing abuse risks losing their children if the home is deemed unfit.[44] Jody Raphael and Sheila Haennicke therefore recommended that all questions be linked to potential sabotage and danger around education, training, work, and child support enforcement.[45]

Events in the last few years indicate that opening up employment opportunities has been crucial to changing the lives of poor black women. Barriers to employment can be overcome, however, only if the state provides strong support and there are jobs available. Hopefully, continued tight labor markets will allow more women who have been stigmatized by employers and brutalized by partners to find employment, and thus free themselves from relationships that have victimized them for too long.

NOTES

1. Emma Starr, "Defenseless in the Park," *New York Times* (June 15, 2000): A24. An *NBC Dateline* (6/20/00) broadcast suggested that the behavior of the women was substantially responsible for male actions. The broadcast opened with lead reporter Bob McKeown describing "young people wearing very little at all." *Dateline* went on to raise the "delicate question" of whether the victims should be blamed for the assaults on them. To answer that question *Dateline* turned to Amy Holmes, a member of the antifeminist Independent Women's Forum, who cited the videos in claiming that the assaults started out as "almost consensual sexual play and roughhousing and exhibitionism."

2. U.S. Census Bureau, *Statistical Abstract of the United States* (Washington, D.C.: Government Printing Office, 1999), Tables 93 and 94.

3. Charles Murray, *Losing Ground* (New York: Basic Books, 1984).

4. Ellen Freeman and Karl Rickels, *Early Childbearing* (Newbury Park, Calif.: Sage, 1998), 93.

5. Joyce Abma, Anne Driscoll, and Kristin Moore, "Young Women's Degree of Control over First Intercourse: An Exploratory Analysis," *Family Plan-*

ning Perspectives 30, 1 (1998): 12–18. On a ten-point degree of wantedness scale they gave a score of only one or two. Another 20 percent gave a score of 3 or 4, so that more than one-half did not engage in sexual intercourse primarily because of their own wishes.

6. For women who had their first sexual encounter when they were sixteen years old, 10 percent characterized it as involuntary and another 34 percent gave it a rating on the ten-point wantedness scale of 4 or lower.

7. Kristin Moore, C. Nord, and James Peterson, "Nonvoluntary Sexual Activity among Adolescent Children," *Family Planning Perspectives* 21, 3 (1989): 110–114.

8. Abma, Driscoll, and Moore, "Young Women's Degree of Control"; Dana Glei, "Measuring Contraceptive Use Patterns among Teenage and Adult Women," *Family Planning Perspectives* 31, 2 (1999): 73–80, found that among sexually active fifteen- to nineteen-year-olds, the probability of becoming pregnant in the next twelve months was 50 percent for women who had not used contraception at first intercourse but only 13 percent for those who did.

9. Jacqueline Stock, Michelle Bell, Debra Boyer, and Frederick Connell, "Adolescent Pregnancy and Sexual Risk-Taking among Sexually Abused Girls," *Family Planning Perspectives* 29, 5 (1997): 200–203.

10. Jacqueline Darroch, David Landry, and Selene Oslak, "Age Differences between Sexual Partners," *Family Planning Perspectives* 31, 4 (1999): 160–167. Glei, "Measuring Contraceptive Use," found that among women fifteen to seventeen years old whose partners were at least three years older than them, use of contraception was only one-third the rate of those whose partners were closer in age.

11. Darroch, Landry, and Oslak, "Age Differences between Sexual Partners."

12. Charles Barone, Jeannette Ickovics, Sharon Katz, Charlene Voyce, and Roger Weissberg, "High Risk Sexual Activity among Young Urban Students," *Family Planning Perspectives* 28, 2 (1996): 69–74.

13. Abma, Driscoll, and Moore, "Young Women's Degree of Control."

14. Moore, Nord, and Peterson, "Nonvoluntary Sexual Activity."

15. Quoted in Charles Krauthammer, "Teen Pregnancy Is a Cause of Poverty," in *Teen Pregnancy: Opposing Viewpoints,* ed. Stephen Thompson (San Diego, Calif.: Greenhaven Press, 1997), 59.

16. William Marsiglio, "Adolescent Males' Orientation toward Paternity and Contraception," *Family Planning Perspectives* 25, 1 (1993): 22–31. One can never really disentangle race and class. In particular, white men and black men with low levels of education and weak employment records are not in the same position in the labor market. Black men are much more likely to be continued victims of racial stereotyping by employers so that they have a bleaker outlook than comparable young white men.

17. Frank Furstenberg, Philip Morgan, Kristin Moore, and James Peterson, "Race Differences in the Timing of First Intercourse," *American Sociological Review* 52, 4 (1987): 512, 517.

18. For a discussion of Gunnar Myrdal's culture-of-poverty views, see Robert Cherry, "The Culture of Poverty Thesis and African Americans: The Views of Gunnar Myrdal and Other Institutionalists," *Journal of Economic Issues* 29, 4 (1995): 1–14.

19. Jody Raphael, *Saving Bernice* (Boston: Northeastern University Press, 2000).

20. John Bound and Richard Freeman, "What Went Wrong? The Erosion of the Relative Earnings of Young Black Men during the 1980s," *Quarterly Journal of Economics* 107, 2 (1992): 201–232.

21. Kim Clark and Lawrence Summers, "The Dynamics of Youth Unemployment," in *The Youth Labor Market Problem*, ed. Richard Freeman and David Wise (Chicago: University of Chicago Press, 1982), 199–230.

22. Michael Males, "Pregnancy Improves Some Teens' Lives," in *Teen Pregnancy: Opposing Viewpoints*, ed. Stephen Thompson (San Diego, Calif.: Greenhaven Press, 1997), 47–51.

23. Quoted in Robert Cherry, "Rational Choice and the Price of Marriage," *Feminist Economics* 4, 1 (1998): 42.

24. Frank Furstenberg, "The Social Consequences of Teenage Parenthood," in *Teenage Sexuality, Pregnancy and Childbearing*, ed. Frank Furstenberg, Richard Lincoln, and Jane Menken (Philadelphia: University of Pennsylvania Press, 1981), 184–210.

25. Jane Menken, "The Health and Social Consequences of Teenage Childbearing," in *Teenage Sexuality, Pregnancy and Childbearing*, ed. Furstenberg, Lincoln, and Menken, 167–183.

26. Frank Furstenberg, J. Brooks-Gunn, and Philip Morgan. *Adolescent Mothers in Later Life* (New York: Cambridge University Press, 1987).

27. Elaine McCrate, "Labor Market Segmentation and Relative Black/ White Teenage Birth Rates," *Review of Black Political Economy* 19, 2 (1990): 37–53.

28. Arline Geronimus and Sanders Korenman, "The Socioeconomic Consequences of Teen Childrearing Reconsidered," *Quarterly Journal of Economics* 107, 4 (1992): 1187–1214. See also Saul Hoffman, Michael Foster, and Frank Furstenberg, "Reevaluating the Cost of Teenage Childbearing," *Demography* 30, 1 (1993): 1–14; Saul Hoffman, "Teenage Childbearing Is Not So Bad After All . . . Or Is It?" *Family Planning Perspectives* 30, 5 (1998): 236–239; and Joseph Holt, Susan McElroy, and Seth Sanders, "The Impacts of Teenage Childbearing on the Mothers and the Consequences of Those Impacts for Government," in *Kids Having Kids*, ed. Rebecca Maynard (Washington, D.C.: Urban Institute), 55–94.

29. Geronimus and Korenman, "The Socioeconomic Consequences of Teen Childrearing Reconsidered."

30. "Domestic Violence and Birth Control Sabotage: A Report from the Teen Parent Project" (Chicago: Center for Impact Studies, 2000). (www.impactresearch.org)

31. For studies that found arresting domestic abusers led to more violent actions if the abuser was unemployed, see Daniel Goleman, "Do Arrests Increase the Rates of Repeated domestic Violence?" *New York Times* (November 25, 1991): C8. However, arresting employed abusers reduced the subsequent incidence of assault.

32. Gina Wingwood and Ralph DiClemente, "The Effects of an Abusive Primary Partner on the Condom Use and Sexual Negotiation Practices of African American Women," *American Journal of Public Health* 87, 6 (1997): 1016–1018, found that 71 percent of abused African American women reported that their partners did not use condoms, versus 43 percent of nonabused African American women.

33. Robert Cherry, *Who Gets the Good Jobs? Combating Race and Gender Disparities* (New Brunswick, N.J.: Rutgers University Press, 2001).

34. Kathryn Edin, "Few Good Men: Why Poor Women Don't Marry or Remarry," *American Prospect* 11, 4 (2000): 28.

35. Ibid., 29.

36. Jody Raphael and Richard Tolman, *Trapped by Poverty, Trapped by Abuse* (Chicago: Taylor Institute, 1997), 14. In a Massachusetts study by Mary Ann Allard, Mary Colten, Randy Albelda, and Carol Cosenza, *In Harm's Way* (Boston: McCormack Institute, 1997), 15.5 and 1.6 percent of nonabused and abused welfare mothers, respectively, reported that their present or former partner would not like it if they had a job or enrolled in a job-training program.

37. Allard, Colten, Albelda, and Cosenze, *In Harm's Way*, found that 40 and 27 percent of abused and nonabused recipients, respectively, suffered symptoms of mental depression. In the New Jersey study included in Raphael and Tolman, *Trapped by Poverty*, 31 percent of all recipients, but 54 percent of those currently in an abusive relationship indicated that they were currently depressed.

38. Joe Klein, "Sexual Abuse Is a Factor in Teenage Pregnancy," in *Teen Pregnancy: Opposing Viewpoints*, ed. Stephen Thompson (San Diego, Calif.: Greenhaven Press), 73–76.

39. Irene Browne and Ivy Kennelly, "Stereotypes and Realities: Images of Black Women in the Labor Market," in *Latinas and African American Women at Work*, ed. Irene Browne (New York: Russell Sage, 1999), 302–326.

40. Cherry, *Who Gets the Good Jobs?* chapter 8.

41. Sandra Danziger et al., "Barriers to the Employment of Welfare Recipients," in *Prosperity for All?* ed. Robert Cherry and William Rodgers (New York: Russell Sage, 2000), 248–249.

42. Robert Pear, "Welfare Workers Rate High in Job Retention at Companies," *New York Times* (May 27, 1998): B1.

43. Robert Pear, "Changes in Welfare Bring Improvements for Families," *New York Times* (June 1, 2000): A1.

44. Ruth Brandwein and Diana Filiano, "Toward Real Welfare Reform," *AFFILA* 15, 2 (2000): 224–243.

45. Jody Raphael and Sheila Haennicke, *Keeping Battered Women Safe through the Welfare-to-Work Journey* (Chicago: Taylor Institute, 1999).

13

Rape on Campus

Numbers Tell Less Than Half the Story

Julie Campbell-Ruggaard and Jami Van Ryswyk

IN THE DECADE since Congress first required colleges and universities to compile and release statistics of campus crime, numerous schools have battled campus watchdog organizations, students, and parents over the accuracy of the resulting data. The primary conflict is over whose data reflect the true picture of campus safety. The law was explicit about which crime statistics are to be disclosed, but it neglected to mandate the manner for reporting them. The resulting ambiguity in reporting policy has left many victims of crime wondering if their colleges or universities are paying proper attention to safety, or even "counting" their crime among the official statistics.

Arguably, the crime category that incites the most controversy on college campuses is forcible sex offenses. Rape and other types of sexual assault are often thought of as being far removed from the experiences of most college or university students. But the data show otherwise.

There are several reasons why parents and students do not expect rape to be a problem at an institution of higher learning. Students and parents might feel that being wary of rape on campus would be an overreaction, since the numbers of rapes reported on campus each year are low. But numbers tell less than half this story. First, rape is often perceived as a crime that occurs only in the seamy underbelly of society, in which an anonymous male attacks an unsuspecting victim, restrains her, and literally forces her (with extreme physical strength and/or a weapon) to submit to his sexual demands. Second, college students might be making decisions about their level of desired sexual activity for the first time and might not be clear about their desired limits. In the process, they might "forgive" actions of their intimate partners as being a terrible mistake—when in fact the actions might be crimes. Third, interviews with college-age males nearly always reveal that these men do not consider themselves rapists. They may recognize that the sexual contact was unwanted, but they do not consider themselves to have "forced" their partners to engage in it. In short, college men tend to subscribe to the pervasive perception that sexual assaults are committed by strangers in dark alleys.

When college students are victimized by sexual assault, they often deny the emotional impact that the assault has on their lives. Many college and university students tend to subscribe to the notion that their "independence" must be maintained above all else, and they may confuse that independence with a responsibility to "handle" difficult situations alone. In addition, students may choose to disclose their sexual assault only to a friend or relative and then follow their recommendations. They may not recognize the need for additional action.

For the above reasons and for countless others, college-age victims of sexual assault are often dissuaded from reporting sexual assaults because they either do not recognize them as rape or do not wish to face the consequences of leveling such charges. In addition, the long-standing and unrelenting stigma attached to this crime makes some students reluctant to notify campus personnel of rape or sexual assault. Educational institutions themselves often give subtle clues that reports of sexual assault are not welcomed, as reporting sexual assault is generally not easily facilitated, even if it is "encouraged" by certain personnel.

An estimated two out of three victims of sexual assault choose not to report the crime.[1] Of those victims who do report the assault, the majority are under the age of eighteen.[2] Most first-year college students are between the ages of eighteen and twenty-one, and are therefore less likely than younger victims to report sexual assault. This may be partially represented in low numbers of documented campus sexual assaults in the United States.

An illustration of the way in which "official" statistics are incongruent with actual assault statistics can be seen in the state of Ohio. At Ohio University in Athens, a rural community surrounded by the Appalachian Mountains, eleven forcible sex offenses were reported in

1997. That same year an additional nineteen offenses were reported to officials other than campus police.[3] By comparison, the University of Cincinnati (UC), an urban Ohio campus situated near a known "high crime" area, reported only two forcible sex offenses including reports made to the university's medical center. Is it possible that Ohio University has fifteen times as many sexual assaults as does the University of Cincinnati? Is UC out of compliance with reporting laws? Should we conclude that women and men are less likely to be victims of a sex crime at the University of Cincinnati? Have students at Ohio University been persuaded to report every behavior that meets their definition of a sexual offense? What accounts for the disparity in numbers?

According to an analysis of campus crime reports appearing in the *Chronicle of Higher Education*,[4] institutions across the United States were using vastly different methods of reporting their required statistics, as described below. The *Chronicle* compared reports submitted by 483 colleges and universities and then contacted approximately one-third of the participating institutions to clarify their statistics. The *Chronicle* found that many institutions had failed to include required categories, had included additional categories, or had used their state's crime-classification categories whether or not those categories were standard. One need not be an expert, university president, or dean of students to recognize that these inconsistencies make it difficult for current or prospective students and their parents to effectively compare the safety records of campuses—records that are reported (theoretically at least) under the same federal law.

Penalties for inadequate reporting of campus crime data, as outlined by the Department of Education (DOE), include monetary fines and possible discontinuation of federal aid. As of July 28, 2000, the DOE had conducted 367 audits and program reviews in roughly seven years, with findings identifying campus security violations. In 2000, one Iowa institution was fined a total of $25,000 by the U.S. Administrative Actions and Appeals Division based on three regulatory violations discovered in a 1999 DOE review.[5] These violations included failure to accurately disclose crime statistics, failure to make campus security information available to prospective students and employees, and incomplete or omitted statements of policy. The college was required to bring its campus security statistical disclosures into compliance with the law, as well as submit a remediation report to the department with its plan to avoid future violations.

"When prospective students are identifying colleges and universities they would like to attend, safety should be very high in their list of priorities," says Ron Ticho, Assistant Vice President for University Relations at Lehigh University in Bethlehem, Pennsylvania.[6] One family in particular, the Clery family of Bryn Mawr, Pennsylvania, would probably have had a vested interest in Ticho's statement, since they have dedicated their lives to campus safety issues following the rape and murder of their only daughter. She was murdered in her dorm room at Lehigh. Reminding college administrators and government officials that they have a responsibility to protect students and to properly disclose crime statistics is never far from Connie and Howard Clery's minds. Ironically, they and their daughter, Jeanne, had chosen Lehigh because it appeared safer than Tulane University. Jeanne Clery's older brothers had attended Tulane, and Jeanne was accepted there and planning to attend until her parents learned of the off-campus murder of a female student.[7]

The Clerys began their crusade after learning during the trial of Jeanne's killer, Joseph Henry, of thirty-eight unreported violent crimes at Lehigh over a three-year period. They filed a civil suit against Lehigh, and with the settlement money began lobbying for passage of the "Jeanne Clery Disclosure of Campus Security Policy and Campus Crime Statistic Act" (originally known as the "Campus Security Act"). The U.S. Congress enacted the bill, and President George Bush signed it into law in 1990.[8] The law applies to all institutions of higher education, public and private, that participate in federal student aid programs.

Under the law, schools are expected to disclose three years of campus crime statistics and basic security policies to the U.S. Department of Education, the governing body that oversees compliance with this law. These statistics are supposed to be updated yearly by each college or university. Crime statistics must also be disclosed to all current students, and to anyone who asks for such information. The most common method of disseminating this information to students is through an annual publication devoted specifically to reporting crimes, not through additions to already existing documents such as student handbooks or course catalogs. Schools are required to disclose both violent crimes and property crimes. The violent crime category includes murder, forcible sex offenses, nonforcible sex offenses, robbery, and aggravated assault.

Many students, however, are like Gwen,[9] and don't even consider campus safety statistics when they pack up their childhood room, favorite belongings, and photos to set off for their first year of college. In 1997, Gwen began her freshman year at Miami University in Oxford, Ohio. She and the other approximately 3,300 other new students probably had no idea that as they moved onto campus, Miami was the subject of an investigation by DOE officials for alleged violations under the Campus Security Act (CSA). One can only guess whether knowledge of the alleged violations would have led students to change their minds about enrolling, or to alter their behavior to be more alert to potential campus dangers.

Too often college students like Gwen arrive on campus unaware that they will face some terrifying realities. Gwen had big plans for her college years, but none of those plans included rape. That's right, rape. It's an ugly word that most are taught to reserve as a description only of the most brutal attacks in dark alleys by strangers who are menacing, callous, and anonymous. Who thinks of college men as rapists? How could that clean-cut young man who sits near me in Calculus be a criminal? Gwen had never had such thoughts until her experience made her think otherwise.

On the first weekend after orientation, Gwen and some of her new friends set out for a fraternity party. They had a few beers, were dancing, having a good time, and talking about how great it was to finally be on their own. Nobody seemed to notice when Gwen slipped out of the room with Mark, a junior with whom she had been spending time almost from the first day of class. Mark was tall, good-looking, and seemed to Gwen to be genuinely interested in her adjustment to college. He even offered some Calculus advice, as Gwen was already feeling challenged in that class, despite having suffered through an advanced pre-Calc class in high school. The night turned into the wee hours of the morning as Gwen and Mark "got to know each other" in Mark's room. Gwen's friends waited for a while, then concluded that she had already gone home without them noticing. They headed for the residence hall themselves, unaware they were leaving their new friend in a frightening situation.

As Gwen later described it to her counselor on campus, "I have never felt so alone in all my life. . . . Hearing voices and music coming from down the stairs, wanting to scream and wishing that someone would come check on me." She continued, "I didn't know what to do. It was my fault for thinking he was a nice guy, but there he was forcing himself on me and not a single person could help me get away. . . . I just want to forget the whole thing ever happened."[10]

According to the American Medical Association (AMA), one in four college students will be raped or sexually assaulted before finishing college, and 42 percent of those will keep silent about the crime.[11] If the AMA's estimates are accurate, then not only is a young woman like Gwen likely to be one of approximately two thousand Miami University women who will be sexually assaulted sometime during her four-year college career, but she is also likely to keep that assault a secret. For the nearly 60 percent of women like Gwen who do decide to tell someone about their experience, the person they tell is often a counselor, resident assistant, advisor, or friend. In other words, someone other than the police or anyone connected with an investigative agency. All the more reason why accurate (but anonymous) reporting on the part of campus officials with "significant responsibility for students" (as stipulated in the CSA) is essential to receiving a more accurate picture of what actually goes on behind closed doors on college campuses. Counselors in particular are grappling with this issue as they struggle to support their clients' rights to privacy and confidentiality, while at the same time attempting to honor the spirit and letter of the law outlined in the Clery Act.

Like Gwen, many rape victims "just want to forget" that the attack happened. But how does a student forget being raped on her first week on campus? How does she carry on, seeing those friends who had no idea they were "leaving me in such a dangerous situation"? Victims of sexual assault may exhibit temporary "deficits in recall" for a number of reasons including dissociation, amnesia, repression, or "motivated forgetting,"[12] but they rarely put the memories to rest permanently.

Evidently, however, there is a fair amount of "forgetting" on the part of campus officials. In 1990, fewer than four hundred of the approximately five thousand colleges and universities in the United States provided their campus crime statistics to the voluntary Uniform Crime Reporting (UCR) program operated by the Federal Bureau of Investigation. As of the year 2000, the participation rate is only slightly better, according to S. Daniel Carter, who maintains the Security on Campus, Inc. website. Security on Campus, Inc. (SOC) is the only national, nonprofit organization geared specifically and exclusively to the prevention of college and university crimes. This is the organization founded by Connie and Howard Clery in Jeanne's memory.

In 1992, the federal Campus Security Act, now the Clery Act, began mandating the public release of campus crime statistics. Most schools still do not report to the UCR program, and statistics reported under the UCR program include only offenses known to campus police. Clery Act disclosures are required to include crimes reported to a broad range of campus officials who are trusted with significant responsibility for students' welfare, although many schools fail to do so. Amendments to the Clery Act, effective July 2000, require the government to compile and release statistics for nearly four thousand schools.[13]

Statistics released for 1998 show the majority of schools reporting no forcible sex offenses. The University of Iowa in Iowa City reported the largest number of rapes (ten), followed by Colorado State University in Fort Collins and Ball State University in Muncie, Indiana with nine reported rapes each. Given the estimates provided by the AMA showing that one in four college women will be raped, the figures clearly indicate significant underreporting. If the University of Iowa, for instance, reported a forcible sexual offense against every fourth female student, then approximately 3,555 rapes and sexual assaults in 1998 would be a matter of public record in Iowa City.

The choice to report a sexual assault (or not) has not always been afforded the victim of assault. Various studies have investigated the apparent change in rape-reporting behaviors, possibly resulting from rape law reforms implemented in the early 1970s. A number of factors influence how, and indeed whether, victims of sexual assault report those assaults to law enforcement agencies. These factors may include the nature of the victim-offender relationship, injuries (if any) sustained by the victim, age and marital status of the victim, and the location of the incident.[14]

The result of less stringent and/or coercive requirements toward reporting rape has allowed victims to weigh the consequences of their disclosures and make more informed decisions. As recently as 1980, most state rape statutes required a victim of sexual assault to make a formal report to the police. She (or he) was bound by law to provide corroborating witnesses and demonstrate that she or he attempted to resist the attacker in order to obtain a conviction or meet the statutory requirement for arrest of the perpetrator.[15] In some cases, perpetrators were acquitted because it could not be proven that the victim(s) resisted "sufficiently." Given that perpetrators of sexual assault nearly always attack their victims in private, it would seem ludicrous for victims to call forth witnesses to substantiate their claims. For no other crime have victims been required to provide such corroborating evidence.

With the reform in rape laws of the 1970s and 1980s, state legislatures made efforts to revise their codes to give victims less burden of proof. Among these important changes were the following common themes: (1) Replacing the word "rape" with graduated offenses and commensurate penalties (e.g., aggravated sexual assault, gross sexual imposition, sexual battery); (2) eliminating or modifying requirements that victims show physical resistance to the assault; (3) completely eliminating the need for corroboration by outside witnesses; and (4) introducing "rape-shield" laws that restrict the use of evidence concerning the victim's past sexual behavior.[16] In addition, the vernacular in these laws was often changed from an exclusively feminine designation (referring to the victim as "she" or "her") in apparent recognition of the fact that an estimated 5 to 10 percent of rapes in the United States involve male victims.[17]

Reporting a sexual assault has, at least in theory, become easier for the victim. However, the process of investigating and/or prosecuting a rape is still inexact, and victims may be left feeling abandoned, blamed, or bewildered by the legal, medical, and emotional consequences with which they must deal after a rape. Many reports indicate that victims of sexual assault are especially reluctant to report that assault if they were acquainted with their attacker before their rape. Survivors who are thrown into the legal system unprepared often face rejection, humiliation, and distress as they move through a system that rarely supports their dignity. In one little-publicized 1999 case in Gainesville, Florida, a woman who was raped at a fraternity party was arrested and charged with falsifying a police report, even though the rape was captured on videotape. Her rapists were not punished, but the victim was given six months' probation.[18] Lee Madigan and Nancy C. Gamble report that a common reaction to the phenomenon known as "the second rape" includes hysteria, rage, disillusionment, and extreme distrust of the world around them.[19]

Mohini, a twenty-one-year-old female student from a small Ohio town, spoke of her shock after being raped during the first week of her freshman year in college: "I just never thought of things like that [before coming to college]. I never knew I should be scared, or worried. I guess in high school I was always thinking, oh, that's something that could never happen to me. But now that it has happened to me, I feel less safe than I did. I don't remember not being a victim of rape." Nearly three years after her rape, Mohini reported continuing difficulties with sleep and eating patterns, as well as a pervasive distrust of men in her social circle.[20]

In addition, Mohini experienced great internal conflict over her decision to speak of her assault with a counselor. Mohini's parents, first-generation Americans with heritage in India, instilled in her a respect for and value of her virginity. To admit to another that she had had sexual experience before marriage would have represented a scandalous act to her parents. Even though the "sexual experience" she described was an act of violence instigated entirely against her will, disclosure to her family had a negative effect on their view of her. As Mohini reported, her time in counseling, intended to help her deal with the physical and emotional aftereffects of sexual assault, was hindered by her family's disapproval and distrust of her rape story. Her situation is not uncommon, as disapproval or disbelief on the part of significant characters in victims' lives can lead them to blame themselves for the assault.[21]

Emily, a student at the University of Notre Dame, did not experience punishing distrust from her family after her sexual assault, but she would certainly concur with the difficulties one faces when deciding to report a rape to campus officials. Emily stated that she called the residence life office nearly every day for a month "so that I could be really prepared for what to expect at the hearing."[22] With the support of her friends, Emily had decided to report the football player who had raped her. Although the university dismissed the man she accused of raping her, she has subsequently been in residence life hearings in support of other young women and is now disillusioned by this process of "justice." What once felt like help and support no longer does. Emily explains that she has come to believe that her school cares much more about their image and the revenues generated by athletics than they do about crimes committed against her and other students. She reports knowing twelve women who have been raped while attending Notre Dame, yet these crimes are not reflected in the university's crime statistics because they have not been reported to police, or for that matter to anyone other than friends, and in a few cases the residence life system.

Historically, college students have been reluctant to seek help, even outside the university. In 1988, Mary P. Koss reported that less than 5 percent of college student victims made use of rape crisis centers.[23] Cultural affiliation may also provide strong mores against reporting sexual assault. A striving for independence or an obligation to the family may cause some victims to "stay quiet" about an assault.[24] The victim may be embarrassed about the assault, may fear the stigma attached to being a rape survivor, or may blame her or himself for allowing it to occur.[25]

Victims are likely to be ashamed of the role alcohol and other drugs may have played in the assault. Antonia Abbey and Kai Pernanen report that up to two-thirds of campus rapes involve the use of alcohol.[26] According to 1994 data from the Bureau of Justice's Violence against Women project, at least 45 percent of rapists were under the influence of alcohol or other drugs. On campus, the use of alcohol is exceptionally high, and therefore sexual assault while under the influence of alcohol or other drugs becomes a particularly common scene. Some researchers hypothesize that drinking before an assault increases the likelihood of sexual assault taking place, and also increases the severity of the assault. When both the victim and the assailant have used alcohol or other drugs, the likelihood of a violent sexual encounter increases exponentially.[27] The act of sexual intercourse with any person who is too intoxicated or otherwise incapacitated by other drugs is a felony sex act. If the victim is incapable of giving consent (for whatever reason), the act is defined as rape.[28] Issues of blame and alcohol use are closely intertwined when discussing campus rape.

Arthur Chickering, in his groundbreaking 1969 book, *Education and Identity*, and in its subsequent revision, wrote of the typical college student's need to develop and demonstrate competence in his or her daily life. One aspect of that competence, according to Chickering, is "the confidence that one can cope with what comes and achieve goals successfully."[29] Unfortunately, this striving for demonstrated competence can cause students to minimize the trauma of what has happened in an effort to "put things into perspective" and/or "deal with it." Some incidents are simply too cruel and scary to be dealt with immediately. Students may rush their healing for the sake of this perceived competence. However, Chickering and others identify a need to reflect on, analyze, reframe, and reinterpret life events to truly learn from them.

When reframing or other intellectual tools fail, some victims deny the traumatic nature of their assault. While they may recognize that the event caused pain, they may be unwilling to admit to themselves and/or to others that their personal dignity was violated. Lois A. Carey reports that in order for the victim of rape to adjust to the experience, she must either (1) change or distort her perception of the experience, or (2) alter the organizing structure around the event to convince herself that she is accountable for the assault.[30]

Despite overwhelming evidence to the contrary, some victims may even be unsure whether what happened to them "qualifies" as sexual assault. One twenty-three-year-old college graduate, comforting a friend who had been raped on a spring break trip to Florida, reported that his friend "completely rationalized the rape, so she didn't have to deal with it. She just thought of it as one big, long, bad night."[31] For these and for many other more intensely personal reasons, silence may seem like the safer choice for victims of rape on campus. However, that silence also has its cost. For every one victim who reports his or her assault, there may be as many as twenty "hidden victims," those who have shared the details of their trauma with no one.[32] It has been widely reported that women and men who are sexually assaulted, whether or not the assault is reported, often have lingering emotional, mental, and physical effects from that assault.[33]

Hugh, a twenty-two-year-old male college senior, reported distrust and emotional disconnectedness after he was raped by a fellow male student. "I guess in the scheme of things, the biggest thing that was affected was the emotional stuff. . . . All my emotional expression became a little messed up, because I had a lot of anger and rage, and I had a lot of self-hate." Hugh reported that he was in extreme distress and considered suicide before seeking assistance with his recovery.[34] While female victims are statistically unlikely to report sexual assault, male victims of sexual assault are even less likely to do so. Part of this hesitancy may come from male victims' perception that rape crisis centers and hot lines have been established to serve only women.[35] But the rape of men by other men does occur at a remarkably high rate in the United States.

The Bureau of Justice's National Crime Victimization Survey found that, of the completed and attempted rapes reported in 1996, 3 percent were perpetrated against male victims. It can be assumed that the actual incidence of same-sex male rape is substantially higher, given men's demonstrated reluctance to report sexual assault. Contrary to the stereotypical image of homosexual men as the perpetrators of same-sex male rapes, the majority of these rapists identify themselves as heterosexual.[36] Same-sex male rape is often employed as a gay-bashing tool when the perpetrator knows or suspects the victim to be homosexual.

Perpetrators of these hate crime-related assaults have sometimes re-ferred to them as efforts to "straighten [the victim] out." In addition to the frequently detrimental social consequences of reporting rape, male victims may face additional discrimination and/or humiliation because they are assumed to be homosexual based on the nature of the crime committed against them.[37] Michael Scarce further reports that many campus organizations or community rape crisis programs include in their mission statements a goal of empowering women and promoting safety for women. The issue of same-sex male rape is seldom addressed because men rarely make use of these services. And because men do not make use of the services, the issue remains unaddressed. Thus the cycle is perpetuated and male victims of sexual assault, for all intents and purposes, are left without support.

College students of either gender who have experienced sexual assault are likely to exhibit strong emotional reactions including grief, guilt, a sense of worthlessness and hopelessness, generalized fears, decreased self-esteem, denial, self-blame, or emotional numb-ness.[38] In addition, victims may exhibit cognitive reactions such as flashbacks and intrusive thoughts of the assault. They may have diffi-culty concentrating, withdraw socially, or avoid contact with friends, family, or any situation that reminds them of the rape.[39] Suicidal ideation in victims of rape is not uncommon.[40] Physical problems are reported frequently, even if the assault left no physical injury. Somatic concerns may serve as the victim's internal barometer, keeping track of the building emotional pressure following an assault. It is more ac-ceptable in the minds of many, for example, to present a physician with a vague complaint of sleeplessness or stomachache than to admit to oneself or others that a sexual assault has been lingering in one's mind. Victims may also develop eating disorders in an attempt to exert control over their own lives.[41]

In combination or in isolation, these common reactions to rape have been called "Rape Trauma Syndrome."[42] Rape Trauma Syndrome is closely related to Post Traumatic Stress Disorder (PTSD). Previously as-sociated only with war and combat, PTSD has received growing recog-nition among mental health professionals as a legitimate diagnosis for victims of sexual assault. The diagnosis may normalize symptoms by addressing the physical injuries and psychological terror that many vic-tims experience.[43]

The severity and duration of symptoms varies greatly. Some victims report no adverse reactions for years after an assault. Some report a relatively brief distress response, while others experience chronic and severe depression, anxiety, or panic.[44]

It is difficult to predict which will "bounce back" from a sexual assault and which victims will be undone by it. Research supports the notion that those victims attributing blame for the assault to external sources, such as a rape-supportive culture or inadequate protective services, are more likely to show a positive adjustment after sexual assault than are victims who blame their own character or behavior.[45]

Vital to meaningful recovery for any victim is support. This support is best offered by people who are important in the victim's life.[46] So critical is support that various studies have reported that a *lack* of support actually impedes a victim's progress in regaining control of her or his life.[47]

Victims of sexual assault on campus have numerous options for support. The majority of students who choose to disclose their sexual assault will do so first to another student, probably a roommate or friend on campus.[48] Many times the disclosure comes weeks or even months after the incident and is prompted by medical or emotional complications that take the victim by surprise.[49] Once victims have disclosed the assault to a significant person in their lives, they are likely to be nearing the point at which outside assistance is sought. The most common outlet for support services is individual or group counseling.

Most public and private institutions offer counseling to enrolled students free of charge or for a nominal fee. Professionals at university and college counseling centers generally receive specialized training in dealing with victims of sexual assault, as there is ample need for their services on campus. Most provide on-call coverage for after-hours emergencies. Many communities sponsor Rape Crisis Programs, with victim advocates available for telephone intervention or to meet with clients at hospitals, police stations, or courts of law. Community mental health agencies in most areas will see students at reduced fees so they can maintain their privacy by choosing to pay for counseling services out-of-pocket rather than utilize school or parents' insurance policies.

With the increase in technological advancements, services have become available to a wider audience. To date, there is only one twenty-four-hour national toll-free hot line for victims of sexual assault, operated by RAINN (Rape Abuse and Incest National Network). Calls to the national number are generally patched through to the nearest direct service provider.[50] The Feminist Majority Foundation has also created a Sexual Assault and Rape Crisis Resource List available on the World Wide Web.[51] A recent search on the World Wide Web revealed no fewer than a hundred registered-member newsgroups, virtual support groups specifically for victims of sexual assault.

Group counseling and traditional psychotherapeutic support groups have become a standard component of rape trauma recovery services. Within groups, victims may experience the intimacy and connection that is necessary for a trusting relationship.[52] This trust may be a motivating factor or even a necessary condition for victims to share their stories with others. Fear of judgment, rejection, and blame must be overcome if the victim is to fully commit himself or herself to the goals of the group.[53] Lois A. Carey indicates that with hard work and supportive peers and leaders, members of rape support groups can increase self-esteem, assertiveness, and self-respect as well as learn new ways to cope with a traumatic incident.[54]

Resources such as these were unavailable to victims of rape until very recently. The sense of isolation and terror that once accompanied rape on campus has not been eradicated, but continuous developments in the standard of care for victimized students may lead to higher rates of reporting in the future.

NOTES

This essay is dedicated to the memory of Jami Lyn van Ryswyk, daughter, scholar, survivor, advocate, colleague, renegade, believer, and friend. Your mountain of dreams will live on through those who loved you. You were called home too soon and will never be forgotten. Thank you for the blessings you brought into my life.—*JC-R*

1. Luciana Ramos Lira, Mary P. Koss, and Nancy Felipe Russon, "Mexican American Women's Definitions of Rape and Sexual Abuse," *Hispanic Journal of Behavioral Science* 21, no. 3 (August 1999): 240.

2. http://www.ama-assn.org/special/womh/newsline/conferen/acog99/051899b.htm website.

3. *Chronicle of Higher Education*, May 28, 1998.

4. Ibid.

5. Stephanie Babyak, "Campus Security Media Request," personal e-mail message to Gregory Flannery, August 16, 2000.

6. http://www.APBnews.com website; November 1998.

7. http://www.campussafety.org website.

8. Public Law 101–542.

9. This and all other names of victims used in this essay are pseudonyms.

10. Personal interview by Julie Campbell-Ruggaard.

11. http:www.ama-assn.org website.

12. Mindy B. Mechanic, Patricia A. Resick, and Michael G. Griffin, "A Comparison of Normal Forgetting, Psychopathology, and Information-Processing Models of Reported Amnesia for Recent Sexual Trauma," *Journal of Consulting and Clinical Psychology* 66, no. 6 (December 1998): 949.

13. http://www.campussafety.org website

14. Ronet Bachman, "The Factors Related to Rape Reporting Behavior and Arrest: New Evidence from the National Crime Victim Survey," *Criminal Justice and Behavior* 25, no. 1 (March 1998): 16–17.

15. Ibid., 10.

16. Julie Horney and Cassia Spohn, "Rape Law Reform and Instrumental Change in Six Urban Jurisdictions," *Law and Society Review* 25, no. 1 (1991): 117–153.

17. Patricia A. Frazier, "A Comparative Study of Male and Female Victims Seen at Hospital-Based Rape Crisis Program," *Journal of Interpersonal Violence* 8 (1993): 65.

18. http://www.now.org/nnt/fall-99/campus.html website.

19. Lee Madigan and Nancy C. Gamble, *The Second Rape: Society's Continued Betrayal of the Victim* (New York: Lexington Books, 1991), 7.

20. Personal interview by Jami Van Ryswyk.

21. Cheryl Regehr, Susan Cadell, and Karen Jansen, "Perceptions of Control and Long-Term Recovery from Rape," *American Journal of Orthopsychiatry* 69, no. 1 (January 1999): 110.

22. Personal interview by Julie Campbell-Ruggaard.

23. Mary P. Koss, "Hidden Rape: Sexual Aggression and Victimization in a National Sample of Students in Higher Education," in *Rape and Sexual Assault*, vol. 2, ed. A. W. Burgess (New York: Garland, 1988), 10.

24. Clare G. Holzman, "Counseling Adult Women Rape Survivors: Issues of Race, Ethnicity, and Class," *Women and Therapy* 19, no. 2 (1996): 53. Helen A. Neville and Aalece O. Pugh, "General and Culture-Specific Factors Influencing African American Women's Reporting Patterns and Perceived Social Support following Sexual Assault: An Exploratory Investigation," *Violence against Women* 3, no. 4 (August 1997): 361–381.

25. Patricia C. Dunn, Karen Vail-Smith, and Sharon M. Knight, "What Date/Acquaintance Rape Victims Tell Others: A Study of College Student Recipients of Disclosure," *Journal of American College Health* 47, no. 5 (1999): 217.

26. Antonia Abbey, "Acquaintance Rape and Alcohol Consumption on College Campuses: How Are They Linked?" *Journal of American College Health*

39, no. 4 (1991): 165. Kai Pernanen, *Alcohol in Human Violence* (New York: Guilford Press, 1991).

27. Sarah E. Ullman, George Karabatsos, and Mary P. Koss, "Alcohol and Sexual Aggression in a National Sample of College Men," *Psychology of Women Quarterly* 23, no. 4 (December 1999): 673–689.

28. Victoria L. Pitts and Martin D. Schwartz, "Self-Blame in Hidden Rape Cases," in *Researching Sexual Violence against Women: Methodological and Personal Perspectives*, ed. Martin D. Schwartz (Thousand Oaks, Calif.: Sage, 1997), 65–70.

29. Arthur W. Chickering and Linda Reisse, *Education and Identity*, 2nd ed. (San Francisco: Jossey-Bass, 1993), 105.

30. Lois A. Carey, "Illuminating the Process of a Rape Survivors' Support Group," *Social Work with Groups* 21, no. 1/2 (1998): 104.

31. Personal interview by Jami Van Ryswyk.

32. Martin D. Schwartz and Molly S. Leggett, "Bad Date or Emotional Trauma? The Aftermath of Campus Sexual Assault," *Violence against Women* 5, no. 3 (March 1999): 266.

33. Ibid., 251–271; Claire Burke Draucker, "The Psychotherapeutic Needs of Women Who Have Been Sexually Assaulted," *Perspectives in Psychiatric Care* 35, no. 1 (December 1999): 18–28; Heidi Resnick, Ron Acierno, Melisa Holmes, Dean G. Kilpatrick, and Nancy Jager, "Prevention of Post Rape Psychopathology: Preliminary Findings of a Controlled Acute Rape Treatment Study," *Journal of Anxiety Disorders* 13, no. 4 (July–August 1999): 359–370; Michael Scarce, "Same-Sex Rape of Male College Students," *Journal of American College Health* 45 (January 1997): 171–173; Brenda L. Shapiro and J. Conrad Schwarz, "Date Rape: Its Relationship to Trauma Symptoms and Sexual Self-Esteem," *Journal of Interpersonal Violence* 12, no. 3 (June 1997): 407–419.

34. Personal interview by Jami Van Ryswyk.

35. Scarce, "Same-Sex Rape of Male College Students," 172.

36. P. L. Huckle, "Male Rape Victims Referred to a Forensic Psychiatric Service," *Medical Science Law* 35 (1995): 188.

37. Scarce, "Same-Sex Rape of Male College Students," 171.

38. Cheryl Regehr, Glenn Regehr, and John Bradford, "A Model for Predicting Depression in Victims of Rape," *Journal of the American Academy of Psychiatric Law* 26, no. 4 (1998): 595–605; Lori K. Sudderth, "It'll Come Right Back at Me: The Interactional Context of Discussing Rape with Others," *Violence against Women* 4, no. 5 (October 1998): 572–594; Shapiro and Schwarz, "Date Rape," 407–419.

39. Cheryl Regehr, Elsa Marziali, and Karen Jansen, "A Qualitative Analysis of Strengths and Vulnerabilities in Sexually Assaulted Women," *Clinical Social Work Journal* 27, no. 2 (Summer 1999): 171–184. Sudderth, "It'll Come Right Back at Me," 572–594.

40. Susan Stepakoff, "Effects of Sexual Victimization on Suicidal Ideation

and Behavior in U.S. College Women," *Suicide and Life-Threatening Behavior* 28, no. 1 (Spring 1998): 122.

41. Regina C. Casper and Sonja Lyubomirsky, "Individual Psychopathology Relative to Reports of Unwanted Sexual Experiences as Predictor of a Bulimic Eating Pattern," *International Journal of Eating Disorders* 21, no. 3 (April 1997): 229–236.

42. A. W. Burgess and L. L. Holstrom, "Recovery from Rape and Prior Life Stress," *Research in Nursing Health* 1 (1978): 165–174.

43. Judith Lewis Herman, *Trauma and Recovery* (New York: BasicBooks, 1992).

44. Patricia A. Frazier and Jeffery W. Burnett, "Immediate Coping Strategies among Rape Victims," *Journal of Counseling and Development* 72, no. 6 (July–August 1994): 633–639.

45. Regehr, Cadell, and Jansen, "Perceptions of Control and Long-Term Recovery from Rape," 110–115.

46. Debra A. Popiel and Edwin C. Susskind. "The Impact of Rape: Social Support as a Moderator of Stress," *American Journal of Community Psychology* 13, no. 6 (December 1985): 645.

47. Libby O. Ruch and Joseph J. Leon, "The Victim of Rape and the Role of Life Change, Coping, and Social Support during the Rape Trauma Syndrome," in *Stress, Social Support, and Women*, ed. Stevan E. Hobfall (New York: Hemisphere Publishing Corporation, 1986), 137.

48. Dunn, Vail-Smith, and Knight, "What Date/Acquaintance Rape Victims Tell Others," 213.

49. Stepakoff, "Effects of Sexual Victimization on Suicidal Ideation and Behavior in U.S. College Women," 108.

50. http://www.rainn.org website.

51. http://www.feminist.org/911/resources.html website.

52. Carey, "Illuminating the Process of a Rape Survivors' Support Group," 105.

53. Ibid., 113.

54. Ibid., 114.

Contributors

JESSE F. BATTAN is an associate professor and chair of the Department of American Studies at California State University, Fullerton. He is the author of "The 'Rights' of Husbands and the 'Duties' of Wives: Power and Desire in the American Bedroom, 1850–1910," *Journal of Family History*, 24 (April 1999): 165–186. He is currently completing work on a manuscript entitled "The Politics of *Eros*: Sexual Radicalism and Social Reform in Nineteenth-Century America."

JULIE CAMPBELL-RUGGAARD is a Licensed Professional Clinical Counselor who worked at Miami University's Student Counseling Center for ten years prior to moving into full-time private practice and consulting. She specializes in sexual abuse/assault recovery and eating disorders, and has spoken at a number of professional conferences on these issues. In addition, she is co-coordinator of a nonprofit group called Victims Rights Advocacy.

BONNI CERMAK is a doctoral student at the University of Oregon. Her dissertation is entitled "Retelling Rape: Legal and Cultural Narratives of Rape, 1920–1960." She has presented a number of papers at professional conferences, including the Western Association of Women's Historians and the American Historical Association.

ROBERT CHERRY is professor of economics at Brooklyn College. He is the author of over a dozen books and articles, most recently *Who Gets the Good Jobs? Combating Race and Gender Disparities* (Rutgers University Press, 2001) and *Prosperity for All? The Economic Boom and African Americans* (coedited with William Rodgers), published by Russell Sage, 2000.

PATRICK J. CONNOR is a Ph.D. candidate in the Department of History at York University in Toronto. He is currently completing a dissertation on the use of the royal pardon in the Upper Canadian justice system, 1791–1841. He is also editor of the journal *Left History*.

LISA LINDQUIST DORR is an assistant professor of history at the University of Alabama. She has published in *the Journal of the History of Sexuality*, the *Journal of Women's History*, and the *Journal of Southern History*. She is currently revising her manuscript tentatively entitled, "'Messin' White Women': White Women, Black Men, and Rape in Virginia, 1900–1960."

HAL GOLDMAN is assistant professor of Legal Studies and History at the University of Illinois at Springfield. He received his law degree from Boston College and his doctorate in history from the University of Massachusetts at Amherst. He specializes in the history of law, gender, and sexuality.

ELSE L. HAMBLETON is revising her dissertation entitled, "The World Filled with a Generation of Bastards: Unwed Mothers and Pregnant Brides in Seventeenth-Century Massachusetts" (University of Massachusetts, 2000). She is the author of "The Regulation of Sex in Seventeenth-Century Massachusetts: The Quarterly Court of Essex County vs. Priscilla Willson and Mr. Samuel Appleton," ed. Merril D. Smith, *Sex and Sexuality in Early America* (New York University Press, 1998).

JACK MARIETTA is an associate professor of history at the University of Arizona. He has published widely on the Quaker experience in Pennsylvania and on computing the population in that area. He is the author *of The Reformation of American Quakerism, 1748–1783,* and is coauthoring, with G. S. Rowe, a work on crime and criminal administration in Pennsylvania from 1682 to 1801.

ALICE NASH is assistant professor of Native American and Early American History at the University of Massachusetts, Amherst. Her dissertation, "The Abiding Frontier: Family, Gender, and Religion in Wabanaki History, 1600–1763" (Columbia Unviversity, 1997) is being revised for publication by the University of Massachusetts Press.

G. S. ROWE is professor of history at the University of Colorado. He has published more than three dozen articles on various aspects of the law, crime, lawyers, and judges in the early republic, as well as two books: *Thomas McKean: The Shaping of an American Republicanism* (1978) *and Embattled Bench: The Pennsylvania Supreme Court and the Forging of a Democratic Society, 1684–1809* (1994). Currently he is collaborating with Jack Marietta on a study of crime and criminal administration in Pennsylvania, called *Law, License, and Liberty: Crime and Its Resolution in Pennsylvania, 1682–1801*.

MERRIL D. SMITH is an independent scholar. She is the author of *Breaking the Bonds: Marital Discord in Pennsylvania, 1730–1830*, and editor of *Sex and Sexuality in Early America*, both published by New York University Press.

TERRI L. SNYDER is an associate professor in Liberal Studies and American Studies at California State University, Fullerton. She has authored articles on gender, violence, and local legal culture in colonial Virginia.

DIANE MILLER SOMMERVILLE is an assistant professor in history at Fairleigh Dickinson University in Madison, New Jersey. She is currently completing a manuscript to be published by the University of North Carolina Press in 2002 called *Rape, Race, and Community in the Nineteenth-Century South*. Her article, "The Rape Myth in the Old South Reconsidered," which appeared in the *Journal of Southern History* (1995), was awarded the A. Elizabeth Turner Prize by the Southern Association of Women's Historians for the best article or essay written on the subject of southern women.

JAMI VAN RYSWYK was a Nationally Certified School Psychologist trained at Miami University, She spent several years working as a Victim Advocate/Program Assistant for a rape crisis program and as a counselor at a shelter for victims of domestic abuse. She was a doctoral candidate in Counselor Education at Ohio University in Athens, Ohio, at the time of her death in April 2001.

JAMES HOMER WILLIAMS is an associate professor of history at Middle Tennessee State University. He is working on a book entitled *The Cultural Struggle for the Early Mid-Atlantic Colonies* and is also compiling and editing the complete correspondence between Winston Churchill and Harry Truman.

Index

Abortion, 269
Adultery, 5, 31, 64, 66, 67, 68, 71, 192
Anderson, Elijah, 269–270
African American: employment, 270–271; incarceration rates of men, 274–275; planned pregnancies of, 271–272; prohibitions of sex with, in New Netherland, 68; sexual coercion of women, 269–270; unwanted pregnancies, 269–270
Arnold, Marybeth Hamilton, 111, 117, 155
Assault, 181, 193

Barry, Francis, 209, 210, 217
Beecher, Catherine, 204
Benefit-cost calculations, 266; and personal safety of women, 266–267
Bestiality, 32
Block, Sharon, 46, 48
Bradford, William, 85, 91, 96
Brown, Kathleen, 50, 56
Brownmiller, Susan, 1, 7

Campus rape, 283–296; and counseling, 295–296; lack of campus help in reporting, 291; penalties for underreporting, 285; reporting of, 283–284, 285, 286, 289
Campus Security Act (1990), 286, 289
Captives: adoption of, 20–22, 23; distinctions between, 18–19, 23; explorers' accounts of 16–17; during King Philip's War, 19–20; Mi'kmaq accounts of, 13–16; ransom of, 23; "white Indians," 22
Child rape, 5, 32–33, 35, 36, 37, 42, 61; in antebellum South, 136–177; of black children in antebellum South, 162–163; charges brought by African American girls, 160; in New Netherland (girls and boys), 70–71, 73–76; in New York, 155; in Pennsylvania, 88, 90, 95; rape laws in antebellum South, 136–137; underre-

ported, 154–155; in Upper Canada, 109, 111, 113–114, 122, 124
Children: can not commit rape, 141; crediblity of, 151, 153–154, 166–167; percent raped in antebellum Virginia, 154; as prey of sex offenders, 149, 152, 155, 165
Christianson, Scott, 71–72, 76
Clark, Anna, 111, 112, 117, 120, 127, 152
Comstock Act, 208, 219
Consent, 4, 5, 47–49, 137–138, 292; age of, 137–138; implied in marriage, 205, 206; in interracial cases, 250; lack of, as cause of ill health, 218; legal arguments about, 190–194, 196; loopholes based on race, 140–141; men and women's views differ, 121
Contraception, 205; lack of and relationship to abuse, 268–270; sabotage of, 274
Copeland, Senator Royal S., 242
Countrey Justice, The (Dalton), 28
Crossdressing, 64
"Cult of sensibility," 93–94

Dalton, Michael, 28, 39
Darrow, Clarence, 231, 240–242, 243
Davidson, Cathy, 93–94
Deutsch, Helene, 255–256
Divorce, and sexual abuse, 217, 228n. 56
Doctors: accounts of marital abuse, 214–215; sympathetic to Free Lovers, 213–214; testify in rape cases, 117
Domestic violence, 275; and employment, 277; of teen mothers, 273–274. *See also* Marital rape; Sexual coercion
Dutch West India Company (WIC), 63, 68, 71, 74, 75; and law in New Netherland, 63

Ejaculation, proof of, 148, 151, 152

305

Sex: as commodity, 47–49; premarital, 120. *See also* Fornication

Sexual coercion: in black community, 269–270; and pregnancy, 268; at risk decisions, 6; of young women, 268–270. *See also* Servants

Slander, 68–69

Slaves, 36; opportunity to commit rapes, 140; punishment for rape, 144–147, 156, 157–158, 164; rape of, 161–162; rape of masters' daughters, 140–144. *See also* African American; Lynching; Rape; Rape victims

Sodomy, 3, 8nn. 7, 8, 32, 61, 64, 73, 74, 79nn. 33, 37; biblical injunctions against, 74–75; punishment of, in New Netherland, 75

Stansell, Christine, 136, 155

Stanton, Elizabeth Cady, 220

Stirling, Admiral Yates, 235, 237

Stuyvesant, Petrus, 71

Upper Canada: attitudes about sexuality, 120–121; court and legal system, 104–105, 108–109, 110; executions in, 124, 125; problems of reporting rape, 104, 105; rape laws in, 106; sympathetic towards rape prosecutions, 103–104, 110; taverns in, 113–114

Vermont: *Alexander v. Blodgett* (1873), 192–193; importance of studying rape in state, 195–198; rape law compared to New York, 197; rape statistics in, 196, 198, 199; *State v. Bedard* (1892), 194–195; *State v. Fournier* (1896), 187; *State v. Gile* (1918), 188; *State v. Hanlon* (1890),

193–194; *State v. Hartigan* (1860), 189–191, 192; *State v. Johnson* (1855), 182, 186; *State v. Reed* (1867), 184–185, 186, 188; woman-centered rape law, 195–197

Vermont Justice (1864), 184

Virginia: African Americans on juries, 252, 254; black men arrested or tried, 249–250, 254; colonial rape trials, 49–50, 57n. 1, 58n. 9; defamation suits in, 53–56; gossip and reputations in, 53–55; rape law, 251; white men arrested or tried, 260; women in court, 53, 56

"Voluntary motherhood," 207

Wabanaki: and captive taking, 12–13; as designation of related tribes, 11; differ from Iroquois practices, 11–12; emergence of new practices, 13; oral tradition on rape, 10; references to rape or sex, 17–18; views of slavery, 19

Waisbrooker, Lois, 208, 211

Walker, Garthine, 61, 62, 116

Welfare, 271–272, 275–278; Family Violence Option, 278

Women: in abusive relationships, 265; beliefs about their sexuality, 95, 248, 254–256, 257, 259–260; decline in health, 204–205, 209, 214, 215, 216, 218; employment of 266; in literature of early Republic, 94–95; Puritan views of, 27–28, 31, 34–35; and rape law, 178–179; and risky behavior, 265; support after rape, 107; teen birth rate, 267–28; use of contraceptives, 205; views of, in colonial Virginia, 50

Woodhull and Claflin's Weekly, 204, 205